how
we
make
each
other

how we make each other

TRANS LIFE AT THE EDGE OF THE UNIVERSITY

Perry Zurn

Duke University Press
Durham and London
2025

© 2025 DUKE UNIVERSITY PRESS. All rights reserved

Project Editor: Bird Williams
Designed by Courtney Leigh Richardson
Typeset in Garamond Premier Pro and IBM Plex Serif
by Westchester Publishing Services

Library of Congress Cataloging-in-Publication Data
Names: Zurn, Perry, [date] author.
Title: How we make each other : trans life at the edge of the university / Perry Zurn.
Description: Durham : Duke University Press, 2025. | Includes bibliographical references and index.
Identifiers: LCCN 2024022291 (print)
LCCN 2024022292 (ebook)
ISBN 9781478031307 (paperback)
ISBN 9781478028062 (hardcover)
ISBN 9781478060291 (ebook)
Subjects: LCSH: Five Colleges, Inc.—Students. | Transgender college students. | Transgender college teachers. | Transgender people—Education (Higher) | Education, Higher—Social aspects—United States.
Classification: LCC LC2574.6 .Z87 2025 (print)
LCC LC2574.6 (ebook)
DCC 378.1/98266—dc23/eng/20240725
LC record available at https://lccn.loc.gov/2024022291
LC ebook record available at https://lccn.loc.gov/2024022292

Cover art: Levi Booker, *Gender Euphoria* (details), 2018. Wood relief prints and fishing net. © Levi Booker. Courtesy of Artist.

contents

Preface vii
Acknowledgments xi

Introduction: *Of Small Places and Edge Ecologies*   1

PART I
1. Problematizing Trans Inclusion   21
2. Becoming a Trans Problem   35
3. Mobilizing Trans Poetics   49

PART II
4. Attunements to Trans History   65
5. Dust   83
6. Stash   95
7. Scatter   107

PART III
8. Attunements to Trans Resistance   121
9. Thread   135
10. Glue   149
11. Pebble   161

PART IV
12. Attunements to Trans Hope   175
13. Fatigue   191

14	Risk	203
15	World	213
	Coda	227
	Epilogue	235
	Chronology	239
	Notes	255
	Bibliography	277
	Index	301

preface

This book began furtively.

Sometime during my college sojourn in the early aughts, I ordered a copy of Leslie Feinberg's *Stone Butch Blues* from the college's interlibrary loan system.[2] While this fact might seem innocent enough, or even quaint, the context made it anything but. This was a school where feminism was a bad word. A school where we had a gendered dress code and daily chapel. A school where, when I took an interest in poststructuralism, my honors professor pulled me into his office and told me he was praying for my (presumably damned) soul. And it was a school where, when I fell in love with a girl, I was put on academic probation and forbidden to spend time with her, speak to her, or even look at her, on or off campus. An impossible demand, if she hadn't already acquiesced.

But this book germinated before all of that, in the early days of my gender wanderings. I loved the library. To this day, it is the campus building I remember best—each floor, each corner, where the reference books were, the classrooms, and the collaborative project space, the philosophy and theology corridor, and the windows overlooking the lake. More than my dorm room, it was my home. And it was a portal to adjacent worlds I was gingerly trying to reach. I had a premonitory sense that *Stone Butch Blues* would get me in trouble, so I kept it in my pillowcase and read it secretly in my top bunk. I was lucky enough to have a (closeted) gay roommate, who wouldn't rat me out, but various RA's would pop in at any moment for surprise cleaning checks and "behavior checks." So I kept the book secret, kept it safe. And cried my eyes out reading it. I felt so lonely and so connected at the same time. When I returned the book to the circulation counter, the student worker said, "Oh, the librarian wants to see you about this." My stomach dropped. When said librarian came over, she looked me firmly in the eyes, and said, "We will have to suspend your borrowing privileges if you continue to order books like this." In a conciliatory tone, she then added, "You understand." She said it like it was obvious. And it was. And it wasn't.

Fifteen years later, and to my own surprise, I was a professor traveling to Holyoke, Massachusetts, to consult the Sexual Minorities Archives (SMA). Researching trans life in the Connecticut River Valley, I was thinking broadly about the ways in which transness collides with and escapes the university. The SMA is one of the longest-standing independent LGBTQ archives in the nation. It is housed in the personal home of Ben Power, founder of the SMA in 1977 as well as the East Coast Female-to-Male (FTM) Group—the first of its kind on the East Coast—in 1992. The old Victorian house in which he and the archives live—affectionately known as the Pink Lady—is in fact painted light pink with bright pink trim. A bit of loud on an otherwise quiet suburban street. I ring, I wait, I ring again. I knock. I pound. I decide to sit on the porch and do emails on my phone. Almost thirty minutes after our scheduled meeting, Ben arrives at the door, cats in tow. He gives me a tour of the house, full of evident love and pride. He pauses at the third floor, eagerly announcing, "And we house the Leslie Feinberg library!" He starts speaking quickly about the displays he is still organizing: a box of pins here, a stack of protest t-shirts, signs, and photos there. I scan the room and stand there stunned. How did I come so far? From a library that erases us, to an archive that defiantly remembers? My heart almost buckles under the weight.

Ben sits down for the interview I had requested. As he speaks, I see the flint in his eyes and the fire—from years of struggle. He has a bad cough. His voice is thin but his words heavy, purposeful, plodding. And I know immediately that and how he understands himself to be a man. He tells me the story of the SMA archives and of trans life in the valley. And he tells me the story of meeting Lou Sullivan. It was 1986 and Lou had sent the archives a pamphlet about his group FTM International. Ben read the pamphlet cover to cover in two hours and was on a plane to San Francisco within a month. Sitting at Lou's kitchen table, Ben talked as only a trans person with no one to talk to can. When Lou paused for a moment to take his AZT (azidothymidine), Ben realized Lou had AIDS and his newfound world came crashing down around him. Listening to Ben, I think about the ways we find and lose one another. And the seemingly fragile character of our connections. I think about how Feinberg found me, and how zie was gone before I thought to look.

I spent the afternoon in the SMA attic, where the local archives are held. It was August and the house had no central air. I heard one window unit barely whirring in another room. I took off my jacket and my tie. A few hours later, my collared shirt and my shoes. Cracking box after box, I wish I had packed water. Finally, I opened the Restroom Revolution folder, a University of Massachusetts, Amherst initiative for gender-inclusive restrooms in 2001–2002. My body lit with excitement. This was the material I was most looking forward to. But when I opened the folder, the first item to appear was an undated memo from American University (my employer), detailing the trans inclusive policies the university ought to adopt (e.g., bathrooms, locker rooms, housing, ID cards, faculty education, nondiscrimination policy, etc.). A cascade of questions washed over me. How did this get here? Was it misfiled? Or are our worlds really that small? And if so, what sort of queer, trans structures of belonging explain this remnant of unexpected coalition? Sometime later, I asked Mitch Boucher, who co-organized the Restroom Revolution and donated its records to the archive, about the memo. He recalled working with all kinds of folks, swapping resources and policy briefs, trying to get universities to listen to the demands of trans inclusion. Part of me wished that sad kid stuffing Feinberg in his pillowcase could have overheard the conversation and known there were others elsewhere, agitating and collaborating in the space of the university.

I never expected to be part of a story. As a queer and trans person, I'm uniquely acculturated to the idea that I am not the sort of thing that has a history. Stories don't call me "mine." But as I returned to American University's campus, walking past Battelle-Tompkins, the Mary Graydon Center, and the library (another library!), I found myself gripped by a certain nostalgia. My people agitated here, worked hard and wasted time here, felt crushed and built friendships here, swore off and moved on from here. Feeling both more and less alone, I wondered what happened to these folks.[1] How did they decide what to demand? And what desires did not make the page? Where did they shit-talk and where did they laugh? Who did they go home to? What hacks did they hatch to navigate a transphobic world? And how were those hacks shared, hitching a ride around the campus and beyond it? Thinking of my own frustrated activism for gender-inclusive restrooms at AU, I wondered how they handled disappointment. How did they keep up hope (or didn't they)? Hope that in ten, fifteen, twenty years (and counting), their recommendations would finally be adopted? Or did they hang their hopes elsewhere, hoping for respite in the clink of a coffee spoon, the warm sun on their forearms, the queer fire in someone else's eyes?

Trans life in the university is always already unhomed, always already misfiled. And yet, the worlds we make with one another take up residence in its cracks. All of these unofficial lines of communication, the offbeat channels of collaboration, and the unexpected friendships that lead to stuffed pillowcases and jumbled archive boxes—these are our traces. We live in the interstices—never in a cohesive way, but in little clumps flung from one another in a yawning archipelago. And those clumps make histories, and stage mutinies, and shout poems at the future, in real isolation and vague companionship by turns.

This book is about unexpected lines of belonging and kinship. It is about refusal. And it is about hope. It is about all the ways of trans being together that demand something of the university and escape it. In the end, this book is also about a history that is always ever finding and losing me.

acknowledgments

If we make each other, what sort of gratefulness flows from there? I could not approach this project, nor can I now retrospect about this project, without feeling a rush of gratefulness—for the fact and the matter of trans belonging at the edge of the university. Nor can I deny the many networks that made this work possible. Of my book projects to date, this is by far the most indebted text. And so I set out to do only the briefest bit of justice to that indebtedness, marking a series of points along the many horizons within which this book took shape. Equal gratefulness goes to those I may have missed in this litany, or who wished to remain unnamed. You, too, are a reason this book—and this history—exists.

The first thanks should go to Aster (Erich) Pitcher, who joined me for some of the earliest interviews and conversations about this project, when it was still research for "just an article or two." Aster's expertise in qualitative research, good humor, and trans fabulousness was critical light at the very inception of this project, and I have done my best to carry it with me through to the end.

Thanks to all my interviewees, the trans students, alums, staff, faculty, and allies—for their willingness to share stories, to cocreate spaces of vulnerability, and to cultivate queer and trans wisdom and hope. Thanks to Sam Davis, who developed an archive of trans oral histories at Smith College that has been indispensable to this work. Thanks to the research staff and librarians in various special collections divisions (especially Rachel Beckwith, Jess Neal, and Shaun Trujillo at Hampshire College; Micha Broadnax, Leslie Fields, and Deborah Richards at Mount Holyoke College; Michael Kelly at Amherst College; Nancy Young at Smith College; Ann Moore and Annie Solinger at University of Massachusetts, Amherst). And thanks to the programs and centers at the Five Colleges in conversation with which this book grew—Amherst College's Queer Resource Center, the Five College Queer Gender and Sexuality Conference,

Hampshire College's Ethics and the Common Good Project, Mount Holyoke College's LYNK program, and the University of Massachusetts, Amherst's Stonewall Center. Thanks also to the lineage of queer, trans, and gender disruptive folks at the Five Colleges, whose scholarly and creative production I relied on for this work and for making sense of my own life—this includes, but is not limited to, Samuel Ace, Cameron Awkward-Rich, Genny Beemyn, S. Bear Bergman, Chase Catalano, Fiona Maeve Geist, Jack Gieseking, Ren-yo Hwang, Alana Kumbier, Andrea Lawlor, Jen Manion, Elliot Montague, Sonny Nordmarken, Enoch Page, Jaclyn Pryor, Nihils Rev, Jordy Rosenberg, Jules Rosskam, Davey Shlasko, and Derek Siegel. Thanks also to (then local) KJ Rawson and the inimitable Ben Power.

Thanks also goes to the venues where I was able to present parts of this work and participate in crucial creative conversations around it. There is both a clarity and a humility about the work that can only be cultivated in these settings. Thanks to my gracious interlocutors.

Thanks also to several institutions that have supported the work of this book. A series of AU Mellon Faculty Research Awards funded much of my archival travel and interview transcription costs. Huge thanks to the organizers and members of the Five College Women's Studies Research Center, where I spent Spring 2020 on research leave, with an office on Mount Holyoke's campus. Few communities can compare in heart and generosity. The way you modeled feminist curiosity, creativity, and solidarity is a lesson for the ages. Special thanks to Darcy Buerkle who, attending a work-in-progress talk, urged me to weave myself into the book. An AU Book Incubator Fund (2022) allowed Cameron Awkward-Rich, Hil Malatino, Gayle Salamon, and me to meet for a day and discuss the work in progress; I am so grateful for their collective wisdom and critical kindness. Thanks also to Cavar, who kindly read and provided trenchant feedback on "Scatter." I was lucky enough to put the finishing touches to the book while on fellowship at Cornell University's Society for the Humanities (2023–2024), and a visiting scholar at the University of Pennsylvania's Center for Research in Feminist, Queer, and Transgender Studies.

Finally, thanks to readers at Duke University Press, whose many injunctions made the book a much better version of itself. And thanks especially to my editor Elizabeth Ault who saw promise in the project from the beginning but also provided the space in which it could remake me—as a scholar, a writer, and a vector of transness in the world.

I also want to thank all the trans, genderfluid, gender fantastic queers who have found their way into my classes over the years. Looking out at you has been part of what kept my soul alive here in the university. Trans theory made a different kind of (non)sense when I read it with you. Thanks to Matt Ferguson, my RA in 2019–2020, for being a trans coconspirator on this project, lending special attention to the chronologies of trans life at the five schools.

Thanks to my friends, especially Andrew Dilts, and my trans family: Talia Bettcher, PJ DiPietro, Jake Hale, Tamsin Kimoto, Amy Marvin, and Andrea Pitts. I have no words to say what it has meant to me that we share our worlds.

Thanks to the riotous lot of my bio family. You are no doubt an implicit source for how I think about poetics. The rough and tumble way we grew up, all smashed together, like a pocket of loud in otherwise tucked-away places, is something I keep close. And I am proud of the creative streak we all share.

Finally, thanks to Asia, who continues to walk with me, to find joy and beauty with me, and, in so doing, safeguards the space within which I can find these words. And thanks to Remy, who joined our life just as I began writing this book in earnest. In our first two years as a family, this project was my anchor in the sea-change that is new parenthood, but it also and increasingly became a place for me to practice a newfound openness and vulnerability. Along the way, you both taught me some of the deepest lessons about what it means to be with one another and to make each other.

introduction *Of Small Places and Edge Ecologies*

It was summer 2018 and there I was, half-dressed in a turret, pouring over the archives in an August heatwave. Records of the Restroom Revolution (2001–2002), at University of Massachusetts, Amherst were the reason I had come to the Sexual Minorities Archives in the first place. I had learned of the group years before while reading a stack of books about toilets. My partner at the time had wisely insisted I not bring "work" on vacation, so I invested in a bunch of books about bathrooms—their mechanical and social history as well as their role as flare-points for multiple social justice movements. Food for my inner nerd, but also salve for my soul. It was in that pile that I came across the story of Restroom Revolution. According to Olga Gershenson, a professor at UMass, the largely student-led group advocated for gender-inclusive restrooms across campus years before the better known group at the University of California, Santa Barbara: PISSAR (People in Search of Safe and Accessible Restrooms).[1] Offering a blow-by-blow of the resistance effort, conservative media backlash, and administrative negotiation, which mobilized hundreds of students and handfuls of local and national LGBT organizations, Gershenson narrates the results: "two single-stall [all gender] bathrooms (on a campus of thirty thousand people)."[2] Was Restroom Revolution really a failure, I wondered? Or had it succeeded in creating something else, something that a focus on trans-inclusive bathroom policy (and brick-and-mortar facilities) overlooks?

A few years after working through that slim folder at the Sexual Minorities Archives, I worked through two overstuffed folders of Restroom Revolution material stored privately at UMass's Stonewall Center. The group is the first recorded instance of largescale organizing by people self-described as "transgender, transsexual, gender-queer, or something other than 'man' or 'woman'" at UMass.[3] Advocating for "all gender," "gender neutral," or "gender free" bathrooms, the group got busy. They posted flyers all over campus, flooded key administrators with phone calls and emails, and tabled at the Campus Center. They also annotated plumbing codes, enlisted trans advocacy networks, and collaborated with other schools implementing trans-inclusive bathroom, housing, and healthcare policies. They got their proposal approved by the Student Government Association and the Graduate Student Senate and met repeatedly with the vice chancellor. That little came of the two-year effort is not, in fact, the point of the story.[4] Something happened here. Something beyond and before bathroom policy. Restroom Revolution created a broad network, a tight community, and a series of friendships that built capacity and strengthened voice. More than that, it embodied the day-in and day-out work of trans people making one another possible. A patch of resistant life at the edge of the university.

And that patch had a certain poetry to it. I got in touch with one of the organizers, Mitch Boucher, and he mentioned he still had a box of records. I jumped at the chance to take them off his hands. I arrived at his house promptly at the appointed time, but no one answered. I looked around the porch, thinking he had left the box for no-contact pickup (it was 2020, and the COVID-19 pandemic had just hit), but there was nothing. I started thinking I was at the wrong house and headed back to my car. Just then, Mitch appeared out of nowhere, in his quiet way. He led me off to a small shed where he rummaged around and emerged with a large Shaklee box, covered in fifty-year anniversary tape. It started to rain, and I was off. Back at my Airbnb, I eagerly pulled the box open, launching a cloud of dust in my face. Its contents were soon scattered about the floor, the bed, and the desk. These were the records of the first trans studies class taught at UMass in 2002. Restroom Revolution activists were both its teachers and students. Alongside syllabi, assignment sheets, student papers, and trans studies articles, there were notes and reflections. Threads of anger, vulnerability, and joy were woven together throughout the pile of pages. What kind of friendships lead to an old box like this, stashed away in a shed for twenty years? After you have studied together, risked together, and burnt-out together, what keeps you nourishing the seeds and pebbles of a world you might still create?

Repeatedly, trans life in the university gets told as a story of trans-inclusive policy—a story of "trans" becoming part of the university. But that narrative neglects the much richer story of trans life lived at the edge of the university—behind and before and beyond policy. *How We Make Each Other* grapples with the difference between ameliorating an institution and flourishing in its cracks. During a renaissance of trans visibility and an ongoing battle between anti-trans bills and trans-inclusive public policies, *How We Make Each Other* aims to understand what happens in the invisible interstices. What survives policy implementation and roll-back? It sets out to tell those liminal stories about trans life in the university: the moments in the shed, around the table, and between people. And it lingers in the space of poetry—indeed, of poetics—to appreciate how it is that, in a setting that can unmake us in a single instant, we nevertheless keep making things and making one another.

How It All Started

In the summer of 2015, I moved to Massachusetts to assume my first faculty job. With all the gumption and anxiety of a newly minted PhD, I was eager to begin my academic sojourn as visiting assistant professor at Hampshire College. On the first day, I turned to my colleague Fae, who exuded genderfluid femme fabulousness, and asked where the nearest bathroom was located. They pointed me to an "all gender restroom" down the hall and announced with evident glee that all the bathrooms on campus were gender-inclusive. As I turned to go, I could feel both shock and relief vying for my body. In that instant, I viscerally remembered my time as a graduate student: the relentless dehydration headaches; the rushing in and out of gendered restrooms, holding my breath; the waiting in line at the nearest gender-inclusive restroom several buildings away, only to run out of time and have to turn back (to attend class, to teach, to meet with my dissertation directors, to hold office hours) before relieving myself, with tears of frustration and shame pooling in the corners of my eyes, and searing heat in my throat. Using the nearby restroom in peace, I wondered, "How is this even possible?" How did Hampshire get this way and when? What stories of trans agitation and world-building lay behind the innocuous bathroom signs? Two years later, I returned to the valley to study not only the history of trans-inclusive policies at the Five Colleges, but the history of trans life, of trans activism, and of the poetics subtending it all.

There are an infinite number of paths one might take to illuminate the relationship between trans life and the university. In situating my inquiry within the Five Colleges, I aim to honor the place where my inquiry originated, as well as the communities with whom I worked. Luckily, the Five Colleges are also a reason all their own. Amherst College, Hampshire College, Mount Holyoke College, Smith College, and University of Massachusetts, Amherst—these five schools are a loosely knit group functioning independently more often than not, their advertising rhetoric notwithstanding. Among them are small liberal arts schools and a giant state school, one historically men's college and two historically women's colleges, some of the most privileged and one of the most precarious institutions in higher education. The Five Colleges are situated in a remarkably queer geographical region of Western Massachusetts, with an unusually robust history of trans life in and outside the universities. It is no surprise, then, that the Five Colleges were well ahead of the national curve when it came to trans-inclusive bathroom, healthcare, housing, name, and pronoun policies. The story of how these policies arose and the many ways in which queer and trans life intersected with (and escaped) these colleges, however, remains to be told.

It is a truism today that universities, like so many other social institutions, are not only historically spaces of gender segregation but continue to be spaces of gender policing. To say this is also to say that a wealth of social inequities, which inform gender norms, shape the institution of the university—only some of which are captured in the terms *settler colonialism, racism, sexism, classism, ableism, homophobia,* and *transphobia*. That higher education institutions not only expect but actively extract cis/heteronormative gender expression from their constituents, however, also means that these expectations are repeatedly frustrated and these extractions resisted. Where there is force, there is counterforce. Like fireflies in summer, the landscape of the university is littered with disruptions. Shit-talking huddles and mutual-aid circles; ramps and smartpens, grab bars and speech-to-text software; young children making cameos in class and elderly relatives turning exam schedules topsy-turvy. Gender unruliness, too, glints down hallways, refracting in and out of classrooms, and lighting up labs and late-night essays. The Five Colleges are no exception. Among early gender disruptors was 1886 Amherst graduate Clyde Fitch, who spent his college years in high fashion dresses, gloves, and rouge before becoming a highly successful playwright and having a brief dalliance with Oscar Wilde.[5] What other gender transgressions and transgressors populate this place?

It is perhaps no real surprise that queer and trans activism in the valley is remarkably robust. There is a long lineage of lesbians and genderqueer folks in the area, many stemming from the two historically women's colleges: Smith and Mount Holyoke. Northampton, moreover, holds a special place in the queer imaginary. In 1992, ABC's *20/20* called it the "Lesbian Ellis Island." The following year, the town was represented in the LGB March on Washington with a giant purple banner that read: "Northampton: Occupied Lesbian Territory."[6] Profiles in the *Chicago Tribune, National Enquirer,* and *Newsweek* quickly followed.[7] As Janet Cawley of the *Tribune* reports, Northampton was a place full of hippies, tax resisters, communes, interracial families, and, yes, lesbians, since at least the 1970s. By the early 1990s, one downtown shop offered a 10 percent lesbian discount (imagine claiming this at checkout). Another sold T-shirts that read, "Lesbianville, USA / 10,000 cuddling, kissing lesbians in the wild" and coffee cups that read, "Northampton: Where the coffee is strong and so are the women." The local lesbian moms group went by the name "Momazons." Not everyone was equally thrilled by the situation. The president of Smith College at the time issued a statement distancing Smith from lesbianism and a local pastor advised congregants to avoid Northampton altogether, because of the "filthy statements on shirts" they might encounter.[8]

It is little remarked, however, that that same year, 1992, saw the local establishment of the East Coast FTM Group and Sunshine Club, both significant and longstanding organizations serving local FTMs and MTFs respectively. It is also the year Ben Power renamed the New Alexandrian Lesbian Library the Sexual Minorities Archives and began explicitly collecting trans materials. It is as if Lesbianville were trans (or transed) from the get-go. Waves of trans activist initiatives followed. There was Transgender Network (TNET) and Transgender Special Outreach Network (TSON) (1996–2001), Transgender Activist Network (TAN) (2001–2004), Northampton Trans Pride (2009–present), and the Miss New England Trans Pageants (2010–2015), just to name a few. In each instance, trans people engaged not only in place-changing but also in place-making, forming bonds and forging pathways. Reflecting on the intimate coexistence between himself and the archives, Power states, "Let it be known that since 1977, it has been a female-to-male TS [transsexual] who has lived with and breathed life into this resource."[9] Conspiring with his material and social worlds, Power brings old worlds to rest and breathe new worlds into being.

For decades now, genderqueer and trans people have been making space in the Five Colleges. It was not until after I had left my visiting position at Hampshire that I learned Fae had been a crucial part of the change in its bathroom policy. As I began to research, I wondered less about the trans-inclusive policy shifts themselves, at the various colleges, and more about the poetic ecologies of their actors. Where did they live and breathe? What intimate coexistences did they nurture and sustain? With what elements of the land did they engage and what histories did they weave? In documenting the trans poetics behind and beside trans-inclusive policies at the Five Colleges, I aim to track the poetry of place-based resistance in and among trans people. I tell folks that the project started in a Hampshire bathroom. But that is not entirely true. It really started with Fae. What I really wanted to know was not how this or that policy happened but how Fae happened. And how more of Fae could happen. This book is part of that story.

Small Worlds, Deep Roots

Before further detailing the ins and outs of how this project got underway, it is worth putting an even finer point on the offbeat, backwoods sort of place in which it is set. There is a uniqueness to the geosocial ecologies here that ought not go unremarked. The Connecticut River Valley is, in the ruddiest of ways, a place of farm boots clomping on sidewalks and into classrooms; of a dozen used bookstores in a half mile radius; of somatic healing and true granola souls; of fresh beet juice and Mal Devisa. There are rotted out barns and junked trucks, boarded-up stores, and unoccupied homes. Towns so small you mistake them for a gas station. An oversized US flag luxuriates over one of the lakes. Folks go swimming in the quarries. Neighboring Sunderland boasts "the widest tree this side of Mississippi," a sycamore older than the union (of settler colonies) itself. And in seventeenth-century graveyards, names are barely distinguishable against the deteriorating stone. Here, leftist and lesbian communes have sought refuge for centuries, while radical experiments in art and education grow like weeds. In this valley—this *place*—the sense that one must abstract from the world in order to remake it is palpable, an excrescence of the earth itself. Here, too, is the sense that such remaking is not a "project." "It shouldn't have to be work," a galoshed old queer once told me. It is just a way of life.

The Five Colleges are situated in a rural, almost idyllic tract. Located in the breathlessly beautiful Connecticut River Valley, just southwest of the Quabbin Reservoir and southeast of the Berkshire Mountains, their respective cities of Amherst, Northampton, and South Hadley zigzag across the river rift and between the rolling hills of the Holyoke Range. Travel writers in the 1920s dubbed the place the "Pioneer Valley," a term I avoid because it evokes a pristine settler past, and even an Edenic paradise, leaving unacknowledged the wilderness and cultivation that preceded European settlements for thousands of years. Idyllic though it may be, the valley has always been a place of agitation. Records of course begin with the long story of Indigenous resistance to colonialization. Then, in 1786–1787, Daniel Shays famously launched Shays Rebellion here, mobilizing four thousand men in armed protest against the government's economic injustice that created and sustained the local debt crisis. From 1842 to 1846, Sojourner Truth spent time here in a utopian community of abolitionists, who raised mulberry trees and silkworms and ran a stop for the Underground Railroad. She remarked, in retrospect, that she found here "some of the choicest spirits of the age."[10] And in 1867, Gardiner Greene Hubbard, after his daughter contracted scarlet fever and lost her hearing, founded Clarke School for the Deaf, the first of its kind in the United States. The compulsion to agitate, to demand something different, is in the blood, yes, but perhaps also in the land, in *this* land.

In the nineteenth and twentieth centuries, Springfield and Holyoke were major manufacturing cities, producing widespread working-class sensibilities in the region. Springfield focused on manufacturing engines, machinery, jewelry, and chemicals, and is credited with developing the first American gas-powered car, the first American musket, and the first American-English dictionary (1847 Merriam-Webster). Holyoke, on the other hand, focused its energies on paper, producing, at its height, 80 percent of the writing paper in the United States. To this day, people still call it the "Paper City." As such, the valley was a place of innovation and fabrication—a *making* place, if there ever was one. The neighboring towns of Amherst, Northampton, and South Hadley, while supporting manufacturing and agriculture, developed as cultural centers where, in each case, the colleges took center stage, making the region a proud part of the Hartford-Springfield Knowledge Corridor, which houses the second-highest concentration of colleges in the United States. As such, the Five Colleges are, on the one hand and in a historically meaningful way, a force of local culture. On the other hand, and in an equally historically meaningful way, they rupture local culture. Class, language, ideology, and gender all become grains across which town and gown sit.

When it comes to the history of the Five Colleges, a counterculture spirit seems to crop up everywhere you turn. First, Amherst College started as the coed Amherst Academy (1812), a grassroots project that aimed to offer sorely needed classical liberal arts education in the area. It was subsequently reformulated as an elite men's college (1821), which then became coed in 1972. Mount Holyoke College (1837), originally Mount Holyoke Female Seminary, was founded by a (queer) graduate of Amherst Academy: Mary Lyon. Convinced that women of all classes deserved educational opportunity, Lyon opened the seminary at a third of typical costs. The oldest of the Seven Sisters (a group of historically women's colleges in the Northeast), the college is now an elite, gender diverse women's college. In turn, University of Massachusetts, Amherst (1863) began as Massachusetts Agricultural College, a land-grant institution with a mission to meet the needs of an increasingly industrial society, focusing on agriculture, military science, and engineering. UMass, Amherst is now the flagship state school, with a sprawling campus and high research productivity. Finally, Smith College (1875) was founded by Sophia Smith. Deaf by age forty, Smith had planned to establish a school for the deaf. After Clarke School opened, however, she decided to endow Smith, which was to offer general education to the women of her time. Smith is now the largest and most renowned of the Seven Sisters.[11] What is signal about this series of stories is the gumption. To hell with historical precedent. Meet the needs of the present moment: classical education, practical education, women's seminary education, and women's general education.

It is that gumption that explains the origins of the fifth and final college: Hampshire. The youngest college—arguably with the biggest heart but scarcest resources (e.g., an endowment of $54 million compared to Amherst's $3.3 billion), Hampshire (1970) was a joint venture of the other four schools. Frustrated by the limitations of traditional education and sensing that learning needed to be far more flexible in a fast-developing infocentric world, the presidents of Amherst, Mount Holyoke, Smith, and UMass came together to form their dream school: a hub of experimental learning and innovation. With no departments, no majors, and no grades, Hampshire was to be a center for self-directed, interdisciplinary learning and creativity. Its founding motto, *Non Satis Scire* (To Know Is Not Enough), challenges students not simply to understand and succeed in the world, but also to generate the wisdom necessary to change it. Describing the sort of student he hoped Hampshire would produce, inaugural president Franklin Patterson once wrote: "[T]hey will be [...] neither privately disaffiliated 'achievers,' technocratic conformists, nor deviants. I hope they will be questioning themselves and the society they find themselves in [...] and be willing to go down hard roads that make genuine sense."[12] Although many queer and trans graduates would proudly identify as deviants today, Hampshire has indeed produced a stream of young people capable of guiding their own souls and the world into new eras. They are emissaries of another way of being, with indeed a willingness to "go down hard roads that make genuine sense."[13]

In a place like this where stories of doing and making abound; where people are open to striking out, fine with breaking rank, and at ease with enclaves; where gender and sexual dissidence (and deviance) are par for the course; and where higher education is repeatedly reimagined in response to organic need—again, *in a place like this*, what happens when trans hits the scene? It is no real surprise trans happened with comparatively more pith and verve here than elsewhere.[14] But how exactly? What is the trans story?

Getting the Research Underway

I took the Five Colleges as a case study not to tell a single story, but to tell many stories. In a case study, the truth of any one story is not in question. Here, I read traces humbly, in full awareness that there is certainly more to each of them (a moreness I welcome well after these pages go to print). The stories I tell, moreover, are limited by what I could see and sew together. I went sifting for largescale events and ephemeral moments, for feelings and for friendships that might outline how it is that trans life forms in the cracks of the university. How it beads up on the banks, how it rushes through gullies, how it settles in and on and with. The result is a love letter. A love letter to a very specific place-based community, but also to other past and future instances of trans life in the academy.

I did not choose this research; it chose me. And while I am a philosopher by training, this project made me part historian and part social scientist, too. To understand the offstage character of trans poetics, I had to understand both institutional and intimate histories. I had to talk to people and shuffle papers. I had to get out from behind a desk and go trekking.

While maintaining a center weight of philosophical reflection, my research methods expanded to include archival work, interviews with trans community members, and consultation of local trans cultural production. Canvassing general Five College archives, LGBT student group archives, and local trans community archives, I tracked how the term *trans* intersected with university cultures and resistant subcultures across its first few decades of use (1990–2020). Then, through more than one hundred interviews with trans students, staff, faculty, alums, and allies at the Five Colleges, I witnessed the innumerable ways in which interviewees made sense of themselves and each other. Together, the official archives, the interviews, and the paraphernalia people shared with me became what I refer to, throughout this project, as the Five Colleges archive of trans life. Finally, I did a deep dive into locally produced transgender scholarship and artistic creation. Too often, theory is thought in abstraction from place, as if soil did not already cling to it. I wanted to think *with* the communities in question, to sink my hands into the grit and humus of landed thinking. As such, I committed to consult local theory for this local project, and to construct local theory from these local projects. I wanted to resist the constitutive abstraction of theory through an obsessive return to place—to the thisness and hereness of things.

As with any place-based study, the setting provides as many possibilities as it does limitations. Squarely in New England, the schools are situated in an overwhelmingly White area, with Northampton being 87.7 percent White, Amherst 76.9 percent White, and South Hadley 90 percent White, according to the 2010 Census. It is the sort of place where, at a 2020 protest in support of Black trans life, UMass professor Cameron Awkward-Rich recalls being, as far as he could see, "the only Black trans person on the street."[15] Town and gown tensions abound, where the often quite wealthy, liberal colleges are surrounded by poorer, more conservative local residents. It is a region in which class, race, and gender are consistently salient, and where disability is consistently underthought.

I started interviewing in the fall of 2017 and largely finished just two days shy of Christmas 2021. These were difficult years, spanning the Trump presidency and the COVID-19 pandemic. I launched an interest survey and it snowballed. Perhaps even more than electronic forwarding, however, the project circulated by word of mouth. People kept telling me, "Talk to So-and-So," and I did. Besides indicating I wanted to talk to trans students, staff, faculty, and their allies, I did not curate my sample; I talked to anyone willing to talk to me. Ultimately, I interviewed seventy-eight people and relied on interviews conducted by Sam Davis at Smith College in 2017 for another twenty-seven.[16] Throughout, I refer to interviewees by pseudonyms unless they requested otherwise, in which case I use their full names. Of 105 interviews, twenty-seven people self-described as non-White (Asian, South Asian, Armenian, Black, Desi, Dominican, Hispanic, Latinx, Indigenous, Middle Eastern, Puerto Rican, and Roma); ten as Jewish (especially Ashkenazi); and three did not say. Thirty-five self-described as having a disability or a disabling illness or impairment. Although the intake survey did not ask (I wish it had), six self-described, unprompted, as coming from a low socioeconomic background. The sample skewed toward people who self-described as assigned female at birth (AFAB) and fourteen of the interviewees self-described as cis or cis-ish. Some interviewees were still teenagers, while others were in their seventies and eighties.

Perhaps unsurprisingly, when asked about their gender on the intake form, interviewees answered expansively. The list of gender descriptors includes, but is not limited to, the following: andro, androgynous, binary transgender male, boi, butch, cis woman, cis-ish, cisgender-appearing, confusing, faggy, female, feminine, femme, fluid, FTM, gender conforming, gender expansive, gender neutral, gender nonconforming, genderfluid, genderless, genderqueer, grungy feminine, lesbian, male, man, man who is AFAB, man raised as a girl, masc, masc-ish, masculine, masculine of center, masculine with florals, metrically 80/20, MTF, multigender, nonbinary, nonbinary cis woman, nonbinary femme, nonbinary man, nonbinary with transgender experience, nonbinary trans masc, nonbinary trans woman, nongender, non-op trans woman, nongender, non-op trans man, not a man / not a woman, queer, shifting, socially male, soft masculine, trans, trans butch dyke, trans dyke, trans femme, trans guy, trans guy (not a man), trans male, trans man, trans masc, trans masculine, trans nonbinary, trans woman, transish, transfem, transgender, transgender femme, transgender man, transgender woman, transmasculine nonbinary, twink-dykey, woman, 100 percent binary. Reviewing the list today, I have a deep sense that any attempt to boil this all down to trans femmes / trans mascs, or AMAB / AFAB, or binary / nonbinary does this archive—and the trans community as a whole—a huge disservice.

Despite speaking only to people formally associated with the Five Colleges (with the exception of Ben Power), I could not assume an easy relationship between interviewees and higher education. I talked to people completely disillusioned with the university. I talked to burn-outs, drop-outs, and stop-outs. I talked to people who gave up the major they loved because the department was unliveably transphobic. I talked to people who left one or more of these colleges in relief. And I talked to people who hated theory—precisely the kind of theory this book offers. In anger and frustration, Jason put it like this:

> When I got to Hampshire, I came from a large, underfunded, overcrowded public high school. I went to a supposedly "intro" to queer studies class (I remember it was a 100-level class). And I'm sitting in there, and they're talking about trans people and I don't understand the language. I'm trans and I have no idea what's happening. And I felt like I couldn't ask. [...] I think that's where a lot of the frustration for me really started. I understand the purposes of theory in a lot of ways, but I also think that sometimes it's used in a way that cuts off people who it's affecting. Then it becomes in a lot of ways really inaccessible to the people who are being written about.[17]

Hearing Jason speak, I had to ask myself: Am I writing a book that welcomes him into its pages? Am I writing a book that resonates, in some way, with each of my interviewees? What about the gender disruptors I met in the archives?[18] If my interviewees were not only associated with but alienated from the university and "theory," my book, too, needed to sit uneasily at the edge of both.

How We Make Each Other, then, is a book of story-led theory. It is so not simply because my research questions required archival and interview data, but because trans stories, again and again, house trans theory, as much as they exceed and challenge it. And luckily, stories are also the stuff of trans poetics.

Trans Poetics

What do I mean by *trans poetics*? What is this pulse I am trying to find below and behind trans policies? In contemporary terms, *trans poetics* typically refers to the artistic approach or philosophy of trans poets. Trans poets, for example, bring (gender) trouble to the poem-body itself, messing with its syntax, troubling its spacing, stretching and reshaping its contours of sense. For trans poets, much like for trans people, a certain ambiguity and shapeshifting, even slipperiness, is par for the course. Troubling the poem-body, moreover, is, for many if not all trans poets, a survival strategy—a way of putting themselves back together, but also of pulling other things apart, leaving them open, splayed, unsettled. Trans poetry in this sense is an act of resistance. But it is also a work of connection: part of the poetics of writing trans poetry is reconnecting to our histories, our presents, our futures by reconnecting to ourselves, one another, and the world. When I say "trans poetics," indeed when I search for trans poetics at the edge of the university, I mean all of this (e.g., the trouble, the ambiguity, the shape-shifting, the survival strategies, the resistance, and the connection), but I also mean more than this.

Historically, the ancient Greek term *poiesis* refers to the act of making or crafting. It can be used with reference to making or crafting poetry, but it can also be used with reference to making or crafting really anything at all. For me, "trans poetics" refers to the ways trans people—and gender disruptors over the centuries—make themselves and make one another. But it also refers to how they make meaning and community—how they hang out alone or in company, how they tell their stories, hatch plans to survive or topple cisheteronormative frames or imagine ways the world might change. It is this deep sense of making, as the thrumming heart of trans existence, that I mean to sound when I say "trans poetics." We are not simply bodies and souls to which things happen, or in which a logic of gender transgression is simply playing itself out. We are not simply those for whom others should make room. We are busy making new spaces and shapes in the world. We are creatively making sense of our own flesh and blood, in and between us. We are cracking open our horizons, materially and conceptually. That is the trans poetics I am looking for, the poetics that germinates behind and to the side of policy.

But I mean still more than this. Stefano Harney and Fred Moten place poetics at the heart of critical university studies. Poetics, Moten states, drawing on their collaborative work, refers to "a constant process where people make things and make one another."[19] But Harney and Moten do not mean anybody, anywhere, making anything. They specifically place poetics in the hands of marginalized people, in the underbelly of institutions, making sense and trouble there at the edge. While focusing on Black fugitive study in the university, Harney and Moten mean for the term *poetics* to be capacious. For them, it refers to all the ways in which oppressed people (e.g., Black, Yemeni, queer, poor, or mad) walk and talk, work and play, survive and triumph, in "any kitchen, any back porch, any basement, any hall, any park bench, any improvised party, every night."[20]

In *How We Make Each Other*, I take more than titular inspiration from Moten. Offering an extension of Harney and Moten's work, following their own references to transness and the undercommons, I track *trans* poetics as the set of practices and affects whereby trans people make resistant meaning and presence specifically in and under the university.[21] I mean to understand how trans folks interface with this institution of education and knowledge production, how they come to know and make known there differently, what their bodies do and where, and how community gets built in a trajectory always oblique to the university, at an angle always askew.

For me, "trans poetics" refers to the ways in which trans folks make resistant sense of themselves and their world through material practices in peripheral and insubordinate spaces. In this sense, I draw on all three theoretical traditions of thinking poetics: trans poetry, classical poetics, and critical university studies. The alchemical amalgam of those sources and their tuning to trans life, specifically to trans life in the Connecticut River Valley, however, is unique to this project. Tracking trans poetics there means listening to the clang of crisis as it produces trans-inclusive policies, but also more importantly to the quiet murmurs of trans existence and friendship, art and analysis that always fall outside those policies. In order to trace trans poetics, I offer in this book a series of attunements and analytics that help illuminate trans life in the university. For me, attunements are practices of noticing that allow certain things to come into the frame, whereas analytics are frames that allow specific kinds of noticing to set to work. I ask, then, not only how to look for trans poetics but also along what vectors to look such that trans poetics has a chance of coming to the fore.

This book studies the sense-making practices of a specific set of trans communities in the university, whether fighting for trans-inclusive policies or surviving without them (and sometimes despite them). To do that, I build on trans studies' longstanding concern with the costs of inclusion and visibility.[22] As numerous scholars have made clear, trans visibility is not *prima facie* good. It matters what becomes visible in trans when trans becomes visible. What shows up and what gets hidden? What is made palpable and what made secret? If attunements and analytics are the method of trans poetics, for me, the source of trans poetics is story, the story of trans life in the valley.

Plotting the Path

There was a time—a long time—when I thought this book was impossible. There were just too many stories, too many nodes. I was awash in people and moments, affects and events, with no through-line. I waited and kept listening (and relistening). The stories started to get caught on similar tags and knotted around the same nexes. Behind all the flashy work of generating trans-inclusive policies, which emphasizes key actors, signal events, and distillable dreams, there is the piecemeal work of telling rhizomatic trans histories, the slow-burn work of building trans-resistance networks, and the resonant practice of generating trans hopes. After characterizing the pivot from policy to poetics (part 1), then, these are the major sections of the book: history (part 2), resistance (part 3), and hope (part 4). From the reservoirs of history and the nets of resistant habits to the ephemeral shimmering of hope, trans poetics reconfigures sense-making and world-making—in ways far deeper than I at first imagined.

Too often, the story of trans life in the university gets told through a series of important personages. There are the big names of an awakening trans revolution (Kate Bornstein, Loren Cameron, Janet Mock, and Laverne Cox) that fill auditorium rooms, their fancy catered receptions funded by handfuls of programs and offices across campus. And then there are the big actors: the spitfire student who galvanizes the campus queer/trans group, or the staff member who writes the final draft, or, more rarely, the (especially junior, nontenured) faculty member who insists change happen now. But the story of trans life is more than this and importantly other than this. To hear it (and to tell it) requires an attunement not to the monumental but rather to the miniscule. It requires listening for the offbeat, off-brand moments of trans in the making and looking for the edges and the cracks of main movements. It requires analyzing how ability, class, gender, and race skew the stories one finds most easily, but also asking what the transgressive histories we do hold tell us about ourselves. Cultivating these attunements in the Five College archives writ large, I find not major actors so much as minor analytics that crisscross the official trans story. In thematizing dust, stash, and scatter, in part 2, I attend to the dust our traces gather, the stashes in which they find new life, and the ways they can become a force of scattering for both cis and trans normativity.

Too often, too, the story of trans life in the university gets told through a series of important events. The big protests and loud insurrections, the campuswide marches and media-magnet sit-ins. Moments where bathroom access, healthcare, pronouns, and housing came to a head. But trans resistance is more than this. It is the flyers, posters, reports, and educational materials; the frustration, pain, disappointment, and triumph; the huddles, friendships, internal rifts, and broken relationships. It is the everyday habits that sustain quiet remakings. To track trans resistance in this guise requires an attunement less to catalyzing events than to structures of being with one another that allow for transformation of ideas and practices. It requires homing in on trans hangouts and looking for the lines they weave around, through, and against cisnormative expectations on campus. It requires thinking trans resistance in the context of other rumblings for liberation, but also asking how trans resistance sometimes replicates oppressive habits in its very undertaking. Nurturing these attunements in the Five College archives writ large, I find not major actions but minor analytics that circulate beneath official chronologies of change. In thematizing thread, glue, and pebble, in part 3, I attend to the resistant threads we weave and wear, the glue we use to gum up the works, and the pebbles lying around with which we build another world.

Lastly, the story of trans life in the university gets told through distillable dreams, especially for representation, visibility, and inclusive policies. But trans hopes are more than this, other than this. Trans folks in the university hope for basic security, for creaturely comforts, for intergenerational community, for radical reshaping of the world, for full houses of meaning and fabrics of relation. They harbor fiery and fragile hopes, silly and excessive hopes, impractical hopes, incendiary hopes, hopes that cool the pain and heat up purpose. Hopes hanging in abandoned airspace and hopes coursing through the arteries of intimacy. To track these quotidian trans hopes requires an attunement to often inconvenient visions and impractical imaginations. It requires listening for the prophetic in the concrete stuff of trans life, even and especially when that stuff is trash (or trashed). It requires looking for trans folks dancing in the dirt, working and singing on the ground, as much as attending to whose grounds and whose dance gets uptake. Deploying these attunements in the Five College archives writ large, I find not major aspirations but minor analytics that suffuse and escape the official story of trans inclusion. In thematizing fatigue, risk, and world, in part 4, I attend to the fatigue we feel and create, the risks we are and we take, and the worlds we (un)make.

This book offers a theory of social change *as poetic life* drawn from the praxis of trans communities. As such, *How We Make Each Other* is a local project with translocal reach. It tells the intriguing tale of how the Five Colleges became trendsetters for trans-inclusive policies in the United States. But more importantly it marks what gets left out and left over in the process. It asks, how might trans leadership in social change, and trans contributions to the theory and practice of history, resistance, and hope, transform higher education? What would happen to the university and after the university? Ultimately, this is a story of poetics, not policy. Of sticky ecologies, not calculative solutions. It is a story of intergenerational community, fatigue and fury, but also generosity and abundance. And this is a story for the world.

Ecologies of Belonging

In *A Queer New York*, Jack Gieseking develops the framework of constellations through which to understand lesbian and trans or gender nonconforming people's negotiation of the city. Gieseking, a Mount Holyoke alum, argues that the story of queer New York City cannot be told through city grids or neighborhoods (or gayborhoods). It is more "fragmented and fleeting."[23] The story is best told by attending to queer constellations, where the stars are spaces and places, people and activities, memories and histories through which queer people build lines of belonging. Much like the seasonal waxing and waning of celestial patterns overhead, those lines, he remarks, often bend and shift over time. There is, after all, a certain regularity to queer deviation. But those lines are also clearly foreshortened or obscured by the twine of gentrification and late capitalism, through which racism, settler colonialism, classism, and ableism constrain the grid. The stars and their lines are nevertheless there. As Gieseking writes, "The political insight of constellations is that lesbians and queers resist cis-heteropatriarchy in claiming and making spaces (for however long), and by finding one another (however few or multiple) in and beyond neighborhoods."[24] Importantly, he welcomes the association between the term *constellations* and astrology, insisting it highlights the queer "ways of making worlds all at once mythical, imaginary, and physical."[25] Such is the minor science, one might say, of producing queer space.

There is a poetry to Gieseking's choice of words here. As he went about his interviews, he repeatedly noticed interviewees sporting the blue star tattoo; sometimes it was boldly brandished on arms and wrists, other times it peeped from behind a time piece. The blue star tattoo was a mid-twentieth century lesbian signal, originating in Buffalo, New York, which over time has taken on nine lives. It is from this unruly archipelago of blue stars that he got to thinking about constellations. While it goes unremarked in the text, astronomically speaking, blue stars are not only rarer and more short-lived than their red counterparts, but they also emit greater heat and luminosity. The symbol captures, then, something about queer life and desire. Our lives often begin later and end sooner than others, but they burn with an exceptional brilliance.

The term *constellations* is poetic for yet another reason, of which Gieseking may be unaware. The first recorded instance of queer life at Mount Holyoke is a letter published in the student newsletter on October 2, 1975.[26] The author, who takes the pseudonym of "Astronomer," titles the piece "Anniversary in Loneliness." Two years prior, she had come out to her then Amherst boyfriend, although her journey began another two years before that. She had since not told a soul. She wonders if there are others like her. "I look for you in the night," she writes, "we are like stars. They can't be seen during the day, but I know they're there."[27] In this single, haunting line, Astronomer crystallizes the searching that marks queer life, the squinting to see if that light is there or no, whether in oneself, in another, or out there in the web of the world. In a follow-up interview the next week, she adds, "If there is a lesbian underground here, it is so far underground that it's like drilling for oil."[28] It's as if the sky is the earth's underbelly, and yet gazing into either extremity is like groping around in utter darkness. When, almost fifty years later, Gieseking publishes a book on queer constellations, he himself becomes a new star in Astronomer's sky.

In *How We Make Each Other*, I, too, find myself staring up and down at the stars, tracking the constellations of trans life that escape the lines and the grids of the academy. I look for the forms of trans life that fall outside of the university, or sit blithely on the edge of it, or grow insistently in its cracks. I am less interested in the policy grids that pick people up and drop them into a trans center, or a trans class, or a trans dorm, and more in the unofficial and non-professional, insurgent, and campy arrangements by which trans people "make things and make one another." What are the shapes of those constellations? In this book, I aim to feel out those lines of belonging that lie scattered around campuses and across queer generations. And to ask not only how it is that we belong, but how it is that we build belonging. Not only what are our constellations but how do we constellate?

In a place so often marked by isolation and alienation, from which trans people continually drop out and drift away, or die inside in order to survive, or never even get a chance to arrive—in a place like that, in a place like the university, the story of who we have been, what we have done, and where we're going matters immeasurably. It matters not only how we make space but how we unmake space. It matters what stars guide us home and, when there are no stars to be seen, how we become companions in shipwreck.[29] This is part of that story.

Part I

Problematizing Trans Inclusion

CHAPTER ONE

No mistake, trans-inclusive policies matter. They help staunch an ongoing system of loss, whereby the few trans folks who make it into the university drop out, stop out, or leak away. But also a system of loss whereby those folks who stay may stay in the closet and/or fail to thrive in multiple ways that richly matter, for them and those around them. At the most fundamental level, trans-inclusive policies can mean the difference between life and death, between thriving and suicidality.[1] More mundanely, they can relieve the daily thrum of anxiety, make certain fields of study possible, and turn social isolation into connection. The university is not, inherently, a trans-inclusive place. Due to its founding investment in men to the exclusion of women, and then women in addition to men, the very fabric of the university is constituted by cisheteronormativity. If "trans oppression" is the systemic privileging of nontransgender people, by which the latter accrue benefits and avoid barriers at higher rates than their trans peers, then the university is deeply—historically—a place of trans oppression.[2] Is it any wonder, then, that trans students and faculty report higher rates of discrimination, harassment, assault, anxiety, depression, isolation, alienation, and precarity?[3] If the university is to become more survivable—let alone sustainable or desirable—for trans people, trans-inclusive policies are baseline necessities. They begin to change a place that has really never taken gender disruption to heart.

As critical as trans-inclusive policies are, however, they are rarely thought critically. Most scholarly and practical work focuses on the fact *that* such policies matter, or *which* ones matter, rather than investigating *how* they come to matter. How, for example, did pronoun sharing practices even appear on the scene and get taken up, especially in the university? By what memos, handouts, protocols, and policies did they circulate and alongside what other practices were they sedimented? I want to set about that critical work of examining the structural and historical conditions that make trans-inclusive policies possible and that define the forms they take.

I begin by recalling Morgan Bassichis, Alexander Lee, and Dean Spade's haunting line: "Be careful of all of those welcome mats."[4] In context, they are marking the ways in which carceral reforms are gutted of their movement's histories—or, as I might put it, how policies are gutted of the poetics that gave rise to them. Their locution "be careful" can be read in at least two senses. First, it functions as a warning, indicating there may be something dangerous here, something amiss may be afoot. Second, it functions as a call for care, to notice, observe, and investigate what might not be immediately apparent. Welcome mats are indeed welcoming, but within what economies of meaning, community, and history? In the case of the welcome mats of trans-inclusive policies in higher education, I want to be careful enough to notice the welcome mats themselves, rather than quickly walk over them—or kick one to the curb. I want to notice how the welcome mat has been constructed and by whom, what it says and what it does (and fails to say or do). When a welcome mat goes down, what gets covered over? When a welcome mat gets placed, which doors open and which remain shut? Ultimately, I want to be attuned enough to notice what might be lost in the patches—or patchwork—that improve a system without deeply healing or transforming it.

I tackle these questions by analyzing policies through the analytic of problems. Trans-inclusive policies happen when trans people are taken to be (or choose to become) a problem for the university. So long as trans people are not recognized as an issue in higher education, their inclusion at the policy level is impossible. As problems, however, they demand to be solved. In the Greek, *pro-blema* refers to a thing thrown forward, thrown up in one's face. Problems cause issue with issuance, stopping up the flow of things, a wrench in the wheel. One way to critically think trans-inclusive policies, then, is to ask: How is it that universities take trans life to be a problem such that certain trans-inclusive policies (and not others) are offered as a solution, certain welcome mats are laid down (and not others)? Throughout this investigation, I have a special interest in attending to what gets left out and left over in the process. After describing and applying the method of problematization to trans inclusion, then, I close by noting the ways in which policy is haunted by the "moreness" of trans life and activism, what cannot be subsumed into the problem/solution structure. It is that moreness the rest of this book will unpack.

A Case Study

Pronoun-Sharing Practices

As we consider the project of trans inclusion, it is helpful to have a specific policy or practice in mind to ground the inquiry. While far and away the most contentious trans-inclusive policy in Five Colleges history (and elsewhere) is all-gender bathrooms, here I focus on the runner-up: pronoun go-rounds. Tracking how pronoun sharing got raised, got instituted, and then got critiqued helps dramatize both the need for trans-inclusive policy work and the need for a critical framework by which to interpret that work.

It was around 2010 and Mateo Medina, a sophomore Latinx student at Hampshire College and founding member of the Trans Policy Committee, was typing away furiously at a new handout for student orientation: "Preferred Gender Pronouns."[5] He himself had had a less-than-welcoming first-year experience and, as a new student orientation leader, was eager to rectify matters. Eager, though, is not quite the right word. He acted "out of necessity," Medina recalls. There was a sense of frustration, anger, and urgency. *Someone's got to do this, but no one else is going to do this, so I guess I have to do this.* The handout explains what pronouns are and why they matter, commonly used pronouns and how to use them, how to ask people their pronouns, and what to do if you mispronoun someone. Unexpectedly, Medina's handout spread like wildfire. People from all over, in and outside of Hampshire, started reaching out saying, "Can we use this resource?" The document has since been used, with attribution, by a range of educational, government, and private institutions, such as Williams College, The New School, Duke University's Office for Institutional Equity, NYC.gov, Dena Samuels Consulting, and Open Washington Pressbooks. In fact, when I got hired at Hampshire in 2015, I was handed Medina's handout and a version of the handout is now posted on the government website of Montgomery County, Maryland, where I now reside. Fire begets fire. There was such a dearth of resources about gender pronouns and such a visceral need for greater awareness that Medina acted. And that act keeps acting.

Sharing and honoring people's pronouns became part of the fabric of Hampshire College in the years that followed. By the time I arrived in 2015, it was the first step in convening any meeting or class period. And, although I was usually the only person in faculty/staff meetings whose pronouns might come as a surprise, I was glad people would know. Of course, knowing does not always mean doing. I remember giving two high-profile talks on campus and being publicly mispronounced both times—once at my own book launch! Nevertheless, it was a relief to know Hampshire was committed to this inclusive practice. But practices can become pro forma. In fact, some of my interviewees expressed a worry the practice had already become rote without root. What would it take to reroot it—and reroot it in what? For Medina, trans inclusion is nothing without trans liberation, and trans liberation is nothing without racial justice. "Queer and trans liberation [...] involve deep racial justice, and reparations, and prison abolition," he told me, "all of those things are actually all really tied together."[6] What would it take for pronoun-sharing practices to be rooted in that expansive sense of trans (and more-than-trans) justice?

Fast forward almost a decade. It is 2018 and Jen Manion, a professor recently hired at Amherst College, makes something of a splash when, in conversation with the pointed push for trans-inclusive policies on their campus, they published an essay decrying pronoun-sharing practices.[7] Regretting the ways in which people engaged in such practices often conflate gender and pronouns (falsely assuming, for example, that her partial use of she/her pronouns indicates she is cisgender), Manion argues that this act of "transgender inclusion erases me." More than this, they insist, pronoun go-rounds are a mere performance, an evidentiary piece of wokeness. Manion calls for people to suspend the practice and get about the real work of transgender justice (i.e., addressing the discrimination and violence transgender people face in educational, carceral, government, healthcare, and public settings). Within a week, trans lawyer and activist Dean Spade published a response. In it, he argued that, however misunderstood or misused the pronoun-sharing practice may be, it is nevertheless a necessary element of trans-affirming community space.[8] Spade cites Davey Shlasko (trans educator and Smith alum) who cites Adrienne Rich: "When someone with the authority of a teacher describes the world and you are not in it, there is a moment of psychic disequilibrium, as if you looked into a mirror and saw nothing."[9] By immediately opening the space for participants to identify their pronouns, facilitators in the university and beyond can allow trans and gender disruptive people to see themselves in spaces they rarely do. Far from an act of erasure, Spade concludes, pronoun-sharing practices are acts of affirmation.

Manion and Spade here spar over now a hallmark of trans-inclusive policy and practice, parting ways over the potential costs and payoffs of institutionalizing this act of welcome. Nevertheless, both call readers to reconnect to the "why" of any rote habit and wrestle with the real demands of trans justice. The alignment as well as the divergence in their positions is reflective of their respective experiences and scholarship. Manion, a history professor, worked for ten years as founding director of the LGBT Resource Center at Connecticut College before joining Amherst. Spade, a law professor, has worked for twenty years as founding member of the Sylvia Rivera Law Project, which aims to improve access to social, health, and legal services for trans, gender-nonconforming, and intersex people. Both have engaged tirelessly in the work of facilitating gender justice in and outside the classroom. That they would think carefully about pronoun-sharing practices, then, is no surprise. Nor that they would think critically. In their own ways, Manion and Spade's early work, in *Liberty's Prisoners* and *Normal Life*, critiques how policy reforms often entrench and extend structures of inequality, rather than reducing them, especially for people marginalized by gender and race.[10] For Manion and Spade, then, trans-inclusive policy work is not a foregone good; it risks weakening precisely the communities it aims to support.

Manion and Spade, however, diverge significantly in their later work, a divergence that tracks their disagreement over pronoun-sharing practices. In *Female Husbands*, Manion shows how individual lives *trans* gender in innumerable ways over the long nineteenth century, especially in the form of the "female husband," a nomenclature common at the time. Importantly, for Manion, too often the ways in which the trans story gets told preclude recognition of the many folks transing gender across history whose lives and sentiments look very little like people identifying as transgender today. Expanding our story, they argue, is critical to honoring the rich history and current complexity of gender disruption. By contrast, in *Mutual Aid*, Spade describes practical basics of radical movement building.[11] Thinking concretely about how we are with one another, the book is chock-full of how-to bullet-point lists and graphs for leadership, group culture, consensus decision-making, agenda-making, work ethos, burnout, and wellness. For Spade, the everyday practices of making group culture *are already* the work of radical social change. Is pronoun-sharing a transformative practice (à la Spade) or does it reinscribe a hierarchy of the recognizable versus unrecognizable trans subject (à la Manion)? Is it a problematic policy or a practice of movement-building?

In analyzing trans-inclusive policies, I want to honor Medina's incisive action, as well as Manion and Spade's shared injunction to think critically about the unanticipated costs of policy and reform work. I want to be welcomed and be careful of all those welcome mats. I also want to heed Manion's warning about transhistorical, dehistoricized, and oversimplified ways of speaking about trans life, and Spade's invitation to craft group practices in ways that make us stronger and more capable of unmaking the systems around us. Are pronoun-sharing policies in higher education welcome mats that have lost their radical roots? Is there a way to *institute* trans inclusion without *compromising* trans inclusion? How do we signal our recognition and what are the habits of our welcome? These are just some of the trenchant questions raised by Medina's legacy and Manion and Spade's disagreement. Let us start from the beginning, with the problem of trans inclusion in higher education writ large.

Problems and the Method of Problematization

How did trans inclusion become a problem for the university to solve? To conduct such an institutional analysis, Michel Foucault's method of problematization is a key resource. I say this knowing full well the personal reasons I return to Foucault. Back in that rural college library, when I was just past twenty, he was the first queer author I ever read, the inception of my queer philosophical family. For Foucault, social problems—by which he means sites of institutional concern and contrivance—get crafted through large-scale discursive and material habits over time. As such, they are never apolitical; rather, they are situated within arrangements of power and resistance, normalization and critique, as a site of constant struggle. Analyzing those problems, let alone shifting them, requires a systemic and genealogical analysis of how things get said and get done. Here, I describe Foucault's method of problematization before threading it through the specific case of trans inclusion.

Problems demand attention. Problems also bely attention. Tracking problems reveals what a particular group of humans take not only to need attention but also to deserve attention—and by what means they go about giving it attention. For Foucault, societies "problematize" certain things (e.g., madness, criminality, sexuality) by making problematic certain techniques, practices, habits, behaviors, phenomena, discourses, and institutions. As a method, problematization analyzes how it is that certain things are made into social problems—what fears get mobilized, what prohibitions, what control practices, what ways of speaking and what ways of doing coalesce into a problem-solution assemblage. The method also tracks the ways in which social solutions bely specific articulations of social problems. As Foucault puts it, problematization takes a set of social anxieties and identifies "the point in which their simultaneity is rooted."[12] The goal of the method is not to offer, in some final way, an ideal solution to said social problems, but rather to open up the possibility of cultivating new soils, new arrangements of how things get said, get done, *get thought*. As such, problematization is a reconstructive project as much as a descriptive project.

If problematization is a method, what are its strategic components? By what steps does it enable us not only to unearth the practices and discourses we have inherited—and the force of their discrete assemblages—but also to unearth different possibilities? Here are three basic elements of the method. First, outline the problem-space. Notice where things are gathered up and where facts are banded together. Where are they clumped and networked as sites of concern and struggle, coalescing as an object of thought? Then, identify the anxieties, fears, prohibitions, control practices, or ways of taking care that mark the parameters of the problem. Second, characterize the problem. Identify the institutional practices, processes, and discourses that both configure and correct for the problem. Then, identify the individual techniques of self-cultivation that negotiate and neutralize the problem. Third, denaturalize the problem. Mark the contingent contours of the problem/solution, their stabilities and instabilities, second-guessing the presumptions and practices that constantly (re)produce them. Then, imagine other problems—or assemblages of concern—that might be meaningful, or that might matter. In clarifying how problems get made (and how they might get unmade), the method of problematization thus equips us to critically engage with what we say, what we do, and the world in which we live.

Sitting in DEI (Diversity, Equity, and Inclusion) meetings, month after month and year after year, I keep wondering how the stuckness of our conversations and the predictability of our solutions got started—and what, if anything, we can do to shake them up. Problematization prompts us to ask how trans inclusion has become a problem in and for and through the university. How do trans people become an agenda item—in the office, the conference room, the boardroom? How do they get on the schedule? And as what exactly? How are they added to a list of things to do or about which things must be done? What are the fears or desires that inform the list? What exactly is the problem-space that "trans issues" carves out?

The heart of such an investigation must analyze both the institutional practices and the individual techniques mobilized around the project of trans inclusion. If problematization, for Foucault, attends to how people "take care," "ask questions," and "become anxious" about things, then how do institutions and individuals "become anxious" about and "take care" of trans people in higher education?[13] First, at the institutional level, what are the "practices and habits," "behaviors, phenomena, and processes" that pull trans life up from the swirl of everyday existence and give it a public face as worthy of (specific types of) care and concern?[14] What are the meetings and memos, the policies and paper trails that characterize the university's machinations around trans inclusion—from student life to academic affairs? Which offices are called upon to act and which people are made to talk to one another? What is that blueprint? Second, at the individual level, what are the techniques by which people in the academy try, as Foucault might say, "to question their own conduct, to watch over and give shape to it, and to shape themselves as ethical subjects" in relation to trans existence?[15] What are the interpersonal expectations, recommendations, demonstrations of wokeness, protocols, standards of policing, and so forth, that circulate around trans inclusion? And how are those standards circulated? What are the flyers, the memes, the diversity trainings, the orientations, and the pedagogical practices that inculcate a specific approach to trans inclusion?

Problematization, however, involves more than analyzing how trans inclusion is made a problem for higher education. It also involves critically assessing that problem. What are the contingencies of its solutions and the possibilities for reconstruction? Are pronoun go-rounds, for example, necessary or accidental features of a trans-inclusive university life? If problems are crafted to "conform to the objectives [they] presuppose," then what does trans inclusion presuppose about trans people—or the university for that matter—and what does it fail to suppose?[16] And what, in the end, might be supposed otherwise about trans people, inclusion, and the university itself?

Trans Problems, Trans Policies

A Brief Genealogy

It was really in the first two decades of the twenty-first century that "trans inclusion" as such emerged in higher education, as a set of (trans) policies to solve (trans) problems. Since then, trans inclusion has quickly solidified as the new frontier of diversity initiatives. The turn has prompted many universities to add "gender identity and expression" to their nondiscrimination policies, map and increase the number of all-gender bathrooms on campus, assign gender-inclusive housing, institute registrar protocols for name changes, add trans healthcare coverage, and embrace best practices for pronoun usage. Some have issued new, transcompetent job descriptions for their LGBT coordinator positions. And others have introduced words like "transgender," "nonbinary," "agender," and "gender identity" into bias trainings and pedagogy workshops. New student orientations now kick off with pronoun go-rounds. Years ago now, as a new hire at American University, I even received a Trans 101 handout in my welcome packet, helpfully offering me a few dated definitions of people like me and a sketch of a Genderbread person.[17] All signs suggest higher education has turned a corner; trans-inclusive changes are afoot.

But how? How did trans life break the surface? What does that emergence illuminate and what does it hide from the light? Institutional pressures to diversify the academy started in the 1960s and 1970s, with the founding of ethnic studies and women's studies programs.[18] Following on the heels of support for students of color, first-generation students, students with disabilities, and women in STEM, trans inclusion is now a focal point of diversity efforts in higher education. Much of the work to integrate trans issues into university life was spearheaded by LGB(T) center staff and student activists starting in the late 1990s. To inherited queer concerns with legislation, nondiscrimination policies, affinity housing, educational efforts, and speakers' bureaus, they added new trans-specific concerns with name-change protocols, healthcare, and bathrooms. The process began haphazardly, with innovations here and there, informally modeled and replicated. People would print dossiers of websites, communiqués, or personal correspondence, describing sample trans-inclusive programs (three here, five there) and append them to university proposals, both as justification for their concerns and as a blueprint for how to address them.

Genny Beemyn, currently the director of the Stonewall Center at the University of Massachusetts, Amherst, a position they assumed in 2006 after a stint in Ohio State's GLBT Student Services, is one of the earliest and longest-standing voices for trans inclusion in higher education.[19] I met them at the Stonewall Center, a dark, half-submerged cement structure, where they spoke openly about the necessity and burnout of being a trans agitator in the academy. Their on-campus leadership, their contributions to national organizations focused on higher education, and their astounding research record all center around what trans inclusion means and what it necessitates. Beemyn's research is unique in its insistence on pulling the "T" out of LGBT in quantitative and qualitative studies, pairing research with story, and sharing their own experiences as a nonbinary person in higher education; together, these characteristics keep the work accountable and accessible. In a 2005 article, Beemyn presents seven key areas for trans inclusion, from locker rooms to programming.[20] In 2019, they present seventeen areas and ask students to rank them in order of importance (all-gender bathrooms easily taking first place).[21] Students are also invited to write-in any additional concerns. Interestingly, the most significant number of student concerns not already represented in Beemyn's questionnaire involved education itself and the personnel who provide it.

Of course, different schools had different trajectories. To put Beemyn's work in local context, consider the Five Colleges as a whole. At Hampshire College, trans-inclusive efforts start in the early aughts with bathrooms and then turn to pronoun and name policies. At the University of Massachusetts, Amherst, efforts start again in the early aughts with inclusive programming, then bathrooms and a nondiscrimination policy. At Mount Holyoke College, the work starts with student organizations, before expanding in the late aughts to health education and admissions policies. At Smith College, efforts start with neutralizing pronouns in student governance documents before moving in the early 2010s to admissions and healthcare. Over a decade and a half, the standard components of trans-inclusive policies solidify to some extent, such that when Amherst College starts the work in earnest in the mid-2010s, staff involved could say, "We did everything," "It was like all the stars aligned at the same time."[22] What constitutes "everything"? Well, they were able to initiate gender-inclusive bathrooms and housing, trans healthcare, pronoun and name protocols, an expanded nondiscrimination policy, Trans 101 trainings across campus, and related programming. This flush of policies and practices has since become more or less the gold standard for colleges and universities across the nation.

What Went Missing?

One way to describe trans inclusion in the university is as a structure of welcome for trans people. Another way to describe it is as a family of problems around which the university articulates itself as a liberal institution concerned with diversity, equity, and inclusion. Both can be true. Assuming trans inclusion is a "problem space," in the Foucauldian sense, what are the anxieties that surround it and the institutional and personal protocols that subtend it? What do trans people become in and through it? Unsurprisingly, in most conversations about inclusive policy, trans people become—at least—people with special needs. Those needs are typically logistical, largely mechanical, always transactional. As Z Nicolazzo states, "the deficit language and models" used within the university and within research about trans life in the university "have the effect of portraying trans students as problems for whom administrators must make accommodations."[23] What goes missing in this characterization is the reality that trans folks bring something to the university. They give something.

Trans-inclusive accommodations aim to produce certain moments of "fit" between trans and university life. Importantly, that fit has a particular skew. When one steps back to survey the scene, trans-inclusive policies coalesce most distinctly around the following five problems (and their corresponding solutions):

1. A legal problem (solvable by the addition of "gender identity and expression" to college and university nondiscrimination policies);
2. A linguistic problem (solvable by name and pronoun-sharing practices, as well as software patches to registration systems for anything from classes to diplomas);
3. A facilities problem (solvable by gender-inclusive housing, bathroom, and locker room facilities);
4. A healthcare problem (solvable by trans-competent staff in health and counseling services, as well as coverage of trans-related mental healthcare, hormone therapy, and gender-affirmation surgeries); and
5. An awareness problem (solvable by trans programming, Trans 101 training workshops, and support for LGBT and/or trans student organizations).

There are, of course, other trans-inclusive policies and practices that have been secured over the years, but the preceding five are the major hubs of concern around which significant momentum has gathered.

The purchase of problematization, however, is not only to identify the form trans problems take, but also to suss out the ways in which trans people do not become problems at all. It is worth marking, therefore, that rarely—*if ever*—does trans inclusion become the following sorts of problems:

6. A curricular problem (solvable by curricular representation of trans people or scholars, as well as a distinctly trans pedagogy);
7. A collections problem (solvable by library representation of trans authors or trans studies, and efforts to secure and build trans archives);
8. A personnel problem (solvable by recruiting trans students, staff, and faculty);
9. A research problem (solvable by supporting, with time and money, research done with, by, and for trans people); and
10. A community problem (solvable by university engagement with local trans communities).

It is certainly the case that these sorts of problems—or ways of constellating trans inclusion—have indeed been proposed, at one time or another, but the proposals have been rare and a distinctive uptake relatively absent.

Upon even a smidge of reflection, this breakdown of problems that do and do not constitute trans inclusion in US higher education today is stunning.

TABLE 1.1

Mainstreamed Trans-Inclusive Policies	Sidelined Trans-Inclusive Policies
Law: Nondiscrimination clause	Curriculum: Trans scholarship and pedagogy
Language: Pronouns and name-changes	Collections: Trans library holdings and archives
Facilities: Inclusive bathrooms, housing, etc.	Personnel: Recruitment of trans students, staff, faculty
Healthcare: Trans healthcare coverage	Research: Support of trans-led research
Awareness: Trans programming	Community: Engagement of local trans communities

Trans people are largely included, or perhaps more accurately accommodated, organizationally. Banks, start-ups, nonprofits, retail stores, healthcare centers, and businesses in the service industry have, much like colleges and universities, integrated Trans 101 trainings, all-gender bathrooms, expanded nondiscrimination policies, trans-inclusive healthcare, and name/pronoun protocols. What is unique to education, and specifically to higher education, however, are the curricula, the collections, the research, the students, and the faculty. Trans inclusion, however, rarely applies to—or gains traction within—these realms. This has a particular feel when you are (as I have been) the trans person being accommodated organizationally but pushed to the side academically. Put differently, in proposing solutions to concerns relatively peripheral to education itself, trans-inclusive policy work in higher education leaves the heart of the university relatively untouched and unchanged. The university's bureaucracy shifts, but not the university itself.

Were trans people to become part of the university in the latter set of senses—such that trans experiences, trans creative productions and scholarship, trans histories, and trans communities were meaningfully integral to its daily function and future vision—something other than accommodation for fit would take place. We might call it a trans-formation. After all, gender disruption—in its known and as yet unknown forms—is inherently a force of transformation. More than upending the cisheteronormative foundation of the university, as it has been historically constituted, however, the integration of gender disruption in higher education would involve welcoming the heart of trans life, which is not and has never been our names, our surgeries, or where we piss and shit. Medina and Spade are right to insist on the importance of respecting people's pronouns, but they, along with Manion, are also right to insist something more is necessary. Trans life involves how we make meaning together, how we come to know ourselves and the world alongside one another, how we tell our stories, arrange our presents, and craft our futures. Welcoming trans life in the university means celebrating, in meaningful and sustainable ways, the poetics of trans life.

By becoming a different sort of problem, trans folks might become both more severe problems for the university and something other than a problem. Were they to be part and parcel of a radical transformation of the university, as its undercommons or underbelly, the institution itself could not any longer be left in peace nor could it ultimately remain recognizable as what it was. What then happens to the university when trans poetics supersede trans policy? How might what lives and grows there change? As Aster (Erich) Pitcher, my early collaborator on this project wrote, reflecting on trans life in higher education: "May those who sit under the press of the normative be committed to the undercommons, that subaltern space where an intersectional coalitional politics, filled with a radical re-imagining of higher education, may blossom."[24] My hope is that this book goes some way toward realizing Aster's vision.

Problem-Being, Problem-Making

By asking how trans inclusion became a problem-space, what institutional policies and individual practices coalesce around trans inclusion, and how it all might be otherwise, I mean to take a hard look at these welcome mats. Where did trans-inclusive policies as such come from, who crafted them, where were they placed, and what other possibilities were foreclosed in their wake? Policies are regularly produced in response to the constitution of social problems. Nevertheless, there is always something about the problem that not only signals other, as yet unrecognized, problems but also exceeds and haunts those policies. Tracking that haunting and becoming attuned to that moreness is the project of this book.

Of course, every method of analysis has its own limitations. As helpful as the method of problematization is for an institutional analysis of trans inclusion, it cannot account for everything. Trans people are not simply constituted as problems by the university. Trans people themselves often choose to become a problem for the university. As such, while a structural approach illuminates institutional projects with personal repercussions, a more phenomenological approach can elucidate individual projects with institutional reverberations. Problematization, then, does not yet help us capture the choice to become a problem, to move from being a problem (or being made a problem) to becoming a problem (or making problems, making trouble, making good trouble).

Beemyn's work keeps making higher education a problem. Medina's handout made cisnormative behavior a problem. Something similar happened at Amherst College. As part of its efforts to institutionalize trans inclusion in the late 2010s, the Queer Resource Center mailed a flyer on pronoun best practices to every student, staff, and faculty member at the college. Amherst students, especially trans students, then launched an accountability campaign. One staff member recalls:

> They did this whole picture campaign, where they would take pictures of the faculty who put [the flyer] outside of their doors or in their offices. And they were like, "Hey, you should go to So-and-so's office hours, because they will actually listen to you, and care, and respect your pronouns. Don't go to So-and-so's office hours because they won't." They would do this frequently. And it became almost a political . . . it became more political on campus than I expected it to be.[25]

Here, rather than being the problem addressed by pronoun handouts, trans and allied students made what they took to be nonsupportive faculty members into a public problem. To understand moments like these, a different framework is needed. I turn, in the next chapter, then, to a consideration of trans folks as the problem-makers at the edge of the university.

Becoming a Trans Problem

CHAPTER TWO

When I think about problems, I think about Pat and a conversation we had back in 2020. Pat, a white, nonbinary student at the University of Massachusetts, Amherst, who was in and out of college for the better part of a decade, consistently felt like a problem for the university. "I tend to be someone who inadvertently causes problems," they remark.[1] As a trans person who uses a cane, has trouble taking multiple choice tests, and has several disabilities related to a chronic illness, Pat has been told by the university administration that they are "a problem person." Pat defines a problem person as someone who causes "an exceptional circumstance," because they need "an exception." They need something out of the ordinary, so they cause an out-of-the-ordinary situation for the university. The ordinary is business as usual; the extraordinary is a problem. A problem for the whole academic machine: the professors, the staff, the students, facilities personnel, et cetera. People think the problem person is making things harder for everyone, when in fact, "it can be harder or it's more difficult or it's more unpleasant, it takes more work" to be the problem person themselves. It takes work to ask someone to change how things work; it can be unpleasant to be the cause of unpleasantness, and difficult to be seen as difficult. Problems are hard nuts to crack. And Pat was a trans problem, a crip problem, a nontraditional problem.

Despite being seen as a perpetual problem, Pat nevertheless worked tirelessly to make themselves a problem for the university. Organizing collective agitation for gender-neutral bathrooms, name-change protocols, and trans healthcare, Pat fought for trans-inclusive policies that would make trans people less of a problem for the institution (and the institution less of a problem for trans people). With these changes, trans people would no longer need to request exceptions because their needs would no longer be exceptional. Much of that effort involved word-work: emails, meetings, discussions, proposals, and the like. Pat was a word machine. But there were also moments where Pat chose to become a physical problem: a visceral roadblock that literally stopped people in their tracks. Co-organizing protests and sit-ins, they used their body—this problem body—to name a problem with the university and to stage a problem for the university. Pat, always getting in trouble, became Pat the troublemaker.

What models of being and becoming a problem might help illuminate—and in turn be illuminated by—Pat's experiences and those like them? What are the theoretical resources for unpacking how trans people choose to make problems for the university (rather than simply be made into problems by the university)? What is it to make oneself a *pro-blema*, to throw oneself in another's face, to press oneself forward from out of the everyday background of things? What is it to choose and craft one's own mis-fitting?

Sociologist W. E. B. Du Bois famously wrote that Black life in the United States involves being the object of "an unasked question," one that hangs in the air without ever falling heavily to the ground: "How does it feel to be a problem?"[2] The question is approached in a "half-insistent" way, he observes, and the problem is a "half-named" problem.[3] The question and the problem circulate within what Du Bois calls "the veil" of the color line; within the veil, racial oppression darkens "half" the sun and makes Black people "half-men." What is this logic of halves and what does it illuminate about being or becoming a problem? What, to begin with, is a half-name? A whole or full name allows for legibility and formal instantiation; a half-name, then, would fall short of such legibility and formality. A half-named problem would be not fully recognized or understood. Some things have to be half-noticed, problems half-known, and words half-formed in order for a system to go on, for the status quo to remain in effect. White supremacy is one of those systems, Du Bois suggests. To extend the problem's half-life, it can only be addressed by halves. What happens, then, when halves start poking holes in the system? Start giving themselves and the problem full names? "When we give problems their names," feminist theorist Sara Ahmed writes, "We can become a problem for those who do not want to talk about a problem even though they know there is a problem."[4]

If for Du Bois, white people see a problem they conveniently refuse to play a part in fixing, for Black feminist theorist Barbara Smith they see a problem they conveniently deny a role in making. Writing in the *Mount Holyoke Alumnae Quarterly*, upon her graduation in 1969, Smith reflects on what it was like to be one of twenty-five Black students at Mount Holyoke her freshman year. "When another life *is* recognized," she writes "it is only recognized as a problem, [. . .] keeping one's self detached and therefore deluded about the part he has played in creating them."[5] The problem of racism, she argues, is just such a problem. Smith calls out the school's "complicity in maintaining a racist society" and insists it make "a serious decision to change" not only society, but the college itself.[6] In the issue, Smith is joined by two other Black graduating seniors: Sharyn Ainsworth and Sheryl McCarthy. McCarthy underscores that the "problem of racism" at Mount Holyoke will remain active so long as white people's "passive hope" and "inactive good-will" remain at the helm.[7] White people need to take more responsibility. For Ainsworth, real hope of addressing the "problems" Black students face lies at least as much in the collective organizing and "communion" of the newly founded African American Society.[8] Together, Smith, McCarthy, and Ainsworth are ready to make trouble. They choose to become a sticking point.

Across her work, and writing within this history, Ahmed provides rich insights into this active stance, this operation of becoming a problem (after being a problem). [9] For her, problems are best made through the willful subjectivity of marginalized people. People who say "No" to systemic oppression. While Ahmed develops her theorization of becoming a problem primarily with reference to women, especially women of color and/or queer women—all positionalities she herself holds, as a British-Pakistani Australian lesbian feminist—she also explicitly recognizes trans people as part of the lineage of problem-makers.[10] Thinking with Ahmed and this history, I want to ask: What might it mean for trans people—particularly in the university today—to choose to become a problem? To insist on a new language and new meaning-making systems through which they can give problems their full names? But also to become the thing that frustrates existing naming practices, that stops such naming in its tracks, perhaps even multiplying terminological half-lives? What might it mean for trans people to insist that those who historically played a part in constructing gender disruption *as a problem* take responsibility for doing so before hustling loudly (as they often do) to "solve" it? What might it mean for trans people to insist on the problem-power of collective trans organizing and communion? These are exactly the questions that the conjunction of Ahmed and Pat call us to think.

Becoming a Problem

Ahmed first engages the problematic of being and becoming a problem in her book on diversity work, *On Being Included*. While it is true that people marginalized in the academy—women, people of color, queer and trans people, people with disabilities, first-generation scholars, and their confluence, among others—are constructed by the university as a problem for the university, they become doubly so when they start naming and organizing around the real problems: sexism, racism, ableism, cisheteronormativity, class, et cetera. As Ahmed puts it, "In making those who experience racism into the problem, racism does not become the problem. To talk about racism is thus to be heard as making rather than exposing the problem: to talk about racism is to become the problem you pose."[11] By not letting structural inequities, systems of oppression, and long histories of exclusion remain in the background or fall away, but by calling them forward, people in these positions are thrown forward and get in other people's faces. As she summarizes elsewhere, "When you expose a problem, you pose a problem."[12] And that posing can be undertaken with relish, if not simply with purpose. For Ahmed, becoming a problem by posing problems is the sine qua non of feminist work.

While Ahmed reclaims the attribution of being a "problem" as such, she extends that recuperative work through her reflections on being "willful" and being a "killjoy." Channeling her own and others' stubborn resistance, whether around the family table or the boardroom, it is as if she says, "Yes. I have been, am, and will be a problem for you: I will willfully work against you and I will ruin your happiness if it is predicated on sexist, racist oppression." Being a willful subject and being a killjoy, as developed in *Willful Subjects* and *Living a Feminist Life* respectively, are best understood as two tactics of becoming a problem.[13] In one passage, Ahmed describes them both as "figures," lending shape to feminist recalcitrance, and each being "a relation, a kind of kin" to the other.[14] In another passage, she suggests they are different sides of the same energy: the feminist killjoy, she writes, "can still appear willful to you [...] she can be tiring" and "costly."[15] Whether two siblings or two sides, willfulness and killjoying share the larger logic of problems. One can be made a problem and make problems. One can be found willful and become willful. One can be and become a feminist killjoy. In each case, the negative attribution can be turned into a positive, life-sustaining force through which people make good trouble.

Becoming a problem involves becoming a willful subject. A willful subject, for Ahmed, is marked by many things, among them refusal, disobedience, and the propensity to block flow. Willfulness involves "a refusal to be willing" and "to become willing."[16] It is a refusal "to be part" and "to become part of a whole."[17] When that (oppressive) whole requires parts to give up their wills for the sake of the whole, parts that refuse become refuse. Unphased, the willful subject assumes the part of refusal—and of disobedience. In saying "No" repeatedly, they are "unwilling to obey," refusing both the tyranny of normativity and the call of law.[18] Such a subject has still other desire lines. Insistently declaring injustice and persistently invoking other modes of sense and sociality, the willful subject reshapes the contours of the network in which they are situated. More specifically, they block "flow," the flow in which bodies, ideas, relations, paperwork, *and time* move.[19] Against the momentum of history, the press of the present, and a fast-closing horizon, the willful subject is a stick in the mud. Going their own way gets in the way of the way things are going. They refuse to get "with" the program.[20] They strike, stop traffic, willfully (and willingly) "cause obstruction," "blocking the flow" of what gets said, gets done, gets thought.[21]

Becoming a problem also involves becoming a killjoy. If being willful entails refusing to work with how things work, being a killjoy entails refusing to feel the way things are supposed to feel. It is working and feeling in another direction and on another register, one that gets in the way of the first one. For Ahmed, a killjoy has a number of distinct characteristics, some of which include staying unhappy, snapping, and world-making. The killjoy is unhappy because the system in which they find themselves is unjust; they stay unhappy by refusing to forget this fact. The upshot is: they are a downer (precisely because they are downtrodden). Critically, Ahmed insists that "curiosity" and "imagination" are necessary for the production of this unhappiness.[22] One must be curious why this world, this way; and one must imagine another world. The longer one is unhappy, moreover, the more likely one is to "snap."[23] Snap your tongue at someone, snap your nerves in half, snap bonds too long borne. The snapping of our fragile selves equips us to snap the far less fragile systems of oppression circulating around us.[24] As destructive as that sounds, snapping is world-making. Being a killjoy opens you to other worlds and other lives.[25] "Killjoying is a world-making project," Ahmed writes.[26] In the work of reorienting feeling, "we enact the world we are aiming for."[27] And the "we" for Ahmed is robust, here, as big as an army.[28]

There is a waywardness about both being willful and being a killjoy. It is not the sort of waywardness that simply wanders from the proper path, content to do its own thing in the shadows. No, it is more insistent than that, and more disorienting. To be willful, to kill joy is to bulldoze over the paths one has inherited and cut other pathways—or, perhaps it is to abandon bulldozed paths altogether and follow other creaturely tracks across the landscape. In any case, willfulness and killjoying are way-stopping. I like to characterize them as *obstructing function* and *obstructing feeling*, respectively. Through that work of obstruction, willfulness and killjoying open up other, queerer modes of pleasure and performance.[29] After all, to be full of will (by having too much will) and to kill joy (by having too little joy) is to be a queerly oriented subject to begin with. When that queerly oriented subject then stops up the flow of things, splitting rivers and curtailing currents, still queerer things can happen. Orientations involve what one faces, how one is turned, who one wants, and where one finds home; they determine what one knows their way around and what one doesn't.[30] Disorientations of flow and function, then, send logics of relation, desire, and knowledge skitter-scattering.

Both willfulness and killjoying are subtended by a structure of openness. Ahmed writes that willfulness is a "signifier of hope," while killjoying is a way of "keeping one's hopes alive."[31] Hopes that have been decimated by the nonspace left in sexist, racist, queerphobic spaces. Hopes of belonging and of blossoming, rather than being isolated and trampled upon, or subject to an elimination regime. Choosing to become a problem, then, through the tactics of willfulness and killjoying, is not simply a matter of anger (although it is that) or curiosity (it is that too), but also a matter of hope. Becoming a problem both founds hope and fuels the work of hope.

Becoming a Trans Problem

How does one become—as I will put it here—a *trans problem*? What is the shape of that becoming? This is to say, how does a trans person or a group of trans people shift positionalities from being constituted as a problem to constructing problems themselves (and themselves as problems)? What resonances of resistant naming and communing, obstructing function and obstructing feeling might be therein at work? And what shapes does this take specifically at the edge of the university?

To illuminate the structure of becoming a trans problem, one might analyze first-person testimonies (like Pat's) or collective actions (like protests in which Pat was involved). Here, I use the latter strategy and focus on a particularly dynamic instance of problem-making in trans history at the Five Colleges: the Shit-In. The Shit-In was organized by Gender Liberation UMass (GLU), a group of trans, nonbinary, genderqueer students and allies (including Pat), on November 14–16, 2016. Variously referred to as #ShitIn, #ShitAtWhit, or #TilUMassGivesAShit, the action involved "occupying" bathrooms in the Whitmore Administration Building, where the offices of the provost and chancellor were located.[32] The Shit-In was modeled on die-in's or lie-in's, during which dying or lying is simulated. Here, shitting is simulated. Simply referred to as "sitters," students occupied thirty stalls, in three-hour shifts, over the course of three days.[33] A stunning 220 students are reported to have participated in the action.[34] As a critical sign of disability solidarity, which is no real surprise given the presence of crip trans life among the group's leadership, one urinal and one stall were left open in each multiuser restroom, and no ADA compliant stalls were occupied.

Becoming a problem, whether trans or otherwise and in the university or elsewhere, is typically interpreted as a simple project of policy procurement. You make noise to get something done. The Shit-In is no exception. Response to and coverage of the action focused on its demands for the enactment of certain trans-inclusive policies and procedures. The Shit-In's demands were as follows: "1) speedy implementation of gender-neutral restrooms campus-wide, 2) advancement of medically and socially competent in-house transgender health services, and 3) the hiring of a professor by the WGSS department, who is an expert in the study of critical transmisogyny from an intersectional perspective."[35] After two-and-a-half days of protest, the administration paid those demands lip service and Shit-In activists disbanded. Many folks interpret that as the beginning and the end of the story.

Becoming a trans problem, however, is not reducible to policy procurement. Indeed, the Shit-In's very demands signal something much deeper and more troubling than expanding trans-inclusive protocols at UMass, Amherst. Through its demands, the Shit-In problematized traditionally trans-inclusive points of policy and turned some of those policies themselves into problems. Putting the Shit-In's demands in a broader critical context, then, helps us get to the heart of the trouble.

1   Bathrooms: In demanding an increase in the number of all-gender bathrooms on campus, organizers explicitly rallied for "a third space," free of "cultural or gender surveillance."[36] As developed by Indian critical theorist Homi Bhabha, the third space is a contestatory zone situated obliquely to cultural hegemony that introduces ambiguity into systems of enunciation and belonging.[37] By calling for a third space, organizers are not demanding a simple act of trans inclusion by adding a new space, but introducing a space of disruption to cisnormative hegemony, a space that points out the ambiguities prior to the solidification of sense-making into the gender binary (and its restrooms).

2   Healthcare: In demanding trans-competence in university-provided health services, organizers did more than request that hormone

replacement therapy or counseling for gender dysphoria be made available. A year prior, GLU circulated a "Transgender Health Survey," in which they gathered information about the healthcare needs of trans people at UMass. In addition to trans-competent personnel (capable of overseeing labs and hormones, as well as offering mental health counseling and providing guidance on insurance, surgeries, and other medical procedures and therapies), survey results included calls for trans staff, legal consultation, and "training for trans-related sexual care."[38] GLU's demand, then, was ultimately a demand that UMass trans healthcare be wholistic and richly accountable to its trans community.

3 Professorship: In demanding that the Department of WGSS hire someone with expertise in intersectional transfeminism, organizers did more than request the hiring of someone with competence in transgender studies. The first tenure-line hire in the Department of WGSS was Janice Raymond, a well-known trans exclusionary radical feminist (TERF) and author of *The Transsexual Empire*, who was and remains remarkably inattentive to gender's racial politics. GLU's demand, then, was an explicit demand that the university right past wrongs and engage in a process of reparations with the transgender community, especially the trans women and femmes who have borne the brunt of TERF rhetoric and organizing for decades.

4 Opt Out: The three stated demands are paired down and condensed from a list of eleven demands GLU circulated the semester before. That longer list included demands for trans competent Title IX staff, funding for the Queer People of Color group, hiring trans staff and faculty, institutionalizing pronoun protocols, and, perhaps most significantly, providing the "option to opt out of tagged markers on housing profiles and UHS [University Health Services] records that indicate a student's transgender identity."[39] This final demand is fascinating. Typically, trans-inclusive policies involve the formal recognition and registration of trans students in a variety of university management systems. Here, GLU troubles "inclusion" by asserting a trans right to anonymity, and even opacity.

By insisting on a third space, on wholistic treatment and accountability, on correcting for history, and on the right to anonymity and opacity, Shit-In activists showed themselves to be the sort of trans problem that is not easily solved with a quick memo or policy brief. A system patch is not going to cut it. A low-cost, low-fuss, low-investment capitulation, or bit of virtue signaling is not good enough. These high-maintenance trans problems agitated for something before and beyond policy that will always trouble that policy itself: the irrepressible value and ambiguity of trans life.

At the heart of becoming a trans problem is not policy but poetics. The Shit-In's problem-making practices dramatize a certain poetic disruption in how people are with one another and how they make each other. In the belly of the binary, protestors built trans belonging. Occupying stalls either alone or with another person, Shit-In sitters were invariably contributors to trans sociality and participants in trans world-making.[40] Separated by stall walls, activists sat within ear and arm shot of one another and "read books, did homework, and talked amongst each other."[41] Marshals were stationed in the halls outside and charged with set-up and take down, overseeing shift changes and the wellbeing of protestors ("Make sure they are alright, and have eaten"), and addressing any issues that might arise.[42] And not for naught. Some people were, unsurprisingly, upset by the action. As David Moye reports in *HuffPost*, "They shouted insults and shook the bathroom stalls."[43] People also spammed the Google form GLU circulated to organize interested participants; on it, comments such as "shut the fuck up and use the bathroom," "you are a disgrace to this country," and "this is not a civil rights movement" were logged in boxes requesting participants share their hourly availability.[44] This fraught sociality is, in microcosm, the structure of becoming a problem. Becoming a problem is disruptive and alienating at one level, but also aligning and redemptive on another. It involves building belonging according to resistant logics that rupture normative codes and customs. And it does so in the sticky places.

At the core of becoming a trans problem is gender disruption and, with it, an inherent gender creativity. It is the poetic work of building trans belonging by rupturing cisheteronormativity and resisting being placated by certain trans-inclusive policies. This resonates with Ahmed's theorizations of becoming a problem more generally and her figures of the willful subject and the killjoy specifically. Might we understand, for example, Shit-In activists as obstructing function and feeling in such a way that trans world-making and trans hope become more possible? Might that be the heart of the action after all?

Transing Function, Transing Feeling

As developed in trans studies, the term *transing* refers to the movement by which supposedly fixed entities are crossed, blurred, and unsettled. While that work of making-slip and making-leak is rooted in crossing the (again supposedly) fixed binary genders of (cis)man and (cis)woman, it extends far beyond that to still other binary structures. "Transing," trans studies theorists Susan Stryker, Paisley Currah, and Lisa Jean Moore write, can function "as an escape vector, line of flight, or pathway toward liberation."[45] It is a processive movement, "dancing back and forth" rather than keeping one's feet planted on one side or the other.[46] It is a doing and a making that is always undoing and unmaking. In sum, they write, transing is an "essentially poetic practice."[47] A more recent conversation between Aren Aizura, Jules Gill-Peterson, Marquis Bey, Treva Ellison, Eliza Steinbock, and Toby Beauchamp similarly characterizes transing as a "process of questioning" that involves both "rummaging around the interstices" (and pressing open the seams) but also "suturing" things together (so as to never be or become one thing).[48] It is critical to keep this seemingly untethered concept accountable, however. PJ DiPietro, for example, insists that transing's emphasis on "doing rather than being" and "connectivity rather than individuality" has to intersect richly with "vernacular histories and ecologies of embodied difference" if it is to have any real traction.[49] Transing where, then, and when? With whom and against what? Why and how?

Marquis Bey does some of that tethering. While DiPietro roots trans- in South American *travesti* embodiment, Bey anchors it in US Black nonbinary experience. In their beautiful reading of jayy dodd's poetry, a reading they explicitly describe as a "romp" through the confluences of Du Bois's "How does it feel to be a problem?" and Leslie Feinberg's "Is that a boy or a girl?," Bey explores transing (and/as blackness) as *becoming a question*, or even *becoming a question mark*.[50] To trans the question that is leveled at Du Bois or Feinberg or dodd is to become a question, to hold open the space of the question and live there, breathe there. Hearing dodd characterize herself as a "blxk question mark" and a "volunteer gender terrorist," Bey pauses.[51] "The question becomes a habitable geography," they muse, the rocky shore on which the waves of white cisheteronormativity break and within which Black and/as trans tidepool ecologies flourish.[52] Actively living one's questioned existence as a question mark "mudd[ies] gender's buttressing luminosity and symbolic integrity."[53] To become a question mark is to mark out one's becoming in the space of "the whatever." "The space of the whatever," Bey writes, "is a miasmic, nebulous, trans kind of ethereal otherwise enfolded in on by blackness' and transness' fugitive inflections."[54] This, for Bey, is the structure that blackness and transness share, the structure of flight from being put in question and made a problem to becoming a question and becoming a problem.

Drawing this lineage together with that of Sara Ahmed, I want to propose that becoming a trans problem involves transing function and transing feeling.

It involves not simply posing a question to gender, or hanging a question mark above gender, but dramatizing the question that is always falsely settled by the mechanics and moods of cisnormativity. As I see it, transing is a specific form of obstructing that holds things in question. At its most fundamental level, the Shit-In was just such a project. In *transing function*, sitters of the Shit-In obstructed the flow of gendered restrooms and administration work, as well as the man/woman and public/private binaries on which both supervened. This involved a certain insistence on dysfunction and an express willfulness to go a different direction. Likewise, in *transing feeling*, sitters of the Shit-In caused unhappiness by insisting on trans presence and trans anxiety, both hidden or occluded by the cisheteronormative campus climate. This involved a certain insistence on bad feelings and a willingness to kill joy and be a downer.[55] In transing function and feeling, moreover, activists opened the space of a question, wherein new, more life-giving affective and operative pathways might flourish.

Becoming a trans problem involves transing function. Transing function crosses, blurs, and makes leak not only how things function but also how it is thought things ought to function (and who ought to function where). The Shit-In meant to muck-up function, and it did so in at least two ways. First, activists obstructed the flow of plumbing and personnel. In their own words, they aimed to "obstruct [the] toilets."[56] They stopped-up the passage of people passing in and through Whitmore. Bathroom users would have to congregate in a line to use a Whitmore restroom or leave Whitmore to join restroom users in other buildings. (Imagine using the only stall not occupied by students doing homework.) Given the inconvenience of both options, protestors inadvertently slowed or stopped the passage of excretion in the people working at Whitmore. Blockages and stoppages proliferated. Second, activists mixed-up space. Protestors got to choose which bathroom they wanted to sit in and with whom. In doing so, they gender-bent the bathrooms themselves. That some of them were trans only added to the palpable hybridity they inserted into these facilities. In addition to befuddling the binary between men's and women's spaces, they also frustrated the distinctions between public and private, individual and social. Private restrooms became public hangouts, while social hallways became individual waiting areas for excretive relief.

Becoming a trans problem also involves transing feeling. Transing feeling crosses, blurs, and makes leak not only how things feel but also how things are supposed to feel (and who is supposed to feel what). The Shit-In meant to galvanize feeling, and it did so again in at least two ways. First, activists made trans presence felt. Sibelle Grisé, one of the organizers, explained that the whole enterprise aimed "to have our presence felt."[57] Sitters were in every restroom, on every floor, saturating Whitmore with queer, trans, and ally spirit, signaling a small but mighty cohort of folks ready to fight for trans life on campus. Second, activists aimed to propagate anxiety. For a mere few days, activists tried to produce bathroom "anxiety" among the administrators working at Whitmore—a small slice of the anxiety trans students feel every day "just trying to pee on campus."[58] As co-organizer Justine Killian put it, "this is just a tiny taste of what it's like to be a trans student."[59] Having stalls perpetually "in use" and therefore always, in some sense, "out of order" palpably demonstrated to the administration what it was like to be a trans person in need of an all-gender bathroom on campus. All-gender restrooms are rarely available and often inaccessible. By producing and multiplying these inconvenient feelings—and, indeed, redistributing the burden of those inconvenient feelings—sitters engaged in affect-activism, shifting, and sifting feeling.

In transing function and feeling, becoming a trans problem also involves becoming a question mark. In their flyer for the event, which they posted on stall and restroom doors, GLU included their demands alongside the single image of a toilet. This was not, however, the sanitized image of an "all-gender" toilet commonly used today. Rather, it was a ravenous, *demanding* toilet that had seemingly come alive overnight. From its bowl emerge a thick tongue, teeth, and fangs, as saliva sloshes over the seat and flies from its gullet. From its tank peer two large oval eyes framed by heavy lashes, while sweat springs from its temples. The toilet itself has become a trans problem. It is willful and full of feeling, out to make folks uncomfortable. But the toilet is also trans-gender, trans-human, and trans-crip. With its hyperfeminine tank and masculinized bowl, the fixture flaunts a fierce femme-fatale energy, with echoes of vagina dentata close behind. The toilet itself has also become animate. The site of inanimate shit is now the site of animate activism. And that animacy will remain until GLU's demands are met. Meet Gloux, then, as I like to call her. Unapologetically monstrous, her mad instability—her raving mind and raging body—lends a crip trans presence to the action.[60] She is a question mark incarnate, not a decorous one but slightly deranged. She is everything powerful and perverse about becoming a trans problem.

Through disruption and negativity, blocking and blurring, the Shit-In also did something beautiful. In snapping (at) the calcifications of cisheteronormativity on campus, it built trans belonging. This building happened before the Shit-In even got off the ground (in organizing meetings, brainstorm sessions, and friendships) and continued through the action itself (sitting together,

WHAT'S UP WITH THE SHIT-IN?

GENDER LIBERATION UMASS IS OCCUPYING WHITMORE'S BATHROOMS UNTIL ADMIN AGREES TO OUR THREE DEMANDS:

1. SPEEDY IMPLEMENTATION OF GENDER-NEUTRAL RESTROOMS CAMPUS-WIDE
2. ADVANCEMENT OF MEDICALLY AND SOCIALLY COMPETENT IN-HOUSE TRANSGENDER HEALTH SERVICES AT UHS
3. HIRING OF A PROFESSOR BY THE WGSS DEPARTMENT WHO IS AN EXPERT IN THE STUDY OF CRITICAL TRANSMISOGYNY FROM AN INTERSECTIONAL PERSPECTIVE

FIGURE 2.1
Shit-In flyer listing GLU's three demands, accompanied by the image of a demanding toilet, with long eyelashes, sharp fangs, and sloshing saliva.

passing one another at shift change, talking on and offline together). The feeling was strong enough that folks involved in the action spontaneously renamed Whitmore "Queermore."[61] But Shit-In activists also built connections beyond themselves. The UMass Fossil Fuels Divestment Campaign, a staunch ally of the Shit-In, posted a call for support of the action on their Facebook page. In it, they wrote:

> There can be no climate justice without gender justice. There can be no gender justice without racial justice. There can be no racial justice without economic justice. There can be no economic justice without social justice. As Arundhati Roy writes, "Remember this: We be many and they be few. They need us more than we need them."[62] Let's topple these systems and build a world that works for all of us.[63]

In calling for transversal mobilizations of trans function and trans feeling, the Shit-In and its allies reconfigured the network of flows that constitute the university itself. Reorienting springs, bridges, and damns, activists made room for new forms of hope and happiness to spring directly from trans life.

BECOMING A TRANS PROBLEM   47

In 2020, Cameron Awkward-Rich, then assistant professor in the Department of Women, Gender, and Sexuality Studies at University of Massachusetts, Amherst, published a reflection prompted by the police killing of Tony McDade.[64] In it, he dramatizes the kind of being a problem that marked McDade's life and death and, conversely, the kind of becoming a problem that marked the crowd of protestors surging through Northampton in its wake. He stands, "the only black trans person on the street," in the clash between "the routine, ordinary violences that inhere in poor, black, mad, gender-nonconforming life" and the sea of young people, led by a Black and Brown high school contingent, that swept Main Street, chanting "Black Trans Lives Matter," scaling flagpoles, and tagging the police station with BLM and abolitionist slogans. And he listens. If a "style of hopefulness" is rooted in transness, as "the insistence on the human capacity for once unimaginable change," Awkward-Rich writes, it is also locatable in the transversal energy of "the motley we" that day, a "we" he associates "with a much darker," madder, "commons." If something like freedom, if something vaguely "better" is possible, it is because a motley crowd is, as he writes, "assembling again outside my window, louder this time, gathering force."

In *The Undercommons*, theorizing a resistant poetics at the edge of the university, Stefano Harney and Fred Moten ask the haunting question: "How do those who exceed the profession, who exceed and by exceeding escape," how do they "problematize themselves, problematize the university, force the university to consider them a problem, a danger?"[65] Harney and Moten's own answer lies in the figure of the undercommons, which is a space of fugitive fomentation where Black, Indigenous, queer, and poor people "cohabit," co-create and co-imagine.[66] To craft one's own and one's people's misfitting is also to fit out new spaces for thing-making and thing-doing. Put differently, becoming a problem, even in the pursuit of important policy changes, always already involves taking a turn toward poetics. Here, the linguistic and the material come together not merely in order to enunciate, like so many protest placards, what it is that we want, but also, and perhaps more fundamentally, to illustrate—physically and aesthetically—how it is that we want to be together. To become a specifically trans problem is to do all of this from and toward trans community, where normatively gendered structures are busted and blurred. That is the sweaty project of a trans poetics.

Mobilizing Trans Poetics

CHAPTER THREE

> call me tumblefish / rip-roar, pocket of light
> —OLIVER BENDORF, "Split Open Just to Count the Pieces"

The ways in which trans people are made into problems in the university and choose to become problems for the university are often reductively understood through bureaucratic policy projects. Trans-inclusive policies—such as bathroom policies, healthcare policies, name and pronoun policies, and nondiscrimination policies—are seen to solve the problem of trans life in the university and satisfy the problem posed by trans people in the university. But there is something before and after policy. There is something before and after "inclusion." There is a residue of trans life that is irreducible to behavioral blueprints, technological patches, and financial redistributions. There is something more fundamentally challenging to university culture here. And that something is trans poetics. It is the fact of trans wisdom, creativity, and community. If the records of trans life and activism in the university demonstrate anything, it is the immense insight into gendered life, innovation in social cultures, and good-humored fun that can be had in the borderlands (and at the expense) of the academy. What might it mean for trans poetics to transform higher education? How might trans ways of making meaning together fashion more room in and beyond these walls, and facilitate more ways to dwell and to imagine?

Poetics. An ancient concept. It refers to what is creative and what is formative. It stems from the ancient Greek *poiesis* meaning the process of making, of crafting, or of fabricating. The term *poetics*, then, does not refer merely to poetry or poets, although they are never far away. It refers, instead, to this nonmechanistic, nonderivative work of making sense—with symbols and bodies brought into conjunction with one another. The magic of words and things. Today, poetics has taken on a distinct hue in critical university studies. Often characterized as the bastion of knowledge production, the university is a place where the supposed sum of things is taught and studied. Insofar as that knowledge is repeatedly and relentlessly thought of (*and lived*) as separable from bodies and from community building, so too is the university. The university project is a capitalist venture with largely utilitarian procedures of production. An attention to poetics here means an attunement not to what gets produced in publication turnstiles, labs, and classrooms, but rather to what happens in the corridors, quads, study carrels, cafeterias, and cafes. It means tracing the creative commons, which is always under, beside, or just behind the knowledge production apparatus and its burgeoning administration systems. Here, counter modes of study and ways of knowing are inextricable from the ways we make things and make one another.

In the university context, what does trans poetics mean? What does it marshal and imply? The term invites us to ask what bodies and symbols are transed in this space, and what does working creatively with them involve and involute? Trans poetics marks the necessity of thinking words joined to materiality, shot through with creativity, and inseparable from the energies clustering under the sign "trans-." Trans poetics involves the words we speak and write, feel and dance. It means the ways we eat and breathe with one another, love and die through one another. It is a cipher for "moreness."

What Is Poetics?

Poiesis stems from the root verb *poien*, meaning not only to compose and to write, but also to make, create, and produce. The term's even older, Proto Indo-European root is related to *ci-*, meaning to collect or assemble; to pile, stow, or gather. There is a kernel of wisdom in this history. When we gather, we make. In assembling, we create. Poetics is the power of the pile to craft new belongings and fashion new functions. But we have to get together first. When we pile our words and our worlds, certain songs can surface. Poetics is the mobilization of imagination through sociality. As such, it is always materially rooted, but conceptually shaped. And it works in and through and by relation.

Poetics connects world and language. In Western philosophy, the thinking of poetics begins with Aristotle's book of the same name, in which he offers an expansive definition of poetry and, indeed, accounts for what makes poetry poetry—that is, poetics.[1] Poetry, he writes, is a kind of mimesis or imitation of life whereby the poet deploys the matter of language, rhythm, and melody to mimic the matter of the world.[2] Crucially, both world and language are substance; both are substantial. Poiesis is the magic by which the dance between symbol and stuff takes shape. That magic, of course, only permits expression to a certain extent. Aristotle's *Poetics* survives incompletely, as if to underscore that the prosaic explanation of poetry can only ever be fragmentary. Millenia later, German philosopher Martin Heidegger argues that there is no simple mimesis happening here, but something more intimate. Poiesis, or the connection between making and languaging, signals a deeper connection between dwelling and dwelling upon, or between building and thinking.[3] For Heidegger, we exist in and through language, which means, in part, that there is earth—and there is material existence—in words themselves. When our being is blocked, and we live in the world only superficially, a return to the soil of sense, *through poetry*, is necessary and that return is always also a new beginning. Beginning to dwell again, to dwell in and to dwell on.

Because of its positioning between world and language, poetics is necessarily rooted in the imagination. For Gaston Bachelard, a French theorist of poetics, one cannot in fact understand the world as it is without attuning oneself to the poetic image and the imagination by which one relates to it.[4] Simplistic reason and mechanistic science are never sufficient for understanding the poetry of existence. For Bachelard, what exists is more than what can be counted; it must be encountered. What falls outside of mechanism and rationality, then, is precisely *what gets lived*, and the only viable access to that matter is the imagination, whose poetic reverberations "interweave the real and the unreal."[5] Queer Chicana feminist Gloria Anzaldúa has a similar account. For her, Western colonialism "split the artistic from the functional, the sacred from the secular, art from everyday life."[6] Thinking decolonially—that is, thinking from the borderlands and with border-consciousness—requires bridging those spaces.[7] With the mindset of the in-between (*nepantla*), the border-writer reaches deeply into her own well (*el cenote*), wherein lie the symbols and metaphors of the imaginal consciousness. Translating those images into story and poetry, the border-writer carries them out into the world. While Bachelard's and Anzaldúa's diagnoses of the need for imagination differ, they make a similar appeal to the centrality of the image to a poetics of existence.

Connecting world and language via imagination, poetics irrevocably needs relation: relations between things, between meanings, and between the betweens. Who better to illuminate this nexus than Martinican theorist Édouard Glissant, author of *The Poetics of Relation*? The poetics of relation refers to a way of belonging and making sense that expands and "explodes like a network."[8] Western colonialism and Eurocentrism function according to a logic of calculation, reduction, and transparency, freezing the network in an institution. Anticolonial resistance, by contrast, honors the relational, the nomadic, and the opaque, returning the network to its latent ambiguity. While "thinking thought" in a colonial fashion typically "amounts to withdrawing into a dimensionless place," a poetics of relation insists on multiplying dimensionalities and thinking in and between them.[9] It is a "poetics that is latent, open, multilingual in intention, directly in contact with everything possible."[10] Glissant finds the poetics of relation beautifully manifest in creolization, where "fractal manifestations of sensibilities [...] reconfigure and reassemble in as yet unthinkable ways."[11] He also takes inspiration from the Caribbean archipelago. For him, the archipelago teaches the poetics of relation through the land itself, and archipelagic thought undergirds the very possibility of creolization and anticolonial resistance.[12] The poetics of relation, then, is at work in languages, cultural practices, and politics, but also in the matter of earth itself.[13]

Even traditionally understood, poetics is capacious. It refers not simply to how we use words, but also to how we assemble things and how things get created through that assembly. It invokes dwelling, imagining, and living in relation. And that work is never straightforward. How might we attune ourselves to such a poetics? How might we trace the ways in which translational tactics, liminal spaces, and hybridity make real and resistant meanings? And what richly rewarding non-sense lies here in the renewal of sense? There is, after all, a poetics to being beside ourselves as much as to being beside one another.

Of Drawers and Letters

Moments that escape or are in excess of the university project, moments in which imagination and relationality are foregrounded, where dwelling and hangouts happen, and words and things blur, are numerous but difficult to notice. Reminiscing about his weekly visits with nurse Ethel at the UMass health clinic in the early aughts, however, Ben, a trans man and University of Massachusetts, Amherst alum, recalls just such a moment:

> She was an older Black woman, with gray hair that was really nicely twisted in with her dreads. She was super cool, super chill. And every week I had my date with Ethel. There was no copay. We would schedule our appointment each week and I would just come in. I'd bring her coffee and we'd chat about the week. She'd do my injection and I'd see her the following week. It was super easy. [...] I wasn't paying for syringes and I wasn't paying for needles. I didn't even have to keep my testosterone with me. Ethel kept it, in a drawer. People came in for all sorts of treatments, so she just had a locked drawer where she kept all of people's stuff.[14]

Super cool, super chill, super easy. Coffee chats without copays. Friendly injections. A drawer for all sorts of stuff, and all sorts of folks. Ben's weekly visits with Ethel bear a distinct poetic resonance.

The name Ethel comes from the old Germanic *athala*, meaning noble, which in turn is rooted in the Proto-Indo-European *at* (over, beyond, super) and *al* (to nourish). Ethel's name suggests either that she has been superbly nourished or that she goes over and above to nourish those around her. Perhaps in her case both are true, the one leading to the other. Hers is an emergent strategy of abundance—precisely in a place where Blackness is scarce.[15] The kindness Ethel showed and the kinship she supported, moreover, is traceable in the microcosm of Ethel's drawer. What lived and breathed here together, bounced and bumped alongside each other? For a campus nurse of this sort, Ethel might have kept materials not only for hormone replacement therapy, but also for insulin injections, iron infusions, or birth control shots. There might be alcohol swabs, needles, tongue depressors, latex gloves, and band-aids. In response to a medley of needs, the drawer hosted an intimacy of things, some shuffling and others clinking beside one another. In this drawer, the needs of people who knew each other would be nestled close, but so would those of people who might never meet. Regardless of who they were or with whom they belonged, Ethel's drawer—much like Ethel herself—set about making belonging, and thereby building a certain poetics.

Helder, a genderless Mount Holyoke alum, recalls receiving gender-affirming care from a local therapist in the mid-2010s and similarly highlights the ways in which the structure of that relationship formed and fashioned a space in excess of university (and medical) logics—a space of revolutionary poetics. As they put it:

> I don't know if she [the psychiatrist] would or did identify herself as an abolitionist, but she was doing that work. She was a provider, a queer

provider with lived experience of psychiatric abuse and madness. And she would let you basically lie through your teeth and copy that down and write you a [surgery] letter and get the stamp of approval. And she would just do that. She was a machine. [...] She provided me this lifesaving technology in the form of a letter.[16]

And, indeed, letter after letter, as if crafting abolition on the page. This was one of Helder's first experiences with a care provider who "was actually caring." Care, here, needs to be understood in a deinstitutional, anti-institutional sense where what gets made is more than (and distinctly other than) what policy provides—or even allows. This provider allowed her own stories to jostle in her body, honored the stories of others jostling in theirs, and let those stories break free into bodies of their own in the form of legally admissible, medically effective epistles. Sheets of paper, drawers full of dreams.

What Is Trans Poetics?

What does it even mean for "poetics" to be modified by "trans"? How do poetics get turned in a trans direction, or invited into a series of trans configurations? To date the term *trans poetics* has referred primarily to trans poets' aesthetic approaches to their work. In her TSQ encyclopedia entry of the same name, Rebekah Edwards writes: "'Trans-poetics' refers to the art and the labor of transgender poets, and it refers to diverse interpretive and compositional strategies attentive to relational movements between/across/within linguistic, embodied, affective, and political domains."[17] Edwards suggests that while poetics become trans simply by being practiced by trans poets, there are also trans ways of working a text that are linked to transness itself, rather than simply to trans authorship. Both senses are plumbed in depth throughout the first two major English-language collections of trans poetry: *Troubling the Line* and *We Want It All*.[18] In *Troubling the Line*, all fifty-five poets pair "trans poetics" statements with their poetry. These statements root trans poetics in the malleability of the trans body and the survival work of trans writing, underscoring the transformative materiality of words and worlds. Trans poetics then gets mobilized, in *We Want It All*, for the "unmaking and making" not only of gendered worlds, but also of worlds without "capital, prisons, borders, and ecocide."[19] This is the capaciousness of trans poetics.

The trans body is malleable, as is the textual body. It can be bent, broken, and repurposed; it can sing offkey or change the entire signature of the melody. Trans-textual bodies use the flesh of sound and syntax, gesture, and rhythm to make speak what could not be heard. What do trans poets do to the (textual) body? What do they do to the (textual) line? As TC Tolbert puts it, they "trouble" it.[20] That is the poetic work. Other trans poets likewise play on the resonance between poem and body, and the trouble they can get up to together. "Consider the poem itself as a body," one invites; "poetry *is* the body" or "is my body, my bodies," others write.[21] "Poem-bodies."[22] These trans-textual bodies, however, differ and defer meaning. They are always already resisting inherited systems of sense. For Trace Peterson, it is critical to notice their readability *and their unreadability*.[23] Trans poem-bodies are confounding. They are "both/and," "shifting," "slipping" and "swerving," "shuttling" and "switching" in a "slipstream."[24] And they can do this because they inhabit "borderlines, betweenity," and "all the interstices and liminal spaces."[25] Part of the trans poetics of trans poets, then, involves exploiting precisely this resistant intimacy between—and shared malleability of—their poems and their bodies.

Writing from that space of intimacy is survival work and it is creative work. As Eileen Myles attests, writing trans poetry is a "survival tool."[26] Living day in and day out, decade after decade, in a cisheternormative world, and experiencing that constant shattering and scattering, produces a deep well of "pain."[27] Writing trans poems is a way to build "wholme," to use Ahimsa Timoteo Bodhran's word.[28] It also promotes "healing," healing of the writer as much as the reader as they build belonging and resonance in a landscape of alienation.[29] Submitting to this transitive and transversal transformation, trans poets are able to unwrite harmful narratives and let the unimaginable take flight. The metaphors for this poetic work are many. Some speak of "fill[ing] the line where splinters exhale off benches," or "filling the holes (the fucking cracks)."[30] How do you fill gaps and craters left by thousands of years of gender normativity? How do you write across them? For some folks, it looks "like stickstickiness, stitches, stitching," or the "pasting" of things together.[31] For others, it looks like "weaving," as if writing were "a way of threading disparates into potential aggregates."[32] These tools—weaving, stitching, and sticking—permit trans poets to do the work of trans poetics, re-assembling in ways that renew and revive.

What then is trans poetics? As theorized by trans poets, trans poetics is the linguistic creative process within which and by which the "breathing" of trans bodies and trans lines happens.[33] It is the space, too, where "eruption" happens.[34] One can think of it grammatically like a comma, a slash, or an ampersand.[35] Trans poetics is a space of opening, a *break*. But it is also a space of connection, a *bridge*. It is a space of counterinsurgency as much as convergence.[36] Writing, D'Lo attests, is a way to connect to "my head," "my heart," and "other people."[37] It is a way to connect to the most ephemeral parts of existence, but also to the earth itself and its "most idle looking pebble."[38] And this break and this bridge together form a "making against unmaking."[39] Whatever space trans poetics makes, whatever life it heals, and whatever slipstream in which it swims, it is resistant as much as it is creative, a "no" as much as a "yes."

Poetry as Tactic

Trans poetics is irrepressibly linked to trans poetry. This not only makes sense theoretically, but it is also borne out in story. Ashling, a white disabled trans woman and Hampshire student, recalls a moment when a TERF zine, including an anti-trans poem or lyric, was discovered in SAGA, Hampshire's cafeteria.[40] It was academic year 2015–2016. There was much hullabaloo about what to do on the part of the administration. Eventually, the director of the Queer Community Alliance Center (QCAC) asked me, as the college's only out trans faculty member at the time, and Fae, a trans staff member, to at least meet and talk with trans students. Although some folks interpreted this invitation to be the administration washing its hands of the affair, Fae and I felt that convening a meeting—in which trans folks could gather and be together—was in itself a powerful response. More powerful still is what we did with the space. Meeting over a pile of pizza and carbonated beverages, we sat there and read trans poetry together for hours. We laughed softly, thinking about shouting the poems in the quad or projecting them onto the side of Hampshire Library for days. Eventually dispersing with our stash of trans poems in tow, we ended up passing out trans poems all over campus.

    I do not remember who came up with the idea, but I do remember that Fae made the selections. We read from Lilith Latini, "Each pinecone's tiered shell already embodies flame, ready to reach and open."[41] From Lady Dane Figueroa Edidi, "Let not the sun dissipate you as it does so many dreams"; "My brothers and sisters we are the celebration. Reclaim. Reawaken."[42] From Charles Theonia, "Everyone else is as beautiful and uncertain as you are."[43] From Mark Aguhar, "Bodies are inherently valid," and "Blessed are the beloved who I didn't describe, I couldn't describe, will learn to describe and respect and love."[44] In this moment, trans poetry was a tactic of resistance against a specific form of erasure. We pitted trans poem against TERF poem, lyrical line against lyrical line. More than this, however, trans poetry was a way to make meaning together and build a sense of belonging. There was no regular meeting place for trans people on campus. I remember one student sharing that she had just come out earlier that day and this was her first meeting dressed in clothes she actually wanted to wear. Her words and the words of these poems reverberated in my ears for days. I can still feel them rumbling.

Trans Poetics and the University

While the term *trans poetics*, especially in trans studies, typically remains tethered to poetry, it need not. The ancient sense of poiesis as material creation belies greater capaciousness. To develop a richer sense of trans poetics, particularly in the context of the university, I turn to critical and cultural theorists Stefano Harney and Fred Moten. In their 2013 book, *The Undercommons*, Harney and Moten use the term *poetics* to describe how the university's underbelly—its undercommons—builds meaning and belonging in ways that escape (and often jeopardize) university logics.[45] Poetics marks a way of being with one another differently. In a certain "(per)version" of Greek *poiesis*, Moten extrapolates in a lecture the following year, poetics is "a constant process where people make things and make one another."[46] In context, Moten is critiquing philosopher Hannah Arendt's valorization of the political over the social, of spaces where the anointed seize public voice and action over spaces where people, processes, and practices that are constitutively excluded set about the work of building life together.[47] For Harney and Moten, then, poetics marks the sociality of the shadows, of fugitive communities, there in the interstices of the university.

The undercommons is not an identitarian space; it is a de-identitarian space. It is filled with "maroon communities of composition teachers, mentorless graduate students, adjunct Marxist historians, out or queer management professors, state college ethnic studies departments, closed-down film programs, visa-expired Yemeni student newspaper editors, historically black college sociologists, and feminist engineers."[48] Harney and Moten elsewhere add feminist, queer, criminal, mad, and fat people to the list.[49] Nevertheless, there is some fundamental relationship between the undercommons and blackness, if blackness is understood "ontologically," as something distinct from Black people, something Black people may intimately understand, but something that may also escape their understanding.[50] "Blackness," Harney and Moten write, "means to render unanswerable the question of how to govern the thing that loses and finds itself to be what it is not."[51] It is fugitivity in a fundamental sense. Interestingly, that fugitivity prompts, for them, a series of "regendering and transgendering" mutations.[52] In this project, one of the ways I want to honor that core blackness in the undercommons is to follow Harney and Moten's own trail to its trans participants.

In characterizing the undercommons, Harney and Moten write simply of poetics—not Black poetics, poor poetics, or queer poetics. In proposing the language of *trans* poetics, I mean to think a thread of the undercommons that can never be fully unwound from blackness, queerness, poverty, or madness but is not reducible to them. A thread which, in the act of tracing it, brings to light elements of the underworld that otherwise go unnoticed, in Harney and Moten's work and beyond. This is not to divide, for example, blackness (or queerness, or poverty, or madness) from transness nor to collapse blackness (or queerness, or poverty, or madness) and transness into an irremediable admixture.[53] It is to think intimacy in difference, and fugitivity across them. Moten does this elsewhere when he connects blackness with transness through ritual practice.[54] For me, trans poetics, as a thread of poetics writ large, characterizes the process by which trans and gender-disruptive peoples make things and make one another, in the belly of the university. It is the sweaty, piling practices by which they build different structures of relation, and create that tangle of threads that writhes beneath the university and out past its edges.

For Harney and Moten, "underconcepts" mark the edgework of the undercommons, capturing a different "mode of living together," a different "mode of being together."[55] What are those underconcepts and how might they elucidate trans poetics? Here I focus on three: study, hapticality, and planning. While the university is, traditionally, a place of knowledge production and curriculum, the undercommons is a place of study.[56] Study is not limited to the classroom or to stereotypically intellectual pursuits; "it's talking and walking around with other people, working, dancing, suffering, some irreducible convergence of all three, held under the name of speculative practice."[57] Study is inherently embodied and shot through with touch, "the capacity to feel through others, for others to feel through you, for you to feel them feeling you."[58] It is "skin talk, tongue touch, breath speech, hand laugh."[59] When studying together, in haptic intimacy, the undercommons *plans*. "Planning in the undercommons," they write, is "the ceaseless experiment with the futurial presence of the forms of life."[60] For Harney and Moten, the opposite of planning is policy. Policy is the suppression and suspension of this experiment. It is bureaucratic governance by "policy deputies." Planning, on the other hand, is innovative and abolitionist, never prescriptive or reformist.[61] Planning is the radical process of "making it up" along the way and staying *in the way* so that making it up remains possible.[62]

Trans poetics, as a way of making that is germane to trans participants in the undercommons, involves study, hapticality, and planning in a trans key. Trans study, for example, would be not just trans and gender disruptive peoples studying, but also a trans speculative practice that looks for "crossings, leakages, and slips of all sorts" that both jeopardize and disregard university logics.[63] In a place like the university, where the body is consistently denied, study also invokes a hapticality that builds affect, somatics, and sentiment together. It is the fleshly breaking and blurring of boundaries that allows for remaking. Trans hapticality would be not just trans and gender disruptive peoples hanging out, but also a transing of feeling and function whereby cisheternormative scripts of joy and belonging that subtend the university become unraveled. Moreover, while I continue to insist that trans-inclusive policy is important—not least because it is important to trans folks at the Five Colleges—there is a danger of policy, almost immediately, coming loose from the trans planning that produced it. Trans planning, in this context, is the kind of generative practice, sustained in communal spaces of gender disruption, that proliferates trajectories rather than solidifies direction.

To think trans poetics in the university, it is necessary to think trans study, trans hapticality, and trans planning. It is necessary to trace how we speculate, generating stories about ourselves and our world; how we agitate, "bumping among and into one another"; and how we hope, or how we get up to crafting trans futures.[64] These are tactics for flourishing, but they are also tactics for surviving. It is not for nothing that Harney and Moten draw social poetics from fugitive and maroon communities, and slaves in the hold. Trans poetics, then, is not only a recipe for greater trans life in the university, or escaping the university, but it is also a way of navigating trans death and entrapment in the university. Through trans poetics, we are better able to honor growing and grieving in the cracks, making do and (not) making it through.

Living Together, Dying Together

Trans poetics is a way of making each other even when we lose. It is a habit of being together even when we are beaten and bombarded. It belies a sociality that sustains the whole life cycle—including everything it means to survive and everything it means not to. Sometimes being together means dying together. There are plenty of examples of trans poetics in the context of flourishing—from the celebrative "Boys Night Out" at Smith (2009), where trans guys hung out downtown, to the silly habit a decade later of watching B movies together in Amherst's Queer Resource Center to build trans belonging.[65] But what does it mean to be together and make each other when in fact we are not okay?

On a clear day in April 2012, then president of Hampshire College and formidable environmental activist and philanthropist, Jonathan Lash, was formally inaugurated. Al Gore, famously the author of *An Inconvenient Truth*, came to campus for the event. During the inauguration, a student group called The Queer Does Not End Here conducted a beached whales action.[66] Dressing as "gay beached whales," students carried signs that read, "An Inconvenient Queer."[67] On the group's Tumblr site, this designation became a question: "Queer beached whales at the inauguration of Jonathan Lash, washed ashore by the waves of uncertain divisional committees. Does Al Gore care about these whales? Or are we just An Inconvenient Queer?"[68] The protest occurred in response to the nonreappointment of the one queer studies professor, Jack Pryor. Queer and trans students, who had independently created a queer studies study group, and organized a staff member to serve in an unofficial advisory capacity (an example of fugitive study), insisted the college hire a full-time queer studies professor not only to offer courses in queer and trans studies (and study), but also to advise senior theses and mentor queer and trans activists. As such, it was a tense moment between an environmental justice subtended by cisheteronormative assumptions and the queer and trans ecologies currently suffering on campus.

Students staged the beached whales protest understanding queer and trans studies/study (and life) at the college to be "endangered."[69] The students' choice to simulate beached whales is singularly instructive. Technically referred to as cetacean stranding, beaching often occurs due to environmental disturbances of geomagnetic fields and echolocation systems, creating navigational errors. Once stranded, whales typically die of dehydration or drowning, and their corpses can then explode in the decomposition process.[70] Crucially, cetacean stranding is often a collective activity. Whether following the injured or the lost, whales will often beach themselves beside one another, as if swimming the seas alone were unthinkable, unlivable.[71] What is this sociality, this manner of being with? What does it invite us to think or to imagine about queer and trans belonging outside university logics? While mammals, beached whales are, metaphorically speaking, fish out of water. Sometimes trans folks are fish out of water, too—while drawing life from one another, they are also dying together.

A week earlier, immediately upon hearing of Pryor's nonreappointment, the same group of students staged a funeral for queer studies at Hampshire. The funeral procession began at the Center for Feminisms and ended outside the Harold F. Johnson Library, where graduating seniors typically ring a large bell when they pass their senior project. A T-shirt worn at the event read: "RIP Queer Studies, 1992–2012."[72] Zique, a disabled genderqueer Middle Eastern student, offered, from their wheelchair, the opening statement.[73] In it, they spoke of mourning, of loss, and of grief, and they described what it is to share that together, to weep with one another.

> As queers and queer studies scholars and allies, we must learn to not shy away from grief. From the histories of our pain and shame and raucous desires that still inform the stretching of our skin over our vulnerable beating bodies. Grief and pain and mutual recognition does not mean complacency. Death does not mean giving up. My heart screams and it sings too. I hold it up. I hold it out. I share it now. And put it in your hands. In your mouth. Spit. Sing, please.

Grieving together, dying together, is one essential way queer and trans folks live together, make meaning together, and build belonging even in the face of a senseless world.

Whether in living or dying together, trans poetics intertwines desire and loss, intimacy and separation. Spencer, a white trans masc nonbinary Smith alum and a good friend of the folks involved, calls the beached whales protest a "labor of love."[74] That labor of love was also the work of grieving. At one of the group's last rallies, Pryor recalls "reading aloud the final passages from Amber Hollibaugh's *My Dangerous Desires*."[75] Hollibaugh knew grief well in an HIV world and nevertheless testified to her desire "to create a movement willing to live the politics of sexual danger in order to create a culture of human hope."[76] What is this politics—and indeed this poetics—willing to grapple with the realities of losing and dying as part of a larger arc of struggle and hope? Whatever a trans poetics is, it must equip us to follow each other when we're hurt, to meet together when we need to weep. To spit, and to sing.

In this book, I want to attend to trans poetics as lived by trans people at the edge of the university. How do we make things and make one another? How do we come to matter and how do we transform different systems of mattering? Attending to trans poetics means noticing how our nouns are often verbs, that things-that-are are often things-being-done or things-in-the-doing, much like hope and risk, thread and dust. Just as a made thing is already also a making, so a making is also a thing made. Attending to trans poetics also means attuning ourselves to trans histories, habits, and hopes as lived things, embodied things, material things that help craft who we are and what we are capable of. How are our stories and tactical strategies in part the result of bumping into one another and of the accompanying microbursts on our horizons? Finally, attending to trans poetics means noticing the ways in which we are punctuated by grammars beyond our ken. And. We. Punctuate. We of the asterisks, the hyphens, the slashes, and the ellipses. We break and we bridge. How might the textuality of trans poetics illuminate our politics? Ultimately, I want to imagine a world in which trans poetics takes greater hold. What would happen to and after the university, yes, but also, what else might happen right here, for us and between us?

Part II

Attunements to Trans History

CHAPTER FOUR

It is important to note from the outset that the archive is not an outside. It is not a place devoid of its own material and sociocultural context. It is not absent certain moral and epistemic investments, nor is it free of persnickety preferences or damning indifference. There is, always, struggle, and even violence, here. The archive is not a space where silenced stories (and subjects) invariably gain voice, building a cacophonous rehearsal in a special collections wing—or oral histories database. No doubt many of us have, over the centuries, gone there looking for freedom. And perhaps we have found it in some small measure. Our ancestors of blood and soul whose names may no longer be remembered are therein roused from their slumber and speak to us, inciting us to find our own courage and purpose, and to struggle anew, and with their blessing. But we have just as often, and in the same moment, turned to the archive and felt trapped, suddenly suffocated. Stories that should be there aren't and the stories that are there are mottled, rotting with the stink of hatreds and ignorances we know all too well, and the rules of capital and power that we had hoped to escape (and one day overthrow). In the archive, there are no heroes.

One has to look sideways at the archive to catch it. That shimmer of poetics, those momentarily lines of flight where what gets catalogued and recorded with sometimes exacting precision, what is made to belong to the order of knowledge and sense, is disrupted and another logic surfaces, if only for an instant. Traces of (un)making. Traces of untoward assemblages through which other breaths find passage. Notice the extraneous bits that lend zero credibility to the story, or even compromise it. Mark the extraordinarily mundane that is, nevertheless, a portal to a different way of being in the world and with one another. Clock the silences, the photographic negatives, the sidekicks. There are always extra appendages to our poem-bodies, tracts shunted to another file called "notes," "extras," or, for one writer I know, "the parking lot." What gets parked outside while the business of life and history happens? What gets pushed out to make room for a cohesive self, a cohesive story, a cohesive struggle? And where does it then linger? The cul-de-sac of the discomfiting. But perhaps also the aperture of joy. To track the poetics of the archive—or poetics in the archive—requires a constant state of disorientation and disidentification. One stares at the record only to peer past it.

Trans stories are already difficult to find—and stories of trans poetics even harder, but there are snapshots, bits here and there, a puff of dust in the eyes. Attached to narratives of liberation that center trans-inclusive policy implementation is the list of high-profile trans speakers who visit campus (e.g., Kate Bornstein, Loren Cameron, Jack Halberstam, Janet Mock, and Laverne Cox) and high-profile agitators who push through the housing and healthcare reform, the name and pronoun policies, the Trans 101 trainings and awareness programming. But there is so much more than this to trans life in the university. How do those poetic tales of trans history get found, get told? How do we—and how might we—go looking and listening for them? What is the best approach here, the best path of drawing near? The best way to angle in? And then of course, once found, how do we keep these off-road/in-home trans histories alive—and what do we keep alive in keeping them? These and so many other questions beset inquiries into trans history, especially ones that aspire to tell not the easiest or the loudest trans stories, stories that capture grand doings by significant actors, but rather the out-of-the-way stories, where gender disruptive people go about the quiet, everyday activity of making things and making one another.

Tracking trans in the Five College archive of trans life is no exception. I was never handed a box of trans-related archival materials, although I was, on occasion, directed to trans-specific folders within boxes. Overwhelmingly, I had to read for trans in nontrans stories. The interviews were different, but they, too, gravitated toward obviously important happenings and overt trans journeys rather than behind-the-scenes subplots. More often than not, attuning yourself to trans poetics means bringing yourself into accord with fleeting moments of dissonance. It means pivoting to an unsteady pitch and adapting your pulse to an erratic beat. You become attuned to the wind when your skin knows rain is coming before you do and your back bows with the grass. Similarly, to track trans you need a spidey-sense for the stray and straying trace. This is especially the case in tracking trans life in university archives (where our traces are buried in newspapers or program records) and in university interviews (where our traces are already shaped by the larger forces at work here). Many of the same structures remain here, however, *mise en abyme*. Too often, the trans remnants that persist and jump out ahead of the others are the remnants of trans life best domesticated and assimilated by the university—most representative of it. To tell the whole story—to tell all our stories—you have to get a toehold or a nail-grip, then, on the edge of the edge.

Attunements can head off archival occlusions head on. They can pull us out toward trans traces while simultaneously pulling us back to the many cracks across which trans sits. In what follows, my aim is to cultivate a set of attunements for tracking trans history in the archives, especially a history of trans poetics. Turning to stories of trans life at the Five Colleges as well as traditional archive theory, I want to think the compartments that pull trans into the frame, as much as the limitations of that frame itself. First, I cull four attunements from archive theory: attunements to the an-archive, to the edge, to feelings, and to silence. I then follow-out, test, and extend these attunements through Five College stories. Trans theorists and folks on the ground challenge us to think trans not as a constant, simple edge that is always the site of marginalization but rather to think the gray spaces of trans itself and the poetic complexities "trans" covers over. They also invite us to interrogate how and why we become attached to specific trans stories (and trans edges) over others and what larger projects those attachments might serve.

Attunements in the Archive

There are many who might be our guides to reading the archive-contra-archive here, some with more poetic sensibility than others. Turning to traditional archive theory, authored by nontrans scholars from a variety of marginalized positionalities, I pull, as it were, one box from the cart where many more sit. In it, the sheafs of Jacques Derrida, Michel Foucault, Ann Cvetkovich, and Saidiya Hartman are jumbled together, as they mention one another, projects touching one another, and building resonance, but also as they break against each other, insistently separating and critiquing. They form a motley crew (Brown, Black, Jewish, white, straight, gay, lesbian, one who died of AIDS, and one who studies AIDS) concerned with dusty collections, oral histories, geographical ephemera, and everything in between. In each case, there is a conversation, loosely linked across time, about the limits of the archive (as formalized) and the power of an-archic possibilities. The materiality of the body as lived, as felt, as silenced, and as lost shuttles forward. Poem-lives and heterotopias surface, the affective and the fictive throw down roots, and the tragedies of erasure are met with a fierce but gentle love. From these sheafs I draw four attunements that help orient me in the Five College archive of trans life, as I look for trans stories—and stories at the edge of trans. Turning to nontrans authors to garner insights for trans study, I exercise a transversal methodology. We can build wisdom together, after all, not just isolated from one another.

The An-Archic

What characterizes a slantwise attunement? An attunement not to presence, but to disruption—not to the reflection in the pool, but to the drop that sets off an endless stream of revealing—and *disfiguring*—ripples? This is the first poetic attunement to history I want to explore. If we are to track trans in the archive, we need an attunement to the an-archive.

As a Franco-Maghrebian, "a little black and very Arab" Jew, Derrida knew well the forces of archival erasure.[1] But they are not total. Variously referring to the "anarchic," "anarchontic," "anarchivic," and "archiviolithic," he points to the force not of collection but of dispersion.[2] If archonic power organizes and solidifies archives, an-archic power scatters, fractures, and dishevels them. It *skews*. The an-*arkhē* is against-law; it escapes and yet haunts the *archon*, his house (*arkheion*), and the archives they oversee. Crucially, the an-archive is not separate (or separable) from the archive, but always inside it, undoing it as if "by heart."[3] Derrida terms this an-archic force "*archive fever*," which he describes as "the desire and disorder of the archive."[4] In French, archive fever (*mal d'archive*) has multiple resonances. The *mal* can refer to fever or illness, but also to evil and, perhaps most germanely, to (mad, maddening) trouble. Archive fever is archive trouble insofar as the an-archic "troubles and muddles" the archive, besets it with nonsense.[5] It is the stray notes, the misfiled papers, the lost box, the other label a file could have had, the sheafs that never arrived (or arrived unreadable), the extra bits lost in the rubble of time and the vicissitudes of life, but also the mere scratches and silences of lives left out. It is the weakness of the archive.

The an-archive is "an ineffaceable hyphen," Derrida concludes. I like thinking, first, of the archive as hyphenated—always building links and new assemblages, but just as often being hounded by the dropped links, the hyphens to nowhere. The archive is a link to what is just outside, just out of reach: people and places, yes, but also feelings and relations, systems of sense that no longer make sense. It is a space of bridges and crossings, where "stones talk" and pages bleed.[6] Shot through with poetics. Attuning oneself to it, and then especially with an eye for what falls outside it, involves looking to hyphens at the edge.

The Edge

Turning to the archive involves turning to the edge. But the edge of what? The edge of what is. Of the present and the palpable. Of what gets legitimated by its own physicality and urgency. Turning, then, to trans life in the archive involves turning to the edge of the edge. To a shadow realm, to what drops off. The archive is already at the edge, an edge-space where edgework happens. It is one of those liminal zones where constraint and contestation tarry. Edges get made and remade here. Contours shaped and reshaped. How exactly does one look for the edge of the edge, though, without rushing over it?

Foucault speaks eloquently of the archive as edge-space. He had a penchant for archives—constantly returning, constantly digging, especially for traces of queer, mad, recalcitrant lives (like and unlike his own). He describes the archive as a kind of surround that hedges and "overhangs" our present; the histories we know and keep tell us who we are and what we can do. They also constrain what we can say.[7] It is like the night sky, he muses; the archive collects the stars that give us context and determine which ones shine brightly, even if very far away, and which ones grow pale, even if they are proximal.[8] And that night to our day, that universe to our planet, might feel like a defining frame from which we might derive the identity of "us" (e.g., we the day-walkers, we the planet-spinners) versus "others," but it does no such thing. The archive teaches us about stardust, "this dispersion that we are and make."[9] The archive is an edge, yes, but an edge in absolute continuity with who we are, like the dead skin cells with which we sleep and eat, paint our living rooms and dust our sidewalks. It is part of our poetics of dispersal. And, if there is a general poiesis of dispersal in the archive, there is a more specific poiesis at the edge of the archive, where border-lives make border-sense, and brief lives make brief sense. "Poem lives."[10] Lives "whose disarray and relentless energy one senses beneath the stone-smooth words."[11] Look for edges like these, that shift and unsettle the discourse and matter of the status quo.

Attuning to the edge of the archive is one way to think about the an-archive, the logics that disturb the archive from within. That attunement attends to everyday protests of sense and systems of power, especially when those protests are spectacularly mundane. It also attends to the resistant intensities that come bursting through the page, narratives of insistence that disposable lives matter. And to the silences that all but succeed in swallowing up these poem-lives.

Feeling

One of the edges of the archive, one of the anarchic potentialities of the archive, is affect. What does it mean to listen for feeling? Feelings do not always make a sound; nor are they essentially a sounding thing. As such, it is not always possible for listening to catch them. Feelings do, nevertheless, signify the unsoundness of our souls, their vulnerability and capacity to be cracked open. They also signify a certain muchness, a muchness that has always fallen outside of reason, outside of disciplinary logics, and outside of normative constraints. Listening for feeling at the outskirts of the archive, then, is a third attunement to history against history, an attunement that I find helpful for sounding out trans archives.

In *An Archive of Feeling*, Cvetkovich analyzes *lesbian* feeling at the edge of traditional and gay archives. In doing so, she aims to attend, citing Kathleen Stewart, to lesbian culture as "a space on the side of the road."[12] Stewart elaborates: "Picture the space on the side of the road as a scenic re-presentation of the force of a lyric image with the power to give pause to the straight line of a narrative ordering of events from beginning to end. [...] Imagine how finding oneself on the side of the road could become an epistemological stance."[13] Too often sidelined, lesbian history can and does, nevertheless, spawn counternarratives. Queer herself, Cvetkovich turns to lesbian history to explore how structures of queer feeling, those "affective experience[s] that fall outside" the norm, can become the ground of a counterpolitics for resistant retellings of who we are and where we are going.[14] The ephemera she consults include oral histories, photographs, pins, diaries, letters, notepads, photo albums, vibrators, T-shirts, matchbook covers, posters, stickers, buttons, financial records, porn, zines, phone numbers, flyers, condoms, and meeting minutes.[15] And it is in this pile of things that she finds a range of queer feelings and affective frames, including fear, shame, intimacy, care, disagreement, burnout, crankiness, giving, and grieving.[16] The poetics of queer archives lies in ephemeral moments and emotional materials. It is that poetics that stands to disturb the archive as traditionally conceived, curated, and secured.

Tracking feeling—whether queer feeling or trans feeling—on the periphery of the archives requires nontraditional archival methods and contents. It also requires a particular attunement on the part of the tracker. Archives are deathly attached to certain structures of voice and presence, of language and image. Cvetkovich's attention to feeling through ephemera, and to the silences that are germane to traumatic feeling, raises perhaps one of the more difficult questions about trans archival methods. What do you do with what is not there? How do you do archival work with archival absences? With silences?

Silence

How does one listen to silence? How can one become attuned to the absence of sound? Or to scraps of sense that, in staccato and stochastic fashion, pock the collections? How does one listen to those scratches in the earth without becoming overwhelmed and how does one heed the whispers of tortured graves without becoming swallowed? We are not trained to listen small. We are not trained to believe there is something there, when almost anyone would say there is nothing (left). But talking about the is-ness of what is not is a fourth attunement ultimately critical to tracking trans poetics in the archives.

Hartman's journey has always been with and against the archive. For so many generations of Black people, "the archive is a death sentence, [...] an asterisk in the grand narrative of history."[17] "How does one write a story," she asks, "about an encounter with nothing?" Leaning on the "gaps, silences, and empty rooms," and to stories too far gone to be reconstructed through ephemera or oral histories, she tells Black stories she can only, in some meaningful way, *make up*.[18] In order to catch sight of the "everyday anarchy," to capture unrecorded affects and intimacies, and to feel along the edge of sense, the edge of history, white supremacy, and patriarchy, and the edge that is the Middle Passage, Hartman develops an increasingly unrecognizable archival method. She calls it *critical fabulation*, this fabrication of a "fugitive text" out of the silences and the scraps, the "bare facts and precious details."[19] It begins by looking for "haints," shadow-spirits who "haunt" the present.[20] It begins by "listening for the unsaid, translating misconstrued words, and refashioning disfigured lives."[21] It begins over and over again precisely where history and the archive end. It involves finding pieces of a story one cannot do anything with, given the paucity of the historical record, and then doing something with them anyway. It involves "imagining what might have happened" and what might have been.[22] The critical fabulator is a fabricator, a textual/textile artist, who "loops the strands" and "weaves" something from *almost* nothing.[23] Such a "poetics," Hartman muses, is "the future of abolition [...] performed on the page."[24]

Hartman's an-archival instincts, her attunement to the edge and to affect, require a gentle, painful creativity. Staring into the black hole of silence and its snuffed-out lives, she picks out, ever so tenuously, scraps from the rubble, from which to craft a makeshift, rickety structure of sense, its solidity drawn not from historiographical proofs or a preponderance of evidence, but from will and from love, from imagination and invocation. She makes something real of something unreal.

Four attunements, then: an-archive, edge, feeling, silence. Four approaches critical to telling edge stories—especially, for me, trans stories and stories at the edge of trans. We never enter or encounter an archive without some set of attunements, ways of angling our eyes, and hands, and thoughts toward what we hope to find. Nor is the archive itself ever constituted without being tuned to specific keys and harmonies, however inconstantly or incompletely. If we want to engage with the archive against its own cisnormative grain, and if we want to engage trans an-archives in ways that refuse to allow them to settle, we need a certain skein and skew of attunements that are atypical of the place and that displace both traditional and nontraditional historiographical habits. Non-trans theorists positioned in other marginalized ways have offered these attunements as survival techniques, but they require cultivation. It is not necessarily natural to look for the an-archive, to search for the edge, to listen for feelings, or to wait patiently beside silences until the worlds within them start to come alive. Still less to hunt the edge of the edge. It is too easy to get pulled away, pulled back into the stronger currents and more pronounced course of trans history in the university, its personages and its policies. It is harder to stick close to the noise, and to sit uncomfortably beside the disorder so that a record of trans poetics can surface if only momentarily. In what follows, I modulate these attunements into an explicitly trans key and explore the complexities that trans stories and trans storytellers bring to them. But first, a side bar.

Of Empires and Friendships

When it comes to trans life, the valley has the dead weight of history tied around its neck. Janice Raymond was a professor at the University of Massachusetts, Amherst from 1978 to 2002. She was the first tenure-line hire in the Department of Women Studies (now Women, Gender, Sexuality Studies). And it was here that she published *The Transsexual Empire*, a scathing critique of the cultural forces she sees as responsible for transsexual phenomena. Sandy Stone's response to Raymond, "The *Empire* Strikes Back," is a foundational text in trans studies. Of course, I had heard about Raymond, but I had not realized she worked in the area until I came across a notice of her UMass employment in the Hampshire College archives. The notice was an old newspaper or magazine clipping, with no context. I remember snapping a quick picture and forwarding it to a friend with some smart quip like, "Whut?!" I did not think to save the file (one of those oversights that haunt all of us who work in archives). But I remember feeling the weight of my inquiry at that moment differently. What does it mean to be writing the story of trans life in the university precisely where one of its staunchest critics lived and worked? Had I stumbled less upon an idyllic trans oasis than upon some originary trans battlefield? If the waves of trans students, at UMass and the other Five Colleges, who keep reckoning with Raymond are any indication, I am not alone in my experience of being suddenly thrown into a maelstrom.

I decided to read Raymond's work for this project. After *Transsexual Empire*, she returned to the subject of trans life forty-two years later in *Doublethink: A Feminist Challenge to Transgenderism*. While the early book focuses (nonexclusively) on transitioning trans women, the later book focuses (nonexclusively) on detransitioning trans men. In either case, given her reputation in trans worlds, I expected vitriolic polemics, disdainful zingers, and prose made unsteady by unbearable frustration. And I found it. *Transsexual Empire*, of course, includes the oft-quoted line, "All [MTF] transsexuals rape women's bodies by reducing the real female form to an artifact, appropriating this body for themselves."[25] It is a line with many lives. Feminist philosopher Claudia Card, for example, reprised and inverted it: "My fantasy penalty [for rapists] is what for lack of a better term I will call compulsory transsexual surgery, that is, removal of the penis and testicles and construction of a vagina-like canal, accompanied by whatever hormone treatments may be advisable for the sake only of bodily health."[26] Trans women as rapists; rapists as trans women. But what of trans men? For Raymond, they are essentially murderers, killing their womanhood, their vulnerability, and their creative power, and laying waste to the landscape of lesbian life. FTM transition, she writes, is "a type of living death."[27] Her only hope is that more will find "resurrection" through detransition.[28] In whatever guise it takes, trans phenomena, for her, proliferates violence against women. And it is at this that she takes dire umbrage.

But an abiding irritability about transsexual and transgender life was not all I found. Archives are like that. The story is never as simple as you think going in. Stated more calmly in *Transsexual Empire* than in *Doublethink*, Raymond's fundamental concern is with the "trans industrial complex," or the confluence of medical, psychiatric, and legal institutions that precondition mainstream medical gender transition. It is a complex system, she argues, that predominantly reinforces norms of manhood and womanhood, which are in turn produced by patriarchy. Raymond's analysis is Foucauldian from the get-go, and

I understood her concerns immediately—concerns, I should add, that are widely shared across trans communities and trans studies. Where we disagree is this: trans is not reducible to recent medical interventions and normative passing. Trans is bigger, older, and more variable than that, and it is not inherently tied to or dependent upon medicine (as much as current political discourse suggests otherwise). And this: even when trans people avail ourselves of medical technologies, we do something resistant and creative to the genders we inhabit. How could Raymond have missed this? The richness of trans life and especially of trans resistance to medical, psychiatric, and legal assimilation? While it is critical to identify the institutional conditions that constrain trans visibility, it is equally important to catch trans life at the edge, the way trans people escape the industries and institutions that consistently try to govern them.

Less famously, Raymond wrote a book on friendship. It was 1986, a time when, as she puts it, feminist politics had become shallow. Feminists had lost their primary anchor point in relationships.[29] Without the personal, however, the political is nothing. Feminist protest, struggle, and policy work needs to be anchored in the people for whom the fight happens. For Raymond, that meant (nontrans) women's friendships, "female friendships." Regretting that the philosophy of friendship had for eons been theorized by men, Raymond proposed to develop a (Foucauldian) genealogical account of female friendship as "counter-memory."[30] To do so, she had to pull together "scattered" fragments, pull apart "tangled" documents, and "excavate the ruins."[31] She went looking for stories that work by another logic, that disrupt the act not only of reading history but also of making history. In reading *A Passion for Friends*, I was struck by the similarities in our projects. In a way, I too am interested in a buried history of friendships, in something before and behind political action. A history of poetics, a telling of intimate histories glossed over. And I, too, hope to follow the genealogical threads that do not tell a linear story, but open up foreclosed possibilities. But I also, and not least because of the limitations of Raymond's own attentions, want to attend, throughout my inquiry, to what trans attention (and attention to trans) occludes (and what it smuggles in).

Claiming SYSTA

Black, queer, gender nonconforming digital archivist at Mount Holyoke, Micha Broadnax, was quick to press me on my project.[32] Why focus on the term "trans" at all? If you choose it, how are you troubling it? In particular, how are you accounting for "butch lesbians" in your genealogy and their long history of transgressing gender? For Broadnax, who now manages the Black Teacher Archives Project at Harvard, the archive is always a space for organizing: *community organizing*. They are committed to telling stories that don't get told—whether pulling out their traces or preserving them in the first place. They urged me to grapple with what edges "trans" itself hides. Reminiscing about queer ancestors like Stormé DeLarverie and Leslie Feinberg, as well as their own friends and family, Broadnax kept inviting me to think "gender disruption" in an expansive sense. Think of all those shared experiences and those shared histories, all that "grayish space" that "trans" as a frame sometimes covers over despite itself. "Trans" is never just an edge, just a margin; there are edges and margins to it. In a sense, Broadnax was concerned that the poetics of gender disruption—and all of its intimate entanglements not only with systems of dominance but also across pockets of resistance—might get lost in the sheen of trans clean. They pushed me to listen for that loss and the stories it represents. And I took that exhortation to heart.

It was too easy not to notice SYSTA. There, in an innocuous corner of the September 10, 1998, issue of *Mount Holyoke News*, an ad read: "SYSTA: a confidential support group for lesbian, bisexual, transgendered, &* questioning Women of Color. Contact: Sandra x4682."[33] It was not the first reference to transgender life at Mount Holyoke, nor was it the first substantial one. Two years earlier, the college's Lesbian and Bisexual Alliance (LBA) organized events for National Coming Out Day to raise awareness about "gay, lesbian, bisexual, and transgender life."[34] And just one year earlier, Spectrum, a student group, sponsored "A Transgender Panel," in which five trans community members spoke.[35] SYSTA was not a public event. In fact, there are no records of its existence except a series of ads over a three-and-a-half year period. From them, we know to ring Sandra, "call Karla Delgado x4682," and "contact Un Jung Lim x4189."[36] The spare lines are sometimes embellished with "Be proud to be you!" and "We love our QWOC!"[37] Otherwise, we have just a long silence. And that is in part purposeful. SYSTA prided itself on providing confidentiality. It met in secret. Its comings and goings were largely opaque.

But we can gather inklings of SYSTA's ethos, enough to draft a suggestive outline of its activities. SYSTA was originally organized by the same woman, Sandra Aguirre, who single-handedly reignited *Voices: Women of Color Past, Present, and Future*, an inset in *Mount Holyoke News* dedicated to "poetry, stories, editorials, photography, book reviews, cartoons, recipes, etc."[38] More than a random assortment of things, *Voices* had a mission, scrawled week after week across its pages: "Express. Teach. Challenge. Change. Unite. Respond. Speak Out. Execute. Share. Discuss. Respect. Celebrate." It was a call—and a testament—to community. It mattered, for Aguirre, that women of color—including trans men and trans mascs, who at the time were referred to as trans women—challenge the system, share their wisdom, and celebrate the beauty they create. Within these pages, students made word and image together, made food together, and made gender and sexuality (and love) together. There was a *poiesis* to it all. The relaunch of *Voices* was announced side-by-side with the launch of SYSTA in the September 10 issue. Then, by April 23, 2002, both *Voices* and SYSTA were gone, without explanation.

How do you approach trans history—and the archives of trans life—in a way that SYSTA catches your eye? In a way that its silences can speak? How do you trace along the edge of things to feel for its affective fabric? And how do you lean in to its disruptive, even anarchic potential? It is too easy to tell the story of trans life at Mount Holyoke by jumping from the LBA, to Spectrum, to various trans committees, focusing on the introduction of trans identity and white-led policy-building. SYSTA offers a different story. The sort of story Broadnax's injunction demanded. A story that, in many ways, resists the organizing force of the term "trans" itself—along with the whiteness it so often smuggles in and the queerness it too often denies—and recenters it within an expansive poetics of gender disruption and community building. To see it, you have to turn to the gray spaces. You have to look to the margins, to the insets and the advertisements. The where of it all is everything.

Who We Call Our Own

Let's say, then, that we are attuned to the an-archive and to the edge, to feelings and to silence. And not only that, but also to the edge of the edge, to things that consistently get unsaid even by those committed to saying them. Let's say we are looking for trans stories, and for stories that stretch and strain the term "trans" into its own gray space, whether in the official archives, in oral histories and interviews, or in ephemera and creative productions collected along the way. We are looking for the an-archive, but also its margins. Looking for queer and trans feelings, but also feelings nonrecognizably queer/trans but that nevertheless circulate in queer/trans orbits. And we are looking for the silences—silences in which we lose trans, but also silences in which trans loses parts of itself. Poised at this pivot, who we look for among our ancestors and what investments we have and absolutions we seek in that looking matter. It matters that we look for less likely stories, *and* that we not find in them a savior.

Years ago, Khary Polk, professor of Black studies and gender studies at Amherst College, taught a queer theory course and assigned an essay from the archives, "Reflections on Gay Life at Amherst."³⁹ The piece, penned by a senior student with the last name of Johnson, is a scathing indictment of the homophobia on Amherst's campus in 1973, just as the college was on the cusp of becoming coed. And while Johnson does not speak here specifically of being Black on campus, they surely could have. In an accompanying photo, Johnson stares at the camera beautifully, defiantly.

Someone got curious and looked up Johnson in the alumni directory. What they found there took them by surprise. In 1982, Johnson had petitioned the college to change her name. She had just undergone gender affirmation surgery and wished to apply to music school in Germany with her chosen name: Raffaela Tamara Johnson. Folks quickly got to work investigating where she was now and what she was doing, only to discover there was barely a record. Amherst journalist, Katharine Whittemore, stepped in to trace what became a trail "as full of roadblocks as epiphanies."⁴⁰ Born in Queens in the early 1950s, Johnson was a smart, generous woman with an ear for music. Fluent in French and German, and conversant in Spanish and Italian, Johnson was something of a Bohemian. After studying abroad in Paris while at Amherst, she moved to Germany upon graduation in 1973. By day, she worked in the basement of a music store, sorting sheet music, and by night she took her charisma to the streets. She quickly started living life as a woman and decided to pursue medical transition in the late 1970s. Johnson's post-Amherst life—tracked however incompletely and piecemeal—is one of delight, pursuing her loves and passions with purpose. She also chose to end that life on her own terms and for her own reasons. She died by suicide in 1994, at the age of forty-three, in Munich, Germany, after a prolonged illness.

When I first contacted Amherst College about my project, staff across the school were abuzz about Johnson. Then in 2022, Whittemore published her extensive profile of Johnson in the *Amherst Magazine*. "Tamara Johnson was a woman ahead of her time," Whittemore writes, "and, to our current knowledge, Amherst's first transgender graduate." At a moment in which Black Lives Matter rocked the nation and Black student protests roiled higher education, and at a moment, too, in which trans visibility was on the rise and trans inclusion in universities constituted the cutting edge of diversity, equity, and inclusion efforts, Tamara Johnson was a signal discovery. For a place like Amherst, moreover, in the process of rebranding itself as an elite institution dedicated to serving especially Black and Brown students, Tamara was more than Amherst's past. She was also Amherst's future.

As I had done with every other school, I did a quick Google search as part of my research. I typed in "trans," "transgender," and "Amherst College" and

FIGURE 4.1 Tamara Johnson wearing a silk pearl-colored dress and large white triangle earrings, posing with a harp below a poster for a 1986 Sade concert.

hit Enter. This usually picked up more recent traces of trans life, especially on social media. In this case, however, it pulled up something much older. A parallel life. Among the first several hits were three profile pieces by the American Heritage Center on Shannon Moffat, a white trans woman who graduated from Amherst College in 1950.[41]

Born in Pittsburgh, in 1927, Moffat, like Johnson, grew up in New York. Upon graduating high school, Moffat joined the US Navy as an electronics technician before attending the US Naval Academy and then Amherst College. She served in the US Coast Guard for a few years, before working at Stanford Medical Center as an information officer and, eventually, becoming a freelance technical and science writer. Moffat married and had two children. She remembers first donning a dress in 1959, wearing lingerie in 1963, and cross-dressing publicly in 1970. Following the publication of Jan Morris's *Conundrum* in 1974 and the changing landscape of medical transition, she identified as a woman in 1978 and lived fulltime as such. In 1981, Moffat returned to work for Stanford University, which paid for much of her transition procedures (1981–1985). When not working, she enjoyed music, theatre, and dance. Moffat passed away peacefully in 2009, but not before leaving eighty-six boxes of materials to the American Heritage Center. In addition to the center's three profile pieces, there is also a collection of oral histories with her family members from 2019.[42] A preponderance of traces.

I decided to visit the center, which is housed at the University of Wyoming in Laramie, the same Laramie where Matthew Shepard was killed in 1998—a young gay man who would have been my brother today, a mere five years my senior. The visit felt weighty. Rummaging through the boxes, I was struck by several things. First, Moffat was a researcher. She saved an exhaustively representative collection of literatures for and about crossdressers and transsexuals in the 1970s and 1980s. Second, Moffat was a writer. She wrote an unpublished novel, she ghost-wrote several medical books, as well as innumerable science articles, and she co-wrote a portion of her own unpublished autobiography. Third, and most importantly, Moffat refused the trans tropes of her day, including the born-this-way narrative and the interiorized monologue expected of trans writers.[43] She insisted, instead, on thinking transness as shifting over time and relationally embedded (with, for example, family, friends, acquaintances, and lovers). Rather than being centralized in an identity formation, transness functions most truly, for her, as an affective fabric between people.

Moffat predates Johnson as an Amherst graduate, but the two cross-dressed in the 1970s and decided to medically transition in the late 1970s. Both Moffat and Johnson make an appearance in *Amherst Magazine*. For Moffat, it is an obituary that makes no mention of her transition, besides the opening five words: "Shannon Moffat (née Samuel Moffat)."[44] For Johnson, it is a full profile that emphasizes the significance of her transness and the claim that she was Amherst's first transgender graduate.[45] Make no mistake: Johnson's story matters. As a Black trans woman who attended an elite all-men's college in the early 1970s, she is the edge of the edge. That she alone would be claimed, however, when she and Moffat transitioned at roughly the same time, says more about Amherst's investments than it does about trans history at Amherst. In their essay on trans necropolitics, C. Riley Snorton and Jin Haritaworn argue that "the lives of trans people of color in the global North and West are celebrated, and their deaths memorialized, in ways that serve the white citizenry."[46] At this juncture in Amherst's history, the celebration of Johnson's life and memorialization of her death must be subject to critical analysis. What role in white cisnormative politics does Johnson's exceptional life play and what still vibrant white cisnormative structures at Amherst does it help to mask? Similarly, at this juncture in liberal politics where whiteness is subject to disavowal, white women are named the nemesis of wokeness, and military connections cannot be brooked, Moffat's transness has no chance of counting. She is too close to what cannot be named, her transness notwithstanding. I cannot help but wonder, here, what it would mean to think Moffat and Johnson together, and the complexities of their respective (dis)appearances.

Let us find our edges, then, and our gray spaces, but also unsettle them and refuse to be saved by them. This is what Raymond didn't do in her history of female friendships. But this is what looking for SYSTA, and looking for Johnson *and* Moffat, necessitates.

From Attunements to Analytics

In practicing these attunements to the an-archic, to the edge, to feeling, and to silence, specifically in a trans key that searches for the gray space within and to the side of trans, and with an awareness of our investments in that search, certain resonances in the Five College archive of trans life began to hang together. It was clear to me this could not be an identity-centric search for identity-centric stories. The vector could not be just "trans" or the frame simply "gender." The goalpost had to keep moving, the target keep slipping away, so I could notice the terrain itself, what it reveals and also what it hides. I couldn't look for definitive objects, under defined parameters, nor for the most significant actors, axes, actions, aspirations, or the like. So instead, I looked for analytics. I have come to think of them as three analytics for a poetics of trans history.

In *A Thousand Plateaus*, Gilles Deleuze and Félix Guattari contrast "royal" or "state science" with "ambulant," "nomad," or "minor science." While the former searches for solids, constants, and stable objects, the latter searches for fluids, the ambiguous, and the continuously variant.[47] Any science, of course, proceeds by way of observing certain things in certain ways. Poetic attunements turn our attention to noticing the lower level strata that so often get missed when telling higher level stories about people, their deeds, and their aspirations. Poetic analytics get to work in that register, not as practices of noticing themselves, but rather as angles that allow certain things (or families of things) in the underbrush to get noticed, or at least become noticeable. While the poetic attunements I have described are practices of noticing that allow edges to come into the frame, the poetic analytics I am about to describe are frames that allow an edgy noticing to set to work. If poetic attunements constitute the ethos of a minor science, poetic analytics are its experimental tools, dedicated to understanding the dynamics of the undercommons. They follow deterritorializing flows. And just as the attunements I offered are not limited to trans life, so these three analytics are rooted in but stretch well beyond trans life in these archives.

Three analytics, then: dust, stash, scatter. These are words that are always in transition between verb and noun. Words that can be taken in one of two ways, and then innumerable directions from there. As such, they capture, in part, the raucous ways in which trans folks have stories, even in the absence of an overarching trans story. As an analytic, dust allows me to attend to the dispersed records and isolated remnants of trans life in the archive writ large—and yet, to also attend to the ways in which those bits clump together, like ephemeral dust bunnies, and puff apart even in our retellings. As a second analytic, stash allows me to think the anarchic and lawless stowaway stories that never make it into the archive proper—and yet, to also think improper stashes in the archive, the oblique, torn tales that heap together in out-of-the-way places. As a third analytic, scatter allows me to interrogate the cisheteronormative forces that scatter us, setting us adrift from one another and from ourselves—but also to interrogate the ways in which we scatter ourselves, especially away from the fundamental intimacies between transness and disability. Together, these three analytics illuminate the stories we are and the histories we make, with a lawless commitment to the doing (and undoing) of trans.

CHAPTER FIVE

Dust

Dust. What even is it? A bunch of airborne particulates that wisp about invisibly before settling in a thin film on the surface of everything—deceptively thin, because the film inevitably grows billowy, as if time itself were padding things. And of what do these particulates consist? They have no through-line but size. Measured in microns, dust is fine bits of material from multiple origins, including human and vegetable, mineral, metal, and chemical, that have become—or may yet become—aerosolized and windswept. Dust is largely unseen, except when it isn't. Agglutinating and agglomerating into fluffy clouds or thick layers of silt, dust floats and settles by turns. Or it tangles itself up into neither serious nor sultry dust balls that tumbleweed-around, held together by gravity, electricity, or a bit of ad hoc webbing. This is one of dust's paradoxes: that it is pulverized isolates—things fractured into some of their smallest possible units and shotgun-scattered away from one another, only to come together again in a soft transhuman mess. Another of its paradoxes is this: largely dead (and sometimes deadly), the mere residue of bygone life, dust clouds and dust bunnies nevertheless become teaming piles of organic life—fungi, molds, bacteria, dust mites, and more go about living and thriving in these dust communities. That is at the microscopic level. At the cosmic level, huge dust disks accreting around a star can give birth to an entire solar system.

I want to propose dust as an analytic for trans poetics and archival praxis—that is, as a frame for analyzing the underbelly of trans life and the way it gets caught at the edge of archives. As trans folks, we are so often isolated in life, scattered from one another and ourselves through cisnormative structures and expectations within which we often shrink, so as to save ourselves from being squashed more vociferously than we already are. While the internet has become, for many, a special haven for trans dust communities today, our histories remain incredibly fractured. Records are barely there or absent entirely, and always inconsistent. When records of trans life are present, they are typically peripheral, tacked on to boxes, folders, and collections about something else. Nevertheless, our dust specks insistently stay there, caught in the cobweb corners. Given time, sometimes on the scale of decades, a tangle of trans resonances develops across trans bodies and archives as they agglomerate together. And, when we are quite lucky, those dust specks and dust clumps go walking, spinning out of bounds with an intergalactic force.

In what follows, I interweave theorizations and histories of dust, especially dust in the archives, and echoes of transhumanism and tranimacies, with actual trans stories of fracture and agglomeration in the Five College archive of trans life.[1] Working with some of the most stochastic records of trans life, I explore how dust, as an analytic, illuminates the transhuman ways of belonging that surface in and between trans lives as we craft our stories and make our histories. As an analytic, dust helps us celebrate our lingering traces which, despite their smallness, are power packs of recalcitrance. It helps us honor the ways in which those traces clump and come alive together, resonances billowing through one another. And it helps us follow where those dust puffs move and flow, escaping any and every system of containment cisnormative structures can muster. Ultimately, dust as analytic highlights sinuous trans resistance and revelry in the midst of a mundane and ubiquitous archival landscape of trans isolates. This gives a whole different sense to the transversality of molecular revolution.[2]

Dust Lingers

Literature on transhumanism and tranimacies invites us to think trans life in intimate relationship with animal life and, ultimately, nonanimal life. The impetus, here, is to pry our hands away from holding the human as distinct from and superior to other beings and nonbeings with which we share our worlds. Later, I will think transness and stone alongside one another. Here I begin with something smaller: dust. I tarry, first, with dust's own insistent tarrying. As much effort may be expended or hygienic regimes instituted to do away with it, dust—always—*stays*.

Dust has always been a little trans-. As aerosolized particulates of plant, animal, and mineral matter, dust crosses boundaries for breakfast. It blurs the elemental distinction between earth and air and fogs up the border between life and death.[3] As this unstable, insistently crossing force, dust, one might say, is busy transing lines. "What does it smuggle in each of these crossings?" theorist Michael Marder wonders.[4] A little stash of something here, a dash of something there, things that are said to belong on one side or the other of some binary bifurcation, but they slip between things. As dust slips, it illuminates. Dust, he writes, "vacillates between invisibility and those discrete instances when it appears in the spotlight," drawing attention to space itself, to the air that hangs there.[5] Invisibilized and invisibilizing on the one hand, spotlighted and spotlighting on the other, never wholly here nor wholly hidden, dust can obscure things in one instant only to bare them in all their grainy, convoluted detail the next. Dust can do this obstructive/deconstructive work. And perhaps it is better at doing than being. At once the sloughing-off and the soil of life, dust epitomizes becoming. It is for this reason that "dust is incompatible with Ideas and Ideals," Marder writes.[6] Something about dust—and, I might argue, trans—is so inscribed in the processual that it resists definitive delimitation. What we do know is that dust is always "matter out of place," catching the space between things.[7]

What would it mean, conversely, to think transness as dust? There is, of course, a certain pixy dust of trans fabulousness that we leave behind on sidewalks, in trains, and around conference rooms—a dust that lilts through the air, lubricating stiffly gendered joints and sliding gleefully along the creases of our genderfuck faces. But this is not the dust I am talking about.

What if gender, as we know it, were only the residual effect of some more organic, material force? And what if transing gender—crisscrossing those effects—were simply the work of illuminating that life/death process and its correlative dustiness? Imagine trans particulates as gathering up, and tufting together, the residue of gender as lived, which is always more than cisnormative veneer would have us believe. Cis norms, after all, are an illusion of dustless, generation- and degeneration-free gendered existence, extracted from the realm of becoming. It is gender's dust-free living room, the sculpted manhood and womanhood made to hide the trace of its making. Transness, in this scenario, is the making made evident. A pile of gender dust newly agglomerated: a different Frankenstein story.[8] Trans folks epitomize all the bits about gender that the binary gender system tries to sweep and Swiffer away. But all that gender creation and devolution (in which everyone—cis and trans alike—are involved) stays, it lingers. Trans people are but one force of its lingering, an insistent coming alive of the lingering trace. Dust, historian Carolyn Steedman writes, signals "the impossibility of things disappearing, or going away, or being gone."[9] While the binary gender system has certain autoimmune allergies to its own dust, gender particulates keep flying, escaping its hygienic regime. This is the way of things.

Of course, being in a trans body doesn't feel all that dusty, most days. If anything, our peculiar arrangement of gender detritus feels more alive than anything did before it. Reflecting on this intensity of aliveness, poet Ryka Aoki vows "dust shall never settle upon this soul."[10] As vibrant as transness can feel, however, it is not resurrection all the way down. Cameron Awkward-Rich, poet and professor at the University of Massachusetts, Amherst, grapples with the question we are so often asked in one way or another: Did your old self die? Where did it go? "Once, I ransacked my own mute skin, searching for an exit," he writes, "All I found was this palmful of dust."[11] Where did the girl he once was go? Did she walk through an exit door—or leave an exit wound? Neither, really. She is still here, just a palmful of dust. "Here. Take it. Throw her to the sky. Let her scatter & drift down," he writes, the way one does the dead, in memoriam. But then, "Let her coat your pink tongue," like summer rain, or fat snowflakes. Whatever we once were is still here, still in us, still part of us, and it can return to us again in an instant of childlike surrender to the sky. Even our own gender dust lingers, always already a force of life, too.

Making—all making—produces dust. And the very condition of our making today is an interstellar dust cloud so many years ago. From dust we come and to dust we return. This is a way of saying we are simply interlopers in a Dusty World. Detritus is its fundamental truth. We can fight it, or we can join it. Transness is—or perhaps might be—a certain way of joining the dust world, a way of playing with the remainders that always are and invoking the remainders that will be.

Dust Bunnies

And when dust stays, it globs. Dust creatures—or the clumps of dust that form in corners and clog the underside of things—are found on multiple continents, variously referred to as dust bunnies, dust rabbits, dust dogs, sheep, mice, kittens, rats, and cats.[12] As the agglomeration of unbelongings, these tangled bits of particulate matter are, perhaps, some of the most visible instances of dust communities. I like to think about the cultivation of dust bunnies as a trans archival praxis—tangling and fluffing together what has been pulverized and then witnessing what can grow and live there. Trans stories are not only isolated and scattered in the Five College archives; they also have already been brought together more than once, especially through documentaries and zines. Paradigmatic instances are Smith alum Sam Davis's documentary *In Our Own Words* and the Hampshire student zine *Something Queer Happened Here*, both discussed elsewhere in this book. These mediums are well-suited to the task insofar as they preserve the particulate quality of trans archival life, presenting a grainy image, with chunks and pieces still palpable, still audible. They make no attempt to offer one living organism, but the animated residue of many.

In the Five College context, and in a region with a preponderance of lesbians and trans-masculine people, trans women and trans femmes, on the whole, experience a greater sense of isolation—and pulverization. More than once, I was told the story of the early days before gender-inclusive housing was available on the University of Massachusetts, Amherst campus. It was the late aughts, and a young trans woman came forward and said, "I need a place to live." Few of the residence halls had gender-inclusive bathrooms (with showers). She was placed in one, on a floor of primarily international students. Staff member Jan, musing on what they view as an act of negligence on the part of the director of residence life, recalls:

> This was a white woman from the US who had a really horrific experience as a trans woman. Got kicked out by her family when she came out. She was homeless for a while because she was perceived as trans by folks. She got a lot of harassment and didn't have a lot of support. So you put her in the place on campus where she's going to stick out the most and feel marginalized. It was a horrible situation. She ended up attempting suicide and ended up leaving college. I thought for years and years that she was dead.[13]

Isolated. Ejected. Drifting alone. Then a call for help. Followed by an assignment to a group of students with whom she did not belong. Attempted suicide—a plea for pulverization. And then ejection again, only this time self-chosen. Years of silence, and then she reached out, as if coming back again from the grave. A tangle of life/death.

But trans women are not wholly absent, nor wholly silent in this history. It is not simply one speck here and another there; the specks constellate. They connect and sediment with one another, thickening together. Among the more powerful instances, consider the two zines *Camp Transfeminism* (2002,

Smith College) and *Gender Liberation UMass* (2015, University of Massachusetts, Amherst).[14] Both zines address the reality of trans women in the university, grapple with histories of transmisogyny, and insist on rethinking gender entirely. Reckoning with the transmisogyny and second-wave feminism that mark Smith's history, *Camp Transfeminism* positions itself as a searing critique of Smith's "sisterhood." Such sisterhood refuses to acknowledge the necessity of trans women at Smith and, more broadly, participates in the exclusion of "unacceptable queers like perverts, trans people, femme dykes, people of color, survivors, intersexed people, genderqueers, fat people, disabled people."[15] Authors call for a collegewide reckoning with the complexities (and indecencies) of gender and position themselves not as respectable instances of any specific gender but rather as "gender trash."[16] And they do so through a zine full of refusal and refuse—an amalgam of manifestos, sketches (often pirate themed), reprints from Bornstein's *My Gender Workbook*, personal reflections, questions, jokes, haikus, a puzzle, a dialogue, and an invitation to "faggy aerobic vegan baking."[17] Dust bunnies indeed.

Ella, a queer cis woman and Smith alum, shared some context for the zine's production.[18] Organizers were both irreverent toward the ideal of Smith womanhood and critical of campus-wide tendencies to think trans issues as trans men's issues. This is why *Camp Transfeminism* forefronts trans women's inclusion. Intriguingly, the seed of Ella's own involvement was planted a year earlier when she was studying abroad in Italy. She attended a caucus in Genoa where a highly intergenerational group of trans women hotly debated the depathologization of "trans" under socialized medicine. It was a "transformative experience," she recalls.[19] Trans women's and femmes' voices are not only quoted and invoked throughout the zine, then, but the particulates of a specific group of turn-of-the-century Italian trans women wafted west to subtend the whole project.

Gender Liberation UMass's zine, predominantly written by trans women, trans femmes, and nonbinary folks with disabilities, is a painful reckoning with trans neglect on campus and its roots in the open transmisogyny of Janice Raymond, the first tenure-track hire in the Department of Women's Studies at UMass and author of *The Transsexual Empire*.[20] Throughout the zine, authors testify to a shared sense of pain, self-loathing, dismemberment, and disassociation produced by the climate of transmisogyny on campus. Part of addressing that climate, they insist, is addressing UMass's transphobic past. They tag Raymond a "war criminal" for her role in cultivating trans-exclusionary radical feminism (TERFism) and insist that UMass offer "reparations" for the decades-long harboring of Raymond and TERF ideology. More than an insistence on reparations, however, the zine understands itself as "an act of reclamation." The authors publish a university-oriented list of demands for a more trans-inclusive campus—including, perhaps most pointedly, "hiring a trans woman professor" in the Department of WGSS—alongside a community-oriented invitation for trans folks to build belonging and "EMOTION" with one another. They do so through sketches, poems, essays, a letter, a future visioning board, and an invitation to a permanent "drag-fest." Here, trans students—especially trans women—negotiate with UMass history and their own futures, leaving behind one of the more vibrant testimonies to a trans poetics of archive and affect.

These zines are not historical treatises; they are not systematic accounts. They are piecemeal projectiles that go some way toward insisting on the value of queer and trans femme histories—of gathering up gender dust in otherwise atomized worlds. Some of that gender dust is trashier than others. Some of it is more finely pulverized, more regularly wiped clean, more likely subject to eliminative logics. Transfemininity remains markedly disdained in the wider culture, and universities are no exception. But trans women, queer femmes, and their allies are still there, building a tangle of thread and electricity.

Dust Traps

While dust bunnies agglomerate bits, dust traps are spots in or on which dust settles and sticks, often in small out-of-the-way places, little desired, and little disturbed. The *Oxford English Dictionary* offers three paradigmatic locations for dust, remarkably absent similitude: hems, hailstones, and venetian blinds. In the context of traditional archives, dust traps might well be the things for which no one ever submits call slips—boxes abandoned, folders unopened, pages unturned. Even a page or an anecdote has traps at its corners, words glossed over and meanings lost. The term "dust-traps" is a strange locution, insofar as it attributes activity to the trap and passivity to the dust—as if the trap were ensnaring innocent particulates as they waft by. But the term "trap" (from Old English *trappe, treppe*) originally meant tread or step, insofar as a trap is what one treads or steps upon. Dust traps, then, are where dust goes about the business of walking. In the Five College archive of trans life, one of the earliest, dustiest, least revisited, and most dispersed stories is of Enoch Page, whom I stumbled upon in a wall of unprocessed archive boxes at the University of Massachusetts, Amherst. This is also the story of a trans person simply going about the business of walking. A palpable recalcitrance.

It was January 30, 1995, and the Chancellor's Task Force for Gay, Lesbian, and Bisexual Matters at UMass met to discuss concerns that had "come to" them about including transgender issues in its mission. The task force was joined by a guest, identified in the type-written agenda as "H___ Paige (from?????????????????)."²¹ Then, in handwritten scrawl, Page's given first name is added in, the (no less than) sixteen question marks are crossed out, and beside them is written "Anthropology." "Paige," then, from anthropology: a professor. The minutes briefly recap each person's contribution to the discussion of task force issues. The final entry reads: "Paige: GLBT—important to address inclusion of transgendered people in Task Force name. Item to be placed on next agenda." In less than a month, the task force proposed the title change, to which then Chancellor David K. Scott verbally agreed in late March and formally confirmed on May 1.²² At some point Enoch Page joins the chancellor's task force. At first, he is listed with his birth name, but no email address.²³ Then, he is listed with a blend of given and chosen name.²⁴ Finally, he is listed with his full name and contact information.²⁵ This entrance into the archival record is signal—so haphazard, inconsistent, and peripheral, and yet eminently effective, constituting an originary spark for trans inclusion at UMass.

A few years later, in 1998, Page joined a panel of out "queer" professors, the only trans person among them. More than seventy students attended.²⁶ As reported by the *Daily Collegian*, Page states pointedly that his transition is harder for his students to accept than his colleagues, but that his race—his blackness—is harder still for everyone. This is a refrain throughout my interviews with trans people of color in the Five Colleges. Western Massachusetts is such a profoundly white space that race is often the most salient factor to navigate and build solidarity around. Commenting on being Black and trans at UMass today, Jadyn attested, "It has felt more important to actively cultivate queer and trans of color spaces than it has to cultivate trans worlds."²⁷ That Page experienced his blackness as more salient than his transness in the UMass context, so many years earlier, comes as no real surprise. Page's own scholarship addresses the costs of racialization in white spaces, especially in academia.²⁸ He also thinks incisively about the whiteness of trans activism and the complexity of Black trans subjectivity, which, he argues, is constituted as an offense against not only the Western gender binary but also its codes of civility.²⁹ The photo accompanying the write-up is memorable; Page is the only panelist not looking at the speaker, the only panelist hunched over, the only panelist visibly not white on the black and white page. His face is turned away from the camera. On the table in front of him is a cap and a few books—"probably Essex Hemphill or Pauli Murray or maybe June Jordan," he said later, reminiscing.³⁰

For years, this was all I knew of Enoch Page. A string of question marks and a pair of slumped shoulders. Who was he, really? What was his story? Page is

A group of University of Massachusetts professors speak about their coming out experiences.

FIGURE 5.1 Enoch Page seated behind a table with other queer professors at UMass. Page wears glasses, a plaid shirt, and black boots and sits hunched over, looking down.

the first trans professor to surface in the Five College archives—and by a long shot. This is surprising, to say the least. Black trans life is subject to some of the most pulverizing and isolating forces of white cisheteronormativity, especially in the academy. These forces not only underwrite racial projects of Black death but also archival projects within which Black trans life disappears. To have even these puffs of a story is astonishing. I wanted to know more, but I also wanted to honor Page's possible reticence to be known. I scoured the internet and found an outdated faculty webpage, in which Page situates himself in the lineage of his mother, father, Black education, and Black social movements.[31] I may have met him in pieces, but he understood himself as whole: rooted and belonging.

I sent introductory missives over several social media sites and email addresses. At first, there was a series of long silences. Then, suddenly, a quick message ("I can meet with you"), a test ("I don't care about your credentials. What do you stand for?"), and then Page was on the line, speaking to me through a black box in my hand.[32] He told me the story of knowing he was a boy the minute he gained consciousness and of informing his parents the minute he could speak—a fact his mother acknowledged only on her deathbed.[33] He told me about going, at the age of twenty, to Dr. Sugar's gender clinic in Saint Louis and passing a battery of psychological tests. He was an ideal candidate for the free sex reassignment program. He simply needed to pass the real-life test, they told him: work in a traditionally male occupation. He replied, "Well, there is no more traditionally male occupation than academia, sirs." They said academia did not qualify; he would have to drop out and get another job. Page was the first in his family to go to college and he was at Washington University in Saint Louis on scholarship. "Not gonna happen," he said, "fighting for my people" is too important. *And he walked out.* This was 1971. It was not until twenty-six years later, after he had finally paid off his student loans and earned tenure, that he got top surgery while on sabbatical—and put it on a credit card.

Page's years in the university system are a litany of struggle, death by a thousand cuts. White students attacking his teaching, overt and covert racism in the department and all the way up the administrative chain, students of color pouring through his (revolving) door in search of support, and a bone-deep loneliness. Page recalls a department "award ceremony" in which, as pretenure faculty, he received the "Honorary White Male Award." His colleagues thought it was funny. Meeting him in the hall after his sabbatical (and surgery), they gleefully announced, "Now you really *are* an honorary white male!" "They were letting me know," Page reports, that "they would accept my gender transition if I didn't lean on them about racism in the department." But Page is nothing if not a truth-speaker. As a result, he felt constantly shell-shocked. The stress and strain became too much. He gained weight, his blood pressure shot up, his knees went out, and he found himself regularly crying at work. He was on the verge of a breakdown. At that point, "The spirit was very clear to me," he recalls, saying, "It's time for you to leave here. You've done what you came to do. Dust your heels, don't even think about the so-called losses. Just walk away." Dust your heels. And he did: *he walked out.* After more than twenty years working in the Department of Anthropology, Page left UMass, without a full retirement package, in 2012. A friend of his, who otherwise refrained from commenting on his departure, simply said, "I think he was treated extremely ugly."[34]

Upon leaving, Page turned to healing. He continued bodywork, therapy, Vipassana meditation, and the 12-step program—all habits he had developed just to "survive at work." He honored his higher power and reinvested in his interests in cosmology and consciousness. As early as 2003, he had coined the term *antiracist spiritual anthropology*, which he defined as a research and pedagogical "practice dedicated to fostering social change through an understanding and pursuit of [. . .] 'higher consciousness.'"[35] Upon leaving UMass, he built a blog called *On Being a Witness*, where he catalogued his interests in consciousness studies and sacred geometry.[36] Here, readers find profiles on the molecular structure of water and salt, fractals and the Fibonacci series, the golden spiral and the golden ratio, morphometrics and madness. Coterminous with his intensified turn to spirituality, Page also turned to "harmony with the biosphere."[37] Most recently, Page curated an online exhibit on the history of trans of color spiritual leadership.[38] His anthropological acumen, personal spirituality, and commitment to trans of color history is palpable throughout the project. From anthropology to environmental justice, from small numbers to sacred geometry, and from individual psyches to spiritual wisdom—it is as if this dust speck, isolated for so long, finally found home.

Dust goes walking. Page turned the page on the university, with its fractured knowledge and fractious sociality. And he walked out, walking away from oppressive environments and walking toward chosen intimacies and opacities. Dust creates the context for new life. It refuses to be confined or controlled. Recalcitrantly, dust *treds*.

Let's Dust This Place

How should we process stories like these—stories of dust flecks hanging on, dust bits agglomerating, and pieces of dust gone peregrine? Clearly, we are not simply pulverized isolates. Taking dust as an analytic of trans poetics and archival practice means reading for dust as only dust specks, dust bunnies, and dust traps can. In a resistant, insistent way that gloms onto things long enough that something other than pulverization and its afterlives can take place. Something like moving, something like walking.

In 2018, I went to visit Ben Power in his punch-pink Victorian house in Holyoke, Massachusetts, where he lives with and curates the Sexual Minorities Archives. During my visit, he had a recurrent cough. He dismissed it quickly: "Sorry, it's the dust."[39] Ever since then, I have been thinking about dust and, specifically, dust in the SMA. It is not simply that dust accumulates in and on the archival holdings, especially with Ben and his cats living beside them. Or that dust is differentially sedimented, producing archival inequities even within queer and trans community records. It is also the insistence of our traces, and their transversal intimacies. Queer and trans dust specks—our bodies, and our stories—gather here, find home and agglomerate here into protoplanetary disks that may one day give birth to a dancing star—if they haven't already, in and among those of us whose orbits have, so luckily, collided with them.

CHAPTER SIX

Stash

Stash is one of those terms "of obscure origins."[1] This is a nice way of saying *stash* is without a clear archive. It is blowing in the wind, so to speak, having arisen *and lived* in such a way as to go unremarked, unrecorded. The term is untethered from the miles of space-time continuum that allow some words to claim origins in Proto-Indo-European, or even Sanskrit, thousands of years ago. According to etymologists' best guess, *stash* stems from criminal slang in the late eighteenth century. With the privatization of the commons, *stash* developed to refer to "hiding" or "concealing" things from established systems of property. *Stash* is a sonorous blend of *stow* (or *stock*) and *cache*.[2] These latter terms, of course, have noble histories, traceable as far back as the ninth century in Old English, French, and German. *Stash*, however, is illegitimate, even criminal, which is to say that it marks and draws meaning from modes of life outside the logic of law and the authority of time. What does it mean to possess and to stockpile that which Euro-American property law negates? The stasher is one who does not belong, and the stashed is made to belong in new ways. What would it mean, in this context, to stow against the logic of the store? To initiate an an-archive? What can be stowed by an-arch(iv)ists?

In *Brilliant Imperfection*, trans and disability theorist Eli Clare asks Molly Daly, held for decades in the late 1900s at the Oregon Fairview Home after being diagnosed as "profoundly retarded" at age two, "Where did you stash your sorrow and your rage? What small pleasures did you steal?"[3] As a ward of the state, Molly was already owned, already held, kept, and stored. Through her "imprisonment," her own life and her life with her family was taken from her.[4] "I can feel the stolen years and histories," Clare writes, "a vast thievery."[5] In this context, what sense does it make for Molly to stash and to steal? What is this theft against theft? What does it mean for Molly to steal pleasures and to call them her own, or to hold her sorrow and rage in a way no case file or treatment program can contain—or tame? Stealing room for life in an institution that disregards one's life and unequally distributes life chances is not unique to the asylum. Clare will often ask questions like these of disabled people in treatment programs, nursing homes, hospital wings, freak shows, and families. In each case, he queries after the stash of stolen time, the off-the-clock poetics.

Trans life, too, has its stashes. Stashes of forbidden clothes, hormones, and other accoutrements that make our gendered and desiring lives possible. Stashes of trans feelings, the good and the bad. Trans life involves stealing back time and stealing the chance to make sense of ourselves together.[6] Trans life in the university is no exception. Here, we steal time, certainly, but perhaps especially methods to make our own histories and fashion our own stories—a few heresies here and blasphemies there, the word becoming flesh. We stash theories in our bodyminds, stash scholarly threads in our dance parties, stash the sounds of our rage in clipped poetry. Insofar as "trans inclusion" in the university has yet to include trans collections and official archives in any reliable way, moreover, where is trans life itself stashed in the stacks? Where does it hide, stowed in an alternative system of value?

It is never easy to track *trans* in the archives—whether instituted heavily in brick-and-mortar buildings or threaded lightly through communal relations. You have to look at it sideways to catch—on one side or the other, this way or that, above or below—the stash that touches but exceeds it. Not that every stash is anarchic, but the stash I mean to take as an analytic is. In what follows, I look for stashes outside the archive, for stashes that sidle up to it without being of it, and for stashed queer/trans stockpiles themselves. I also tarry with lexicons and all the ways trans folks turn the existing archive of a language against its own grain so as to build there an underhanded stash of, for, and by queer and trans life. Attuning to the an-archive in these ways means following the furtive throughout—the disruptions of belonging and the makings of new belongings.

A Theft

The trans an-archive is a theft, but also a gift. It is composed of texts, memories, and ephemera that are stolen and stashed away by a force foreign to the institutional archive, in places that disturb or depart from that archive, and for reasons that confound that archive with the anti/ante-sense of trans life. Trans stashes not only break in and shatter stories of what is and might be (thieving sense), but they also beckon and carry out shards of transformative becomings (giving sense). Critical and cultural theorists Stefano Harney and Fred Moten insist that any relationship to the university worth its salt must be a "criminal" one, marked by relentless theft of its resources for the undercommons—for the purposes of study, hapticality, and hope.[7] In squirreling away, however, that theft cannot function according to the logic it contradicts—a logic of property and individual ownership. Instead, squirrelled resources and squirrelly time survive in the space of "sharing," a "continual giving away of it all," acorn cap after acorn cap.[8] It is the sort of stockpile that is always getting free of itself. Trans stashes, too, are best thought as a taking that is also, as fundamentally, a giving. It is cache scattered and stow splattered. A poetry that is as much a defiant disruption of the library as it is a generous "corruption of language" itself.[9]

Davey Shlasko, a trans, genderqueer Jewish educator, recalls a moment at the turn of the century when trans students at Smith assembled one of the first stashes. Current and graduating trans Smithies felt the need to build a loose-knit, tactical force. In an age before personal email addresses, when losing your Smith affiliation meant the trail going cold, they got smart.

> We started literally a box of index cards on which we wrote the permanent contact info for trans folks and allies, who were graduating, because we had the sense that there was going to be a moment, like there was with the "lesbian issue" earlier on in the '90s and earlier than that too, where the shit was going to hit the fan. There was going to be some *Time* magazine article. There would have to be some alums calling in to counterbalance all the alums calling in being scandalized, right? I have no idea what happened to that box of index cards.[10]

Index cards were a common feature of university education. Students typically used them to record information relevant to exams and then quizzed themselves or one another. Here, the materiality of university study is transposed into another key. Index cards become what they were not meant to be: entries in a monstrous trans rolodex, which did indeed come in handy. In 2005, the docu-series *TransGeneration* was released featuring, among other folks, trans Smithie

Lucas Cheadle.[11] Many alums were furious, as if transness—especially public transness like Cheadle's—sullied the purity and prestige of Smith College. Shlasko and company pulled out the box and launched into action, as if they had been preparing for precisely this test all along. They called in to defend trans students' right to exist at Smith—much as, a generation before, people had had to defend lesbians' rights to exist at Smith. Today, however, the box is a mystery, an instance of ephemerality, so outside the official archive as to exist only in memory.

Some stashes do make their way in. In the mid-to-late 2010s, Everett Owen, a white genderqueer student, went looking for trans records in Smith's special collections and found something confounding.

> I decided to see if I could find any traces of transgender women in the Smith College archives because I knew from class and also just from talking to people, that the archive, for a long time, really intentionally did not include any sources about transgender women. [...] I found this thing... this is the only real paper trail you could argue for. The archive has this thing called Magic Files which are basically just files where they put stuff that doesn't have any other spot in the archives, sort of like extra archival space. It's not really a part of the archive, but it's there. It's for things that don't really belong in the archive but it's still in the archive. So it's a really weird space to negotiate. And they have a Magic File about transgender students.[12]

Owen's story was so intriguing, I went to see for myself and, indeed, there was the folder: "Transgender Students. MAGIC FILE," sandwiched between other folders for "T-Shirts" and "Trivia Questions." Still one of only two substantial collections on trans issues at Smith, the folder contains a random assortment of contemporary articles from Smith's student newspaper, *The Sophian*, and elsewhere, about trans life on campus. Word was that the magic files were records the archivist either needed to keep or was prompted to keep by insistent reference queries. In a sense, then, this particular folder was the "magic answer" for trans-curious minds. As if trans desire, in a theft of the archivist's time, stole back a space at the edge of the archive and summoned a stash to live at its edge. An answer always there and not there, in a constant thieving act.

Shlasko's and Owen's stories are preserved in the first official trans archival collection at Smith. In 2016, Sam Davis, a trans masc Jewish student, took a class called Documenting Queer Lives, offered by Jennifer DeClue. He immediately decided to do a documentary: *In Our Own Words: On Being Trans at Smith*.[13] Building the film, however, was not enough. As he recalls, "I was looking through the archives and I was like, 'Huh, there's no trans people.' [...] But [at Smith] there's just trans people everywhere." Davis set about rectifying that representation by establishing the college's first official trans archive composed of twenty-seven oral histories ranging from under an hour to more than two hours. The stash was, importantly, a theft of student energy. Developing alongside a final course assignment, the archive was always apposite the system of grading and de-grading. Davis went over and above to get to the (trans) undercommons and record a stash of stolen moments there. In it, there is an overwhelming sense of frustration with Smith's failures of trans inclusion. But flashes of friendship, of faith and fellowship, also suffuse the collection, in which knowledge is not deposited so much as continually derailed and then shared.

Whether a lost thing, a sidelined thing, or an installed thing, trans stashes are both thefts and gifts of sense. They steal away moments of trans life at the edge of the university and stow them in such a way as to strengthen the undertow of its knowledge production apparatus. They are lawbreakers and unmakers, but with an open hand. More specifically, they are sites of rebellious refusal. The index card box refuses the isolation that so quickly becomes the default for trans folks. The trans Magic File refuses to be excluded from the archive point-blank and thus hang about the door. The trans oral histories refuse to let trans stories either be buried or bullied into specific, college-approved lines. This "No" is an-archic. It is also a dramatic "Yes" to another story. A theft—and a gift.

A Crisis

Becoming part or parcel of an official archive is not without its complicities. What, then, is the relationship between stashes and stacks? In the stacks, knowledge gets made and placed, not only in consonance with existing institutional investments but also constructive of them. Little of the an-archic survives, but that is not to say nothing. When the stash is installed in the archive, does it lose in legitimacy what it gains in legibility? For the stash to retain its essence of theft and gift, it must consistently put in crisis the archive in which it finds itself a stowaway. A crisis is a decisive moment, a turning point, the crank and crack of the hinge. If the stash, as stash, is to survive in the archive, it must pose an identity crisis to the archive—what and who is it for? And what must escape from its hold[ings]?

The library is a tensed site of power and resistance, where complicit and creative knowledges jostle for space. How might stashing in the stacks happen, and how might it fail to happen? In *The Order of Things*, French theorist Michel Foucault insistently reckons with the contingent and capricious organization of knowledge (and what gets counted as knowledge). As illustration, he cites a short story by Argentine writer Jorge Luis Borges about an encyclopedia that includes strange entries for "fabulous" and "frenzied" animals, as well as "those that from a long way off look like flies."[14] Black queer theorist Rod Ferguson then focuses, in *The Reorder of Things*, on the university and its capricious conceits. The university deploys "diffuse strategies" not only for the "management of knowledge" but also for "subject formation"—that is, it involves itself in shaping who we are and what we "know."[15] Projects dedicated to liberation for minority peoples (especially those instigated by departments of race, ethnicity, gender, and sexuality—and surely we could extend this to trans studies), he argues, must not see the university (and its many libraries) as an instant haven, but as a fraught borderland in which they ought necessarily to "disturb expectations and systems of intelligibility."[16] Academic sense needs to be brought to "crisis" through the activation of "minor details" or minor lives, he argues, rather than the establishment of official archives.[17] Is this the work of the stash? The activation of minor details from minority people that puts the university itself in crisis? And how might the stacks stage such a scene?

Lark, a former Hampshire librarian who initiated trans holdings there, reflects on the complexities of working in and against the library. In 2017, they helped organize a monthlong exhibit on the Young Lords and Black Panthers' shared legacies of resistance.[18] It was a "takeover" of the whole first floor: essays, books, documentaries, archival footage, FBI files, and ephemera from protests and community events were plastered over walls and windows. Flattened there, they blocked out the sun—and became the light. For a moment, the library was self-critical, interrogating its tendency to occlude radical resistance movements among—and especially *between*—communities of color. The stash got out—a bit.

But Lark also witnessed a student-led critique of the library.

> Last fall [2016], the doors to the library, the stairway up into the library, and the Airport Lounge (which is a room that is part of the library building but not in the main reading area of the library), those spaces were all stickered or Post-It-ed with Black Trans Lives Matter and Black Lives Matter and Black Femme Lives Matter stuff. We felt like it was very important that folks had done that activism in the library. So we basically left it up for a week or so until it was time to.... My boss consulted with me and another person on staff at the time about just what message do we send to the community as this gets cleaned up, and what that looks like.[19]

Imagine it. Two sets of large automatic doors; a wide, brick double stairwell; and a long, open community space—all feathered in Post-It notes. A bit of bright against the dull façade. The visual is powerful, insistent—each instance a punch of sense. Like voices clamoring outside the library and flooding up against its inner doors—voices lifted lightly but stating something heavy. Black Lives Matter, Black Trans Lives Matter, Black Femme Lives Matter. Do they matter here, in the library? Are they the matter of its stacks or no? And how would they, could they be? Concretely, who penned all these Post-It notes? Who stuck the Post-It notes up there one-by-one until the space took wings? It is not insignificant that Post-It notes come in booklets—stacks of them, no less. Did they fill the books—*write the books*—before tearing off each page? Is the action not simply a set of repeated iterations but a testament to the torn-pages experience of Black and trans and femme students on campus? Who then peeled these Post-It notes from the walls? And at whose behest? What is the message communicated by a hygienic regime that can only suffer the mess for a week? And in what landfill do they now lie, pages pressed back together, immobilizing all those fluttering wings?

There is no record that the Post-It notes action did anything or demanded anything. No policy was won or change secured. The rubric of success and failure is inappropriate here. Something happened. Something was said, seen, felt. Our movements are better for such moments, where the stash almost gets in.

This splash of skirmishes in and around the library poses the question of exactly what relation the stacks have and ought to have to trans life in the university. How can libraries honor and preserve, as Ferguson puts it, these "burnt offerings of communities in struggle"?[20] How can they support the resistance work of "minor details"? But also how might the trans stash harbor the library's own tendencies in its wake—so often failing to account for trans of color lives, especially when those lives are lived across racialized categories? The library is inherently a space of tensed relation. It is stretched (*tendere*) between dominant and insurgent forces of knowledge production, dissemination, and preservation. Critically negotiating the library, therefore, means attending to these divergent structures of attendance (*attendere*). It means cultivating a capacity for crisis by letting the stash out—and letting the stash in.

A Hold

Some stashes get serious, get substantial—no longer a vanished box of index cards or slivers of paper just outside the archive doors, but a whole building of memories—a storehouse, a storehold. These solidified stashes of trans life tend to thumb their nose at archival norms of structure, classification, access, and materials.[21] They are criminally loose with convention, leaving a properly trained archivist drenched in an anxious sweat. They steal from stolen histories something small, insubstantial to hold onto—plant it and watch it re/degenerate. These are more than stashes outside the official archive, or in but not of that archive; these are stashes *as* archives, creations against institutionalization. They hold their own and are beholden to their own with a kind of tenderness, even as they comprise a stronghold against other ways of doing and keeping history. What logics do trans stashes store and safeguard? What logics do they scatter? If archiving is "an inevitably political craft," what are the politics of trans an-archives and how might "stash" be a vector of that politics?[22]

In *Confessions of the Fox*, University of Massachusetts, Amherst professor Jordy Rosenberg offers a queer and trans retelling of the escapades of eighteenth-century London thief and escape artist Jack Shepard. But the footnotes tell another story. Professor R. Voth finds the manuscript of the *Confessions* in a pile of disgorged holdings outside the university library.[23] He pockets it and becomes consumed with annotating it. Asterisks and daggers galore, he inserts philological, theoretical, and personal notes that are as much about the manuscript as they are about himself. The university gets wind and tries to make a buck by strong-arming Voth into producing a P-Quad edition of "the earliest authentic confessional transgender memoirs in Western history"— P-Quad being a publisher-pharmaceutical surveillance organization.[24] Voth agrees briefly, only to despair quickly. He disappears with the manuscript, stashed under his arm, then in his car.[25] In a final footnote, he speaks in a cryptic tone of a library in the sky, where he's found archivists who aren't really archivists. And his readers—the queer "unheld" by familial capitalist logics—can find him and the manuscript there.[26] It is an an-archive outside the archive, full of an-archivists, in a place where queer trans stories are, indeed, "for us."[27]

The Sexual Minorities Archives (SMA) is one such stash. Founded in 1974, the SMA understands itself to be both activist and intimate in character. Ben Power has held the collection in his personal home since 1978, and in his Western Massachusetts residence (first a rental in Northampton, and then a power-pink Victorian house in Holyoke) since 1979. In the SMA, which is one of the largest independent LGBTQ archives in the world, he preserves national LGBT history, but also local records—stories of trans life and activism in the Five Colleges and in the valley more generally. For Power, it is a calling. Queer and trans history should be preserved *for* queer and trans people *by* queer and trans people. Everything else—from the corporate world to official archives—is "run by my oppressors," he states.[28] This archive and its holdings, however, take a political stance. They refuse the silencing to which queer and trans life has been subject and the misrepresentation and lies that so often accompany it. The SMA, he proudly announces, is "a house of truth" which refuses that silence and cultivates our stories."[29] Its commitment to truth telling, moreover, is also a commitment to movement building. To Power's mind, queer and trans archives are "the basis for political activism."[30] They are the basis for "changing the world."[31]

The SMA, however, is not simply positioned against—against traditional archives, silence, oppression, and the present. It is also positioned toward—toward its users and its/their futures. In Power's words, the SMA is a place of "healing," from which users can draw academic, intellectual, and spiritual "strength."[32] The archive is meant to be engaged physically, intimately. Suffused with the "lifeblood" of Power's own queer and trans body, the SMA invites users to let their own bodies be made and unmade by its holdings.[33] In a world in which queer and trans people can so rarely touch—or be touched by—their own histories, they can lose themselves here, exploring the loosely tagged materials preserved in relatively untamed piles. The goal, for him, is not simply that people see themselves in the holdings, as if in a mirror, but also that they "grow."[34] Here, queer/trans folks can ask queer/trans questions about queer/trans life, exploring and expanding who they are and who they might become. It is "a survival-level nurturance place," Power summarizes, an archive *of* feeling, but also *from* feeling and *for* feeling.[35]

Trans stashes have the potential to be a stronghold in which certain form(ation)s of queer and trans holding(s) become possible—pending a holdup, in which certain institutional logics are suspended and cisnormative patterns put on pause so that trans lives can stop holding their breath.

A Lexicon, A Larynx

Not all stashes are brick-and-mortar or flesh-and-blood. Some stashes merely reverberate in the ear and thrum in the throat. A collection of vibrations that have come to mean—over eons of time and tracts of space—something queerer than a meerkat. Language can trans itself, as much as its bureaucrats and its police. It can set sense veering. And part of that veering, part of that turning (French *virer*), is a material making.[36] This is the built-in and in-built entanglement of sound and body, waves and particles. It is entanglements like these that Karen Barad, who was a professor of women's studies at Mount Holyoke from 1999–2005 during which time they wrote the bulk of their magnum opus, *Meeting the Universe Halfway*, theorizes in their notion of transmaterialities.[37] If "matter is promiscuous and inventive in its agential wanderings," so too is the matter of sound and how we sound out our gendered lives.[38] There is a power of possibility and imagining stashed away in the soft vibrations of our vocal folds.

I want to return, here, to Davey Shlasko. This time, he recounts a tale not of a card box but a voice box. He remarks on the privilege it is, as someone not from a recently colonized group, to have many of the words that most resonate with his gender be English words that are recognized by those in power. But then there are the Yiddish words. He recalls a mishmash scat-smattering of gendered and genderqueered words in Yiddish through which he (s)mashes together his own gender. In this instance, the linguistic archive that is Yiddish hides a stash of queer and trans possibilities.[39] As he puts it:

> I learned Yiddish a little bit from going to Yiddishist socialist summer camp as a child and a little bit from my family and a little bit from studying it as an adult and studying it with queer teachers as an adult. So some of it is just like, some of the gendered words that are most uncomfortable for me are words that my elder relatives would call me in Yiddish, like, "You're so pretty." "*Shayna punim*," "You're so pretty." Or like, "Such a pretty girl [*shaina maidel*]," or like, "Such a wild child [*vilde chaye*]," all these very gendered compliments and insults that feel so much stronger to me than any English ones, I think because I wasn't super socialized in mainstream femininity. And at the same time, some of the masculine, but young, so masculine diminutive words, are so, feel so cozy to me. And then, there's also just some really fun grammar, where grammatical gender in Yiddish isn't always aligned with the gender of the person. So like, the word for girl is grammatically neutral, and you can do some funny things with that, it's just really fun.
>
> *Yingele* is a little boy. Or *boychik* is a different diminutive word for boy, which also sounds super genderqueer in English, but really isn't in Yiddish, but kind of is. And some of that is about Yiddish, but some of it is about Yinglish really. Even like, the ways in which when I was a teenager, I was around a lot of adult lesbians, who would talk about someone being a *mensch* in a completely gender-neutral way, just like, "They're a good person," but also in a way that I think that those folks were kind of into it, because it did something about gender to use this word that's sort of technically, grammatically masculine, but also just means a good person. And to use that word about a woman, particularly a butch, does some things with gender.[40]

There is a cache of Yiddish words stowed away for (gender)queer and trans folks today. By shifting, ever so slightly the timbre with which words are said, the location of their saying, and that about which they are said, that stash can spill out, a wealth of culturally inflected gender possibilities gone veering. This is no mere wordplay. As Agni, a trans nonbinary Jewish alum of Mount Holyoke, puts it: "It's part of my political practice."[41]

When prompted to dream of more liberatory futures, trans interviewees often hoped for more words. Jack, a trans butch dyke from a working-class background, who studied at Mount Holyoke in the 1990s, said this: "I think we need more words for who we are, and more stories. [. . .] The diversity and distinctness of the experience" is just so much greater than we can express.[42] Those words may well be new, as we see in trans Tumblr archives or Reddit threads (stashes in their own right), but they need not be. They can also be old, familiar words made to move again.

Stash is an analytic for abolitionist informatics. It is one form that desubjugated knowledge takes. Tracking the stash—or stashes—allows us to attend to stories squirrelled away in unofficial pockets and recalcitrant coves. The stash is one way that people whose histories, voices, and flesh have been stolen and silenced make a theft of the system anyway, clawing back fragments and filaments for a cache. It signifies a refusal of the laws and logics—the grammars—by which they and their peoples have been pulverized. And it is a commitment to make something else—make something else happen, make something else live. It is a commitment to give—and give away. The stash is one way we make our stories and histories, one way we give ourselves to one another, one way we hold each other.

Trans poetics in and at the edge of the archive can look like many things, but it looks at least like a stash of Post-It's, papers, index cards, and unfiled files, it looks at least like a bright pink Victorian home with long-haired cats lounging on acid-free boxes—safeguarding our pasts and snuggling our futures. It looks like words gone veering off the page and out of the sides of our mouths, glinting as they pass. And it looks like fire in the eyes, tension in the fists, and fierce songs in the heart. To pose stash as an analytic of trans poetics, then, especially a trans poetics of history and archival praxis, demands a certain unfaithfulness to official archives themselves. It means looking where the stories shouldn't be, and where one shouldn't look. It means looking for the disobedient, recalcitrant storytellers. And it means looking for their stolen stories, stories in crisis, stories that hold and that swerve. There is no trans poetics of the archive without a stash.

CHAPTER SEVEN

Scatter

Scatter. Disperse, diffuse, dissipate. A word of obscure origin, the etymology of *scatter* is itself scattered across languages and millennia—Old and Middle English, Dutch, Low German, and Greek—and no one is quite sure when or where it all started.[1] To say its origin is obscure, then, is perhaps to say it has no single origin, no definitive anchor, no first place. Scatter has always already been scattered, never once unified or settled. Even the term *scat* (or *skat*) itself is split, meaning *treasure* in Old English but *dung* in Greek. Over the centuries, scatter has referred to the scattering of sheep and ships, of clouds and snow, and, perhaps quintessentially, of seeds—which are spread, sprinkled, and strewn about. It marks the pattern of fugitive flight. And the way laughter shatters the air, sending its peels bounding and bouncing along the ground. There is something onomatopoeic about it. Strangely, the reflexive use—that is, to scatter oneself—is now rare or obsolete, as if it were too hard to think. Nevertheless, one can imagine, without too much effort, oneself as scattershot, the very point of a scatteraway.

How scatters get made and what they make in scattering constitutes the poetics of scatter. Perhaps unsurprisingly, there are multiple levels and layers to that making. In nature, the scatter typically happens in tandem, an intimate dance between the scattered and scatterer. Birds and bees scatter pollens and seeds, squirrels strew the ground with acorns, while deer drop burly bristles across the forest floor, and a light breeze coaxes spores along. A bit of *trans pollination*.[2] An ancient orchestration, companionate spreading allows for new life. But there is another kind of scattering. A noncompanionate, nongerminative one. Monocultures scatter plants from one another, while highways cut up wildlife habitats. In both cases, human projects undertaken without regard for other lives scatter those lives. Flora and fauna become isolated, and biodiversity declines. Thinking the vibrant and violent scatterings of concept and creature, theorists Jacques Derrida and Édouard Glissant make a critical intervention: the violent scatter is never complete, never final; the vibrant scatter always exacts its revenge. Entropy wins over order every time. Frozen momentarily, the cycle of life and death inexorably returns.

For Derrida, a theorist and self-described Franco-Maghrebian Jew, a certain scatter subtends everything—every formation of matter into being, every substantiation of sense into meaning. Before and beneath concepts, institutions, and things, which are always determined via distinction and delineation, there is the indistinguishable and the irreducible. In a way, this is the point of Derrida's concept *différance*—the constant differing and deferring of sense that makes writing both possible and impossible.[3] One commentator calls this primordial scatter "a certain madness," which irrepressibly interrupts normative sense and sense-making procedures; a "motley" multiplicity that cannot be reduced to identifiable, legible, respectable units.[4] Derrida's friend Glissant concretizes the scatter. As a Black Caribbean theorist, he thinks in and with that geography. When colonization swept through the region, it set out to replace the natural scatter of languages, histories, and customs with a culture of the continent. Solid, singular. Stationary and consistent. In doing so, it created peoples "scattered"—and isolated—from themselves.[5] Colonization, however, is never complete. In this case, the revenge of the Caribbean archipelago is creolization itself, a reassertion of nonreductive scattering, and, through it, a "poetics of Relation."[6] Ephemeral, multiple. Mobile and erratic. A scattering for, rather than against, life.

To think scatter, then, is to think a smattering of things. It is to think the vibrant force of multiplicity that drives things in various directions and without clear origin. It is also to think the violent force of dispersion that quells that multiplicity (although never absolutely). And it is to think creative processes—like creolization and writing—that, while they gather things into identifiable forms nevertheless harbor a stash of dispersive power that frays them at their edges, making room for something else.

Scatterways

Binary gender logics scatter us, as trans people. But we scatter them in turn, making them more than and other than themselves. Indeed, we might understand trans as a kind of gender scattering—smattering, slathering. There is, however, also a scatter at the heart of transness itself, by which I mean the crip instability of the term *trans*, the unstable cripness of trans experience, and the coeval intimacies of crip life and trans life. In largely disavowing this scatter, trans studies and many trans people scatter transness from itself: what it is and what it could be.[7] But it is in this primordial "scatterscram" that we might more richly make things and make one another—in all the madness that trans makes possible.[8] I offer scatter, then, as a trans/crip analytic through which to catch sight of trans poetics.[9]

Consider trans is/as scatter. If transness is anything, it is an insistence that gender is—vitally and intimately—inherently more scattered, more diffused and dispersed, than a binary gender system can account for. The multiplicity that we are disrupts that system from within, always extending beyond and entangling between the clean lines, defined categories, and limited histories. But by instituting the swift and solid bifurcation of male from female, man from woman, that binary gender system scatters us and our scatter-selves—we gender disruptors and gender dissidents. It scatters us to the winds, throwing us from homes and havens, schools and restrooms, legibility and legality. We are scattered—isolated from each other, from our histories, and sometimes from our very own selves. But the story does not stop there. Trans- always returns, gender disruption always erupts, even under conditions of erasure. And it is that return and eruption, we often think, that promise trans liberation.

These two scatterings, however, are tempered by a third sense: our trans selves as the site of a scatteraway. To the layers of vibrant and violent scatterings, we need to add the reflexive sense, a self-scattering. We scatter ourselves from ourselves. We, too, are a source of our own scatteraway—especially, in this context, from the crip side of trans. There is a fraying force that fractures overly clean conceptualizations of what trans is, trans does, and the (non)sense trans makes. It is a mad force for which we are not always ready and which we do not always welcome. Likewise, there is an inherent instability by which transness misses the mark and breaks normative function (and misses its own mark, breaking its own normative function). There is something fundamentally dysfunctional about it. And of course, this is not to mention the embodied and enminded ways in which transness collides with and explodes into disability.

The two misfitting and mal-adjusting together. This—all of this—is the crip content at the heart of trans. Too often, we institute divisions, denials, and disavowals about transness in order to scatter it precisely from its crip scatterself. It is this crip reflexivity I hope to illuminate.

Scat!

While there were decades of bathroom skirmishes at Hampshire first through bathroom stall graffiti, and then through bathroom sign removal and tampering, it all came to a head on November 21, 2011, with what everyone ominously refers to as "the bathroom incident."

"Get out!" he screamed. "Scat!" he might as well have intoned.

Hampshire students in Jack Pryor's Performing Identities class were tasked with developing site-specific final performances.[10] Three students chose to work in what was at the time labeled a "Bathroom with Urinals" in the Music and Dance Building (immediately opposite which stood a "Bathroom without Urinals"). A professor was just leaving the restroom as they entered; he returned after ten to fifteen minutes to use the restroom again. With some frustration, he asked the students to leave. They left momentarily to check with Pryor but then went back to work in the restroom. The professor returned a third time and, upon seeing them, exclaimed in frustration, "Okay! This is it! You need to get out of here! This is a men's room! You can't be in here. [. . .] It's a men's room. It's my bathroom."[11] When they resisted, he called campus police and reported "three girls in the men's bathroom."[12] By their own description, one was a "Jewish cisgender woman," another a "white transsexual man," and a third was a "genderqueer person of color" of Middle Eastern descent.[13] On the heels of the queer studies awakening on campus, in which Pryor played a significant role, and the heightened gender justice awareness that had produced the inclusive bathroom signs in the first place, the incident was shocking and struck like a flint.[14]

Students read the scene in multiple ways. In the first, the professor is the Man, in more than one way. Patriarchy relies not only on the superiority of one sex over the other, but also on the presumed rationality of one and an active infantilizing of the other.[15] His restroom, his assessment, his rights—and his material resources. Historically, men's rooms—much like other public spaces such as courtrooms and universities—were for centuries presumptively masculine, only named (or signed) as such when women's restrooms were introduced in the late eighteenth century.[16] Against the professor's claims to reason and property, then, Hampshire students dubbed their resistance effort #OccupyBathroom.

Occupy Wall Street was in the air and an Occupy Hampshire chapter had just started earlier that month. In continually occupying the restroom, students insisted that power and resources be redistributed in nonpatriarchal ways, especially around bathroom use and determination.

In a second reading of the scene, the professor's claims evince a certain coloniality. Developing in Europe in the late eighteenth century, binary-gendered restrooms were then introduced either as civilizing initiatives among the colonized or as distinguishing architectures of colonial culture.[17] Such initiatives and architectures were always already racialized and gendered, and coincided with a larger effort to assert the colonial modern gender system and to police especially Indigenous, Latinx, and Black people.[18] The assertion that this is "my bathroom," this is a "men's bathroom," belies a conviction that whatever local gender flexibility might be signaled by the quaint "Bathroom with Urinals" sign, it is nonsense. Civilizing distinctions must be reasserted, even violently implemented. It is for this reason that the students' resistance effort came to be known as #DecolonizeBathroom.[19] To decolonize, in this context, meant to breakdown the gender and racial hierarchies that inform the production/possession of space.

The (admittedly tense) work of occupying and decolonizing involves a return or revenge of the scattered. Such work is a testament that the force of the scat(ter) is unable to be contained. Incidents like this are endemic; queer and trans people join a long line of gendered, racialized, and disabled bodies that have been scattered from bathrooms. We go looking for a gender-inclusive restroom in a different building, or a gendered bathroom in an out-of-the-way place, or we use the bathroom associated with (or not associated with) our sex assigned at birth because we will get yelled out of the other one. But queer and trans people—at Hampshire and elsewhere—also scatter. Our insistent presence in binary-gendered restrooms, using whichever we choose, is a dispersive force in the heart of these social institutions, demonstrating with insistent flesh that gender is more than dominant stories—and histories—would have us believe.

Hampshire's bathroom incident concluded with an insistent critique of the event itself and of campus policy. The students finalized and staged their performance piece, which offered a "queer magic ritual" through which they and others might heal from the racist, homophobic, and transphobic "wounding" of the incident.[20] This was a fundamentally poetic response. But the students also demanded that the college clarify its policies (and where appropriate create new policies) about public space, bathrooms, signage, enforcement, and accountability—demands the college went some way toward fulfilling.[21]

The story could have easily stopped there, but it didn't. A student-produced zine covering the incident reports, on its final page, that the professor was said to require "medically necessary bathroom access."[22] It is a cliffhanger, left unaddressed. I interviewed an administrator who confirmed the report. What happens when disability hits the scene? When queer and trans students practicing a performance piece make a bathroom inaccessible for a professor with a medical need for it—even if there is another, differently rendered restroom five feet away? Neither the zine nor my interviews helped illuminate this quandary. Here was the source point for another scatter.

Splits and Tangles

Before proceeding with the story, I want to take a quick step back. In *The Terrible We*, neighboring University of Massachusetts, Amherst professor Cameron Awkward-Rich refuses the split between transness and disability—and especially the divisions, denials, and disavowals that scatter transness from its (crip) self. He recalls two founding moments for trans and disability studies. In 1990, as the Americans with Disability Act (ADA) sat on the Senate floor, conservative senators insisted on a rack of exclusions, including "transvestism," "transsexualism," and "gender identity disorders."[23] In the moment disability became protected, transness became unprotectable. Then, in 1995, Susan Stryker insisted, to a roomful of conference attendees, "I'm a transsexual, I'm not sick"—an anecdote she deploys to introduce trans studies a decade later.[24] In the moment transness became authoritative, then—enough to warrant its own academic discipline—it also became nondisabled, nonsick. Against these originary splits, Awkward-Rich insists on the scatterplot intimacies of transness and disability, especially through trans of color stories. His questions are haunting: "Might insanity, tragedy, and absurdity be integral [...] to trans life and thought? [...] And how might a trans studies, accountable to the world- and knowledge-making force of the maladjusted, the bad, the mad, the painful, [...] otherwise unfold?"[25] How, indeed, might trans studies and transness reject its founding disavowal of disability and instead embrace its existing crosshatch with disabled and mad knowledge-making and world-making practices?

In the annals of trans maladjustment, running apposite these split histories, Awkward-Rich finds a complex poetics. From the archive of transmasculine (especially of color) life, he culls moments of depression, reclusivity, trauma, and suicidality, as well as pathologizing run-ins with the courthouse, the prison, the asylum, the freak show, and the sensational newspaper. In doing so, he builds a poetics of "entanglement," which consistently marks *and recreates* the co-constitution and co-occurrence of trans/crip intimacies.[26] He thinks that poetics of entanglement (which refuses to scatter transness from disability) alongside a "dissociative poetics" (which places a crip scatter inside transness itself).[27] Rereading the writings of Eli Clare and Elliott DeLine, he identifies a disaggregation constitutive of the transmasculine experience and of how that experience gets told—replete with a "fracturing epistemology," "narrative fragmentation," "halting repetition," split voices, and messy stories.[28] Paradoxically, then, one of the entanglements of transness and disability is dissociation. One of the ways they are gathered is through scattering. In locating a dispersion of crip elements in the very heart and histories of transness, he asks a simple question, over and over again: What would it mean not to quell this scatter?

Awkward-Rich takes his title, *The Terrible We*, from Carson McCullers's *The Member of the Wedding*. Twelve-year-old white tomboy Frankie Addams wants to belong to the girls' club, which meets in a clubhouse across the yard, but she is clearly not welcome. Frankie focuses on the pain of rejection and isolation, when in fact she belongs to "a much queerer collective" that meets around her own kitchen table. A cast of queer, crip, and of color characters, both real and fictive: this is "the terrible we."[29] A we more dispersed than the other, but also more intimate. Reviewing the scene, Awkward-Rich calls for "sitting together" in the kitchen—with this "motley" we that is the mess of transness and disability, shot through with race, their histories and phenomenologies all wound up and scattershot with each other.[30] Sitting like an archipelago around the table. Critical and cultural theorists Stefano Harney and Fred Moten make a similar call to the kitchen, where fugitive communities—members of the undercommons—have repeatedly generated and nourished "the to come of the forms of life."[31] Amid anxious calls to rectify who is at the policy table—or the clubhouse table—Awkward-Rich invites us to think about the heterogeneity already integral to the offbeat spit-balling and yarn-telling, shit-talking and big-dreaming tables at which we sit.

Back to stories, then. We—trans folks, trans studies folks—scatter ourselves. The obsolete reflexive sense of the term is alive and necessary here. We are scattered in our accounts of ourselves. We tend to tell stories (and histories) of trans existence and resistance without reference to disability, whether in our own community or among those with (or against) whom we struggle. What would it mean to attune ourselves to the complicities and complexities that already exist, already form networks, between and among madness and transness, dysfunction and disruption, sickness and gender trouble? What does it look like to stand—or, perhaps better, sit—on this bridge of maladjustment?

The Scatteraway

Let us return to the scene in question: the bathroom with urinals in Hampshire's Music and Dance Building. The professor walks in. Is he simply the voice of patriarchy and colonialism? Is he merely the conduit of a violent scattering? If, and insofar as, he has a medical condition that structures his access needs down to the minute, he is a crip figure. A professor, yes; a man, yes; but also less and more than these norms signify. In a not uncommon twist, the story goes, he appeals to a discourse of colonial patriarchy in order to advocate for his needs. In this scene, what are the students doing? They are occupying and decolonizing a space that they are nevertheless not using to relieve themselves. Are they figures of ableist entitlement? Are they enacting a differently violent scattering? What would it take to think professor and students as one community and the histories and ideologies that keep us apart? What would it mean to imagine both parties joining at the point of *access* and sharing the ground of *maladjustment*?

Rereading the zine, it is impossible not to cup one's ear to its crip undercurrent. The Middle Eastern student, who assumes the name "Beast" in the performance, uses a wheelchair, self-describes as neurodivergent, and describes their body as "twisted and taut," "fruity," and "brown."[32] All three students are described as "survivors of chronic and acute traumas."[33] They in turn describe the incident as a "trauma" and a "wound," causing one student to "shake" and another to have "an anxiety attack" in the stall.[34] The students also describe the incident as a "crazy-making experience."[35] The students felt "triggered" and "emotionally unstable."[36] Somehow, an ally's foot got caught in the professor's office door afterward and they came back "limping."[37] The student exchanges with the administration after the event are characterized repeatedly as "unhealthy" and as constructing a "toxic energy flow."[38] Against the professor's "rabid defense of male territory, cissexism/sexism, and a constant fear of abjection," then, is a less than sane and staid collective.[39] A motley we indeed. A motley we who, nevertheless, tried to craft a place of healing in a space of experiential violence: the bathroom. Indeed, there is one way to read the scene as a clash between access needs, the professor and students composing a circle of maladjustment and misfitting that produces further rifts and harms where there might have been, in another world and around another table, a bond of alliance.

Across the more than one hundred interviews with predominantly trans interviewees that inform my larger study of trans poetics at the Five Colleges, testaments to disabilities, disorders, and dysfunctions abound. They are named in tumble-fulls, with crip vectors cropping up in clusters across and within individual interviewees. A representative but nonexhaustive list is as follows: "always sick," angst, anorexia, anxiety, attention deficit hyperactivity disorder, autism spectrum disorder, autoimmune disorder, back injury, bad memory, bipolar disorder, burnout, cancer, childhood abuse, chronic fatigue, chronic illness, chronic pain, clinical depression, cluster migraines, diabetes, dyslexia, eczema, fatigue, flu, "fragile body," gender dysphoria, hard of hearing, heart defect, labyrinthitis, learning disability, long COVID, Lyme disease, mobility impairment, "mixing up" words and letters, neurodivergence, obsessive-compulsive disorder, panic attacks, post-traumatic stress disorder, psychiatric abuse, sexual assault, "six years of a bum right ankle," suicidality, trauma, and traumatic brain injury. Many interviewees list "disability" and "mental illness" on the intake form without further description, and some describe themselves as "mostly able-bodied" or as "appearing able-bodied."

What is perhaps most interesting about this list is not its length and diversity but how often these disabilities, disorders, and dysfunctions were disavowed in the very moment they were disclosed. Granted there were important exceptions, but a solid number of interviewees found themselves mentioning something and then saying, "Sorry, that's not the trans story."[40] They were apologizing because they assumed (perhaps in some way I communicated) that I wanted the trans story, not the disability story. Interviewees who easily spoke of their transness and experiences of racialization often avoided discussing their crip experiences. They assumed these stories were separate stories, not hyphenated stories, asterisked stories, elliptical stories. When explicitly invited to say more, for example, Joshua acknowledges his impulse to "play up" his transness but not his disability, to lean in to "passing as able-bodied" but come out as trans. Another interviewee, in telling their gender journey, told me they got sick, so sick, and still are sick, but "anyway, all that other stuff is not about trans identity." Yet another mentioned a virulent, chronic infection that required them to go off antidepressants and testosterone, which then sent them into years of depression and anorexia. They quickly righted course and confessed, "but that's not about trans things." But it *is* about trans things, it *is* trans stuff, it *is* the trans story.

Discussing trans-inclusive university policy, especially trans-inclusive sports, Mount Holyoke alum Blake poses what he considers the "crazy" idea of making trans count as a disability under the ADA.[41] What a wild thought. "That'll consume a whole sixpack and an afternoon if you let it," he says. But it would be effective and efficient, he adds. "Would it be pathologizing?" Sure. But would it be worth it? Probably. Blake's proposed tactical alliance is Awkward-Rich's constitutive intimacy—an intimacy disavowed by much of trans studies and trans people alike, but an intimacy that keeps returning to scatter transness at its core, shattering any illusion of a solely healthy, able, and sane trans bodymind and community.

Scattering Sense

As trans folks, we are always already scattered. Our bodies do not consolidate the way they are supposed to, whether pre- or post- or non-transition, and the way we think about ourselves and our worlds is, perhaps at its best, scatterbrained—jumping from here to there, breaking apart what appears together, taking a broom to the anthills of cisheteronormativity. We live and function in a world where we are scattered, despite ourselves, into two genders, two social roles, two bathrooms, and two boxes. And when we can't take the hint, we're scattered from two to nowhere. But the flesh is insistent and the spirit recalcitrant. We scatter people's categories; scategories. Much rides on this return, even revenge, of the dispersed. We pin our trans hopes and dreams on it, as if someday, finally, multiplicity will win out. And the scatter of gender fluidity will reign. But what we spend too little time appreciating is that we often scatter ourselves from the depth of this potential. We tell our stories piecemeal, refusing, so very often, to look again, to look still more closely, and find there in our stories vectors and energies that tear trans from its own origins and send it scattershot in another—or several other—direction(s). Asterisked indeed.

To take scatter as an analytic of trans poetics is to look for these many scatterings in trans comings and goings. It is to follow the wind, the winged creatures, and the stockpiling, stashing squirrels of all gender disrupting persuasions. It is also to track the split tracts and sealed silos. And the cracks—the fissures in every edifice through which the wind and the sun rush in. Something trans surfaces and squares off in each of these spaces. More than simply marking the scatterways, however, such an analytic must think the scattershot with scatterthot. With a hint or a haint of transMadness, refusing the too-easy division between trans and everything else across and within which it sits. Cavar, a genderless and neurodivergent Mount Holyoke alum, defines transMadness as "a wandering and wondering praxis, anticipating and refusing neurotypical, sane, cis supervision in both the structure of our thought(s) and in the comportment of our bodies."[42] For them, transMadness "rewilds" the "wordstrokes" that condemn thought to reified disabilities, inflexible genders, and tyrannous commonsense concepts.[43] TransMadness mobilizes ways of (un)knowing and knowing-less, in spaces of "less" than cisnormative sense and sanity.[44] Taking scatter as a trans analytic, then, might mean attending to these mixed and multiple scatterways in such a way as to set trans theory on edge. To make it unsteady on its own feet. Such an analysis would track what trans unsettles, but also *where* trans settles—and upset the sediment there, where it happens.

Sonny Nordmarken, a University of Massachusetts, Amherst alum who helped organize a trans studies working group during his sojourn as a graduate student in the Department of Sociology, thinks deeply at the intersection of trans studies and disability.[45] He writes eloquently of the monstrosity of trans existence and, specifically, the way in which it disrupts "gender accomplishment practices"—the way we try to prove our genders (and our transness).[46] He also published an autoethnography of living with Lyme disease, a tick-born illness endemic to Western Massachusetts, among other places.[47] In one especially memorable description of cognitive impairments precipitated by Lyme, he writes:

> Throughout my days, I forget what I'm doing in the midst of doing it, what I'm looking for in the midst of looking for it. [...] I strain to remember the first part of the sentence at the same time as retaining the last few words, but I'm not fast enough and many of the words evaporate. [...] It is a task to think of appropriate words in the moment I am forming sentences. Sometimes I say words that don't make sense. Sometimes I misspeak. Sometimes my grammar is not right. Sometimes it is embarrassing.[48]

Nordmarken is lost in words, lost to words, at a loss for words. First and foremost, this is disorienting for him, as he loses an access to his body he previously had. It is also deeply frustrating, because these symptoms are repeatedly disregarded and misdiagnosed by medical professionals. But Nordmarken's headspace might also signal possibility. What if his cognitive lapses were characteristic of trans(Mad) life itself and trans(Mad) studies, too? What if they, too, were full of absences, silences, muddles, and lost origins, as Cavar might insist?

What if this were all precisely as it should be? What if trans life and trans studies, shot through with crip intimacies, were full of illogics, silences, muddles, and dissonances? Lost in words, lost to words, at a loss for words? Indeed, what if it were only patriarchal, colonial, and ableist instincts that press for more consistency, more reliability, and less (crip) poetry? What would our stories—our histories and our archives—look like if we really reconciled with the scatter that is ourselves? And to the transMadness of that poetics? This is not simply a call to tell better (or more accurate) stories, but also to break our storytelling praxis. Archipelagize it; mad-scatter it. And it is not simply to cite better (having more well-governed and well-disciplined reference lists), but rather to honor the scatter that is trans/queer/crip/of color community knowledge building.[49] Such calls to destabilization put in question languages of centering. They insist that stories not simply be stabilized in another place but be held precariously in their inherent instability. This is a scatter that vibrates multilocally—twitching in the heart, shaking in the belly, skittering in the mind, and flapping across the page.

I have written before that a series of injuries and illnesses brought me to my knees just as I was graduating with a PhD and the several years thereafter.[50] And that in that moment, the vastness of what I had never wondered—about capacities and futurities—took my breath away. What I have not yet put to the printed page is this: I was so physically wrecked when I arrived at Hampshire that one of my sisters moved in with me for an entire semester to help care for me, get me around, and make life possible for me. I did not simply arrive at Hampshire trans. There were holes in my stomach and ribs scattered from my sternum. I remember grieving my (previous form of) trans masculinity, now that I was unable to carry things, push things, or hold myself up with my own two arms. I remember collapsing on a walk I thought I could make and thumbing a random car for the first time in my life. I stared down the barrel of a future nothing like what I had envisioned. It took me years to heal, but the vulnerability of my strength stays with me. More than that, I realize now, almost a decade later, I have been my own scatteraway. I am not claiming disability here; but I am resisting the mirage of the sane and able trans body. Perhaps in writing this, and sending these many words splattering across the page, I will have gathered something together that can germinate otherwise, in another disordered and disordering ecology.

Part III

Attunements to Trans Resistance

CHAPTER EIGHT

Resistance. Revolution. Rebellion. Words laden with the heft of upheaval. They indicate something really signal happened—so signal, in fact, that it is not too much to say that nothing was the same from that point on. The world turned upside down. In resistance (from the Latin *sistere*, to stand), people take a stand against something for long enough, and hard enough, that the thing itself gives way. Walls fall, states topple, ideas are swept away with the changing tide. Leaders and laws are struck down or instated, by turns. To tell the story of resistance, then, one seems to need incisive moments and largescale happenings. Chronologies of resistance are measured out in a series of high-profile protests and incisive actors. There are sit-ins that instantiate that work of standing out. Public speeches, public letters, and public opinions saturate the political landscape around which media attention circles like crows around carrion. Charismatic leaders, with (often oversimplified) counterculture messages, move from podium to bullhorn and back again. They are thrown in a cop car, in jail, in prison, or killed only for their spirit to rise up again like a phoenix and guide the movement home. Resistance is dramatic stuff, the doing of spectacular deeds often by spectacular people. But it needn't be.

Tracing the poetics of resistance is difficult, insofar as it lies beneath the surface. A devastating undercurrent, a low-profile countercurrent. The shoals against which the symbolic order slowly breaks. Real change starts with how we are with one another. It starts within the movement, between people. Witnessing it requires looking for the people remaking the world by relating to one another differently. Where are people walking and talking, cooking and eating? Where are they laughing? Where are they jamming things up and jamming out?[1] Where are they playing around with new gestural, guttural, and gendered motifs? There is a certain musical improvisation coincident with throwing a wrench in the machinery. Poetics is a pulse too often overwhelmed by projects (and pontifications about such projects); too often overshadowed by policies (and self-congratulatory assessments of achievement); and too often eclipsed by Important People (and their corresponding sense of self-importance). I am curious here about the attunements necessary to catch resistant ways of being together and making each other that (and as they) escape. How does one attune oneself to the explosively ephemeral, especially when it inhabits the thickness of our bodies together? To the leaks between solids?

The poetics of explicitly *trans* resistance is no exception. It is those flashes of recognition that pass between us in the check-out counter, on the metro, on the city street or at the country market, or, if we are especially lucky, at the daycare or in church. It is all those selfies we take in bathrooms we are not supposed to be in, according to one law or other, in one state or another. It is the sometimes fuzzy, sometimes fiery talks we have with one another about what gender is, what it means, and what it does. About our unbidden desires and about things excruciatingly hard to put into words. And it is all the ways we begin building networks together, organizing our shared presence into lines of force. In the university, the poetics of trans resistance takes on a unique hue. It is our theory-driven mornings and our body-driven nights. It is how we experiment with form and function, line and curve. It is our sketchpad proposals and our chalkboard dreams. It is those long, sometimes taxingly extensive stretches of time where we hash out what we mean to the university and what we need from the university. And it is all the moments where the university itself fades into the background, because we are each other's foreground—our fury, our tears, our lives, and our suicides. In the trans work of making ourselves and making one another, we are already the revolution we have been hoping for.

In what follows, I search within political theories of resistance and the Five College archive of trans life for attunements that, far from leaving us waylaid by institutional policies, important personages, and incisive protests, pull the poetics of resistance into the frame. Here, the embodied ground of refusal and its commensurately toothed creativity come to the fore. Woods and mountains, backrooms and city streets, bodies bumping into one another and things passed hand-to-hand—there is a recalcitrance cultivated in these places and in these ways that spurs but also escapes larger projects of determinable, isolable, official change. My hope in attuning to the background is to get back to the ground of resistance, which is always, like any other ground, thickly solid but ever shifting. First, I cull three attunements from political theory: attunements to webs, to tactics, and to hangouts. I then thread these through Five College stories, where the network and tactical structures of trans resistance get insistently localized in spaces tertiary to the university. Those stories also emphasize that resistant formations are never simple or isolable; there are always multiple webs and competing hangouts. In order to understand what resistance work trans is doing (and not doing) in any given moment, trans cannot be studied in isolation. It must be situated in what is more and other than trans. In pulling the poetics of trans resistance into the frame, then, I hope also to flex the frame itself and to lay the groundwork for the analytics to follow.

Attunements to Resistance

Writers have been running after revolutionary poetics for centuries. To begin, then, I want to work transversally to cull bits of wisdom from perhaps unexpected allies in political theory: a French anarchist, a Jesuit priest, and a lesbian Argentine philosopher. When looking sideways at an archive of resistant praxis, it helps also to look to the side of trans and garner resonances that allow trans to reverberate in another key, resonances that illuminate it as well as set it off-kilter. I offer, then, one strand of a conversation. Spanning three decades and three continents, Fernand Deligny, Michel de Certeau, and María Lugones together attune themselves to the poetic architectures of resistant practice, each referring to and critically building on the one before. It is here, in their analysis of everyday movement, practice, and language, that another picture of resistance surfaces. Webs and wander lines, tactics and strategies, walks and hangouts take center stage, together illuminating the power of making through intimate motion. Afterall, the small ways people move still change the way things are. In this case, the attunements to poetic resistance provided by Deligny, Certeau, and Lugones can inform precisely what we might look for when investigating the poetics of trans resistance in the university.

Webs

In the poetic substrate, where does resistance happen and what shape does it take? Deligny, an activist involved in the antipsychiatry movement in France in the mid- to late twentieth century, put it this way: look for the webs and the wander lines.[2] Having worked in educational, psychiatric, and correctional institutions for children with psychiatric disabilities, Deligny pivoted to developing alternative structures not founded on the presumption of pathology. He championed communal residential programs rather than state-run asylums. Straying further and further from city center and state funding, he ended up building a commune for nonspeaking autistic children in the mountains on a shoestring budget. Tracing their everyday movements, Deligny saw in these children a certain poetics, a way of being and making that resists the capture of language and the constraints of sanist social structures.

Why webs and wander lines? Deligny became obsessed with spiders while reading Karl van Fritsch's *Animal Architectures*. The spider is never separable from its web, insofar as the thread is internal to it.[3] Neither is the web separable from its context—the branches that anchor it, the wind that moves it, the creatures that disturb it. In building a life of these layered intimacies, the spider offers us a lesson—a lesson similarly taught by the autistic children with whom he worked. Those children's movements, whereby they *wove* space and relation in ways that countermand normative logics, are fundamentally resistant to and transformative of societally customary behaviors and expressions. They did not participate in society's "thought-out-project[s]," but rather crafted their own "wander lines [*lignes d'erre*]."[4] Importantly, wander lines do not merely curve; they *cross*. As a central feature of the web, Deligny describes *chevêtres*. Translated heavily as "crossbeams" and "binding joists," *chevêtres* refers to the points at which one shaft or filament crosses another.[5] They are the "*heres* where the wander lines intersect and overlap, in space and across time."[6] It is where transing happens. For Deligny, *chevêtres* appear in webs, in networks, and in communal hideaways. They are the places where we touch, the magnetic spaces to which we repeatedly return, forming the nodes of the network, the "curls and tangles."[7] If one is to look for a poetics of resistance, one might look for these knots, these *chevêtres*. For wherever they are, anti-institutional spaces of belonging and making are not far behind.

Trans life moves in ways the thought-out-project of binary gender cannot sustain and aims to erase. Transing weaves gender—and all its filaments and affinities—into intolerable shapes, so those shapes keep getting swept away. As soft as that weaving may be, however, it is recalcitrant and resilient. Indeed, in some fundamental sense, it is the heart of trans resistance. A poetic approach requires attunement to those gender-silk threads and their Arachnean network, where the crosshatch happens. Where do trans folks move in the university? Where do they wander around campus—through what halls and offices, quads, and gardens? What affinities do they build and where on campus?

Where do their minds clump and their paths meet? And what does that meeting make?

Tactics

While Deligny saw that autistic children's everyday movements were revolutionary in a sanist society, Certeau took that message mainstream. For him, there is an incredible power for social change implicit in people's everyday practices—practices as mundane as cooking, shopping, and art making.[8] Certeau wrote in the aftermath of the French resistance movement called May 1968, one of whose rallying cries was *sous la pavés, la plage*, or "under the paving stones, the beach." Borrowed from earlier Situationists, the slogan indicated that life lay under the rubble of social artifice and institutions. Beneath the unyielding solidity of stone lay the flexible silt of sand, itself just stones deconstructed. Drawing from this tradition, Certeau insisted that while one can never get behind or before the surveillance structure of late capitalism, one can get between its teeth, so to speak, grit and sand surfacing in the cracks. This tactical transgression is available to anyone, anywhere—and everyone, everywhere.

On Certeau's reading, a tactic is a calculus (in Greek, *calx* means pebble or stone), a way of arranging, counting, and sedimenting things precisely against the way things are officially arranged, counted, and sedimented.[9] Importantly, that against is always also through. Tacticians can never get outside their environment, only move through it differently. Tactics, he writes, are like Deligny's wander lines. "They circulate, come and go, overflow and drift over an imposed terrain, like the snowy waves of the sea slipping in among the rocks and defiles of an established order."[10] Tactics traverse the system, diverting it and making it drift. One of Certeau's favorite and most famous examples of a tactic is walking.[11] Weaving across streets, bike lanes, sidewalks, curbs, potholes, and thresholds alike, bumping into things here and people there, the walker navigates the city with greater ingenuity—*and rebellion*—than the urban planner ever intended. The walker "moves [things] about and [. . .] invents others."[12] There is a resistant "*poiesis*" to it.[13] Indeed, a "long poem of walking" overlays the city, drowning out the clipped syntax of the urban text.[14] Remember your skip, or your stumble, your rushed jump over the curb, or the swerve of your chair. The awkward dodge of someone who appeared out of thin air. Remember the shortcuts through impermissible spaces, or the ones so circuitous you got lost. This whole process of moving one's body along and against the city's capillaries lays "a second, poetic geography on top" of the first.[15] The city is thick with it, hazy with it. Millions of poems, millions of pathways. Poems cliff-thick and river-long. A record of embodied resistance—of insurgent making—in space.

If one were to look for poetics of resistance in the spirit of Certeau, one would look first to everyday practices rather than grand gestures and pontifications. One would look, among archives of trans resistance, in particular, not for the punch in the face but for the sand in the teeth. One would look for trans tactics—tangled efforts to make/unmake sense and space. Where does the trans body break through the strictures and discourses that attempt to contain it? Where do those with less position or power turn things around and veer off in another direction, whether in the context of meaning or materiality? Where, indeed, are the long trans poems overlaying the well-organized structures of cisnormative life?

Hangouts

Wandering and walking, cooking and art-making, are important, but our resistant potential is arguably more than our everyday movements and everyday practices. Writing at the turn of the twenty-first century, Lugones took exception to Certeau on precisely these grounds.[16] For her, tacticians are not simply embedded actors, but leaders of social change and social theory.[17] They are tactical *strategists*—they can do some urban planning of their own. And while there is no evidence Lugones read Deligny, I want to put them into express conversation. While Deligny might well have pressed Lugones to undertake an honest reckoning with madness in her work, Lugones might have insisted that autistic people can in fact organize and direct their own educational centers, rather than simply wander through them.

Lugones roots her critique of Certeau's tactics in the streets and, specifically, among streetwalkers. Streetwalkers (*callejeras*) are people who live and work in the street, especially women of color, poor women, sex workers, and queer folks.[18] It is here in the street that the streetwalker develops a different *rationality* rooted in a different *relationality*. And she is in good company. Other street folk, including "the outlaw, the despised, the useless, the insane, the hustlers, the poachers, the pickers of garbage, the urban nomads," "defy and unmask common sense."[19] The streetwalker, too, builds resistant sense and perspective by cultivating "an ear and a tongue" for the languages and logics that litter the streets.[20] But how exactly? The streetwalker's "*poiesis*," their ability to "make and unmake sense," and their capacity for planning and theorizing beyond mere tactical flexing, is rooted in "hangouts."[21] Originally said of claws, teeth, and tongue that loll from the lips, then of clothes and shingles hanging overhead, *hanging out* only came to modify people spending time with and beside one another about two hundred years ago. For Lugones, streetwalker hangouts are not apolitical entertainment centers; they are labs for revolution.

> Hangouts are highly fluid, worldly, non-sanctioned, communicative, occupations of space, contestatory retreats for the passing on of knowledge, for the tactical-strategic fashioning of multivocal sense, of enigmatic vocabularies and gestures, for the development of keen commentaries on structural pressures and gaps, spaces of complex and open-ended recognition.[22]

Hangouts are transgressive *and* attentive. They are counterspaces *and* communal spaces. And they are deeply generative. "Walking and bumping, among and into each other," streetwalkers capitalize on the frictions and adhesives of being-beside to generate being- and thinking-otherwise.[23]

If one were on the lookout for a trans poetics of resistance, à la Lugones, where would one turn? One would look for these moments in which we are present to each other, in the rich multiplicity of ourselves, and trying to live and think from that polylogical and polyvocal place. One would look for curdled spots, border spaces where ambiguity flourishes. Where are the streets and the streetwalkers? Where are the trans and gender-disruptive hangouts? Where do folks bump into one another, jostling beside each other? Where is sense made and unmade in ways so enfleshed as to be difficult to see? And where does theory happen not from on high but from below, and between, and beside?

There are numerous ways to track political resistance. Reams of paper and raffs of digital space record leading personalities and major events (the protests, marches, die-ins, lie-ins, and other direct actions). Tracking the poetics of it all, however, is a different task altogether. It looks to the interstices and to the flesh *between* people. It looks to the habits of bodies together in space and the (non) sense they make. Deligny, Certeau, and Lugones carve out unique shapes in that landscape, inviting different attunements in our study and our practice. Sometimes, resistance requires getting out—of the city, of the schools, and of the trappings of commonsense—and making not bee lines but wander lines. Webs of our bodies moving and making meaning in space, knotting here and stretching out languorously there. Sometimes, too, resistance requires getting savy and getting smart, turning tricks with what you got: tactics. Where you turn up and turn out, and how you turn things against their grain in order to make them say a new thing—this is the everyday stuff of struggle. And sometimes resistance requires getting crunk in the cracks. It means hanging out— with or without a purpose, with or without a plan—and hashing out what we mean and what we dream. The poetics of resistance is thick on the ground and thin in the seats.

So what do these attunements look like in the Five College archives, transposed into a trans key? In what ways is it crucial to look for webs, wander lines, tactics, and hangouts here, and in what ways do trans stories push these attunements further, lending them a unique ring?

Disturbing the Universe

In spring 2016, Gabriel Stein-Bodenheimer, a Smith College alum, became perhaps the first out transgender man to teach at an all-girls Catholic high school—and not be fired for it. A college-preparatory school, Mercy (1952–2020) was part of the Roman Catholic Archdiocese of San Francisco and sponsored by the Sisters of Mercy in Dublin, Ireland. When Stein-Bodenheimer came out, school administrators feared Mercy would lose its Catholic status and its funding. It was an immediate crisis. The Sisters of Mercy flew in from Ireland to meet with the Reverend Salvatore J. Cordileone, archbishop of San Francisco. To everyone's surprise, they determined Stein-Bodenheimer would remain welcome at Mercy High. Cordileone justified the decision by stating that the case fell under the purview of "prudential judgment."[24] To address their community, Mercy's administrators called a school assembly. After hundreds of students filtered into the assembly room, administrators opened with a long prayer and spoke of God's unequivocal love for all people. They then informed students that counselors were standing by for those who would need emotional support in this critical moment. They enjoined the students not to tweet about what they were about to hear. Finally, they announced with great solemnity, "Gabriel Stein-Bodenheimer identifies as a trans man." The hall was silent. Students were entirely unfazed.

While relieved at the outcome, the whole process left a strange taste in Stein-Bodenheimer's mouth. Framed as the exceptional object of institutional largess, he was abstracted from his own story, as well as from trans history. The inherent instability—indeed, the queerness—of his transness was neutralized. He would have much preferred to come out, as he always had, in the classroom with his students. Coming out to them as a lesbian in previous years, he would begin with T. S. Eliot's poem, "The Love Song of J. Alfred Prufrock."[25] A paradigmatic text of modern alienation and mundanity, and of the weight of expectation and social scripts, this poem asks haunting questions: Can I refuse to measure out my life "in coffee spoons"? Can I learn to ask not "What is it?" but "Do I dare?" "Do I dare disturb the universe?"[26] For Stein-Bodenheimer, his sexuality—and ultimately his gender identity—were "Do I dare disturb the universe" moments. Students would then share their moments in kind. This was a space of vulnerability and community, built on belonging and trust. Each person's story mattered. And in sharing those personal histories, students and teacher alike built aptitudes for resistance and self-creation, nurturing a more capacious world here-and-now with a sense of hope and freedom. A far cry from a silent auditorium.

Stein-Bodenheimer came by his love of queer-trans resistance tactics in deinstitutionalized spaces honestly. He had first learned of trans life during a gathering of Jews in the Woods, at some off-season campground in Western Massachusetts. A "laboratory for vibrant, inclusive Judaism," Jews in the Woods (1997–2013) facilitated unofficial gatherings—hangouts—outside of synagogues and Hillels where young progressives could reawaken their spirituality and reimagine their traditions.[27] While Jews have historically hidden in the woods from persecution, living on food from nearby fields and farms, Jews in the Woods reclaimed the woods as a different kind of fugitive space. "Outside of established Jewish Institutional structures; outside the rules, processes and assumptions that exist elsewhere," writes one member, "we create our own space. We find God in the *midbar*, as our ancestors did."[28] The Hebrew *midbar* (and the Greek *eremos*)—or, wilderness—indicates a place of political exile, even social abandonment, where humans wander but God nevertheless shows up in unusually intimate, powerful, and revelatory ways. It is an uncultivated place, where lines and confines are thin, and therefore where more becomes possible. Extracted from empire, it is the ground upon which empire will ultimately falter.

Here in the *midbar*, Stein-Bodenheimer received a copy of Micah Bazant's *Timtum: A Trans Jew Zine*. First issued in 1999, *Timtum* is a self-published, grassroots-circulated zine that explores resources in the Jewish tradition for understanding and appreciating trans and genderqueer life. The *timtum* is a gender-indeterminate person, often cast as "stupid or ineffectual," who appears hundreds of times in the Torah and Midrash. Byzant recasts the *timtum*, however, as "a sexy, smart, creative, productive Jewish genderqueer," with undeniably crip undertones.[29] He does so in this lengthy multimedia text, which weaves together Word (.doc) files, typewriter sheets, photocopies of printed text (sometimes hand-edited or hand-annotated), handwritten notes (with varying font sizes and intensities), sketches, collages, photos, several languages (Hebrew, Yiddish, English, French, German), dreamscapes and diary entries, Trans 101 lessons, a top surgery narrative, book recommendations, and references to Jewish trans precedents—including early twentieth-century surrealist Claude Cahun. In this project, the liminal figure of the *timtum* is powerfully mobilized in the liminal medium of a zine. Both live on the edge and in the cracks, in unofficial spaces and unsettled places. Creatures of twilight (of the in-between moments, their instability, and their power), they disturb the limits of law and category.[30] Stein-Bodenheimer's world cracked open.

In many ways, Stein-Bodenheimer's story is consistent with the above attunements. He locates his capacity for disrupting the universe not in the auditorium, the synagogue, and the Torah so much as in the classroom, the woods, and the *Timtum* zine. He roots his ability to make change in the poem lives he lives with those around him. That is where the webs and the hangouts happen. And that is where transformative tactics get generated (rather than ameliorative strategies inherited). Importantly, Stein-Bodenheimer's story insistently pushes these attunements into (trans)local spaces. The wilderness, the woods, the classroom, the twilight spaces and texts, the disturbed universes, these are concrete places (situated to the side of educational institutions), where webs, tactics, and hangouts get off the ground. His story is a testament to the poetics of trans resistance in local settings.

But the Five College archives do more than mobilize and reroot these attunements in a trans key. They also challenge it. Over and over again, the archives tell stories of resistance in which multiple webs, competing hangouts, and tensed tactics jockey with one another. Attuning to these tales requires a facility with dynamic networks and a capacity to track what is happening to trans in conjunction with other discourses and other skirmishes. It requires looking at what is *tangible about* but also what is *tangential to* the revolt. It requires a transversal bent.

Pronoun and Sponge Battles

On March 6, 2003, the Smith College student body gathered to discuss replacing the pronoun "she" with the phrase "the student" throughout the Student Government Association (SGA) constitution.[31] The amendment was proposed by SGA president Lindsay Watson and supported by the T Committee, composed of transgender students and their allies. Throughout the campuswide debate that ensued, it was referred to as the motion for a "gender neutral constitution." Those for the amendment argued the case of gender inclusion, noting that there just are non-she's at Smith and they should be represented in the constitution. Those against the amendment worried it threatened the identity of the college and the value of women, thereby compromising admissions and alumni giving. Some worried Smith would become, or was becoming, the "trannie school."[32] On April 17, after passing a senate vote, the motion passed a student body vote by a simple majority (1,115 votes; 50 vote margin), earning Smith a two-minute segment on *Fox News*.³³ Something of a domino effect followed. That fall, Smith's annual Celebration of Sisterhood (originally a 1991 lesbian vigil) became simply Celebration and the Big Sis, Little Sis program became Big Sib, Little Sib.³⁴ Gendered bathroom signs also started disappearing all over campus.³⁵

A powerful minority was concerned enough that on March 9, the following spring, they formally proposed an amendment that would revert the SGA constitution to its former state: all references to *the student* would go back to simply *she*. Proponents of the new amendment cited harassment by the "thought police."³⁶ Opponents of the new amendment, once again, argued that she/her pronouns just did not reflect all Smith students. "You are imposing language on my body," Tobias Packer said—a body that is already here, already a Smithie. "This human is not an opinion," he continued.³⁷ On March 30, the senate voted down the new amendment (31 to 17; 1 abstention), precluding a campuswide vote.³⁸

In what might seem like a tangent to the gender controversy, a dining controversy simultaneously rocked the student body. Following the 2001 recession, and its aftershocks, the Smith administration announced, in the fall of 2003, the consolidation of dining due to budget cuts. Traditionally, Smith offered in-house dining, with assigned kitchen staff, in residence halls. It was an old-world practice that, while having shorter mealtimes and more limited food options, aimed to cultivate a family environment and house community. It was, as one student insists, a "social adhesive."³⁹ As the changes got underway, students complained of the "devastating loss" of dining rooms, of traditions "washed away by the economic tide."⁴⁰ Students and alumni again worried it would impact admissions and alumni giving, not to mention involve laying off kitchen staff. Student house presidents collectively responded to the proposed consolidation in *The Sophian*, arguing that house community was more important than budget cuts or improved dining experience.⁴¹ A reaction group called Save Our Smith (SOS) formed, but to no avail.

Silas, a Smith alum, who describes himself as a Southern trans guy with a blue-collar white trash background, recalls the moment as follows:

> People were upset that the tradition of having your own kitchen staff in house (talk about class politics at Smith) would not be preserved. And so those two issues [gender and dining] were intermeshed. We're talking about the tradition of a women's college. It's really interesting in terms of looking at a race/class narrative and preservationist politics. And they

were campaigning. They were using sponges and kitchen gloves as campaign ephemera. They were handing them out.[42]

Silas here suggests a race/class politics behind the dining controversy—a politics that likewise undergirds the gender controversy. If Smith is a "cashmere and pearls" kind of place, gender disruption is a form of class disruption.[43] Just as there is something vulgar about gender riffraff, people who are something other than, more than, to the side of "woman" (let's be honest, especially short dudes with kindly faces), moreover, so there is something plebian about eating in big mess halls together. Notably, in *The Sophian*'s extensive coverage of the issue, there are only two photos of the dining room/kitchen in action. In the dining room photo, dining services staff member Bruce Cichy, to all appearances a white man, "inspects the salad bar."[44] In the kitchen photo, work-study student Tonya Wilson, a young Black woman in cornrows, stands at the sink and "reaches for another dish" to wash, wearing an apron and white rubber gloves.[45] Gender, race, class. Save our Smith, then. Here, take a sponge.

In retrospect, the sponge is really the one element of this story I cannot wipe from my eyes. There is something spongy about every corner of it, a far cry from the clean, firm lines of wood-paneled walls and wood-paneled tales. Replacing *she* with *the student* in the SGA Constitution was like poking holes in the document, compromising its internal stability but also making it more porous, more absorbent. Similarly, closing private kitchens perforated dining with a strange anonymity. To be sure, forfeiting (the illusion of) women-only space and small-group repast is a loss. But it also creates a million tiny inlets and outlets, where multiple substances can coexist and not every surface has to touch. These are sponge stories, then. The poetics of trans resistance looks like sponge formation. This is true at both the micro and macro level. Sea sponges are known for their symbiotic relationships inside and out—with bacteria, algae, micro-organisms, but also barnacles, crabs, and anemone, just to name a few. Trans resistance, too, is spongy with nontrans activity. To hear the gender and dining controversies together, then, and to sit with their consonant and competing resonances, you need underwater gear. It is too easy to flip through *The Sophian* and record only the SGA constitution kerfuffle (as I did the first time). If this turn-of-the-century moment at Smith teaches us anything, it is this: you have to look at the tangents to understand trans resistance. You have to look transversally. You have to look across trans itself.

I have proposed that in the search for a trans poetics of resistance, one needs to cultivate attunements to trans webs, trans tactics, and trans hangouts, noting especially where they show up in local contexts and placed-based settings.

In doing so, moreover, one needs also to stay alive to the multiple webs, competing hangouts, and tensed tactics that overlay, intersect, and struggle with one another within and beyond the organizing matrix of "trans." In this case, class so often gets occluded both in the construction of what trans means but also in the oppressive structures trans replicates. Underground records of trans resistance, however, bring this and so much else to the fore. The call to poetics is a call to honor just this.

From Attunements to Analytics

Looking for the poetics of trans resistance requires looking not for the flashy events and easily toutable tales, but the stealthy details. Our transness spreads thickly over the everyday ways life gets organized, gooing at the seams and leaking through the cracks. And sometimes we target that goo and that leakage, gathering it up and turning it against the systems set interminably against us. Trans resistance works obliquely; it has to. There are no behemoth superstructures here, or freight trains of destruction. Instead, there is a kind of tactical weakness filled with the enduring strength we draw from our time in the fire and the warmth we make with one another. That furtive, flexible force hangs about our shoulders and in the corners of our eyes. Looking for the poetics of trans resistance *in the university* requires still something else. It shows up not just in the classrooms and on the quads, but in dorms and queer centers and off-campus hangouts. It shows up in the study sessions that devolve into shit-talking and friendship-building. And in the moments when trans folks care for one another. It is even in the dropouts and the suicides, and the many revolutionary thoughts and acts of refusal that can lead up to them. It lies, too, in the wild theories each of us throws at the world until something, finally, sticks.

Of course, a poetics of trans resistance also includes moments when trans folks and allies get up to something, scheming about what the university could be in a trans-flourishing world. In those moments, it is crucial to notice what is happening around trans or to the side of trans. Track the sponge stories alongside the constitution stories—the stories full of holes alongside the definitive ones. Notice how trans gets inflected through class, and race, and the rest. Notice the inflections we do not even know yet to look for. What trans resistance is up against is more than trans erasure or transphobia or cisheteronormativity. It is also susceptible to the most mundane and egregious, as well as the most delicate, reinscriptions of gut-sickening ableism, settler colonialism, and gender-based oppression. There is always more than one web in the webbing, and more than one tactic on the ground. Staying awake to the complex system within which trans is always slipping in and out is part of tracking trans resistance underground. The multilevel attunements that open up here are breathtaking.

In attuning myself to trans webs, tactics, and hangouts, to the trans wilderness spaces and the disturbed universes, alongside their more-than-trans counterparts, as they surface in the Five College archive of trans life, certain resonances began to clump together. I have come to think of them as three analytics for a poetics of trans resistance. In this context, the attunements I have culled are practices of noticing that allow webs to come into the frame; correspondingly, analytics are frames that allow a webby noticing to set to work. One way to understand these analytics is, again, as tools of a minor science, an ambulant mode of study that tries to understand flows more than stable units, the thing activated by trans rather than capital "T" trans itself. Another way to put it is this. These analytics are the apparati used to study underflows. For queer and trans river scientist Cleo Wölfle Hazard, the term "underflows" names not the surface flow of rivers but what flows beneath it, the hyporheic zone where river seepage moves through the silt and clay of the riverbed and its watershed.[46] The vast majority of an underflow is underground. On a theoretical register, underflows are the subdominant discourses and practices that, while typically erased from history and excised from science, nevertheless hold keys to the entire ecosystem. The ecopoetic practice of studying underflows, moreover, arguably requires attunements to underflow areas and analytics to isolate what moves in that water and where. Analytics are like the porous tubes sunk deep in the earth through which our buried but still mobile rebellions can be witnessed. Whatever is happening above them, these analytics can help explain the resistant understory of trans life.

The three analytics I will use to illuminate a poetics of trans resistance are these: thread, glue, and pebble. Nouns that are also verbs, these terms capture specific structures through which trans folks resistantly make one another through things other than and more than their transness. In asking how it is that trans folks get (un)webbed together, I came to realize that one answer is to follow the thread of the fabrics we wear and the relational fabric we make (or break). In asking about tactics, or the ways in which trans folks resist being stonewalled, I came to realize that one way to think them is through trans folks' own use of stone—to build new worlds. And in asking about the structure and function of trans hangouts, I came to realize that one answer would be stunningly simple: glue, the adhesive that makes the hangout possible. These are mobile analytics which, while rooted in the Five College archive of trans resistance, are applicable well beyond them.

CHAPTER NINE

Thread

>My right to be me is tied with a thousand threads to your right to be you.
>—LESLIE FEINBERG, *Trans Liberation*

Deep in the UMass college archives, leafing through LGBT boxes from the 1980s and 1990s, searching for the earliest traces of trans life, I came across phone tree after phone tree. Whether printed or etched into the page, the lines of intimacy were palpable. These were informal networks of care. Some pages were meticulous in their typographical clarity, reminiscent of species trees. Others, hand drawn, seemed to run off the page, with new folks squished into the margin and others sprouting like buds between branches. Some recorded brief directives: if you are positioned at the end of the tree, go "back to start," I read, or, if you cannot reach someone, go to the next tier "to keep the information moving." We call them phone trees, but they could just as easily be phone hyphae. I thought about trees thatching canopies and mycelia holding the earth in place, and I thought again about care. I thought about those calls and their electrical signals shuttling across phone lines crosshatching the valley. Filamentous tendrils of light and tenderness. I left the library, eyes bleary from hours of absorption and paper shuffling, while, unbeknown to me, a pile of blue, pink, and white paperclips I'd absentmindedly acquired in the archives tangled together in my pocket.

Lines become threads. Threads that tie us in all kinds of ways to place and to people. Eddie/Edsuvani Maisonet is a trans nonbinary Black Puerto Rican alum of Smith College from the mid-2010s. After the tireless ignorance he faced around transness as well as around the Afro-Latinx experience, and especially the stumbling mispronunciations, the laughter, and the shame prompted by his given name, he admits to developing a certain "bitterness."[1] But that bitterness never attached to his name itself, but rather to the larger, interlocked systems of cissexism and racism. He writes, "I have no problem claiming my given name, for it's my bond to my family and our tumultuous relationship."[2] Edsuvani actually has three middle names, each given by a different member of the family while seated around an IHOP table, "where my family put me together."[3] One day, a trans man and close friend of his asked when he was going to change his name. "I wanted to yell and be articulately angry—I am proud of my name and that's not something I need to do, not everyone is transitioning to be a white man—but I could only stammer out, feeling young and confused and all soft lines, 'I don't think I'm going to do that.'"[4] Edsuvani's name is a line of connection, a thread of belonging.[5] He, like many other gender disruptors with marginalized racial, ethnic, or national heritage, carries "difficult names, loaded names. Heavy names. Beautiful names."[6] "We are bois figuring out how to wear those names, our histories," he says, like a mantle of honor about their shoulders.[7]

While threads tie us to what precedes us, they also lead us into new spaces and relations. Joshua, a Jewish trans man and another Smith alum, remembers Smith's Hillel as a remarkably welcoming space. As such, it played an important role in his gender journey in the late aughts.

> One of my early gender things [laughs].... For Hanukkah, my friend felted me a huge bushy beard and matched it directly to my hair color. So I ran around the Kosher K, the space that we had all Shabbat evening, and people were telling me how handsome I was, how good my beard looked. [laughs again] I think I used that feeling as a way to guide me forward based on that feeling of validation—and my pride and joy now, a little red beard here [touches his cheeks].[8]

Joshua found himself gleefully weaving among friends, food, and flickering candles, his felt beard threading through the night with a warm orange glow. Felting is the patient process of agitation whereby wool fibers are invited to interlock into fabric.[9] While the Mishnah prohibits beating wool, twisting threads, and sewing on the Sabbath, there is a sense in which Joshua's own transgender life was stitched together in that moment, around the queer Kosher K and its reverberations in memory.

When we ask how we are with one another, what are the fibers of *with*? What are the threads that let us hang together and warm each other, pull apart but not isolate? I want to track, here, the lines of trans resistance not only but especially through the cotton, polyester, and wool fibers in and through which trans people negotiate home. The term *thread* stems from the Old Germanic *præ* meaning to twist. *Twist*, in turn, comes from the Proto-Germanic *twis-* and its Proto-Indo-European root *dwo-* meaning "two." The twist can either denote the integration of two or the division into two. Old Icelandic *tvistróttr*, for example, means "scattered." Trans folks are always two or more things twisted into one another, gaining strength and propulsion capacity. With gender (and nongender) scripts curling round, under/over, and between one another, trans folks reweave what it is possible to be and, simultaneously, unravel what they were told to achieve. But threads are also the medium through which trans folks find each other. From internet chat spaces and underground sex cultures, print newsletters and trans care practices, to listservs and streetwalking, trans people have built ephemeral lines of belonging, decade after decade. And what would that trans history be without the materiality of threads—that aesthetic resistance of crossdressing, ball culture or, as Eddy Francisco Alvarez puts it, "sequins in the rubble"?[10] Threads are one way we make ourselves and one another.

Meaning / Making

What happens when things get woven? Independent threads become fabric. Whether with threads of meaning, or threads of matter, the weaving of warp and weft produces text(ile)s. And whole worlds come together. Fabric gains form and function as a whole, while nevertheless gathering in its folds a constellation of negative space that refuses final closure. In *A Philosophy of Textile*, artist Catherine Dormor offers an extended meditation on the processes of meaning/making as textilic.[11] She is inspired, in part, by literary theorist Roland Barthes's claim that "text means tissue."[12] Indeed, the Latin *texere* means to weave or interweave while the Proto-Indo-European *teks-* refers to wattling or wickering branches. Building on this ancient metaphor of thought as thread (and thinking as weaving), Dormer argues that text and textile are best read together, as shedding interdependent light upon one another. They cover up, for instance, as much as they reveal, and touch as much as they create distance. To further illuminate the interchange, Dormer considers various modes of textile life and explores what they suggest for the weaving of words and worlds. She focuses, in particular, on the functions of folding, seaming, and fraying.

First, then, folding. Fabric folds over itself whether purposefully or inadvertently. The fold, of course, always implicates and portends unfolding.[13] The overlay of fabric, moreover, marks an interplay and an intimacy much like the overlay of threads. As such, folded fabric is never unitary, always multiple. It is "connections within connections" but without collapse.[14] Folding, however, is not the only form of textilic intimacy. There is also seaming. With a seam, fragments are joined together in a kind of functional camaraderie yet without erasing the cut or hiding the stitch. The seam always speaks the potential of being unstitched. The seam is a "passage" between two pieces, a "passage space between reinvention and sameness,"[15] which is nevertheless made by multiple passages of needle and thread back and forth, up and down.[16] It marks a generative lingering on the edge. The edge, however, does more than draw together; it also frays. Fraying reveals the structure of fabric itself, warp pulling away from weft and seams left dangling. Loose ends mark the space of transformation, where the piece either returns to its material elements or is repaired and repurposed. In this "transitional" space, this "edge of becoming," fabric epitomizes the precarity and yet possibility already at work in the seam and the fold. [17]

Citing visual artist Axel Vervoordt, Dormor muses on the resonances between the prefix *tra(ns)-*, which signals across, and the suffix *-tra*, which signals a way of doing something. Dormer applies these resonances of movement and modality, egress and effectiveness to a fraying cloth, but they might fruitfully be reframed in relation to cloth as a whole and to the clothes of trans worlds in particular. What if trans were a way of moving and doing that is, fundamentally, textilic? What if trans worlding involved modes of folding, seaming, and fraying gender scripts that only ever complexified them rather than resolved them? What if, in coming together, we fold over one another so as to safeguard resonances without capture? What if, in agitating, sweating, creating, and thinking beside one another, we seam round a passage that is always open and fluid? What if, in sparring with one another, loving and losing one another, we fray in ways that transform us *together*, inside out? This is to say that we shimmer, but it is also to say more.[18] If trans ontologies are emergent, affective, and processual, so too are trans poetics. In making, we weave; in meaning we thread. And we do so, again and again, through these mundane things called clothes.

Balls, Swaps, and Pitstops

From ball culture and drag to everyday transgressions of dress, the design, cut, and weave of fabric matters for the life of desire and of gender alike.[19] Within that history, weaves of queer connection and trans relation create the canvas upon which everything from self to sociality supervenes. Our clothing is but a momentary sedimentation of our being-together. We are threaded through with one another.

The Five Colleges have an unusually long and robust drag ball history. Held at multiple colleges for decades on end, drag ball lore is at the core of the trans story here.[20] Many are the testaments to the sheer vibrancy of these events, their role in gender journeys, and the battles for their authenticity. Oliver, a white trans man, for example, recalls attending Hampshire's drag ball at the Red Barn in the early 2010s.

> The Hampshire College drag show I went to was really mind-blowing because it was a whole mix of genders, including folks who were AFAB, who were trans masc, who were then putting on a drag queen persona. And I was just like, wow, I had no idea that all of these expressions of gender were even possible, and that it was possible to be trans in all these beautiful and complicated ways that I just hadn't encountered before in my life. I think that experience, going to that particular performance, was really.... I think of it as a pivotal moment for me.[21]

It is important to be clear about what is happening here. It is often astounding to see bodies dressed differently. That is the long and the short of it. Norms of gendered dress are so inflexible and so suffocating, that bending them 180 degrees (let alone any angle more askew) creates a luxurious fissure of air in the tank. The breadth of what is possible takes one's—takes Oliver's—breath away.

The underappreciated sibling of the ball is the clothing swap. Queer clothing swaps recycle pieces of apparel, jewelry, and other accessories among people of various genders. Turning the closet into a place of belonging, and turning articles refused by some into articles of refuge for others. It is "just good old-fashioned community care."[22] Swaps are critical for people who do not have the funds for new clothes, as well as for those who want to explore differently gendered clothing in a safe space rather than a traditional fitting room. Swaps are also a beautiful way for trans folks to care for one another, by trading clothes that are suffocating for clothes that are enlivening. Clothing swaps have been a cornerstone of Hampshire's Queer Community Alliance Center (QCAC), Amherst's Queer Resource Center (QRC), UMass' Stonewall Center, and the annual Five College Queer Gender and Sexuality Conference. Trans activists at Mount Holyoke College even invited the predominantly nontrans campus to explore dress in a similar way with their 2004 action "Pat the Mannequin."[23] The action included two elements: a "male mannequin" acquired from the theatre department and "a box of free bin clothes." The invitational flyer said, in a delightfully vague way, "Come and dress a mannequin in a gender."[24] As one of the organizers reflected after the event, "It made people consider what it is to gender somebody."[25]

It is not exclusively in queer and trans spaces, however, that trans genders and communities get built. Ryan, a Black trans man and an early 2010s Smith alum, asked his (nontrans) guy friend where to get underwear. His friend replied, "Oh, I'll show you." They went to Walmart and bought "some Hanes underwear or something," for "maybe five or six dollars," but "it was probably one of the most affirming things I ever did."[26] Similarly, Blake, a white trans man and a mid-aughts Mount Holyoke alum, recalls getting fashion advice from another trans guy's (nontrans) girlfriend. She offered it, he says, with all the nonchalance of "You need a tic-tac? Here, take a tic-tac."[27] Blake later found himself passing it on within more intimate circles:

> I remember I would get people who would bring me people [...]. I would always get calls that were like, "Hey, I think so-and-so really needs to talk to you." And that happened almost a dozen times. It was pretty much strangers, and they'd just come to my room and be like, "Hey, yeah. [...], I just had a quick question about a tie. Do you have a tie?" And I was like, "Oh, okay. Yeah, I have a tie." And then it would devolve into, "I think I'm trans!" or, "I don't know!" So I'd just usually get them drunk and get it out. And then, yeah, I wouldn't really see them again. But there was some kind of network for support, it was just very unofficial.[28]

Here, the tie is a linchpin. It is a piece of clothing of essential significance in itself, but it is also a gateway to gender and relation for many trans-questioning people. It is the fabric and it is the thread.

Whether drag balls, clothing swaps, or random pitstops for a tie, it is clear that clothing itself is a point of trans care. But it is just as true that trans mutual aid is a textilic project.[29]

The Stitch

In trans studies, the textile metaphor *par excellence* is the stitch. micha cárdenas, writer and performance artist, theorizes the stitch as one of three poetic operations fundamental to trans of color resistance strategies: the cut, the shift, and the stitch. The cut is an act of refusal and breakage; it "uses interruption to create opacity" and to say "no."[30] In turn, the shift changes things; it makes them flicker and flinch, multiplying valences of sense and configurations of flesh. In doing so, it resists surveillance by playing with opacity and transparency, norms of embodiment and forms of monstrosity. If the cut and the shift separate and create, the stitch reconnects, but it does so by a different logic. Building belonging across heavily enforced borders, its sense-making supervenes on otherwise possibilities. Arguing for the poetic character of these operations, cárdenas shows how they work through *making* on multiple registers, whether the human body, nonhuman materials, language, or concepts. "Poetics," she writes, "are the observable meeting points of matter and agency."[31] These three operations of trans of color poetics, then, generate a mélange of discursive and material algorithms that reduce violence, enhance survivability, and protect the flourishing of trans, especially trans of color life.

For cárdenas, stitching is a feminist operation and a decolonial operation. It is also a deeply trans operation, and cárdenas expertly stitches these layers together. For millennia, women have predominantly done the work of sewing and weaving, not only sewing together clothes but also weaving together families and communities. The stitch is a feminized act. To recover it "as a material and conceptual operation," cárdenas writes, is "a feminist proposal."[32] It is also a decolonial proposal. If colonization is a force of separation, distinction, border-making, and border-policing, then decolonization involves stitching across those borders and boundaries, reconnecting what has been torn asunder. "Decolonial acts of solidarity are acts of stitching," cárdenas asserts, "connecting communities across national borders and across lines of gender, racial, and sexual identification."[33] But the stitch is also uniquely meaningful for trans and travesti people, who stitch genders and gendered bodies together in resistant ways. One need only think of trans theorist and historian Susan Stryker's epic remobilization of the figure of Frankenstein ("flesh torn apart and sewn together") to appreciate the fundamentality of sewing, assembling, and self-fashioning for trans life.[34] In these disparate but interconnected contexts, then, the stitch is not only "a necessary part of healing," as cárdenas writes, but also of rebuilding deep, sustainable networks of relation.[35]

While cárdenas's attention to the stitch moves far beyond its textilic roots, I want to tarry still over the textile. After all, before there are words, there are lines, and before there are stitches, there is thread. What sort of thread is it that permits what sort of stitch? Over what seam does each supervene? I want to follow that line of thought, hold that thread. And I want to explore its various functions (and cadences) in the larger project of trans belonging and resistance—especially in connection with cloth itself.

Weaving Nets, Cutting Seams

Trans stitches are always unstitching, too. Leo Rachman, a white nonbinary man, was working as an intern in the Mount Holyoke archives over the summer of 2018.[36] While each intern was responsible for curating one lobby exhibit, Rachman chose to curate two: "Desire and Action: The Development of Black Studies at MHC" and "Trans Lives at Mount Holyoke College Today."[37] Where the former traced Black activist roots in Mount Holyoke's Barbara Smith, James Baldwin, and the early agitation for a Black Studies Department, the latter traced an absence. "The trans archive was pretty much nonexistent," Rachman recalls.[38] The exhibit involved an abstract painting by Jack Gieseking, an essay on trans belonging by Cavar (who, in *The Mount Holyoke News*, also wrote about being genderless and autistic, and several mixed-media pieces by Levi Booker including "Dysphoria," "Gender Euphoria," and "Gender Anarchy."[39] Insofar as Mount Holyoke was traditionally a place for neither Black nor trans students, Rachman aimed to tell a resistant story—a story of another Mount Holyoke. He wove a different tale of pry bars and belongings in the undercommons. Here, I want to take up Booker's work as an ongoing meditation on the ways in which trans life stitches and unstitches things.

"Dysphoria" is a mâché piece of rag and corn husk paper. The rag paper, cast over the artist's bust, is blistering in places of unusually intense dysphoria, trailing down their body, and flaking to the ground. There are rips and holes, frayed edges and folds, torn bits scattered on the floor. "The casted body is drowning in the fiber," Booker observes.[40] But beneath the wreckage, in spots over the head and the heart, natural corn husk fibers shine through, indicating the resiliency of trans life and creativity. To make the piece, Booker collected articles of clothing that trans people on campus experienced as especially dysphoric. Converting the pile into rag paper took time. They cut out the seams and turned the rest into confetti. Then they cooked it with soda ash for hours, before straining, rinsing, and blending. The paper pulp turned a dark turquoise. "Going through the experience of ripping apart clothing that has made many people including myself feel distress and inner unrest," Booker recalls, "was extremely cathartic and ritualistic."[41] In removing the seams, they removed the cisnormative logics that defined each piece; and, in cutting the rest into confetti, they made the whole thing unrecognizable, a mere portent of the possible. Transforming those articles of clothing into an instance of aesthetic resistance, Booker redrew lines and rewove threads to convey an inner truth of trans existence.

FIGURE 9.1 "Dysphoria" by Levi Booker (2018). A suspended bust of a person covered in a dark film that flakes from their forehead and above their heart down to a pile of dark flakes on the floor.

FIGURE 9.2 "Gender Euphoria" by Levi Booker (2018). Two photos of the art installation: One a close-up of netting interlaced with sigils for "honest," "beautiful," "capable," and "stable." The other showing the netting interspersed with prints of smiling faces, from the nose down.

"Gender Euphoria" is a mixed media piece composed primarily of large woodcut prints of four beaming smiles, one belonging to the artist and the other to three of the artist's trans friends. These prints were then hung on a rope interspersed with fishing net covered in square sigils of the words "honest," "beautiful," "capable," and "stable." The piece was originally installed on the Art Building Balcony at Mount Holyoke; portions were then donated to Special Collections and Archives. As Booker writes in an artist statement included in the exhibit, "This piece reinforces the sacredness that building community can have for trans people (especially on campus) and how that sort of love fosters self-love, growth, stability, and warmth."[42] From medieval to modern occultism, sigils are signs that, through their delicate calligraphic scripts, name and summon certain spirits. The lines swirling on the square stretch through to the other side of the veil. Smiles, real smiles, are contagious, likewise summoning the bright spirit of another. Too often, trans people are thought of neither as smiling nor as in trans company. Too often, we are seen as deceivers or make believers, never honest. Or as monstrous, never beautiful. Or as volatile, never stable. And needy, never capable. What makes us warm, growing, stable people, Booker proposes, is not some healthy, sane and able core, but the ropes and nets between us. The threads by which we make things and make one another.

The themes of dysphoria and euphoria are woven together in Booker's third piece, "Gender Anarchy," a linoleum relief print that dramatizes a snake in honeysuckle. According to Booker, the snake conveys "power and transformation," while the honeysuckle "resilience and beauty."[43] The honeysuckle drips with smiles, while the snake sheds its skin like the corn husk blisters through the rags. Both forces mark trans life and, in particular, trans life in the university. How is this gender anarchy? Anarchy means being without an originary law, leader, or archive. Through Booker and others, exhibit organizer Rachman is able to dramatize in an archive not only the absence of a trans archive, but also the incompatibility of transness with a certain sense of archive. Transness can function in an archive only without an *archon*. It is not loyal to a first, a proper, an unbroken thread. Rather, it is loose and frayed, seamed and folded. It is always doing the work of (un)weaving. Trans folks in the official archive are not bees in the beehive, but a snake in the honeysuckle. In some sense, this is the ultimate stitch, the drawing together of transness and archives in the face of their legislated separation, yet according to a different logic. In an even more fundamental sense, this is the work of textile, of insisting that things only exist in relation, threaded together for a moment. A twist that also scatters.

Robes and Wardrobes

Among the Five Colleges, Amherst College has the strongest and longest—most well-wound—ties to conservative wealth. Much of that story can be read in *The Amherst Student*, a newspaper published continuously since 1868. In a remarkably telling op-ed from 1991, situated amidst ads for cheap liquor and investment banking tutorials, regular columnist Jonathan Keats takes aim at—wait for it—paperbacks. In a piece fatefully entitled "Paperback Classics Reflect Downfall of Societal Values," Keats bemoans the demotion from leatherback to hardcover, and now paperback.[44] Paperbacks "are made of card stock that would put most business cards to shame," he writes, "and are bound to the volume itself with glue that wouldn't hold together a model airplane. They are ugly, flimsy, and awkward."[45] While he can understand (although not endorse) publishing Danielle Steel, Steven King, and other "airport throwaways" in such a state of undress, he cannot brook the vulgarity of clothing Aristotle, Jean-Paul Sartre, or Émile Zola in such rags. The way you dress a book, he argues, should at the very least reflect the rigor and excellence of its contents. That the college has stooped to requiring students to buy paperback classics says everything one needs to know about the demise of the institution.[46]

Keats's attachment to the image of wealth and intellectual excellence, at a school that has ping-ponged around #1 among US liberal arts colleges for decades, is reflective of Amherst culture to this day. That attachment, moreover, has had redoubtable effects on trans life at Amherst. Ean, a nonbinary trans femme with a working-class background, recalls how hard it was in the late 2010s to build trans community at Amherst. Old money and status saturate the place. Reunions include $40,000 ice sculptures, they told me, and students at convocation "make fun of the faculty that don't have crimson and blue robes—robes from Yale, Columbia, or Harvard."[47] In fact, Ean once offered to talk to a student looking for a trans mentor, but the student said no, he needed to talk to someone with a "real degree"—that is, from an Ivy League school. In places like these, class—and the class of the clothes and of the diploma—make the trans real (in a fake way). Trans folks not dressed in crimson and blue (e.g., trans folks from state schools, and certainly trans folks with no college degree, as well as trans folks not from private schools or with no high school diploma), have little to offer those who do. Thread for thread, they are found wanting. Excruciatingly, then, it is not just cisnormative accoutrements that trans folks tear to tatters; it is also each other.

The issue of classed clothing also comes up regularly among interviewees at the second wealthiest school of the Five Colleges: Smith. Davey Shlasko, a Jewish genderqueer Smith alum recalls that, in the late 1990s (although the pattern surely holds to this day), trans students at Smith would, "from one month to the next, announce they were trans, change their name and pronouns, and throw out all their old clothes and [buy] a new wardrobe."[48] As a first-generation low-income college student, it took Shlasko himself ten years to turn over his clothes. Crucially, while he changed his name, pronouns, and wardrobe, and medically transitioned, Shlasko did not transition into a traditional masculinity, either of the straight or gay variety. "I'm not an especially masculine person. I'm not even sure if 'trans-masculine' super makes sense to me. I'm kind of faggy," he says, having "a pretty faggy kind of masculinity" but without the stereotypical "cultural references or urban fashion sense" of gay guys.[49] Traditional forms of straight and gay masculinity are often classed in a way Smith is but Shlasko is not. Wealth, success, strength, beauty. There is something plebian about trans that, in fact, many trans folks, especially at places like Smith and Amherst, expend great labor and resources to disavow. But Shlasko leans otherwise. After all, what good is trans disruption if it does not open a space for more gendered lines of being in the world?

Threads have the ability to create volumes from very little, from almost nothing, from a line.
—RIKE FRANK, *Textiles—Open Letter*

Resistance work is making work. It is not simply a wall thrown up in another's face—a simple refusal or a long elaborate dance through which we say, "No." It is also pulling together and bridging across. Or simply wearing each other—and wearing each other out. From drag balls and clothing swaps to everyday dress, textiles play a critical role in our histories, our presents, and our futures. But our textilic refusals and creations are more than that. They are also traceable in how we seam our gender ways, fold our gender communities, and fray our gender thoughts. Indeed, trans threads can do many things. And it all begins with a line, a line that sometimes breaks when it shouldn't. This is what it means to take thread as an analytic of a trans poetics of resistance. Our threads are one set of patterns through the understory.

CHAPTER TEN

Glue

> It is poetry that I want now. I want the concentration and the romance, and the words all glued together, fused, glowing.
> —VIRGINIA WOOLF, *A Moment's Liberty*

Our doings adhere us to certain things and certain beings, and sever us from others, whether suddenly or ever so imperceptibly. And we ourselves are only ever glued together, becoming unglued and reglued in the vagaries of a moment. Sometimes we see it happening, sometimes we don't.

Glue safeguards the threshold between things; it presides over the crack. Through it, things come together and things come apart. In this sense, glue is perhaps the clearest cipher of possibility in an atomized world. It resists the separation of two separate things and produces the tendency to cling. But just as surely, in the rush of water, heat, or pressure, it permits of dissolution and cleaving apart. Glue is the force that joins and unifies, while granting the right to divide. Unlike the stitch, the yoke, or the screw, glue's force lies in its flexibility, its nonbrittle jointure. Tar, pitch, resin, paste, mortar, caulk, glue—adhesives are both derived from and applied to just about every sort of being on the planet, as if the whole universe had glue in its seams and seeping from its pores. And there is nothing glue cannot gum. That gumming can be protective and nourishing, as in the case of plant mucilage. Or it can be defensive; trees, for example, gum up the works, when their sap hardens on the machinery that cuts them down and cuts them up. Natural resins coat and stall things aiming to intervene. In this sense, glue is strong enough to build a home and weak enough to resist certain builders and buildings surreptitiously.

Although unsung by philosophy and trans studies alike, despite their attentions to the seams of relation, glue is a powerful analytic for thinking both intimacy and rupture. The Five College archive of trans life returns to the spot over and over again: this dynamic of adhesions broken and bonded, of belongings rewired beneath the (f)act of trans resistance writ large. I have collected here but a representative sample of those traces. The stories are so insistent, I am tempted to think the whole project of trans activism might boil down to the reclamation of glue. In case after case, there is a refusal of certain ways of putting things together, and a concomitant insistence that things come apart. But there is also a faith strong enough to find something in the wreckage worth connecting—in an effort to craft a more livable life and to find home. A trans poetic praxis of "making things and making one another," just as much as unmaking things and unmaking one another, starts and ends with glue.[1] Within a cisheteronormative construct, trans praxis messes with the social and the intellectual, the material and the symbolic, ultimately re-signing and regluing what matters and who belongs.

Homemaking

Without a decent restroom, things can come undone fairly quickly. Ben, a trans man and UMass alum, recalls the moment things snapped. The School of Education had moved into Hills House, on the eastern edge of campus, in 1972. More than thirty years later, and despite the program's marked (and marketed) emphasis on social justice education, there was not a single all-gender restroom in the building. At some point someone had had enough. And that someone was not a fresh undergrad or graduate student, amped up and activated by a Trans 101 training or a recent gender identity crisis of their own. No. Instead, it was a "super butch" professor emeritus who, in full on fix-it mode, came in one night and slapped a "big ass sign" on the wall that read "Gender Neutral Restroom"—and it stuck.[2] Most bathroom signs measure 6 × 6 or 8 × 8. This one was a-foot-and-a-half long. "She just did this operation one night," Ben recalls, "just did it and put it up, and no one claimed it and no one took it down. And it remained the gender-inclusive restroom until they tore down the building," more than a decade later.[3] Ben never explained how he knew it was her, and she apparently never said. The story passed effortlessly into lore.

But the "incident," as Ben calls it, made an impression. It was not just the butch/trans camaraderie, or the intergenerational solidarity. It was also the sheer know-how. The sign was the sort you make, not the sort you buy. "I mean it was serious," he said; "I was like, 'You have homemaking skills, clearly.'" Homemaking skills. Not canning, crocheting, and interior decorating, but woodshed tinkering. What kind of home was this old butch making? The sort of home where you and yours can pee in peace? The sort of home where you do things yourself because you are self-reliant and handy and don't need nobody's permission? Or the sort of home where you do it your way because things outside are pretty messed up? Hills House was a dormitory well before it became an administrative or academic building. But of course, for gender disruptors of all stripes, it was never a home. Is that what pulled this retired butch back to campus? What made her hatch a plan, build a sign with her bare hands, and stick it up there for posterity? The craft—the sheer pragmatics—of it all suggests an attempt to make home out of what was not home, what had not been home, and what would keep unhoming unless someone somewhere did something.

How did Prof. Fix It get a sign that big to stick—to the wall, for ten years? What kind of adhesive was this homemaker brewing in her backyard? Whatever the source of its staying power, the sign was clearly a doing and a making, as much as an undoing and an unmaking. It unsettled house in order to make home. Hills House was eventually razed to the ground and a parking lot was put in its place. I like to think about the dust of this whole endeavor lying somewhere underneath. Polymers waiting to reactivate.

"Little Crew of Us"

Replacing a sign is one thing. Subjecting signs to sustained guerilla activism is another. For years, and by some accounts decades, queer and trans folks at Hampshire College insistently made the bathroom a crux of contestation. It was here, in the accretion of plumbing codes and social mores, that claims to belonging (and counterclaims of alienation) materialized. And yet, it was never anything in the bathroom itself that warranted serious calumny. Instead, it was what lay just outside. Year after year, bathroom signage was vandalized, obscured, confiscated, and replaced. Such prolonged activism certainly insisted on a change in policy, a shift from binary to gender-inclusive signage. Just as certainly, it problematized the bathroom as a space of material need and ideological conflict. But more than this, it practiced a different way of being together, a kind of trans poetics that changes what affixes to what and when. In true Hampshire spirit, moreover, those bonds are broken and reborn with a delightful lightness.

The epic tale begins in the late aughts with a seemingly insignificant observation: across campus, most bathroom signs were glued to the wall. Vincente, an alum, recalls noticing the "adhesive"-like substance and "just kind of pop[ping] [the signs] off."[4] Reese, another alum, reports, "tearing down bathroom signs all the time. [...] I mean, there were basically never bathroom signs."[5] Imagine the emptiness, the mysterious unmarked doors littering campus, but also the freedom to come and go as you please. Fae, yet another alum, describes the whole activity of removing signs as a social practice, a series of lighthearted interventions rooted in trans companionship and world-building:

> One of our nightly activities, which was undertaken in this jolly, just friendly manner, was we would go to the different bathrooms and take down the gendered signs on them ourselves. You know, just sort of here we go, little crew of us. It wasn't rage or this is a direct action. We were just tootling around removing signage that didn't really apply to our community. [...] we were like, "Well, those signs are irrelevant, and we're going to get them. Let's go get them." So we got a lot of them, I think. We would always take them home. This went on for years.[6]

Alongside study groups, movie nights, and midnight hikes, trans students "tootled" around in a "jolly," "friendly" manner, peeling away and appropriating bathroom signs. There is a singular level of good humor here. It's not just that the signs are wrong or oppressive; it's that they are silly. And that silliness is met with a formidably equal silliness of wresting them from their walled habitats and repurposing them as bookmarks and coffee coasters. (Imagine setting the table for tea.) In a moment of trans world-making, this "little crew" holds both university habits and resistance tactics lightly.

As the gentle war over bathroom signs continued, the college took notice and, after significant deliberation, including consultation with a recently formed Trans Policy Committee, re-signed the bathrooms as "Self-Identified Men" and "Self-Identified Women" in 2012. The shift was accompanied by a ponderous plaque installed beneath each bathroom sign which, while clearly stating "we meet all building codes for particular occupancy levels," expresses Hampshire's "vision" and commitment to "make all buildings as welcoming to all genders as possible."[7] The solemnity of the statement and its overt code courtesy stand in sharp contrast to the general playfulness with which it was met. Many trans students felt the "self-identified" designation denied the realness of their gender. They also took exception to the language because it assumed that those using the men's or women's restrooms in fact self-identified as such, when many of them did not.[8] Cassidy, a nonbinary trans woman and alum who'd realized that most signs were simply "glued on" and could just as easily be "peeled" off, made the additional discovery that, in cases where metal signs were bolted into the wall, the sign's letters were glued on.[9] This provided the opportunity to create more havoc. Cassidy recalls trans folks removing specific letters to create, for example, the "Self-Identified" restroom, the "Self-Identified Me" restroom," the "Self-Identified Omen" restroom, and the "Elf-Identified" restroom.[10] It was "hilarious," she recalls, chuckling, absolutely "out of control."

But not all bathroom re-signings were semipermanent; many were instantaneous, even ephemeral. Talia, a queer, nonbinary femme and an alum, recalls moments when trans students would go to use the bathroom, suddenly crouch down, pull a sheet of notebook paper from their backpack, write BATHROOM in big, sharpie letters, and stick it up there with a single piece of tape.[11] It happened in the urgency and exasperation of a moment. Students then blustered into the bathroom, leaving the paper sign to rustle softly in their wake, as if signaling the thin tether by which any gender demarcation hangs. Perhaps unexpectedly, staff similarly took advantage of the ephemeral possibilities of signs. Feeling that women-only space was being threatened, some staff used copy paper from the department offices to paper over the "self-identified" designations and simply reclaim "Women's Restroom." (Un)glued here, (un)glued there. Gender was just a gummy mess.

The many actions that composed Hampshire students' long protest of traditionally gendered restrooms ultimately aimed to loosen the grip of cisnormative gender not only on bodies, but also on the bathroom itself. By highlighting the malleability, the gooiness of gender—not unlike the glue that made it all possible—these actions invited people to gender the bathroom fluidly, more viscously.[12] Even more fundamentally, they invited folks to take signs and customs as lightly as the glue behind or atop them.

Bathroom Domination Project

Adhesive-backed material (in this case, tape) is the hero of yet another tale. Around the same time, in the mid-aughts, the first inklings of trans organizing took root at Mount Holyoke. The Trans/Gender and Allies Group, a spinoff of the True Colors queer student organization, held their initial meeting on November 6, 2004. They hit the ground running, planning a full week of transgender awareness activities for later that month—a first for Mount Holyoke.

In a meeting recap, student leader Milo Primeaux reflected on the necessity of the new trans organizing on campus, writing: "Remember, oppression is best fought when we all come together as one strength, one mind, one voice. Rarely can a battle be won by a single person. Let's build this community to make the task less daunting, and victory more plausible."[13] The effect was significant. As testified in a front-page story in *Mount Holyoke News*, the inaugural Transgender Awareness Week was a huge success, raising awareness of transgender people and transgender issues on and off campus. Events included a Trans 101 workshop, a faculty "T" party, a trans movie night, a genderqueer fashion event, and a drag night.[14] In addition to these events, the group undertook a direct action: the brazenly titled "Bathroom Domination Project."[15]

It began innocently enough. Students first imagined simply posting flyers in a range of campus bathrooms. Something provocative but educational. Then, they imagined "dominating" bathrooms by "taking over one or many bathrooms on campus for the week, decorating them with pictures and facts, etc."[16] Notice the two verbs here: "taking over" and "decorating." What sort of domination is this? Finally, they decided to target the walls just outside the downstairs bathrooms in Blanchard Hall. This would have been a highly trafficked, highly visible area. Blanchard Hall, the Great Room, and the Dining Commons together make up the campus Community Center, the central hub of student life. According to group member Vanessa March, the Bathroom Domination Project involved "covering the wall [. . .] with Trans awareness posters, quotes, and other terms to get people thinking about gender."[17] The goal was to get people to think about gender *precisely* where gender is least thought but most prominent: the bathroom. Covering the wall disrupted the automaticity with which people file into gendered restrooms day in and day out. And it impressed upon users that, for some people, the choice is neither clear nor kind.

Although the material remnants of the Bathroom Domination Project (be they pictures, posters, quotes, facts, or terms) are lost, a photograph of a single sign was printed in *Mount Holyoke News*. The sign resembles a protest sign; it is clearly hand-drawn, in a mild hurry, with thick markers on stiff white paper. It reads: "WARNING: Hiding or Misunderstanding your gender identity may cause you to feel SHAME, Despair, and ANGER."[18] The sign-maker's choice here is intriguing. Rather than simply inform bathroom-goers about transgender people (i.e., that they often experience shame, despair, and anger while using restrooms incongruous with their genders), the sign-maker prompts all bathroom-users to reckon with the possible incongruities of their own genders. As if to say, "Warning: Your inner truth, too, might be hidden, covered over, suffocated and suppressed by the demands of cisheteronormativity." If bathroom signs in general underscore the stability of gender and erase transgender experience, this sign—and perhaps others in the Bathroom Domination Project—emphasized the instability of gender and made space for everyone's possible transness. The effect was less informational than existential.

Recognizing that bathrooms (and, by extension, the people who use them) are dominated by the cisnormative binary, the impetus behind the Bathroom Domination Project is to dominate differently. To cover the walls so as to uncover truths and ideologies, practices and possibilities. But can domination be fought in kind? Or is this an ill-fated attempt to use the master's tools against the master's house, trying to beat the binary at its own game?[19] While the term *domination* typically refers to the exercise of sovereign power over someone, its history hides other resources. The Latin *dominus*, referring to "lord" or "master," stems from *domus*, meaning "house," and from its Proto-Indo-European root *dem-*, meaning "to build, to arrange, or to put together."[20] While the term has come to mean the act of ruling people, it might just as easily have meant making home, or home-making. The related word *domicile* (a compound of *domus* and *celare*) means to make home by covering or hiding. The Bathroom Domination Project, then, can be understood as an attempt to create a different kind of dwelling and a different kind of shelter. What sort of home is it crafting? Did students reclaim these restrooms as home to the many genderqueer and trans students who frequented them? And thereby undo the legacy of shame, despair, and anger? Or did they change home for cisnormative folks, unhoming habits and razing assumptions, so that others might be built in their place? In either case, the signs seemed to feather the wall until it sprouted wings, wings for shelter and for flight.

And what tethered those feathers? In contrast to the mystery of how a retired butch professor got a massive sign to stick to the wall of Hills House in perpetuity, Bathroom Domination deployed tape. Tape at the top and bottom of each sign, tape along the sides, tape in between. The wall was webbed with tape. Domination—or home-building—by adhesion. It was the sort of glue homemakers use in an unhomed place. A *hometactic*.[21] Taping over, above, below, alongside, or across from whatever bathroom sign was already there, students multiplied the signs of another world, a queer and trans home.

That sticky web, moreover, traveled across campus. The Bathroom Domination Project was paired with widespread chalking and flyering. Hoping to catch people going about their day, it aimed to insinuate gender questions and transgender issues into the everyday fabric of Mount Holyoke students for a week, as if to create an atmosphere, an ecology.[22] Getting folks "to question" and to "stop and think," student activists did not just poster by restrooms in the heart of campus, but chalked the sidewalks and put flyers to the posts, catching eyes as they skimmed the ground or looked around.[23] Tape, chalk, pushpins, staples. None of it was permanent. All of it was temporary. They built fragile worlds and fleeting homes. Webs spun in a day. Some interventions would have lasted a few days (with rain), or a week (with janitorial cleaning), or maybe a few months (depending on the flyer location). Who would have cleared the wall in Blanchard Hall? Irritated phobes perhaps, but eventually staff whose job it was to keep things "clean." Reintroducing the college's hygienic regime, staff would clean up after student homemaking, clean up after student world-building. And dump the waste. Where did the remnants go, the morass of tape? Were the signs recycled? Or do they sit in a nearby landfill decomposing? And where did the energy go? Was it recycled or lost? Not knowing our histories consigns them to silence, while recovering them allows us to recycle their substance and energy. Memories stickily strung together—these form another kind of home.

Glue Sticks

Across these stories, within which glue signals the weakness and impermanence of cisheteronormativity just as much as the strength and resilience of trans, genderqueer community, no one took glue more seriously than Gender Liberation UMass, or GLU for short. Many years after bathroom activism started at UMass, Hampshire, and Mount Holyoke, a group with strong trans femme and disabled leadership banded together to form GLU. Meeting in the inauspiciously named Crampton Hall, the group aimed to address trans isolation on campus and fight for coalitional justice. As they put it:

> We stand in opposition to the structures of the university and of a greater society that isolate us, belittle us, and divide us amongst ourselves. [...] We are dedicated to claiming the space that we deserve as human beings and students on campus. We are here to support, fight with, cry with, and laugh with our trans siblings.[24]

The group's oppositional work, therefore, went hand-in-hand with support work; they aimed to fight with and to feel with. Their work was a call to action and to affect. In this way, GLU aimed to "glue back together the cracked and fissured community" of trans folks on campus, and their allies.[25]

Practically, this mission involved trans organizing and deep coalition. Over the course of two years (2015–2017), GLU organized a series of events and direct actions. Among those co-organized events were a trans lecture series (including Ryka Aoki, Talia Mae Bettcher, micha cárdenas, and C. Riley Snorton), a "Tranel" (or trans panel) featuring GLU members, and a week of trans awareness events.[26] In turn, the direct actions included a general GLU protest for trans inclusion (including revising online infrastructure), the #Shit-In action demanding gender-inclusive restrooms, and collaborative work with the Smith College group Trans Women Belong at Smith.[27] The GLU team also created a zine. Along the way, GLU built relationships and collaborated with an extensive number of trans and/or progressive groups on and off campus. These included local organizations (e.g., PFLAG, Rainbow Elders, and the Unitarian Universalist Church), Five College organizations (e.g., TransActive and the Queer Gender and Sexuality Conference), and UMass organizations (e.g., Access and Affordability, Black Student Union, Coalition to End Rape Culture, Divest, Multicultural Organizing Bureau, QPOC, RA Union, Stonewall Center, Students for Justice in Palestine, Student Labor Action Project, and UMass Pride Alliance). GLU lay its gooey tracks between and among trans folks on campus and well beyond.

How did GLU conceptualize glue? What inspiration did it draw from its namesake? Although the group did not write about it directly, GLU's graphics are gluecentric. Analyzing three images in particular, it is possible to draw a sense of glue rich enough to form the basis of a trans analytic.

1. Glue on a Shoe: One of the profile pictures of GLU's Facebook page depicts a glob of sticky pink glue, stuck to the floor, and stretched up to something hovering just above. The image is reminiscent of cartoons in which bubblegum is stuck to the sole of a protagonist's shoe. It captures a certain insistent irritation: while UMass might want to leave trans folks in the dust, trans community will stick to it doggedly. And the sticking compromises autonomous movement. Clearly gumptious, GLU aims to muck up the machinery and gum up the works of the university. In doing so, however, GLU also aims to be the gummy glue between otherwise isolated trans people. This glue permits separation and distinction, but also secures connection and intimacy.

2. Glue Gun: On the cover of GLU's zine, there sits a hot glue gun writing out the words "Gender Liberation UMass" in drippy glue letters. It enjoins readers to think of craft, but of craft elevated and craft powered. The gooiness of the glue-gun metaphor is important. The visual similarity between a glue gun and a pistol suggests that art and aesthetics constitute a technique of struggle, the felt force of

FIGURE 10.1
A zine cover featuring a glue gun that writes, in sticky glue letters, the words "Gender Liberation UMass." The zine is dated November 2015 and held by the hand of someone with black nail polish.

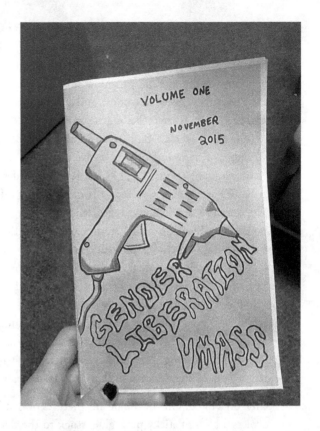

resistance. GLU itself presents an aesthetic-militant sociality, where what connects also critiques. Liberation by glue; freedom via adhesion. The glue gun, however, also writes. The zine that follows is a mélange of genres (e.g., story, history, statement, sketch, poems, essays, letter), bonding trans folks together through militancy as much as artistry.

3   Glue Spill: Another profile picture on GLU's Facebook page depicts a bottle of Elmer's glue tipped over, with white glue spilling out and pooling under its loose orange nozzle. The scene recalls crafting accidents where, in a flurry of cheap and childish creativity, the bottle is set down, but not secured. This is the kind of mess you can get up to when working toward gender liberation. The pool of glue captures the capacious possibility of that work. It signals that things are underway; they are already in action. But this image also palpably marks what falls outside the bounds, what exceeds its proper container, what transgresses space. This suggests that GLU, in its work of gender libera-

tion, necessarily spreads beyond its own bounds; it is a little uncontrolled and uncontrollable, slightly monstrous.

GLU drew strength from the disruptive, excessive, and yet connective force of glue itself. It is, then, no wonder that GLU members called each other, with a bit of lighthearted silliness, "glue sticks." Within any one of them, there is less something solid and certifiable than there is potential—potential for doing, for making, for joining and jamming. And that work is ultimately restorative. In some ways, perhaps, GLU's adhesive work is reminiscent of Dermabond, the skin glue deployed in gender(disruption) affirming surgeries to help facilitate natural healing and scarring processes. But it is certainly not limited to individualized applications. Much like glue itself, whose fundamental principle is relationality, GLU's adhesive work is inherently social and collective in nature. It is together that they bond and bust.

How would one use glue as a trans analytic? What does it ask us to attend to? What complexities and ambiguities does it draw to the fore? Following glue's tracks involves keenly noticing the ways in which stickiness and stuckness facilitate the work of trans flourishing. This involves marking not just where trans life interfaces with the material substance called glue, creating a transhuman assemblage, but where that interface itself marks a particular form of transing. Alongside the "crossing," "leaking," and "slipping" movements Stryker, Currah, and Moore identify as distinctive of trans-, gluing and gumming are similarly resistant forms of negotiating two separate and separable things.[28] Transing is sticky business. It holds apart things forced together and holds together things forced apart. Deploying glue as a trans analytic involves tracking both formations. If glue frustrates by drawing together and slowing down, where does that structure appear in trans resistance? And if glue formulates by fastening while holding apart, where does that structure appear in trans community-building? If glue forms and unforms in response to contextual elements, whether wind, water, heat, or pressure, what are those corollary contexts for trans makings and unmakings? What bonds our work and how do we go about unbonding?

Whatever the specific trans formations of thinking-via-adhesion, a few things are certain. These stories demonstrate that trans activism functions to throw into relief the contingency of cisheterosexual norms and practices. It looks for the seam, the weak bond behind the buffed and bolted. And it presses on that seam, insisting that things be glued (and become unglued) differently. That belonging be built and unbuilt differently. That making and crafting, improvising and workshopping, be done and undone differently. In some cases, that trans activism brings a lightness to the weight of unchanging and unchangeable binaristic structures. But in other cases, it is exquisitely incisive, leveling strategies and tactics of transformative action. And that critical work is necessarily a social practice. It is a practice that refuses to cleanly separate the social from the intellectual, the material from the symbolic. It is a practice of pressing beyond the demands for policy and the experience of being a problem, to being with one another differently. This is a poetics of trans resistance, a poetics of trans world-making.

CHAPTER ELEVEN

Pebble

Stones, rocks, pebbles. Hard, inanimate objects, the vast majority left unattended, while some are monumentalized and others are stepped upon, kicked around, or clambered over. Consolidations of recalcitrance, these stubborn creatures do not bend to the breeze but will just sit there or tumble together, often with a glint in their eye—a remnant of inner fire forged during periods of intense pressure. People write eloquently about the similarities—and indeed intimacies—of trans folks and starfish (and spiders), but what of stones?[1] It is one thing to recall the ways in which we are treated like stones, or to wonder about the callouses and the scars we acquire. It is another thing to remember the lineage of stone butches and femmes, who stonewall certain intimacies while nurturing a garden of others. And, of course, to remember Stonewall itself, and the rocks, bottles and bricks launched by queers and street queens. It is still another to think a comradery between pebbles and people, or even, one might say, a (trans) pebble-politics. Not boulder-tossing or cobble-laying, but pebble-dashing.

Philosophers of the twentieth century had a bit of a row about stones—which would have been more interesting had it not always been on the way to arguing about animals. Martin Heidegger famously asserts that "the stone is without world [*weltlos*], the animal is poor in world [*weltarm*], and man is world-forming [*weltbildend*]."[2] The idea here is that humans are world-makers, whereas animals are not. Stones are the end of the line; they are in the world but they do not have or make worlds, weakly or otherwise. A world, in this context, is a web of experiential relations and involvements (and involutions). For Jacques Derrida, the stone-animal-human ranking is unjustifiable because it supervenes on the undecidable. Tirelessly deconstructing clean divisions, Derrida argues it is ultimately impossible to specify the line between species or between the vital and the inert.[3] Why insist, then, on the worldlessness of stone, its solitude and insensate stupor? This is what affect theorist Mel Chen might call a blatant animacy hierarchy: an arrangement of value along spectrums of motility.[4] The important thing, for Chen, is to analyze not only how these hierarchies are (unjustifiably) justified but also how those justifications are involved (and involuted) themselves in systems of oppression, especially along lines of race, gender, sexuality, and ability.[5] How is mistreatment of certain people and the planet predicated upon their presumed insensibility? Their proximity to stone?

In trans studies today, talk of trans worlds and trans world-building is common. But it is important to ask: Who and what belong in those worlds? What presumptions of worldedness (and unworlded being) inform them? I am left wondering: Do stones share in trans worlds? Practically, how might stones inhabit and habituate those worlds? And, perhaps more fundamentally, how might stones be a material analytic for the trans world-building ventures of activism and poetic resistance? Here, I have pebbled together a series of vignettes that explore precisely these questions, locating stone in the most personal—and most political—moments of trans life, which is also to say of trans resistance.

Of Eggs and Stones

While at that small Christian college in Ohio, I developed something of a friendship with a professor who taught logic and philosophy of religion. Walter was a lecturer I considered "old" at the time, but he was probably not much older than I am today. One day, Walter organized a field trip for philosophy majors to nearby Cedar Falls. It is a testament to how much I liked Walter that I signed up for a social outing at all. We all piled in a van and drove several hours south. I remember he and I standing for a long time to the left of the falls, skipping rocks in the pool below it and talking about philosophy. Toward the end of our conversation, he took the rock he'd readied in his hand for another throw and turned instead to press it into mine. He told me I had a talent for philosophy and this rock was a testament to it. "Keep it," he said, "and remember this moment." I have it to this day. Unbeknownst to me at the time, the water crashing down around us belongs to Queer Creek, itself fed just upriver by Old Man's Creek. As the story goes, Queer Creek got its name centuries ago when early settlers witnessed it not heading into the valley, as local topography would dictate, but veering off in another direction. The stone he handed me was Black Hand Sandstone, the sedimentation of sand and silt into solidity. While I doubt Walter would have been able to support my still buried queerness and transness, he gave me a bit of the courage I would need for both. After all, being queer and trans is a lot like becoming a skipping stone. Stones are meant to sit heavily on the ground, just where they are, but these stones, these pebbles go flying, touching down gently to walk on water.

Stones in My Pocket

Perhaps the single richest engagement of trans life and stones is offered by trans and disability activist, educator, and poet Eli Clare. Just a stone's throw away in Vermont, Clare speaks regularly in the Connecticut River Valley (his curriculum vitae records no less than fifteen talks here over two decades, starting in 2000), so much so that his ethos and ideas are in the water, so to speak. For him, it is impossible to think his trauma, his crip body, his gender, his relationships, his history, or his future apart from stones. It is not simply that stones have been his material companions for as long as he can remember, or that stones serve as apt metaphors in many of the stories he tells; it is also, and more fundamentally, that Clare experiences an ontological intimacy between his body and his stones, such that the distinction between them blurs. In his crip/trans world, stones are at once world-building and world-unbuilding, and it is only through stones that Clare himself can undertake the project of self-knowing and self-fashioning.

    Growing up in southwest Oregon, Clare recalls an always already vibrant connection with stones. "At 13," he writes, "my most sustaining relations were not in the human world. I collected stones—red, green, gray, rust, white speckled with black, black streaked with silver—and kept them in my pockets, their hard surfaces warming slowly to my body heat."[6] Often alone, finding his way through forests with feet and hands made unsteady by cerebral palsy, Clare found friendship in stones. Returning later to occupied Kwatami Territory, Clare again found himself drawn to the stones, to assembling with them and through them. At low tide, he picked up one glistening "vivid green and black," in which nature had bored a small hole.[7] Threading a leather cord through it, he now wears the stone around his neck and against his chest, where the green and black "blur" from the oil on his skin. Stones hold his heat and absorb his oil, weight his neck and his pockets, hug his edges. He lives in and through and with them, in an intimacy and interdependence that "white Western culture goes to extraordinary lengths to deny" and occlude.[8]

Not all stones, however, were collected by his own hand; some were chucked at him or stuffed inside him. He remembers the stones whizzing through the air in grade school.[9] And he remembers the repeated physical and sexual assaults from his father and his father's friends. Clare wonders, "Is it any surprise that sometimes my heart fills with small gray stones, which never warm to my body heat?"[10] The assaults stole his inner world, body and soul, leaving behind an empty shell chock-full of stones, stones he characterizes as the "stereotypes, lies, [and] false images" that he deserved what happened, that he deserved no better.[11] Emptied out and weighted down, the way a grave or a sandbag might be, Clare continued to collect an outer layer of stones, draping their solidity over his shadow. Recalling the heavy hollowness of his early years, he writes, "I lived in exile, the stones rattling around my heart, resting in my pockets, were my one and only true body."[12] His flesh and blood a warzone between petrification and solidity.

The outer stones provided an anchor, a sense of body, soul, and gender to boot. Collecting them, it was as if Clare were barnacling himself or covering himself in cairns, companions, and guideposts all in one. "Those stones warm in my pockets," he writes, "I knew them to be the steadiest, only untouched parts of myself."[13] And unlike the small gray stones accumulating inside him, which told only lies, these outer stones spoke of something deep, something true. "There was a knowing that resided in my bones," Clare recalls, "in the stretch of my legs and arch of my back, in the stones lying against my skin, a knowing that whispered, 'not girl, not boy.'"[14] His stones knew and spoke of his transness before he could. They knew, and they whispered. The process of becoming-trans then, of drawing the truth out of marrow and mineral, was unsurprisingly slow and stony. Once taken for a boy in his youth, Clare remembers smiling about it for weeks afterward and "reach[ing] down into my pockets to squeeze a stone tight in each fist."[15] Later, bullfrog staring at butches around him, with their buzzcuts and biceps, he remarks, it "was like polishing my favorite stone to its brightest glint."[16] The stones were his guides—his hyphens (compare *guión* in Spanish). A small stone heartbeat in the flesh of his hand and he felt his way forward, through the transversality of tactility, with glints ricocheting from stone, to eye, to other, and back again.

Draped along all Clare's inner and outer edges, then, were stones that lie and stones that don't, stones that silence and those that whisper, stones that hold heat and carry oil, stones that glint. So many stones make Clare who he is; and it is only through stones that he can become something else. Reflecting on the process of self-fashioning, he paints the following picture:

> I turn my pockets and heart inside out, set the stones—quartz, obsidian, shale, agate, scoria, granite—along the scoured top of the wall I once lived behind, the wall I still use for refuge. They shine in the sun, some translucent to the light, others dense, solid, opaque. I lean my body into the big unbreakable expanse, tracing which stones need to melt, which will crack wide, geode to crystal, and which are content just as they are.[17]

The task of working through—whether self, trauma, or gender—is a task of working through stone. But it need not be undertaken alone. Projecting a future in which he is surrounded by queer and trans community, Clare imagines a scene in which people "laugh and cry and tell stories. Sad stories about bodies stolen, bodies no longer here. Enraging stories about false images, devastating lies, untold violence. Bold, brash stories about reclaiming our bodies and changing the world."[18] Together, they swap stones, memorializing some and melting others. Stone people, story people.

By way of refrain, Clare invites himself to write not about the stones but about "the heat itself." Heat. Something shared between human and mineral. The spark between two stones, two bodies of desire. The conduit of connection, heat emphasizes less of what separates and more of what is shared. Clare offers, here, a contribution to trans ecology and transhumanism, but also to trans politics and poetics. It is by way of stones that Clare undertakes the craft of being and it is through stones that he resists the narratives propagated by sexual assault and cisheteronormativity. It is perhaps no surprise that one of his survival tactics—which is always also an act of resistance—is this: "Talk to the trees; listen to the stones."[19]

Gneiss Guy

The earth's crust is hardly foreign to Five Colleges ecologies of trans resistance. Hollis, a Mount Holyoke alum who describes themselves as a trans, low-income white settler, is a river restorationist. Reflecting on negotiating the simultaneous healing of land and body, they tell the story of shared self-making between themselves and the rivers they work with. "I seek to be neither alienated from my work nor alienated from my body. I think that connection, between body and labor, as a trans person, for me are very wrapped up in each other. River restoration as restorative labor has been very closely connected for me to restorative practice with my own self and embodied experience."[20] To cultivate one's trans self and community not only alongside other features of the natural world, but in intimate companionship with them is a remarkable practice, a practice with deeply anti-individualist repercussions. It is in this context that I want to think about Gneiss Guy.

"Gneiss Guy" is the moniker of Jake, a trans student at Smith College in the early 2010s. Double majoring in engineering and geosciences, Jake unironically subtitled his blog "Geology Rocks My Socks."[21] The blog's background photo is of a gneiss cliff face. Why gneiss? Jake obviously thought gneiss was neat. Gneiss is a metamorphic rock, a product of transformation. When, for one reason or another, igneous or sedimentary rock is subjected to extreme heat or pressure, gneiss is the result. This happens most often among shifting tectonic plates and the formation of mountains. Gneisses are the oldest crustal rocks, and some of the hardest. They are marked by distinct foliation, with different strata compressed into gneissic bands. In the case of augen gneiss (*augen* meaning "eyes" in German), the foliation is less banded and more elliptical. In either case, gneiss does not break along those foliated lines. Unlike its lesser grade companion schist, gneiss is without distinct cleavage and has a weak tendency to fracture. The term *gneiss* comes from the German *Gneist* meaning "spark" because the rock itself glitters.

Jake's gneiss guy qualities were put to the test his junior year. Never the center of attention or the type to grab a bullhorn, Jake was catapulted into the spotlight when, as a trans man, he was prohibited from hosting prospective students in his role as Gold Key tour guide. When asked why he had been singled out, administrators simply shrugged and said, "We know about you."[22] From Jake's perspective, the prohibition aimed to maintain "Smith's pristine image as a pearls and sweaters kind of place," not a place where trans men get an education.[23] Day after day, as he met with both administrators and trans student organizers, he wrote repeatedly: "I hate this kind of thing."[24] "I hate to be the one responsible."[25] "I am not an activist. I am not a rabble rouser and I hate confrontation."[26] "I am not a rabble rouser or a politico. I don't start fights."[27] Jake preferred to fade into the background. He worked with Smith's trans student group, Transcending Gender, to develop a consent protocol for prospective students and hosts.[28] And he pleaded with fellow students not to go off half-cocked, but to follow Transcending Gender's lead. That plea was successful: the group's petition and Facebook event went viral in a matter of days.[29]

Gneissic politics, one might say, involves sticking together—even sparkling together, refusing to fracture or be fractured, and it mobilizes a bond forged by fire and built under pressure. Being a gneiss guy, Jake carried a queer/trans spark, itself the product of a deeply transformative experience. Like other gneiss guys, he was not one to cut loose and do his own thing; rather, he held the parts of himself and his social world together, maintaining a distinctly trans kinship and sociality. In contrast with a transphobic college protocol that singled Jake out, to make an example of him as an instance of trans difference, Jake sunk deep into his friendships and student community to respond collectively, and therefore more strongly. Crossing rather than cleaving, Jake embodied a gneissic ecology that was akin perhaps to pebble politics.

Pebble Politics

In the early aughts, Hampshire students could score identity-based housing via lottery application. This is how queer and trans students formed Mod 54, a unit whose archive and oral history were collected and preserved by then senior Yana Tallon-Hicks in 2006. As Danny, a member of Mod 54 recalls, "Living in 54 is like warm, fresh-baked bread," bread milled and baked in stone, bread knock-hard on the outside and pillow-soft on the inside.[30] Bread soaked in butter. From shared meals and late-night gender hashing to arts and crafts and Drag Ball organizing, the house became a unique form of home to its inhabitants. Year after year, they marked that sense of belonging. In the basement, just outside the boiler room, is a wooden post and door on which occupants of Mod 54 (un)ceremoniously etched their names, using sharpened stone. "It's got about a hundred or so signatures carved into it," Danny remarks, "of all the people who have lived in the Queer Mod in the past ten years."[31] A house of bread, then, a house of stone.

In the mid-to-late aughts, queer and trans Hampshire students agitated for dedicated affinity housing. Among the most memorable of their actions, students repeatedly placed pebbles in front of President Ralph J. Hexter's office door, in the Cole Science Building. As one student tells the tale, which is passed down orally from cohort to cohort:

> They would leave outside of his door little pebbles, every day. The same fifteen or twenty people would do this. Not a big mess, just little pebbles, and he would get so angry. They weren't graffitiing anywhere, they weren't having a die-in or anything, they were just doot, doot, doot, with these little pebbles.[32]

How did this action get off the ground, so to speak? Did a bunch of gneiss guys, gals, enbies, and kin band together? The sort who were apparently not about to make a big mess or cause too much of a stir. Or was the whole action initiated by a Clare lookalike, walking around with pockets full of rocks? Did students barnacle themselves around campus, only to shed a few in the president's office? Did they leave behind a piece of themselves, their stones conducting a sit-in in their stead? And what is it that pebbles might signify here? What kind of ecology and sociality do they model? What wayfinding do they signal?

Concrete can be formed through crushed pebbles. Are these pebbles, then, a future housing unit in potentiality? Perhaps. And yet perhaps more fundamentally, pebbles happen together. They are made by the crush of waves or the ripple of currents, the lilt and tilt of water, whether salt water or fresh. With gentle, rhythmic motions, edges are softened, rounded, smoothed; extensions are made more compact and oblong. High curvatures erode most quickly, while negative space waits. The rock surface itself becomes more porous. Abrasion is of absolute importance for the existence of pebbles; for, it is through that friction that their shapes evolve, and their geometric qualities are transformed. As such, pebbles, not unlike queer and trans people, are in an eternal state of existential transition. Always already transported, they transition in space but also in nature, between rock and sand. Leaving an ever longer trail of sand behind them, pebbles eventually dissolve away entirely, silt the only remnant of a rock's existence. Together, pebbles protect beaches and banks from aggressive erosion, supporting tree roots and moss colonies, cliff faces and cutaways. In the intertidal zones, they are especially adept at crafting tidepools, housing delicate forms of oceanic life: barnacles and seaweed, algae and snails.

The students' action is undertaken not simply to insist that the structure of housing change, but that there be space and love for what queer and trans communities can do and can make together when living together. What queer and trans life is and what a loss it is to live without it. The students' action was really not an insistence that new boxes be added to Residential Life forms, but rather on a new opening, a new way of being, the results of which could not yet be conceived, appreciated, or fathomed. And as such could not themselves be the object of advocacy. Rather, the object of advocacy was possibility. And the hope fueling that advocacy was not to secure property, or a place of mere protection (from the endless task of navigating transphobia and cisheterosexism), but rather to steward the space necessary to build deeper queer and trans community. A space not free from abrasions, but full of the friendly and nevertheless fierce jostling one against another. A space where configurations of queer and trans pebbles might hold up the banks and host tidepools that nourish young questioning lives.

Down the road at Mount Holyoke, a handful of years later, a first-year student found themselves assigned to share a room with someone who refused to honor their pronouns.[33] "I stopped living in the room," they said simply. Their roommate said they/them pronouns were "a problem" because the student "still look(s) like a 'she.'"[34] Residence hall staff largely did not understand the roommates' understanding of the problem to be a problem in the first place. After what felt like endless couch surfing, and drowning in anxiety, the student was finally assigned a single room in the basement of 1837 Hall. The student penned a long, untitled poem about the whole experience, a composition that sits alone in an archive box otherwise devoted to LGBT student organizations. A lone pebble, with little to chink to.

The Hampshire pebble protest belies a trans pebble politics, one that foregrounds transformative intimacy. It is not an instance of "rocks just laying around," to invoke Jesse Jackson.[35] In his 1984 bid for the Democratic presidential nomination, Jackson recalled the story of David and Goliath and argued that every progressive vote uncast was a rock—or "a God biscuit"—just laying around, capable of felling the giant if only it were picked up and hurled appropriately.[36] On Jackson's reading, rocks are singular and militant, instruments of acumen and defeat. By contrast, pebbles in the pebble protest are effective solicitation for and instantiation of community-building only through their resting collectivity. Fifteen to twenty people brought pebbles, whether one at a time or by the handful. Unlike David, who fetched "five smooth stones" from a brook bed in Elah Valley, and slung only one, the pebble protestors did not steal a few stones so much as they transposed a bit of a brook bed from the forest or path nearby.[37] The pebbles jostled one another, pressed up against and beside each other, and in doing so modeled a demand as much as an ethos. They practiced intimacy and demonstrated the transformative potential that lies in the collective force of small things. A certain trans political ecology.

In the desert, pebbles sometimes move great distances seemingly of their own accord, no gravity or running water necessary. It is as if they simply get up and start walking. In the eleventh hour of this project, I learned key context for the pebble protest. An incident of racist graffiti rocked Hampshire's campus in Spring of 2007. President Hexter met with students in the Merrill living room (the same room in which I met trans students after the TERF zine was found in SAGA).[38] During that meeting, he said, "I wish I had a pebble to remind me every day that racism exists."[39] Students gathered pebbles and "marched" into his office to each "place a pebble in a vase."[40] The action was coterminous with SOURCE (Students of Under-Represented Cultures and Ethnicities) members making seventeen demands for identity-based student groups, staff support, and faculty expertise. Among the demands was, the "designation of a Queer-Identified (and not just Queer-Friendly) residential hall in the dorms."[41] It was a volatile moment and the students shut down campus in Spring 2008. Here the pebbles do more than insist upon queer and trans housing. They pebbled together students from SOURCE, the Queer Community Alliance, the Cultural Center, and the Women's Center and committed to building together. As a result, the president tasked a newly appointed administrator with overseeing diversity issues on campus—an administrator who, in the years to follow, began formal work generating, among other things, trans-inclusive policy.

What are trans worlds, then? And what is the work of trans world-building? With whom and with what? And how are stones not only present in those places and processes, but also participants in their moving and making? What are the trans pebble politics, the trans petra-politics at work in the testaments of Eli Clare, Gneiss Guy, and Hampshire's housing activists? And how might these testaments challenge the constructions of animacy among trans agitators and gender disruptors more generally?

Recall for a moment that rocks make roads. A commonplace in contemporary construction, large rocks are collected, crushed, and tumbled into concrete to pave roads. They are typically excavated from quarries or riverbeds. But it is a rarely appreciated fact that rocks form natural pathways in precisely those quarries and riverbeds, whether snaking up mountains or winding through forests. The two formations of wayfinding—roads anthropogenically and geologically constructed—are instructive as we consider pathways to trans (or trans-inclusive) change. On the one hand, the work of trans activists can be culled, crushed, and concretized into policies that can outlast those activists and permanently change the terrain. Often this involves decontextualizing trans community wisdom in order to expand policy reach. On the other hand, trans activists can aim to maintain and restore the guiding riverbeds of trans world-building. In doing so, the complex ecologies that make trans people possible have to be cultivated. In river-rock terms, pebbles cannot form without the water that jostles them, the algae that coats them, the companion stones that carve them, and the earth that holds it all together. A trans pebble politics, then, would nurture patterns of trans world-making that are always in motion and in relation, rather than set apart or on top. And that relation can be like the relations between stones, but it must also be a relation to and with stones.

After leveling a devastating critique of animacy hierarchies, Chen blithely classifies stones as animate—as "dynamic and even moving, changing and shifting"—especially on beyond-human timescales.[42] They then close *Animacies* with the question: "What might it be like to take stones as 'more than a thing to ignore'?"[43] To think beyond the classical stone-human polarity? What

I have offered here is a rumination not only on how trans folks might "take stones," but also how they *take to* stones and are *taken by* stones, in the intimate construction of bodily being and political ecologies.

But this is only the beginning of a geology of trans activism, or the connective tissues between geological and trans life. Attending to those tissues might require, as Derrida repeatedly enjoins, stumbling on stones. He invites us to allow stones to "interrupt [our] progress and oblige [us] to lift [our] foot."[44] Make touchstones of stumbling blocks. And return relentlessly to the space in which our footing is displaced and our direction disoriented. Doing so, he suggests, will afford us a greater sense not only of the many ways in which we lack our worlds (or are worldless), but also of the many ways in which we are always gathered up together and worlded alongside the stones we touch.[45] Perhaps trans pebble politics might encompass a similar injunction. Might it support a practice of living and thinking in constant tension with the limits against which trans worlds get repeatedly drawn and defined?

Part IV

Attunements to Trans Hope

CHAPTER TWELVE

I grew up in a fundamentalist Christian world in which what you hoped for was thousands of years old. It was so clear and crystalline as to be already put in writing and translated into thousands of languages. I was to hope for a place called heaven, with no pain and no tears. I was told I would be reunited with all my god-fearing loved ones, although I had not yet lost anyone I loved. I was told I would spend my time worshipping god, but the actual content of said activity remained opaque to me. And I was told I would play music most of the day, but not need to learn any of the songs. As a kid, this all sounded terrible. No projects, no grit, no calling on the strength of my legs or the courage of my heart. Life zapped of its pleasures. When I voiced my concerns, I was told not to worry, that when I finally got there my desires would have changed and I would be completely at peace with the plan. I felt sorry for my future self, who sounded like a bit of a schmuck. And rather than pine for that time, I dreamed of being a writer and a musician, a poet in the hills, of getting lost in the wilderness, and of being loved illicitly by a woman. Of being my body against the wind. My words woven across the page. My hands deep in the earth and interlaced with hers.

Trans people, too, carry around inherited hopes. Many of them do not serve us. Whether stamped by social media or circulated by the medical industrial complex or juridical discourse, these hopes often instruct us to want a world we never created—and our people never generated. Hopes of fitting perfectly into the gender-binary system. Hopes of moving effortlessly across borders and through institutions. Hopes of a kind of trans recognition that involves recognizing only certain kinds of trans. Of course, the system is such that these hopes cannot really be fulfilled. A cruel optimism indeed. In the university, inherited hopes have in many cases become vapid and piddling. There is the hope of securing this or that fancy trans scholar to come speak, while the voices of our own are repeatedly passed over in university organizing and, too often, in our community-building. And of course, there are the hopes of passing a standardized set of trans-inclusive policies that certainly supports trans folks as neoliberal monads but does little to support specific, place-based trans communities. Where, then, are the trans hopes not easily inherited, not rooted in already (pre)dominant projects? Hopes not funded by institutions and governments with blood money and land, or stamped with the approval of big grant money, big research universities, and big hospitals? Hopes not coursing through giant algorithms on multiple media platforms and seeming to craft everyday life in advance? Trans hopes not set on tweaking the university structure but radically transforming it?

Thankfully, there are muddier, ruddier hopes cultivated among gender disruptors. Hopes that get *made* in and by trans bodies in community. Not by the most obvious personalities or the most vociferous voices. But by the people on the ground in the moments when they are breaking ground, stirring up the dirt. They are weirder, nongeneralizable, and not eternal. The hope, for example, of being a specific kind of real.[1] The hope of being a value that does not resolve.[2] Or of having come back already as something else.[3] And the hope of keeping space rocks close.[4] Hopes that I wake in the morning with enough gravel in my voice to polish a stone. That every few days she looks not at me but into me. And that the thing in me that's trying to grow can do so under her second moon and third sun. That my muscles get the chance more often to melt at the surprise of trans-saturated, queer-maturated spaces. In places like the university, it is hopes that trans knowledge flourish, and trans language explode, and trans feelings and trans bodies expand and contract in surprising ways and that the choreography of our byways and thoughtways get weirder by the hour. Hopes that we move mountains. That we become pebbles. That we silt like sand.

In this chapter, I turn to the Five College archive of trans life as well as more canonical theories of hope to explore attunements that best equip us to notice trans hope in precisely that poetic register. Such hopes happen in an improvisatory space, where people craft their dreams into existence, dreams that stretch and strain the parameters of the real. In that sense, hopes in the making create something new. But they are also grounded, rooted, even buried in the materiality of the now. First, then, I cull three attunements from theorists of hope: attunements to trash, to the concrete, and to the ephemera(l). Turning to test and expand those attunements in the archive of Five College trans stories, I then offer a picture of local trans hope (or of trans hope localized): trans hope is like dancing in a littered parkway, ephemeral freedom caught up in the concrete mess of the here and now. In putting the *what* and *how* of revolutionary hope in a trans key, moreover, these stories also highlight the insidious inequities that continue to mark its *who*. Before setting up the analytics to follow, then, I explore several incongruities in whose hopes get to dance.

Attunements to Hope

Hope in the undercommons, hope in the underflows. Hope at the edge and in the cracks of the university where typical utopias are always already out of the question. It's grim here, with lots of proforma, perfunctory gestures of inclusion and long lines of erasers at the end of sticks—syllabi, office hours, restrooms, official communiqués, residential life forms. I find, in three theorists of hope, attunements subtle and subterranean enough to trace hopes as they get made. And this should be no real surprise. These nontrans theorists write from marginalized positionalities that can illuminate much about hope in a hopeless place. Audre Lorde, Ernst Bloch, and José Esteban Muñoz: a Black lesbian cancer survivor, a Jewish refugee, and a gay Cuban man. In keeping with a transversal methodology, I turn to them to build coalitional wisdom across time and space, experience and the page. Together, they locate the substance of hope in unexpected places: in the not-right, the not-yet, and the never-quite. The not-right is the refuse of systemic oppression that must be sorted through in order to find flashes of another world. The not-yet is the slate of possibilities always in the process of being concretized. The never-quite is the ephemera(l), both the never-quite here and the never-quite gone; it is the promises and the remnants all tied together. To find hope in these out of the way places, one needs unusual attunement. These three ways of looking and listening for hope can help track the dance of trans hopes—and the transing of hope itself. Look for the concrete. Look to the ephemera(l). Look through the trash.

Trash

When thinking hope, we typically think of desire for something not yet present, not yet here, as if *to hope* meant *to reach* for something inherently futural. There is an implicit sense that hope lies in the new, in reaching out from and leaving the old, the tired, the dilapidated behind. Hope is caught up with what is still clean—not yet sullied. But this is not wholly true. In an entropic, thermodynamic world, energy lies here already, in the used and the refuse. As much as hope can be found elsewhere, then, it must also be found—and perhaps even first found—right here, in digging through the present and digging out its subterranean possibilities. The hopeful, then, are the trash pickers as much as the dream chasers.

Such at least is the contention of Audre Lorde. "Hope," she writes, is "a living state that propels us, open-eyed and fearful, into all the battles of our lives."[5] She hopes that her cancer story will give other Black women strength, that her children will be warriors and save the world, that Black women everywhere will form transnational coalitions, and that her poetry will reach people.[6] For Lorde, the activity of the hopeful par excellence is scrutiny. One can hardly miss how often the term surfaces in her work. The verb *scrutinize* stems from the Latin noun *scruta*, meaning old or broken materials, trumpery or trash.[7] To scrutinize, then, is to pick through the trash—the broken habits, rotten ideas, smashed values, discarded histories, wasted affects. It is to sift through what one has inherited—and decide what can be salvaged and repurposed, and what must burn. It is to struggle in the here and now rather than nurse pipedreams of what might never come. Lorde's calls to scrutiny are also testaments. She speaks of scrutinizing actions, relationships, whole lives, and poems—and of scrutinizing our fears and our silences, our common histories, racist attitudes, and the truth we share as much as the language we share it in. She speaks specifically of scrutinizing the similarities and differences between Black women and of her own expectations of other Black women. Across these contexts, she sees the act of scrutiny as multifaceted: picking through, reclaiming, recognizing, questioning, healing, evaluating, taking responsibility, and ultimately altering.[8] Poetry is a tool of scrutiny. It gives her the strength to dig herself out—of the tired tropes, the stereotypes and the lies, pressing open the tiny chinks in false taxonomies and sham stories.

How does one become sensitive to trash? And, in this case, to the racialized gender bullshit one slogs around in, knee-deep? The ability to recognize trash under the glint of novelty, the glare of power, and the dull hum of the quotidian is itself half the battle. But then, how does one also attune oneself—and selves together—to the revolution in the refuse? From every corner, there are things given no value, no use, no place, but that promise the inklings of another world. Shards of Black imagination, gender disruption, queer desire, and crip time strewn about the yard. Scrutiny is only the beginning.

Concrete

To scrutinize the trash, you have to start by standing still, in the concrete stuff of life-as-it-is. A German Jew, fleeing from the Nazis, Ernst Bloch wrote the bulk of *The Principle of Hope* during his sojourn in the United States, most of which he spent in Cambridge, Massachusetts—just seventy-two miles east of the Five Colleges.

For him, hope is eminently concrete. It is not willy-nilly daydreaming. Nor is it an obsession with abstractions, a habit of fantasizing about the future or pining for the past. These are merely the guises of "fraudulent" hope.[9] Instead, hope, true hope, is a thinking in the cracks, a kind of dreaming that finds reason for being in the unplumbed possibilities of the present. It begins on the ground and proceeds through the trees. And it is there, in that generative grit and grime, that hope awakens.

Attuning to the practice of hope means sticking to the concrete, then. Bloch describes consciousness as a field with two edges, two thresholds between what has been and what has yet to be. In this schema, the "Not-Yet-Conscious" is both backward-fading and forward-dawning.[10] It is alive and well in the present, always auguring new possibilities. Revolutionary openings, then, are everywhere, on all sides, in the fractures, the unfinished loops, and the fuzzy edges. Hope is a kind of "sideways relationality" to the possibilities implicit in material life at both edges, *in this very moment*.[11] Hopes concretize themselves, he says, growing together (Latin, *con-crescere*). Unsurprisingly, there is a concrete *poetics* to such hope. While all people engage in bringing possibility to the surface, artists are especially adept at crafting portals to other worlds. Art crafts a window into the Not-Yet-Conscious, or the realm of possibility. Before the future appears, it preappears in the work of art.[12] It is in this way that art can be said to capture truth. "Art is a laboratory," Bloch muses, "a feast of implemented possibilities."[13] It is the crack, the opening, the front. It lets the light in, a light that is already here, shining up from below through the stuff of creation. Poets, in particular, live on "the front-side of possibility-matter," Bloch writes.[14] Matter is never just matter to poets, nor are words merely words. Both are shot through with possibility—the kind of possibility that bends and breaks what we already know and makes room for something else—something unexpected, something still nascent, something not quite conscious: the ground of hope.

How, then, does one catch hope in the happening? Stop staring at the sky, with its holy shafts of light and white whisps of moisture. Look below at the trees, the earth, and into the rock itself. Look not simply to the pristine reserves, but to the disturbed places. "We will be able to hew out of the mountain of despair a stone of hope," Martin Luther King once said.[15] This is the pebble politics Bloch too invokes. Sort through the trash, the mess of things here and now, and find, in the concrete stuff of existence and aesthetic creation, windows to an elsewhere. Passageways of possibility. Here is where you find hope.

Ephemera(l)

While the stuff of hope may lie in the concrete mess of the here and now, that is not to say it is not also the signatory of an elsewhere. That elsewhere is ephemera by nature and ephemeral in nature: ephemera(l). Never-quite here and never-quite gone. Insofar as that elsewhere, moreover, disturbs the present with a certain antilogic, an unapologetic extravagance that refuses to quite make sense, it is arguably a little queer, if not also a little trans. The stuff of hope does not give it to you straight; it does not play square. It does not show up in the flesh, under the glare of a full sun, but rather hints at its own existence in shadow-words and seemingly insubstantial things. Court it accordingly.

There is an *ephemeral* structure to hope—something transitory and evanescent. The queer utopian project, for Muñoz, "call[s] into question what is epistemologically there and signal[s] a highly ephemeral ontological field that can be characterized as a doing in futurity."[16] Queerness is the ephemeral stuff of hope. If the queer disrupts what counts as mattering, it likewise disrupts the metaphysical dichotomy of matter and immateriality, and of presence and absence. Nothing, not even the most well-conditioned and trimly wrought projects, is safe from the "ephemeral trace" of another logic.[17] Everything is susceptible to what might come in the form of another world. That is where hope comes in.[18] But there is also an *ephemera* structure to hope—an organics of minor science, even if easily missed or discarded. If hope is never-quite here, it is also already-here, in the chuckable, evanescent stuff of our present—especially among queers. Queer practice is a "building" and "doing"; it is a "*making*" of queer worlds.[19] Queers "invent" gestures and dance, they conjure and they ornament, and they straight-up "make up genealogies and worlds."[20] The queerness of queer futurity, Muñoz argues, is "a relational and collective modality" that makes things happen together.[21] The year Muñoz died, he keynoted the Five College Queer Gender and Sexuality Conference and spoke of the brown commons. A commons that is—and has been—already here, already on the ground in the organic embeddedness of our "pulsating social world."[22] He asks, "What if we think about hope [...] as a need to achieve that 'we,' that essential being-with, the commitment to a making common [...]?"[23] Making it here and now, in the small things.[24]

Where, then, does hope lie? One cannot look at what is already solidly here and squarely before us, nor can one look solidly or squarely at all. One must look sideways, squinting at the horizons underfoot. And there, what one sees is always already behind them: a way of making each other underground, in the forward-dawning fast-fading beauty of queering the moment, side by side with one another. That moment is inherently ephemera(l). It is constantly coming and going. And there is something mad about looking for such hope and finding it in the "maniacal and oddball endeavor" of the queer, brown utopian project.[25] But Muñoz is committed to such madness and, indeed, the madness of hoping together.

These three thinkers—Lorde, Bloch, and Muñoz—left behind not only their recommendation for how to locate hope in practice, but also a record of their own search. For each, hope is communal. For each, the reason to hope and the stuff that makes hope is already here—here in our bodies, our poetry, our communities, and our militancy. None of them can be accused of facile utopian thinking. None of them is stuck waiting. Each of them belongs to one or more social groups (across class, disability, gender, ethnicity, race, religion, and sexuality) that have long taught them the bone-deep necessity of hope and of rooting that hope in praxis, in everyday ways of being with one another and making each other differently. It is this collective wisdom that I incorporate into the search for a poetics of trans hope. But what do these attunements look like when transposed into a trans key? How do trans folks oxygenate hope on the ground, in the messy spots? I am looking for the arts of noticing best attuned to concrete expectant existence, where *trans* takes on or retains an anticipatory trajectory rooted in fleshy relations. In exploring the extension (and mutation) of these attunements in the Five College archives, I also remain alive to the tensions in and among trans hopes, straddling as they do the various edges and incongruities along which we—we gender disruptors and dissidents—sit.

Dancing, or Divots in the Dirt

Directed by Jules Rosskam, a former Hampshire College faculty member, *Dance, Dance Evolution* is eighteen minutes of documentary glory.[26] Six trans people dance and talk about dancing—what it is and how it feels. They dance on the beach, on a dance floor, in a hallway, at a bookstore, and in a park. They dance barefoot or in socks; some sport tennis shoes, others leather oxfords.

In the dark of night or under the white-hot sun. While they each dance alone in the film, they talk about dancing with others, at clubs or in dreamscapes—one even yearns for an underwater dance party with their ancestors. Over and over again, they describe dance as a portal. It is the "eruption of possibility, of potentiality," Lua says, "the production of indeterminacy."[27] Dance is, fundamentally, a space of futurity. It is an opening, both "an escape" and "a way to ground myself," Max says.[28] A doing, here and now, that creates a way of being beyond the present. As portal, dance is also trans. It transforms and transports people, excerpting them from everyday life and thrusting them into a liminal world. Here, gender bends, bodies morph, movement transfigures. Trans people can be at home here. This is a place for the moreness of bodies in space. "How do we take that idealized moment," that *gift*, Mattilda says, and "bring it somewhere else? Everywhere else."[29] This is the ultimate evolution the film invokes.

The revolutionary potential of dance—the reason why it can be a space of hope—is not, for these trans artists, something cheaply won or easily plumbed. Lua, for example, does not cast dance as some pie-in-the-sky utopia but rather as a complex space of decomposition and creation, resistance and homemaking, danger and belonging. It is a space that is *made* in and through every concomitant movement. After dancing in a littered parkway, to music only they can hear, Lua muses about the experience:

> What I feel when I'm dancing is this very decomposition of my understanding of myself and of my body, and then, you can say of my gender, of my race, of my place in this world, and in the world we're trying to build. When I'm dancing.... Dancing, for me, feels like I'm questioning my body. That I'm putting my body in question, somehow. I remember feeling the ground and its softness, and starting to make these little potholes that will hold me and push me back. As I was starting to move, I was feeling very much those twigs, metal caps and plastic caps. There was something about my presence here, and the presence of these materials that relates to each other. Some sort of danger to it too. There's a danger of this glass in the floor, there's a danger of my presence here. I feel like this non-conforming becomes a danger to sociality, becomes a peril to narrative, becomes really the very demise of the white normative cis-oriented systemic relationality of this place.[30]

Making space in and with the dirt, in and with the trash—concrete enough to hold up Lua's feet and ephemeral enough to give place to their movement—Lua becomes a force of change as an actively decomposing brown self, among other decomposing and decomposed brown materials, in a brown commons.

This is the reason Lua's dance can challenge "the white normative cis-oriented systemic relationality" with something else.

There is no question that the dancers in *Dance, Dance Evolution* craft their hopes through the mess of gendered inheritances in their bodies, the concrete structure of the dance floor, and the ephemeral memories of themes, tropes, gestures, and movements, a bricolage inherited from numerous dance traditions. It is there that they make, and dream, and hope. But there is more to the documentary than a confirmation of the attunements provided by Lorde, Bloch, and Muñoz. The documentary offers very specific invitations to space and place. How do we (and who are we anyway) craft the kind of spaces Mattilda and Lua are talking about? Spaces like dance that are portals to another world—or to this world transmogrified and made brown? It is at least on grimy, ground-level dance floors and in parkways littered with bottle caps, twigs, and glass. This injunction to locality prompts us to look for all the surfaces on which the insistent creation of gender disruptors necessarily makes an impression—a divot in the dirt. Dirt-divoting, it turns out, is essential to a poetics of trans hope.

Who Gets to Hope and For What?

Let's say, then, that we are looking for a poetics of trans hope by attuning ourselves to the trash, the concrete, and the ephemera(l), especially in the places where gender disruptors are dancing and divoting up the dirt. Who is it, in these spaces, whose hopes are most often given the floor? Because again, it is not enough to look for "trans" as itself a simple margin. There is a world in this word, with innumerable contours and edges of its own. In *Dance, Dance Evolution*, there appears to be a perfect balance—no doubt consciously constructed—of people assigned to two different genders moving, variously, in the opposite direction. Two sets of dancers, two sets of dreamers. In the Five Colleges, that balance—which itself already erases so much about the variability of sex, gender, and sexuality—goes missing.

As part of my interviews, I asked participants about their hopes and dreams for trans life at the Five Colleges and in the United States (or world) more broadly. Among the hopes and dreams people shared, trans women and femmes occupied a unique place—paradoxically not because of their predominance, but because of their relative absence. Indeed, the predominance of trans men and trans mascs in the valley in general and at the Five Colleges in particular is undeniable. Anya, a trans feminine Five College staff member, regrets this "big imbalance."[31] The imbalance is attributable in part to a transmisogynist "stigma," which makes trans femmes less likely to be out, as well as to local conditions created by the traditionally women's colleges and the lesbian history of the area, which makes trans femmes less like to be there to begin with.[32] Effects of this disparity appear in all kinds of ways and are particularly acute at Smith and Mount Holyoke. For example, Phoenix, a trans woman at Mount Holyoke, shared with me screenshots of a "Trans at MHC" bingo card that circulated virtually in the spring of 2020.[33] On it, tiles include "Getting misgendered bc u 'look like a woman,'" "Going to ur dorm to change/put on The Dysphoria Hoodie," and "Thought u were a lesbian when ur actually just a het trans man."[34] Of twenty-five tiles, the only reference to trans women is indirect, "Proud to be going to the first of the seven sisters to let trans women in." In the meme's comments thread, which Phoenix also shared, one student recalls a Trans Day of Visibility during which the library passed out they/them and he/him buttons—but not she/her buttons. This is the kind of context in which dreams for trans women and femmes push to the surface.[35]

The trans women and femmes I interviewed repeatedly called for greater representation in all aspects of university and community life, for more possibility in their everyday being, and for less transmisogyny in the relational fabric around them. They also repeatedly called for accountability to the valley's TERF histories and presents. They are not the only ones, however, to make such calls. In fact, some of the most acute calls and pointed dreams for trans women and femmes come from nontrans women and femmes. Spencer, a trans masc nonbinary Smith alum, for example, insists that the single most important thing for trans futures is "trans femme people being at the center," especially at the center of Smith and Mount Holyoke.[36] "Everyone go read Julia Serano," they said, and come back when they are clear on "whose story [the women's college controversy] actually is": that is, trans women's. Similarly, Helder, a genderless Mount Holyoke alum, states, "First and foremost, Mount Holyoke needs more trans women."[37] "The sheer toxicity of the queer social culture there," they continue, "is informed by white trans masculinity and all of its deleterious effects on community. It's really vile." Reese, a trans masculine queer alum of Hampshire, dreams of establishing a Hampshire fellowship exclusively for trans women in science, and a companion program for trans femmes of color at the college.[38] Each of these nontrans women alums highlights the value of trans women and their irreplaceable role in trans liberation.

Surprisingly (or perhaps unsurprisingly), among all the Five College interviews, there is not a single dream specific to trans men or trans masc people. There are, correspondingly, no proposals to center trans men and mascs, or to form programs or fellowships for them. There is no reason, it appears, to specially train or support trans men and mascs and there is no special contribution they can make to trans liberation (or liberation writ large). This is a signal absence in the data. How are we to interpret it? Are there simply enough trans men, trans mascs, and their dreams on the ground, such that it does not occur to interviewees to generate more? Or is it that trans men and mascs, by virtue of being assigned female at birth, and having their transition possibilities (presumably) limited to nonwomanhood, are seen as less valuable, less radical, less trans real? Leaving them less positioned to offer and to occupy trans dreams and hopes? And more likely to take their transness as a source of shame? The data support both interpretations.

There is an understanding—in some places dominant and in other places not so—that trans men and mascs are detrimental to the cause, traitors to gender liberation, insofar as they have transitioned into and capitulated to masculinity and manhood.[39] From this perspective, there is nothing to trans masculinity and trans manhood other than masculinity and manhood—and masculinity and manhood are, at best, an embarrassment to radical politics. This is, of course, a position radical feminist Janice Raymond took back in 1979 and it remains an element of TERF ideology to this day. As one trans woman and Hampshire alum put it on Facebook, "masculinity" is a "hellmouth that feed[s] on destroying feminist, queer, transfeminine, sapphic joy." On the ground, this discourse has wide-ranging effects. One white trans man, with a low-income background, was regularly called "the patriarchy" by his student peers—not because he was a misogynistic asshole (he is kind, humble, funny, often soft-spoken) but simply by virtue of his trans manness.[40] Another Black trans man reports being repeatedly perceived as transitioning from "powerlessness to power," a perception that ignores the complexities of both gender and race, erasing what transness and blackness does to manhood.[41] Finn, a trans man and faculty member, recalls being questioned as a trans mentor because he was often read as a cis man.[42] Musing on that moment, Finn said, "It would be a relief to be pregnant," because the students would actually "see me, see I am trans." It is as if traditional signs of femininity, femaleness, or womanhood are necessary in order for transness—anyone's transness—to count as trans and not just patriarchal drivel.

This presumption, threading across the Five Colleges, that trans men and mascs are at best a waste of space and at worst an embodiment of patriarchy takes on a special valence at Smith. Here, some assume that, by virtue of being a trans man or trans masc, one automatically "takes up more space" (too much space) and has a louder voice (too loud of a voice).[43] Concerns about toxic masculinity become, in a trans key, concerns about masculinity as toxic, and trans masculinity as toxic. According to Sam Davis, a fundamental idea informing Smith culture around trans men and trans mascs in the late 2010s is, indeed, that "masculinity is toxic."[44] One of Davis's interviewees, Cai Sherley, a Black trans poet, confirms: identifying as a trans man or as a medically transitioning trans masc nonbinary person, is perceived as "in and of itself an act of patriarchy" and garners immediate "animosity."[45] It signals that "you think womanhood is wrong." "There's an understanding of masculinity as something that only does violence to other people," they add. But this obscures trans masc people's experiences of misogyny and, where appropriate, their embrace of femininity. "To cover up all those parts of my experiences with this masculinity that you decided is violent and that has no value or use I think is so invalidating to me and frustrating and totally about transphobia," Sherley concludes. Indeed, at bottom there is the presumption that *transing* masculinity does nothing to it. That transing, when undertaken by people assigned female at birth, is inept, incompetent, impotent. Something to be apologized for.

The valley is a strange place for many reasons, but this is certainly one. It is a place where trans men, trans mascs, and trans nonbinary people assigned female at birth are everywhere, and that predominance has an undeniable effect on the perception of what trans is and the building of trans community. But it is also a place where trans men/mascs are, too often, considered not trans, and perceived as sellouts, not radical, not woke *inherently*. Their hopes do get to (in some cases overwhelmingly) inform trans-inclusive policy work, but also their more personal hopes are often, structurally, considered invalid, by their very nature. That is the complexity of this place. Correlatively, trans women, trans femmes, and trans nonbinary people assigned male at birth are less commonly at the organizing table. But they are also, too often, fetishized and given carte blanche legitimacy (with little to no critical reflection or evaluation), again inherently, as if such treatment were warranted by their very nature. By virtue of being assigned male at birth, then, and (being perceived as) having only one direction of transition to go (i.e., down the social ladder, toward womanhood), trans women and femmes are to be given voice, space, and leadership: centered. While by virtue of being assigned female at birth, and (being perceived as) having only one direction to go (i.e., up the social ladder, toward manhood), trans men and mascs are not to be given voice, space, or leadership: marginalized. Here, there is an uncanny repetition of an inherited patriarchal binary structure of value—and of who should speak and who be silent.

Within marginalized communities, insurgents will often inadvertently swallow the blue pill. This is a fact of our histories. Reflecting on the "unavoidable tendency of subaltern counter-knowledges to wind up co-opted by and/or confirming the leading ways of knowing,"[46] Otto Maduro enjoins members of subaltern communities to cultivate a fundamental epistemic humility with respect to their own discourses. What does that look like in the context of trans discourse around trans women/femmes and trans men/mascs? As Cameron Awkward-Rich has deftly pointed out, "The terms transmasculine and transfeminine [...] are more or less self-defeating, in that they simply reinscribe the binary sex/gender system in a trans context."[47] To say "trans femme" and "trans masc" these days is to functionally name the person's assigned sex at birth *and* to simultaneously impute the associated (trans)gender to them. The apple does not fall far from the tree. Moreover, the widespread discursive division between trans femmes and trans mascs introduces further problems: it preconditions a reactive hierarchization in trans communities; it erases the trans femmes assigned female at birth (and trans mascs assigned male at birth), some of whom populate the pages of this very book; it occludes the transness of both groups, remaining unaccountable to what trans does to womanhood/femininity *and* manhood/masculinity such that neither is positioned as before; and, finally, it fails to explode the binary in the way that trans, adequately understood, does.

When it comes to trans hopes, it is not simply important to track hopes in the background or hopes shooting up from underground. That is critical so as to avoid the prefabricated, trumped up hopes we inherit. But it is equally important, in that project of tracking hope in the undercommons, to notice dominant structures that inform, often despite our best efforts, who gets to be the actual and who the idealized generators of those hopes—especially when that splits along two groups. That, too, is part of looking through the trash, assessing who gets to divot the dirt and why. It should be noted, too, that the valley is not alone in this troubling bifurcation. I once witnessed trans conference organizers regret asking a Black trans man to keynote, saying, "At least he's Black and an artist. That's kind of femme, right?"

From Attunements to Analytics

A poetics of trans hope refuses to think trans hope is reducible to individual aspirations or whimsy. So many hopes surfacing in and among trans bodies are neoliberal hogwash; our transness does not exempt us from oil slicks of desire. By contrast, trans poetics locates hope in struggle, the ways trans folks are constantly making more room in their own bodies and at their workplace, on the dance floor, and in the streets. But it also locates hope in trans story and creativity. There is the red-hot flare of stories told in the moment. And then there are the embers still burning—of love and rage long kept alive. These are stories made ages ago, in backwater towns and buckthorn brambles, on the brick façade of now defunct bars and among antibureaucracy rabble-rousers. What we make together is everything there is to be made, but it is especially our art and our poetry, our visions, and our imaginations. The way we can invoke the absent into the present and woo it to tarry with us—a little while longer. These and more are the reasons why a trans poetics of hope insists that the stuff of hope is already here, beaming from between and within gender disruptive lives and communities. It does not lie in trans folks achieving benchmarks of success in the areas of visibility, legibility, and respectability, but rather in the behind-the-scenes ways we make meaning, build belonging, and take care of each other. That is what puts hope on the table.

Attunements to trash, to the concrete, and to the ephemera(l) in conjunction with trans life cannot help but highlight, first, the ways in which we are judged as too trashy, too concrete, too ephemeral, especially in the university. There are the waste-spaces we occupy (old, out-of-the-way campus housing, basement bathrooms, the end of the agenda), but also the perceived tawdriness of our desires and cheapness of our wrought genders. There is the perceived bluntness of our being—bodies and genders busting out of their proper contours with an uncomfortable thickness; the way they stick to the eyes, stick out in a room. And there is the perceived insubstantiality of our concerns (whining, complaining, petty preferences). In the university, there is a way in which trans life already occupies the space of concrete trash and ephemeral willy-nillies. But what of us among ourselves? How do the mess, the material, and the momentary take on a richer hue in our communities? Is this not precisely where we build our trans hopes together?

Indeed, part of what *Dance, Dance Evolution* shows us is the trans capacity to dance our dreams into existence *by* and *through* divoting the dirt. Turning to trans life at the Five Colleges to track the traces of hope, three more analytics surfaced for me. In this context, the attunements I have culled are practices of noticing that allow expectant ephemera to come into the frame; correspondingly, analytics are frames that allow an expectant, ephemeral noticing to set to work. One way to understand these analytics is as tools of a minor science (à la Deleuze and Guattari); another way is as apparati to study underflow dynamics (à la Cleo Wölfle Hazard). Still another way is this. Attunements turn us from the forest *and* the trees to the dirt beneath, the ground without which neither forest nor trees could be competing for our view in the first place. But once you have your eyes on the dirt—the poetic ground—however, you can get lost in the mess of it all. Analytics turn structured observation toward specific dynamics within that dirt: water drainage patterns, earthworm behavior, nutrient cycles, and electrical signals. Anna Tsing, a world-renowned anthropologist first hired on the tenure-track by University of Massachusetts, Amherst in the late 1980s, turned to the mycorrhizal networks and spore patterns of matsutake mushrooms. Insofar as matsutake thrive in recently devastated forests, and other precarious landscapes, where collective survival is barely being rebuilt, she argues, they offer notes on hope, or "on the possibility of life in capitalist ruins."[48] In this context, poetic analytics would be the tools to illuminate both the underground mycelia of trans hopes and the microscopic dream-spores floating just above ground. These are the places where our hopes are mobile but too often missed. When I went looking for trans hope-making in the mundane, everydayness of material life, as much as in our danced dreams, three analytics commanded my attention.

Fatigue. Risk. World. These are concrete words, nouns in their solidity, but they are also ephemeral, moving quickly in the way verbs do. They rock back and forth between a being and a doing, a thing as it is and a thing as it might be—not unlike hope itself. As an analytic, *fatigue* allows me to think some of the concrete things that make trans hope hard—the conditions that tire out our very souls, degrade our friendships, and enervate our projects. But it also equips me to think the fatiguing force that trans life already is in a cisnormative world and the generative fatigues it harbors. Likewise, *risk*, as an analytic allows me to follow the harm and the hazard constitutive of trans life here in the mess of the mundane, alongside the stunningly creative risks of reimagining gender at all. Finally, *world* invites me to notice the ways in which trans worlds have gotten constructed at the Five Colleges, and, each time, to carefully distill what is at stake in the how and the *who* of it. It also allows me to think the ephemeral force of trans worlding. If the matter of trans hope lies in fatigue, risk, and world—and in the hinge between how we are fatigued, risked, and worlded and how we might be—then these form crucial analytics for any trans poetics. Through them, words go whirring and whirling in ways that part the clouds and divot the dirt, if only for an instant.

CHAPTER THIRTEEN

Fatigue

To become fatigued, tired, weary. To approach the limits of one's capacity for exertion. To slow and become heavy. To yearn for rest, or for sleep. Such is a capacity shared among all humans, and indeed most, if not all, nonhuman beings. Despite the ubiquity of the experience, literature on fatigue remains sparse, primarily treating fatigue management among people.[1] Crucially, that literature makes the simple case that fatigue is socially allocated as much as physically felt. Fatigue is widely distributed in a capitalist system of production where work is often without meaningful purpose; it is, likewise, differentially distributed among marginalized peoples—as if fatigue itself were a symptom of inequity, a cipher for the fatiguing conditions of systemic oppression. Black feminism offers an especially strong diagnostic strand. "I am sick and tired of being sick and tired," Fannie Lou Hamer said in 1964, commenting on the anti-Black racism and sexism she daily faced.[2] Responding to that long history, Black feminist authors Alexis Pauline Gumbs and Tricia Hersey insist "sleep is political" and "rest is resistance."[3] There is the macrolevel fatigue, generated by histories of domination and exploitation. And then there is the microlevel fatigue, generated by anticipating a space never made for you, navigating it, negotiating potential harms, maintaining hypervigilance, and indeed constantly needing to (re)calculate and (re)calibrate. That exhaustion takes its toll on bodies themselves and their inner workings, such that fatigue is a risk factor for and often comorbid with all kinds of dysfunctions, disorders, and diseases.

But fatigue is more than something we suffer. Fatigue is also something we do. The Latin *fatigare* stems from *fati*, from which we get *fatiscent*, meaning "having chinks or clefts" or being "cracked."[4] To fatigue something is not only to exhaust it or tire it out; it is also to put a crack in it or crack it open, crack it up. In mechanics, fatigue cracks precede fractures, also referred to as fatigue-related failures.[5] If you stress a structure long enough and hard enough, cracks form and then eventually breaks follow. Those cracks begin as microscopic dislocation movements that occur in places of discontinuity along the grain. There is a stochasticity and a scatter to how these cracks develop and precisely where and at what angle. This is true of physical structures as much as social systems. To fatigue the system that sustains inequity is to "drive it to the point of breakdown."[6] There is a crip imperative and potential here. To fatigue something is not to overtly attack it or directly drain its strength; rather, fatigue is an undertow, a force from beneath or inside that can rupture and disrupt productivity. It is a remainder that can drive something mad. To fatigue the system is to make it sick and tired, make it woozy from a sea change and loss of solidity. There is cause for hope here.

I want to tell stories of fatigue from trans life at the Five Colleges. These are hard stories, draining stories. They speak the truth about the exhaustion that comes of being trans and caring for trans folks within a university system where we were never expected, are rarely welcomed, are regularly disrespected, and from which we are not irregularly excluded. Such fatigue often leads to withdrawal, leaving, or shutting down; sometimes it leads to suicide. There is no saving grace to these stories; no silver lining. But there is an equally true reality. And that is this: we fatigue the system, as much as the system fatigues us. Grinding stones have to be replaced for a reason. The stress applied by structures of trans oppression is nontotalizing; trans folks too strain and stress those structures.

But I want to do more than this. As I think the dialectic of fatigue in the context of struggle, I also want to think trans fatigue as a third space. There is a fecundity to fatigue that permits of valences beyond chronic stress and strain. Fatigue, for example, can be a welcome space, a generative space, and a queer space. Whether in the euphoria of a body recently fatigued by desire-driven activities or in the precious slowness of just laying around, body and soul in drowsy stupor, fatigue can offer a creativity irreducible to militancy. A space where something is giving out, so that something else can give in. In thinking trans fatigue as a component of trans poetics, it is important to think fatigue as a hinge place in the context of cistemic oppression and gender disruptive resistance. But it is equally important to consider other, more abundant kinds of breaks (and breakthroughs) that fatigue makes possible. There is a hope there, too.

On Being Exhausted

Stories of trans life in the valley are rife with testaments to sheer exhaustion. The exhaustion of being (hyper)visible. The exhaustion of being invisible. The exhaustion of self-advocacy, and of being the only one in the room. The exhaustion of negotiating ciscentric syllabi, and transphobic professors and programs. The exhaustion of losing other trans folks to drop-out, stop-out, depression, and suicide. The exhaustion of losing other trans folks to exhaustion. The exhaustion of community organizing against the relentlessly mundane forms of trans exclusion in everyday life. The exhaustion of caring, of feeling, of hoping, of trying. And, ultimately, the exhaustion of just barely and just simply being.

Jason, a white trans man at Hampshire in the late 2010s, who describes himself as having a soft masculinity and experience with disability, discusses the exhaustion of peer-to-peer trans care, especially in the absence of trans elders.

> My friends and I left [school] exhausted. I think that's for a lot of reasons and part of that is just being trans in the world. Maybe it's silly and maybe it's a pipe dream, but I love the idea of [trans college students] just being excited. [...] Murder, violence, hate. [...] We need to have spaces to mourn and we need to have spaces to be upset. [...] We need spaces to commiserate. We need spaces to be sad. We also need spaces to vision for a better future or else we're not getting anywhere. And people need to start providing those spaces or helping make those spaces. Because it's too much to just ask trans people to do it. It's hard. We get tired. We're exhausted. We're all exhausted.[7]

For Jason, it is exhausting being trans, but that exhaustion is compounded by being trans in a world without spaces to mourn and spaces to imagine, a world in which being twenty-three makes him a trans elder. It is exhausting to take care of ourselves and each other because others don't take care of us.

Cai, a Black trans nonbinary person at Smith, also in the late 2010s, spoke of a specific exhaustion at the intersection of being Black and trans.

At home I just feel very, very, very depressed, because it's like, you get so lost in the world that you're in, and I think sometimes my instinct is to be like, "Okay, this is where I'm at, so I just have to like, deal with it. People are misgendering me, so I just have to suck it up. I'll just be a girl for...." Like this summer I was like, "Okay, I'll just be a girl for three months." I worked at a camp that I used to go to. I spent every day at camp not wearing my binder, going by the name that I don't go by anymore, and listening to people referring to me with she/her pronouns. I did that for three months, working a 9 to 5 basically every day. So that's exhausting. I think being at home and being nonbinary and being Black and all those things is just exhausting. It's just hard and a little bit tragic, which sucks, because I'm with people that I love. It's just tiring.[8]

For Cai, it is exhausting to be trans nonbinary, to be Black, and to be home. In each case, there is an undercurrent of fatigue from being with people who do not recognize and honor them (as Black, as trans, as home). Such exhaustion comes not from any specific effort or project, but from being something at all—a life in a world, as cultural theorist Lauren Berlant might put it.[9]

Cai and Jason are exhausted. At one level, their fatigue stems from negotiating cisnormative violence. They have to calculate, for example, what's harder: advocating for your gender or passing as another. An immense "depletion" results from such an "(un)homeliness in the [cissexist] world."[10] At another level, Cai and Jason's fatigue stems from trans-eldering prematurely: caring for each other, crying for one another, and wishing they had a moment to dream. This is that "radical exhaustion, depletion, and depersonalization" so often affecting trans folks working on behalf of trans communities.[11] Crucially, however, that is not the end of the story. Insofar as Cai and Jason are exhausted, they are also exhausting the systems and situations in which they find themselves. They are grinding away at things. Their negotiation and their trans care changes what must bend and break. Fatigue, in this case, cuts both ways.

But Cai and Jason seem to also be describing a fatigue simply constitutive of being trans, rather than traceable to any specific enterprise. This is the fatigue of living trans-wise, of existing diagonally or of being set sideways. This is not the exhaustion that comes from an assault on the trans heartbeat, nor resistance to that assault, but an exhaustion that indicates the heartbeat itself. What if fatigue were a constitutive factor for trans being, as much as a consequence of anti-trans worlding? What if to be trans already means to be resting across things, and to be at rest between things? What would it meant to think *that*?

Snap-Slap

There is fatigue-being and then there is fatigue-doing. Snap! It is part of what fatigue does. A branch or a log, rock or concrete, a beam or a bridge—with enough time, enough pressure from the outside and weakness on the inside, crack! Things pop apart. Interestingly, before the "crack" was a space, it was a sound; for hundreds of years, the word referred simply to the sound of snapping, crackling, popping.[12] One can imagine the trans community, then, in its state of utter exhaustion, as a crackling field: minds, bodies, hopes, and dreams snapping apart everywhere. But one must also imagine said community as a snapping collective, the sort of group that makes other things—gender, certainly, but also in this case the university—break apart. Sara Ahmed insists on just this turn. Have we snapped and are we at a breaking point? she asks. Sure. Are we also breaking points? Certainly. Snapping is a symptom, but it is also a force. And for her, it is a force of "feminist hope."[13] Might snapping, too, be a force of trans hope?

The Five College archive of trans life crackles with snaps. Oliver, for example, a white trans man, spent a decade working as a staff member at the Five Colleges.[14] He had a track record of snapping cisnormative university policies apart to make room for trans inclusion. The extent of that cisheteronormativity, especially in the university, is always stunning, but so is the relentless siege queer and trans folks lay to it, year after year, decade after decade. The ways in which it has eked and seeped into every corner of the institution, affecting functions it has no business touching, is matched only by the queer/trans ability to fray it not only at the edge but deep in its middle. This is the fatiguing force Oliver brought with his every breath.[15]

Oliver started working at the Five Colleges in the early 2010s. He started medically and socially transitioning on the job. He dealt with students who would say "shitty" things about trans people's appearance; office colleagues who would think two trans people was two too many; and bosses who asked invasive questions, manifested controlling behavior, and made inappropriate remarks.[16] He also had to work with alums and donors who were vehemently racist and transphobic; it was "overwhelming," he recalls. But that did not stop him. He tried (unsuccessfully) to negotiate trans healthcare for staff. He spent untold hours making admissions more trans-inclusive—that is, adding gender-inclusive language and more gender options to multiple forms and portals. On a campus roiled with bathroom controversy, he joined a collegewide working group for gender-inclusive bathrooms. He established programming for LGBTQ+ alums, replaced ad-hoc with systematic name-change protocols, and conducted collegewide Trans 101 (and 201) trainings. This is just the tip of the iceberg. Oliver's record would run you ragged. Chock-full of initiative and developing expertise, he was repeatedly passed over for promotions and advancement opportunities. "I keep trying, I keep volunteering, I keep doing stuff," he said, in exasperation. He had hit a glass ceiling, the whole situation exacerbating his already existing experiences with trauma and anxiety.

By the time I talked to him, he was bone-tired, both physically and existentially. "I feel burnt out and exhausted," he kept saying.[17] He felt himself on the precipice of quitting—quitting his job, yes, but also quitting trying and maybe quitting caring, at least in the ways he had cared up to this point. He was completely, utterly drained. A year later, he did quit. He had been fatigued long enough; he finally snapped. He had entered academia thinking it would be liberal and inclusive; what he found was "toxic and abusive." And he was done with it. Something broke inside him.

In this cycle of breaks, this scene of struggle over who snaps what when, there is a remnant of fatigue in a third sense or a third space. Oliver's break had a certain flair to it. He snapped back. Fabulous and a little fierce, he quit in order to protect his own sacred energies. He turned to somatic healing and poetry. This is one sense of "snap" Ahmed does not exploit. Snappy dressers are fashionable, with a little extra flair and flavor. Their snap is all dare and no care. They are done with caring. In this sense, their snap is a lot like a beaver's slap. When meaning to flag danger or intimidate or simply show a little attitude, beavers slap their tails on the water, making a loud splash. There is something flamboyantly dissident about the beaver's slap, something resonant with queer and trans attitudes of refusal.[18] A raucous flaunting, this slap is a snap. Take that. There is more than one way to say you are fed up and tired of it all. Snap/slap the door on your way out. And Oliver did.

To Bend, and to Break

Fatigue bends things—bends things out of (straight) shape, bends them past breaking. Bending is not just something fatigue does; bentness is something fatigue makes. As the study of wear and tear, tribology analyzes "bending life" and "bending fatigue." In contrast to load or alternating load fatigue, bending fatigue involves the cyclical stress of pressing something out of shape. It is the reason, for example, that gear teeth break. While we are often enough bent into ungodly shapes in a cisnormative world, trans people, too, do our own bending. We gender-bend as if gender had an eternal "bending life." We also bend our gender from room to room, codeswitching from context to context. And we bend the rules; we have to. More than this, however, and in some sense because of this, we cultivate hopes that are themselves bent out of shape. These are our fatigued and fatiguing hopes. Our tired whims. Our maladjusted desires. Some of that bend we acquire naturally, some of it violently—all of it honestly. I am interested here in thinking not simply the hope of bending, but the bent nature of trans hopes.

Born in 1995, Chinese American Calliope Wong came out as a trans woman in her sophomore year of high school. In 2013, she applied to Smith College, but her application was twice returned, due to a stray "M" sex marker first on her school records and then on her FAFSA.[19] She worked with Smith's Queers and Allies (or Q&A) student group and GLAAD to campaign for change. Her story was featured in *HuffPost*, the *New York Times*, *Time* magazine, *USA Today*, and on MSNBC, and she was named as one of 2013's Out 100. She is credited with the subsequent cascade of trans-inclusive admissions policies adopted by historically women's colleges. Of the dozens of colleges in the Women's College Coalition, only one at the time of this writing does not have such a policy. Mills College was the first to change, in 2014, and Mount Holyoke was the first of the Seven Sisters, also in 2014; Smith followed in 2015. When Wong got the news that Smith had finally adopted a trans women inclusive policy, she wrote on her Tumblr to "all of you Tumblettes and Tumbluttes," "I am happy; I am so tired, but happy."[20] Wong and supporters, including the *New York Times*, then called, unsuccessfully, for Smith to award her an honorary degree.[21]

Wong's activism was not only to agitate for policy changes but also to communicate the particularities of her own trans experience. To tell her story and indeed her stories. "I'm one woman among Earth's 3.5 billion women," she wrote, "and that's got to say something about how many stories and social experiences go into womanhood."[22] In 2015, she released "Hyaline Songs," an album of instrumental music, accompanied by in-depth liner notes that form a mini autobiography.[23] In it, she describes her childhood as that of a "paper prince"— great at homework, but hollow inside. After years of severe depression and suicidality, she found room to "flower." "I am a woman," she writes, "and that's my parlance, my way of talking and working." Four years later, she published "Odyssey," an extensive poem that is yet another retelling of her life.[24] Having come through multiple seasons of intense depression, she finds herself still "hoping beyond the death of hope."[25] She's ready to risk, again, "to make of this world a brighter day and safer night, to make with [my] hands music and mythology, and healing."[26] Indeed, "never knowing exactly the next thing happening [...] this is the price and gift of living," she writes.[27]

FIGURE 13.1 A pen-and-ink, hand-drawn depiction of "Year One" by Calliope Wong. One primary trans-human character says, "*Hope* Let's see what happens," and the other replies, "Yeah: *hope*."

She died by suicide, on February 2, 2021.[28] After three years as an honors premed English student, Wong had graduated in 2016 from the University of Connecticut and matriculated as a Point Foundation Scholar in Stanford's School of Medicine. She had started using the name "Rose." In remembrance, a close friend of hers underscored that "even those who seem load-bearing can still struggle"—those who bend beneath the weight too long can break.[29] And the fatigue of that struggle is real. But it is not total. In another tribute, a UConn alum wrote, "Because of Rose's persistence, over 15 American colleges and universities instituted explicitly trans-inclusive admissions policies following her rejection, including Smith College."[30] They, too, bent and broke. For the story of Calliope—or *Rose*—to be only a story of her denial from Smith and her death is not to honor the power of her life. Her achievements do not justify her pain, but they do signal that the system of trans exclusion and assault is not totalizing. Her life fractured Smith, leaving a fatigue crack through which trans women now pass in and out of its walls with greater ease. That the system can be and is being fatigued by our very being, as well as by how we show up for one another—that is cause for hope. It is something to hold out for.

But what characterized Rose's hope? Here, beside a militant hope to bend and break transphobic (and transmisogynistic) policies in higher education, fatiguing the cistem, there is another, still more personal hope. In her book on transphobia, gender theorist Gayle Salamon hopes against hope that queer and trans life not end in suicide. Drawing on queer and cultural theorist José Esteban Muñoz, she argues that hope lies in believing things can change in a way one does not yet know or understand. "The abstractness of the world invoked," she writes, "its distance from what I can know or imagine in this moment and also from my own will, allows my own horizon to widen and to offer a way to an outside."[31] This same hope for something different, however, can drive one to, as much as from, suicide.[32] Both choices can be choices of hope for an I-know-not-what. Perhaps Rose was not so excruciatingly tired that she gave up trying to reach for anything, but rather chose to reach beyond being tired. Perhaps in that sense, she chose hope. A bent hope.

Lying Across

In disability studies, fatigue is widely acknowledged. Besides the fatigue of carework and navigating access needs, there is also the fatigue of being sick and mad in a sanist, ableist world. Crucially, however, not all fatigue is thought to need solution or resolution. Sometimes, fatigue is simply there; other times, fatigue is an augur of power. Local Northampton poet, writer, educator and activist Leah Lakshmi Piepzna-Samarasinha discusses the fatigue of being chronically ill. While they are keen to acknowledge how exhausting it is to be exhausted all the time, and for that exhaustion to be accentuated by an ableist culture, they also explore the value of exhaustion, as if it shaped the contours of a crip-creative world. In their tribute essay to queer Chicana feminist Gloria Anzaldúa, Piepzna-Samarasinha rethinks their bed not as a pathetic nonspace (to be avoided) but as a powerful *nepantla* space (to be embraced)—a space of radical imagination and resistance. For them, it is a place for cracks that can crack open the world. For fractures that scatter. "I give in to the bed," they write, "to the dreams, to the long, long sleeps and times curled up, the words curl close to me because of them. [...] Turn over, write another line. Poems flying in our teeth."[33] For Piepzna-Samarasinha, being fatigued is not necessarily something to be fixed. As a structure of crip experience, it disrupts productive (and reproductive) time. And precisely because of that disruption, it opens space for crip creativity.

I see this crip configuration of fatigue as an invitation to think trans fatigue in a third sense, again beyond the oppression-resistance dyad. Each of the stories I have told here offers, in its own way, notes for configuring fatigue otherwise.

First, there is a fatigue to just being trans in a world that precisely isn't trans, no direct action necessary. A fatigue of crossing lines, fields, borders, and bodies. The fatigue of this ex-ertion and ex-istence is part and parcel of the creativity transing makes possible. So often down, so often lying around, we are an unrivaled force of music, poetry, science, laughter, and change. If it were easy, if we were rumbling down well-rutted roads, new directions would be few and far between. But because we are crossing, because we are *lying crossways*, ingenuity and innovation are curling up all around us like dreams. We typically think of trans as straddling or striding across a gender divide, but what if it were supine? What if transing was a lolling across lines? A quietude in the crack? Trans fatigue does not simply signal resistance work and carework, but cracks and creativity. I am talking about ontology, not just militancy. Of making, not just undoing. Indeed, a fatigue (as much as a fugue) state may be constitutive of being and becoming trans.

Second, a slap, too, is one way to lie across. The slap of a beaver's tail—this seemingly universal sign of attitude and agitation—breaks the surface of the water into a million ringing ripples precisely because the whole tail hits at once. A fast-closing perpendicular line. Smack! There is a mode of trans fatigue, more specific than the existential variety, that is tired of all the bullshit and gets spicy about it. And that spiciness, that excess attitude fueled by exhaustion, is often precisely what makes noise and makes waves. It shakes things up, setting fatigue cracks walking on water, and looks good doing it. This, too, may be constitutive of trans' crossing—and crossness.

Third, bent hopes, too, are a mode of trans fatigue. As trans folks, we are full of maladjustments and bad feelings.[34] We have, quite literally, "grown sideways," crossways.[35] The dysphoria, dissociation, even suicidality integral to the fabric of trans histories and trans futures bends the arc of our hopes back down so as to track the ground of our sideways bodies and our sideways minds.[36] What, then, are the fatigued and fatiguing hopes that we have yet to embrace? Our bent hopes. Maladjusted, sideways hopes to be trans at all, to mourn and to imagine. Hopes to break ceilings and tell complex stories. Hopes to go back to bed, as much as to bring down the house. Hopes to snap back. To withdraw from the light as much as to reclaim spaces of visibility. Insofar as trans poetics marks an underflow, it is quite often, and perhaps constitutively, a space just above or below ground, in "the non-lines of life in ellipsis," where hopes are not always bright.[37]

Fatigue. Trans people at the edge of the university are fatigued—in so many ways, it would tire you out to tell it. They are tired of the everyday discrimination and microaggressions. They are tired of structural exclusion. They are tired of being a political volleyball, used to score points in someone else's game, while they get batted around and beaten up in the process. They are tired of having to make space for themselves and to care for their own. They are tired of having to learn trans theory, trans history, trans cultural production on their own time and dime. But they also, and increasingly, are tiring out the university. It is not only trans-inclusive policy that is on the rise, but also, and perhaps more importantly, trans *presence*. These competing forms of fatigue are not only coterminous and correlative, but also mutually causative. One cannot have one without the other, just as one cannot grind without wearing down the grinding stone. While it is important to recognize the disservice (and damage) done by the systems within which we work, it is equally important to honor the damage we do to the normativities subtending those systems. To understand fatigue is in part to think this hinge. Indeed, the possibility of that bidirectional negation has to constantly be in play in any trans poetics—any method that attempts to attend to the scrappy, under-the-wire ways trans people live exhausting lives.

But fatigue is more than a hinge. It does more than open in two directions: onto domination and onto resistance. Yes, cistems fatigue trans people and trans people fatigue cistems; and in both cases this is critical, destructive (even deconstructive) work. But trans fatigue can also be generative and constructive. Trans fatigue can circumscribe a place of creativity, the (sometimes happy) exhaustion of lying crossways atop (and beneath) long-sedimented binaries of gender expressions, sexual comportments, and desire lines. It can manifest in the raucous slap of a snapping back, with all the flair of queer trans exuberance. And it can press inherited hopes out of shape until they bow and buckle under the weight of trans disorder and trans disruption. Whether it be by creativity at rest, snap-slapping, or bent hopes, trans folks turn their constitutive lying crossways and growing sideways into a fatigue force that crafts and that makes. This sense of fatigue, too, this fatigue in a third space, must form part of any trans poetic method.

In order to catch trans fatigue on and off its hinge, then, I propose fatigue as an analytic of trans poetics. Through it, the complex structure of trans life—as it is lived especially at the edge of the university—can come to light. And importantly, this is not simply the light of reason, or mechanical calculus, but also of madness. Fatigue, especially in its creative guise, is a maddening process. It drives something to the point of breakdown—it breaks out but also breaks open things—including trans things—to improvisation and mutation. The hope of a trans poetics, then, and indeed a trans poetics of hope, is to follow that fatigue crack wherever it leads—then lounge across it, and spit poetry in the wind.

CHAPTER FOURTEEN

Risk

It is often risky business being trans. Colloquially, to be at risk is to occupy the possibility of harm or the influx of unpleasant consequences. To be at risk is to face danger, especially in the form of uncertain danger or to hazard danger, never quite knowing when it will strike but knowing the odds are in its favor, not yours. Trans people are a people often at risk—a people of risk. And the risks are myriad. To construct a list already limits one's ability to think trans risk in its essence. One need only take a cursory glance at the national conversation to surmise that trans people are, on the whole, at higher risk of microaggressions, loss of friendship, discrimination, harassment, violence, physical and sexual assault, abuse, murder, neglect, abandonment, homelessness, school dropout, unemployment, lower wages, refusal of service, refusal of care, rejection from public accommodations, poor health outcomes, HIV, arrest, incarceration, trauma, and suicide than their nontrans peers.[1] These risks range in severity and are differentially sustained depending on a compound calculation. Among us, different risks are associated with our sex assigned at birth and higher risk is associated with trans people of color, lower wage earners, and out or "visual non-conformers."[2] Trans life is risky. Harm happens—as surely as it does haphazardly. We are exposed, constitutively, to the possibility of loss. We run risks and run with risk, even when standing still.

This is to think risk negatively, and therefore narrowly. What would it mean to trans(gress) that instinct? Could we not think of trans people as risking the possibility of happiness? To think us as a people at risk of knowing ourselves, feeling ourselves, returning to ourselves and leaving ourselves behind in a fracture of freedom? Do we not risk facing our fears and finding kindness beneath them? Do we not risk finding our why (and sometimes our what, although that is hardly necessary)? Trans life is the stuff of dreams insofar as we hazard what was only, at some point, a shimmering image, an inkling of possibility, a horizon we could barely imagine. We risk this admittedly hard road of listening to something beneath and behind normative scripts and try to cut a path through that concrete jungle which, in our wake, turns vertiginous. And we risk being loved for that, loved for this body of ours and the way its bones sit in its flesh. We risk touch not searing our skin or glancing off its hardened surface, but sinking in, suffusing the stones within us with a gentle heat, inviting us to rest sunbaked on their surface. We risk someone seeing and wanting and guarding and celebrating the tales told in the corners of our eyes and the hope that flashes through them. We risk building nets of belonging with cords of truth, woven in a dance of faith and forgiveness. A people of risk indeed. Poised precipitously over who knows what edge.

I would like to propose risk as an analytic for a trans poetics of hope. Risk sidesteps the teeter-totter between hope and hopelessness and keys in instead to the complex dynamics of being at risk and risking being. In that act of risking being, trans folks risk futurity, life, and, not least of all, hope itself.

To Risk a Future

Trans is a risky position, always a bit off balance, at an angle askew. *Black's Law Dictionary* defines "risk position" as "the extent of any exposure to a risk expressed in terms of money."[3] But of course, one can talk of risk position metaphorically. Consider, for example, the risk position of a research participant. A standard consent form, such as the one I used with my interviewees, includes a risk assessment notice, which typically reads, "The investigators do not perceive more than minimal risks from your involvement in this study." Legally, minimal risk is defined as an amount of risk that does not exceed those the subject ordinarily encounters in their life. Risk position: zero? But if, in fact, everyday trans life is marked by high risk of a variety of harms, variegated in their intensity, this "minimal risk" notice to trans participants—this calculation of a trans risk position—seems misleading, to say the least. Indeed, on the heels of the many traumas trans people routinely experience, there is the trauma of (re)telling it.

Perhaps it is for this reason that, as a community, we often become attached—given all that risk, given our risk position—to positions themselves, as disavowals of risk. Positions can be an insurance against risk. A cliff facing the sea. There is a way in which having a position on something—on the correct trans terminology, on the constitutive elements of rad trans politics, and on the precise diagnosis of which people (groups) are most at fault for being (trans) shitty—makes living it all less risky. And of course, if you have a position, you are less at risk of being caught out, innocent, unaware, and therefore somehow culpable. You are less at risk of being shamed by other people occupying positions. Our attachment to cancellations and corrections, for telling each other (or others) how it is—and telling each other (or others) off—bears a certain refusal of wrongness in its belly, a surreptitious suffocation of humility.

Mount Holyoke professor Andrea Lawlor's "Position Papers" tease out this play.[4] A mainstay of academia, law, and politics, position papers typically state an argument, in a problem-solution structure, and often disarm opposing views, leaving them little dignity. Lawlor's position papers are different. Prose poems, they are utopian and uncertain, hesitant and hopeful. They imagine a "new country," not only what it would be like and what we would do, but also how we would be with—and make—one another. Lawlor takes the risk of imagining a fragile, fantastical future. Each "position" addresses something upon which position-taking is common, e.g., cars, inherited wealth, insurance, landfills, police, property, taxes, but also, perhaps unexpectedly, lawns. Each poem/position is positively constructed, in the future tense and the first-person plural. And every one of them carries a trans-abolitionist, ecofeminist vibe. While many of Lawlor's constructions are definitive (e.g., "we will x" and "there will be no y"), many are importantly weak (e.g., "maybe," "I haven't worked out the particulars yet," "how will we. . . . ?," and this is all "to be revised"[5]). They are also haphazardly numbered (5, 1, 4, 9, 10, 12, 7, 47, 6, 3, and 14, 18, 19, 20) and multiply published, as if they were dropped down a stairwell or caught in the wind and scattered across a field, assembled only momentarily and at random. What is it to risk *that* future and the future like that?

Every one of the poems is haunting—and light. One can't help but laugh a bit as they linger about the ears. In "Cars," for example, Lawlor imagines cars that can snap on and off each other, allowing us to merge and separate our paths as facts and friendships dictate. "In my country, we will have modular cars. [. . .] Our modular cars will run on composted Apple IIes, predictor kits, rainbow barrettes, PalmPilots, and parts of station wagons which we will train special bacteria to first eat then shit out in the form of a paste."[6] Here is my position: a shit-pile of rainbow barrettes running our mustangs and minicoups! Lawlor strikes again in "Cell Phones," where they imagine strings of messages, photos, and dreams draped and snaked among trees. "In my new country, we will have various and more efficient systems of communication, including trees. [...] In the hollows of the eldest redwood trees, I will leave my epics, my catalogues, my Icelandic sagas of how I miss your smell and your meatloaf and your every little way."[7] Here is my position: trees turned organic newsstands, missives dangling like leaves. In "Transitioning," Lawlor submerges gender transition in a string of life transitions we naturally take up ourselves and kindly support in others, "with or without vast talking."[8] In each poem, there is a certain return to intimacy with the natural world and a resumption of authentic connection between humans.

Etymologically, a position is something posed or placed. But it is also something you leave somewhere, something you set down and then go on your way, like a string of cairns behind you. The Latin root *sinere* means both to let in and to leave alone. I wonder if we—the riskily positioned—were to imagine taking a position less as an act of space-claiming and place-setting and more as a testament to intimacy and a trace of hope. What if a position were precisely a concept, an image, a feeling that once took up residence in you, and you now leave for someone else, in a (de)pressed hollow by the side of the road? What if position papering were the risky business of witness and fragile fancy?

To Risk Life

To turn from the insurance of a position, and the protection of its insistence, is to turn to the project of living, in the here and now (what is most palpable) as well as into its future (at its edge). To what is most known (most directly perceived) and what cannot be (what is ultimately unsayable, apophatic). A professional psychoanalyst and philosopher, but a poet at heart, Anne Dufourmantelle argues that the biggest risk one can take is not the risk of dying, but the risk of living. In her book, *In Praise of Risk*, she writes, "to risk one's life [...] is an act that pushes ahead of us on the basis of a still unknown knowledge, like an intimate prophecy."[9] In the risky embrace of life, we are called out beyond our own edges, where what defines us and the world around us turns malleable and porous. To risk living is a "physical engagement at close quarters with the unknown, night, and nonknowledge."[10] As such, it requires a certain amount of hope—hope in the face of who knows what. This is not a hope that pins our survival on a determinative future, but rather "the seamy side of hope" which pulls us more deeply, more vulnerably into the present, to see what may come.[11]

The life we risk, in this sense, can only be welcomed in the spirit of hospitality, which bears a certain poetics at its heart. Hospitality, Dufourmantelle muses, like risking life, opens us to what is intimate and yet unknown, "the night" or "nocturnal side" of things that underlays as much as it undoes the visible, sayable, distinguishable, and doable.[12] We might say, in this regard, that hospitality is incommensurate with a normative script or an institutional policy. You cannot show hospitality to scripts and policies, however much you can enact or enforce them. They are already too precise, too brightly lit and cleanly cut. You can only witness their entrance, not welcome them in a way that your own hearth and home are put in question. By contrast, things you risk welcoming are things you cannot describe fully or in advance. They cannot be scripted or distilled. You can only greet with a poem the things you risk letting in. "An act of hospitality," Dufourmantelle quotes Jacques Derrida as writing, "can only be poetic."[13] There is a double fold of *poiesis*, here. The stuff of poetics—and the life we risk—can only be seen and said via poetry.

Trans folks know this dynamic intimately. We live into who we might become and hold open the definition of who we might have been. In this sense, we live—and hope—"elliptically."[14] Without a root or recipe, trans life is this state of risking, this state of hospitality, without anchor or definitive destination. We refuse the perfect circle of gender norms in which you must become what you have always already been. Instead, we embrace a life of missing the mark, in our every reach and our every return. This is the risk of living a trans life, or the life of risking transness itself.

To Risk Hope

To risk life and the future is also to risk hope. In asking interviewees to describe their hopes and dreams for trans life at their college, in the United States, and in the world, I witnessed unmistakable resonances across a wide range of responses. People dreamed of gender expansiveness, in affect and practice, as well as more language, more stories, and more histories of gender disruption. They dreamed of official trans archives, of better information preservation and circulation; of representation and visibility; and of undoing the hegemonies within transness itself. They dreamed of trans-competent medical care and academic infrastructure; of dedicated—and *accessible*—trans community spaces on campus, where gender and intellectual empowerment could coincide. They dreamed of intergenerational solidarity and interconnectivity across marginalized communities; of racial justice, decolonial justice, economic justice, and abolition; of explicit college support for trans women and a widespread resistance to trans disposability. Within this overwhelmingly shared picture, however, some differences did surface. Among the colleges, by far the quickest and heartiest visions came from Hampshire. And among interviewees, the most expansive visions came from those more sensitive to the heartbreak of the present. How curious that those with the least felt reasons to hope in fact expressed the most hope.

I conducted my interviews between 2017 and 2021—that is, circling the Trump presidency and the COVID-19 pandemic. During this time, trans rights, always elusive, came under heavy fire. It was a moment charged with risk. It is no real surprise, then, that our conversations had an insistent air of instability and insecurity about them. The acuteness of interviewees' sense of precarity was exacerbated by their already precarious positionality as trans. Despite this—or better, perhaps, in and through this—they were eager to share their hopes and dreams. I spoke with Jimena, a Black Latinx transgender woman, who worked on one of the college's medical teams. She was used to risk, used to meeting it face-to-face and negotiating its costs. She was used to witnessing loss and helping her patients through it. Unsurprisingly, then, her dreams oscillated between the eminently concrete and the ephemeral. She wanted to see more people of color in the sciences, and more people of color and trans people in campus leadership positions. "I have one person to look up to," she shared, "as a staff member here, who is a trans person of color."[15] When it came to dreams for trans people in general, she replied quite simply, "I want to be seen as a human being. I want to be treated with respect, with dignity, with compassion, and community." If there is to be a life at risk, Jimena suggests, let it be a life fueled by hopes for the radically simple embrace all beings deserve.

A Hampshire staff member, Fae shares a similar dream for a world of trans flourishing beyond visibility. A genderfluid nonbinary transgender femme and white settler, Fae worked on a contingent contract in a volatile economy. More than anyone I knew, however, they seemed able to see contingency—or the potential for radical transformation—in the world around them.

> I think what I wish for us is a turn to history that allows us to really dream of the future that our trans ancestors gave a lot to make possible. As a trans millennial in the soup of all of this, I have to fight really hard to hold onto that, because the technological age is so worrying and distracting and alarming and precipitating this time of incredible climate turmoil. Trans people know a lot about changing, transforming, and adapting to a world we didn't even think was possible or that we've been told doesn't exist. I think that's the kind of thinking that the planet

needs right now. We need really exuberant deeply connected systems at every level to have any chance to sustain the species, some of whom are trans. My hope for trans people is sanctuary and standing strongly with our ancestors to dream of a future that includes a renaissance of us beyond just visibility.[16]

Trans sanctuary. Intergenerational and interspecies healing. A sense of belonging—and being held in the hold of a more-than-human world and becoming a steward of that world. These are big hopes, melon-size hopes—geodes carried on the backs of pebbles and pebble piles.

Anya, a disabled staff member at the Five Colleges who describes their gender as "confusing and feminine," also jumped at the chance to vision.[17] While their interview is marked by a consistent return to gender as a source of pain and discomfort, a gaping hole of confusing feelings, uncomfortable embodiments, and upsetting social interchanges, that dispirited position was matched by a light utopianism. As shadowed as their own trans world might be, they enthusiastically imagined new ones.

> The campuses would endow and fund the Sexual Minorities Archive[s], and help it be a thriving institution and incorporate it in their research and teaching. That's thing one. There should be no gendered bathrooms anywhere. In my ideal dream gender world, everybody would talk about their gender more—ask questions about it and think about it. Everybody would make mood boards about their gender. There would be even more trans-affirming medical care. There would be more trans therapists. There would be trans people in the leadership of organizations. At least one of the colleges would have a trans president. There would be more than two, three tenured trans faculty in the Five Colleges. The mayor of Northampton will be trans, and there won't be a police department anymore in any of the towns. There'd be more trans teachers in the public schools. And there would be different approaches to sex-ed in the public schools. There would be trans medical options available for even young people. In this world we will have figured out how to make it viable for trans women to carry children. There will be trans-competent emergency medical responders. There will also be affordable housing. I don't know how, but there will be. And people will be more flexible and less rigid. There will be more of a fluidity and an openness to change. In this dream Valley where everybody is not so rigidly stuck to their understandings of gender, they will also be less rigid with respect to everything else that they're so rigid about. The campuses are not good neighbors.

> Students in this world will understand that they're coming into communities that exist and will care about them. And people won't all have to go back [post-COVID] to working in person just because. I love being at home surrounded by the three other trans people I live with, and all my chickens.[18]

All my chickens. The image, here, of transhuman intimacy stretches well beyond the more recognizable desires for representation and visibility (e.g., trans mayor, trans president, trans therapists, trans teachers, trans tenured faculty, etc.). Those definitive desires are important, but they are joined to much less definitive ones. What is a world of gender moods? Of flexibility and fluidity? Of caring for our archives and our communities? A sci-fi world of transgeneration? And a here-and-now world of trans people and chickens? Anya hopes for a healing of multiple ecologies, sensing the many rifts across which trans sits.

Trans folks are no strangers to hope in a hopeless place. My interviewees repeatedly, relentlessly, risked hoping for massive changes in the very fabric of how we humans are in the world—especially with each other and with the earth. These are not simply definitive hopes for x, y, and z improvements in visibility or policy (although they are that). These are also indeterminate hopes, hopes that deeply affirm as-yet indecipherable forms of life, hopes that meet the unimaginably painful with fecund fantasy.

A Pebble in the Cheek

Risk. To risk hope, life, and a future is the stuff of trans life. And it is also the stuff of poetry. Risk is an analytic of trans poetics insofar as it returns us again and again to what cannot always be said or known, what cannot always be seen or planned, but what lives there riotously on the edge of our horizon. As an analytic, risk pushes us to think precarity, diminished life chances, the vice grip of legal and financial instability, the threats to mental health and physical safety, and the social isolation that in many ways haunt trans lives. But as an analytic of trans poetics, risk cannot simply be thought on its face, as the determinate risk positions of trans precarity. It must also be thought of as the risks that disrupt those structures and open trans lifeworlds to otherwise modes of being and belonging. The analytic requires us to hold together, like the illuminated moon and its shadow face, the risks of trans (social) death with the risks of living a trans life. Hopelessness and hope side by side. Trans oppression is never totalizing. The poetics of the trans undercommons—or trans underflows—press up through these surface positions and rupture the external determinations of trans life with an unbridled generativity.

The generative potential of trans risk fueled Hampshire's Trans Policy Committee (affectionately known among its members as the "Trans Cabal"), which formed in 2011 after two faculty and two students approached the Dean of Faculty office about the need for trans-affirmative training for faculty. Upon working to implement a preferred name system, preferred pronoun system (he/she/they/ze/none), and training for professors, the committee found it was impossible to leave unaddressed other necessary areas of trans inclusion, including healthcare, curriculum, student orientation, accessibility, and data gathering. Indeed, even before the "bathroom incident," the Trans Policy Committee had completed most of the work to roll out gender-inclusive bathrooms across campus.[19] But policy change was not the committee's sole hope. Talia, a member of the committee, recalls it was driven by a vision for "foundational transformations" in "the way that people think about who is normal and who is human."[20] "I don't know if we'll ever get there," they said, but "I think if we constrain ourselves to what we thought was possible"—that is, if we stop taking the risk of asking questions and imagining different futures—"well, it's just not very spiritually compelling."[21] Talia here characterizes the committee's hopes as reaching for (and risking) a place it may never get to and things that may not be possible, and they insist there's something "spiritually compelling" about that.

Religious studies scholar David Newheiser, in *Hope in a Secular Age*, argues that hope is just this sort of thing that risks, that reaches for and into the unknown; it is a desire shot through with vulnerability, a way of working for something you may not even have words for.[22] As such, for Newheiser, hope "unsettles the secular" with an element of the spiritual.[23] In contrast to the certainty and determinacy that has characterized the secular age, hope injects mystery and openness into the edge of the present. As if echoing Talia's sentiments, Newheiser writes, "hope is [. . .] a risk but it is one worth running, for our lives would otherwise be constrained by the scope of our certainties."[24] If we constrain ourselves to what we thought was possible—if we are constrained by the scope of our certainties—we remain, ultimately, riskless but also hopeless. By contrast, we are full of risk *and* hope when we work toward what may not be possible, what is still uncertain, and what cannot be fully captured in words. After tracing hope through the apophatic tradition, Newheiser closes his book with a memorable metaphor. Hope, he writes, "is like a pebble tucked into one's cheek, reminding its practitioner that there is always more to be said."[25] A pebble not meant to increase one's ability to say certain things (or cure a speech impairment, as in the case of the ancient orator Demosthenes), but to embrace one's inability to say everything and to celebrate the stumbling way in which we reach for—and, indeed, risk—what we hope.

In the 1990s, Smith alum Davey Shlasko recalls, trans masculine students were told that, should they choose to medically transition, they would be expelled. Around 2001, a group of seniors "just started taking testosterone and had chest surgery over J[anuary] term."[26] In doing so, they "dared the administration to mess with them." "That was the environment," Shlasko says, "we felt constantly at risk."[27] Taking risk as an analytic of trans poetics means reckoning with this structure of being at risk, but also recognizing that these students took the risk of trans life—medicalized or not, visible or not. They dared to be. Shlasko didn't have words for this. The students may not have either. But the pebble stops us from stopping with trans vulnerability and precarity. It pushes our tongue elsewhere, to something that is much more difficult to express and impossible to capture. And that is this necessarily undefined risk of living a trans life.

CHAPTER FIFTEEN

World

> It's very hard to wish anything for trans people without wishing for the end of everything. And I think that's how it should be.
> —HELDER, Personal interview

What is your world—or your worlds? Who and what peoples it, inhabits it, colors and contours it? How we define our worlds determines who we can become. Put differently, how we define our worlds defines the "we" who we make when we make each other. Who and what we think of as constituting our worlds constrains and intensifies, in advance, our capacities for worlding. It puts guiderails and goalposts on who we do our worlding for and whom we do it with. The English word *world* stems from the Proto-Germanic *wer* meaning "man," which in turn stems from Sanskrit *vīrá*, which also means "hero." How often, across history, have we witnessed the construction of worlds for and by (purportedly "cis") men, worlds in which men are the heroes? How often, too, have we witnessed the dominance of human worlds over the growth and nourishment of the nonhuman? However the story gets told—and whomever it is said to be about—determines what the story can do and where it can go. What is it then to change the "we"? To expand or contract the circle of belonging— of actors and of heroes? If trans hopes have taught me anything, it is this: to change the "we" is in fact to change the world.

In affect theory and phenomenology, worlding involves, most simply, the forming and fashioning of life-worlds and worlds of sense. To call a world a life-world is to emphasize that and how it is *lived*. And one does not merely live in a world; one *lives it out*. Worlds are not just artifacts to be found or slices of reality that come fully formed. They are experienced by someone(s) and something(s)—and it is in that experiencing that worlds become worldings. They become things that are being made and always in the making. Inherently poetic. To attend to worlding, ethnographer Kathleen Stewart writes, is to attune to "the generativity of what takes form, hits the senses, shimmers."[1] This applies in a material sense as much as an immaterial one. Life-worlds are worlds of sense insofar as they are composed of meaning-making and unmaking practices. They are shaped by—and in turn shape—our orientations and disorientations in the intertwined matrix of physical and conceptual space. Just as "in putting certain things in reach," whether objects, concepts, or capacities, feminist theorist Sara Ahmed writes, "a world acquires its shape," so rearranging the objects and methods of reach itself must necessarily reshape the world.[2]

What happens when worlds—and, in particular, modes of worlding—are queered or transed? When their affective density and material sensibilities make queer and trans modes of being (and becoming) not only possible, but proliferative? Queer worlds and worlding set normalized ways of knowing and affective geographies askew.[3] They lean, sag, tumble, and slide into desire lines otherwise invisibilized, made impalpable. Trans worlding, too, generates similar untoward possibilities. Trans worlding is "a trans vision," Aren Aizura writes, of "the generative capacity to navigate the world," to act upon it and be acted upon by it.[4] When that generative capacity is rooted in "trans/queer generativity," Eric Stanley in turn writes, it becomes a "disruptive worlding."[5] For world-building is world-breaking too. It is abolitionist in nature—destructive and creative at once. Both Stanley and Aizura warn, however, that thinking trans worlding without thinking race—and the twine of gendered and racialized possibilities that define worlds—undoes trans-worlding's generative building and breaking capacity. This raises a longer line of questioning: What other occlusions keep trans worlding from transing worlds?

The fundamental question of trans worlding in the Five College archive of trans life is this: Who gets taken to constitute trans worlds, and whose webs of relation, kinship, and belonging define the stories we tell and the futures we turn toward? In this final chapter, I take up three moments in those archives that best dramatize the stakes of this question. I want to track how the generativity of worlding gets constricted or expanded depending on who is chosen to direct it. Ultimately, I want to grapple with the real, everyday problem of dreaming trans futures from specific locations—and to explore how location itself might allow us to honor that specificity without limiting the species of hopes (and hope-ers) we engage.

#TransWomenBelongAtSmith

I met a friend who preferred to pi than to 3 or 3.2 the infinite slide through the river of identitude.
—SAMUEL ACE, "I Met a Man"

On May 2, 2015, Smith College formally revised its admissions policy to explicitly include trans women. The move came as a culmination of more than a decade of student activism that had come to a head in the year or two immediately prior. The revision doubled down on Smith's commitment to being a women's college and coincided with Smith's record-breaking fundraising campaign: "Women for the World." The policy included the following stipulation: "Applicants who were assigned male at birth but identify as women are eligible for admission."[6] More broadly, "People who identify as women—cis, trans, and nonbinary women—are eligible to apply."[7] The Smith world is a woman's world. And Smith women are trained for the world—to enter it, lead it, and achieve in it. Student protest signs underscored this worlding: "Support Your Sisters, Not Just Your Cis-ters," "A Women's College is for ALL Women," "All Women for the World."[8] According to the policy, to be a Smithie is to be a woman, just not necessarily a "cis" one. This is not to say that there are no trans men or other non-women at Smith, but that they have largely been understood as accidents of history and retain a tenuous relationship to the institution as a whole.

If one is not born but becomes a woman, how does one become the sort of woman that can belong in—and make—Smith's world? Besides the implicit ableism, classism, heterosexism, and racism that have informed the category of woman and the special figure of a Smith woman, what determines the essence of woman in this new admissions context?[9] According to the revised policy, a woman is a woman because she self-identifies as such and that identification need not be corroborated by school or medical records or ID documents. "Smith's policy is one of self-identification," the website states; "the applicant's affirmation of identity is sufficient."[10] Fueled by the case of Calliope Rose Wong, whose application was twice rejected for inconsistently documented sex, student protest signs called for precisely this shift away from documentation and toward self-identification: e.g., "Womanhood Is Not Defined by Documentation" and "Smith's Admissions Policy Defines Womanhood by How

Supportive Your Schools + Families Are, Not By Identity."[11] Identification here means not simply internal processes of self-description but the social practice of self-attestation either by selecting the appropriate gender marker on the application form or by declaring said alignment in the written portion. Importantly, "cis" women are not newly required to offer written attestation of their womanhood, but trans and nonbinary women are given license to do so.

Smith's Admissions Policy Study Group as well as Smith's student group Queers and Allies (or Q&A) both appealed to Mills College as a precedent for their work, although they might just as easily have appealed to their more immediate sibling school: Mount Holyoke. Mills and Mount Holyoke became trans-inclusive in August and September of 2014, respectively. Both define their worlds more expansively than Smith does. Describing itself as a historically women's college concerned with all those typically excluded from or underserved by higher education, Mills admits "self-identified women and people assigned female at birth who do not fit into the gender binary," including "transgender and gender fluid" people.[12] Likewise, Mount Holyoke, describing itself as a "gender diverse" women's college, welcomes applications from "female, transgender, and nonbinary students."[13] Limit cases are "cisgender" men (in the case of Mount Holyoke) as well as transgender men who have completed legal transition at the time of application (in the case of Mills). Informing the policy changes at both schools were years of deep campuswide conversations about gender diversity. Mills's policy change was immediately precipitated by a report of the Gender Identity and Expression Subcommittee in 2013.[14] Mount Holyoke's policy was preceded by a long chain of organizing and activism led, in large part, by the Transgender Committee (2006–2014), a student, residential life, and sexual health services collaboration.[15]

If Smith's world is a woman's world, the worlds of Mills and Mount Holyoke are trans, nonbinary, genderfluid, and women's worlds (and their overlaps), worlds built for and by gender disruptors and rabble-rousers of all sorts. Smith's worlding, moreover, is localized in the work of identification, such that belonging is built through shared self-descriptions (i.e., of being women). Conversely, Mills and Mount Holyoke's worlding centers instead on the non-ideal paths women and people of other marginalized genders take—paths, in turn, constrained by many of the same normalizing institutions that nevertheless fail to suppress gender failures. Here, belonging gets built transversally, across identifications that are nevertheless impacted by similar structures of marginalization and oppression. It is this fundamental difference in the construction of worlds and worlding that determines the divergence between these schools' trans-inclusive admissions policies. Crucially, questions constrain our answers.

FIGURE 15.1 A flyer by Smith College activists, resting on a bed of other flyers, that reads, "A Women's College is for ALL Women." The flyer paper is blue and the hand-penned words are in dark blue.

And the locus of care contours our practice in advance. However a world gets named is also how that world gets made.

There are, of course, reasons for women-only spaces and identity-centric organizing. Importantly, however, when Mount Holyoke alum Barbara Smith and the Combahee River Collective conceptualized "identity politics," they did so not to proliferate personal, depoliticized self-descriptions, but rather to attend to complicated social positions that are defined by "interlocking" systems of oppression: patriarchy, racism, classism, and homophobia.[16] To build a world around a politics of identity, for them, was perhaps paradoxically to think across positionalities and to stage resistance there where experiences of exclusion intersect. For historically women's colleges to remain women-only colleges, fueled by self-attestations of identity, creates and sustains one kind of world. Reframing women's colleges as gender-diverse colleges forefronts interlocking systems of gender oppression, creating and sustaining another.

Amherst Uprising and Abolition

[...] is that motion, really? This tendency to cross & recross the small terms of our lives?
—CAMERON AWKWARD-RICH, "Essay on the Theory of Motion"

Following the 2014 deaths of Tamir Rice, Eric Garner, and Michael Brown at the hands of police, 2015 saw widespread protests for racial justice. That spirit gripped downtown streets as much as it did university campuses. At Yale University, for example, vehement student protests shed light on the casual racism and sexism saturating Yale's campus and the failure of administrators to address it, while at the University of Missouri, student protest over anti-Black racism on campus led to the resignation of then college president Tim Wolfe. These years also saw the expansion of the Black Lives Matter movement and a mainstreaming of abolitionist thought and practice.[17] While BLM and abolition are rooted in racial justice, both also stretch through and beyond it to encompass gender justice (including queer and trans liberation), disability justice, migrant justice, environmental justice, and Indigenous resurgence.[18] These movements attend so carefully to Black communities and carceral institutions that their attention refracts into the multiple vectors of power and resistance that constitute them. To think blackness here is to think more than blackness, just as to think the prison is also to think more than the prison.

It is in this context that, one soft fall day, November 12, 2015, three women of color, from Amherst's student body, met and initiated a sit-in in the Frost Library. Beginning as an act of solidarity with Black students at Yale and Missouri, the initiative became a protest of the structural racism and everyday racial discrimination at Amherst itself. By November 14, there were hundreds of students in the library, conducting teach-ins, leading discussions, and sharing testimonials, many of whom stayed the night. They called it Amherst Uprising. The movement's eleven demands included the removal of the school mascot Lord Jeff (named after colonizer Lord Jeffrey Amherst), campuswide training in "racial and cultural competency," and a "zero-tolerance policy for racial insensitivity and hate speech."[19] But the movement was more than that. Under the hashtag of #radicalcompassion and a commitment to attend to marginalization wherever it happens, Amherst Uprising quickly became expansive and transversal in nature, seeking to address, in its own words, the "institutional legacy of white supremacy, colonialism, anti-black racism, anti-Latinx racism, anti-Native American racism, anti-Native/indigenous racism, anti-Asian racism, anti-Middle Eastern racism, heterosexism, cis-sexism, xenophobia, anti-Semitism, ableism, mental health stigma, and classism" at Amherst College.[20]

Results of the Amherst Uprising were wide and deep and included the removal of the Lord Jeff mascot, the creation of the Office of Diversity and Inclusion, and the release of a seventeen-point antiracism plan for the college.[21] But the uprising also fueled a sweep of trans-inclusive policy changes at Amherst. Already, there was a strong queer and trans—especially of color—presence on campus, and that presence translated into significant queer and trans visibility in Frost during the protest. Moreover, both the Queer Resource Center and the student group TransActive signed the eleven demands. Empowered in the uprising's aftermath, students and staff successfully transformed the landscape of trans inclusion at Amherst, solidifying gender-inclusive bathrooms and housing, trans healthcare, pronoun and name protocols, an expanded nondiscrimination policy, Trans 101 trainings across campus, and ramped up related programming. Consistently, that trans inclusion remained meaningfully tangled with other axes of liberation. The "Common Language Guide" is a case in point.[22] Overseen by the Office of Diversity and Inclusion, this forty-page document defines important terminology related to class, disability, gender, sexuality, and race, as well as political ideologies, global power dynamics, and inequality. In it, definitions of *hard femme*, *critical race theory*, and *neocolonialism* sit comfortably beside one another.

Given its own emphasis on tearing down oppressive structures and building up new ways of being together, Amherst Uprising can be read as protoabolitionist. And yet, abolitionist protestors saw significant inconsistencies in the movement. The third of the eleven demands, for example, reads, "Amherst College Police Department must issue a statement of protection and defense from any form of violence, threats, and retaliation of any kind resulting from this movement."[23] Langston, a Black trans man and Amherst alum, reports additional concerns: free coffee and muffins for protesters were subsidized by the university president; a hand lotion and wipes stand encouraged protestors to practice self-care; and protestors wore cheap t-shirts that read "Nah.—Rosa Parks."[24] Most concerning for him was the moment when a row of non-Black students of color sleeping in the library whispered, one by one, "thanks" to the white Amherst policewoman patrolling Frost that night. "I don't even think I was an abolitionist at that point," he recalls, "but I remember feeling really weird about it. Something felt off."[25] It felt as if Amherst Uprising were not thinking deeply enough about its own complicity in the carceral, capitalist, white, cisheteronormativity that prompted the protest in the first place.

Amherst Uprising was a reworlding. But what might that reworlding have looked like in a different key? Abolition is a practice of unbuilding and rebuilding worlds.[26] According to abolitionist scholar Dylan Rodríguez, it is "the site where culture recouples with the political" to produce "liberation practices from within collective rebellion, insurgency, and community."[27] That Amherst Uprising prompted a reassessment of interlocking systems of oppression—and advanced liberation along multiple axes of oppression—already signifies a commitment to digging up the foundations. But it could have dug deeper. The trans-inclusive policies implemented in the aftermath of Amherst Uprising, like most trans-inclusive policies in higher education, still presume an individual citizen-subject, enmeshed in a capitalist gender economy, and interpolated by neoliberal selfhood—a subject made readable in records, housing, and health insurance databases. Perhaps, if Amherst Uprising were reprised in a more deeply abolitionist key, with a more meaningful critique of the carcerality of racial capital, the transing it made possible might have been more materialist—and therefore poetic—from the start. What might trans presence, as enfleshed community, mean in a decarceral, radically abolitionist world?

River Restoration and Decolonization

[...] we assemble (fields of stubble, fields of thread).
—OLIVER BAEZ BENDORF, "After a While, We Stop Asking"

Of all the interviews that inform this study, only two mention Indigenous communities explicitly. Just a few more mention decolonization as an important component of trans liberation. In the archives proper, representation of trans Indigenous life is largely restricted to some early showings of the 2009 documentary *Two Spirits*, which was making its rounds through LGBTQ college programs across the nation.[28] This dearth is signal in itself. If trans worlds are not thought as intersecting with—or, more strongly still, being composed of Indigenous, as well as *landed*, histories and futures—those worlds will remain constitutively colonial and as such abstracted from earth-based community living. Such a framework limits accountability to queer, trans, Two Spirit, and gender disruptive stories, and their fundamental intertwinement with multispecies intimacy.[29] It furthermore limits ability to trouble the word *trans* as some kind of universally meaningful anthropocentric term for gender disruptors across time and space. Without Indigenous peoples, nonhuman beings, and land-based practices of community-building, trans worlding here and elsewhere remains, at some level, a violent imposition on land and history itself.

Mason, a mixed Indigenous trans man and Five College alum, admits to experiencing his Indigeneity and his transness as largely separate. Both, however, are regularly written out of the academic worlds in which he circulates, considered to represent too small a population to justify largescale reformation. In a DEI world of higher education, neither Indigeneity nor transness regularly "count" as a kind of diversity that warrants survey inclusion, media coverage, funding support, or structural revisions to existing educational programs, material architectures, or epistemological practices. On the one hand, Mason insists, this exacerbates the dearth of Indigenous and trans people in academia; on the other hand, he says, there are more (especially mixed) Indigenous and trans people in the university and elsewhere than most folks realize. They simply go uncounted and unreckoned with. Just as trans life poses a fundamental challenge to traditional systems of knowledge production, moreover, so, too, does Indigeneity.

> Academia has a complete disregard for Indigenous ways of thinking and knowing and being. We think that there's only one way to do science, and there's only one way to do academia. And it's Western. It doesn't encompass anything Native. I mean, Natives have been utilizing science for hundreds and hundreds of years. And the Western part is just so arrogant. Just such an arrogant stance.[30]

Perhaps most signally, trans and Indigenous people put the knowledge project back in relation to the body and to land. This is a correspondingly humble stance, where what we know is intertwined with the material strata and beings through which and with whom we come to know.

In their discussion of resurgence, Indigenous theorists Leanne Betasamosake Simpson (Nishnaabeg) and Glen Coulthard (Dene) propose the framework of grounded normativity. Normativity within and across Indigenous communities is grounded, they write, insofar as "our relationship to the land itself generates the processes, practices, and knowledges that inform our political systems."[31] Whatever specific land we are talking about, depending on its longitude and latitude, Indigenous communities the world over share a history of rooting in it, learning from it, and building social ways after it. Simpson explains grounded normativity further when she characterizes "land as pedagogy."[32] For her, Indigenous theory is, literally, "generated from the ground up."[33] The land—its plants, animals, rocks, and water—teach. Few know this return to the earth, and its anticolonial forms of desire and embodiment, better, she states, than queer and Two Spirit Indigenous peoples. They are, she writes, "our teachers and our most precious theorists."[34] Grounded normativity, for her, must then also be "Indigenous queer normativity"—queerly grounded in place and space and in a reweaving of the material lines of relation that (dis)possession breaks.[35]

While settlers, immigrants, and their progeny cannot, in any immediate sense, become indigenous to place, Indigenous poet and scientist Robin Wall Kimmerer (Potawatomi) recommends they "become naturalized to place."[36] Such a process of naturalization, for many non-Indigenous trans people, involves a (re)turn to body and land. Hollis, a trans, gender-nonconforming, low-income white settler and an apprentice to Indigenous ways of knowing, reflects on their work in river restoration, which they began at Mount Holyoke.

> I think that connection, body and labor, as a trans person, for me are very wrapped up in each other. And that river restoration as restorative labor has been very closely related for me to restorative practice with my own self and embodied experience. And I think that the me engaging in restoration work and restorative labor when it comes to river restoration really intersected with me figuring out how to be in my body in a way that wasn't destructive or harmful. So in that sense, yes. I don't necessarily see river restoration as like, a trans issue, but I don't think I see anything as a trans issue, per se. But everything as issues stemming from colonial capitalism. [...] I think that both prison abolition—and abolition as a broader framework for liberation—and decolonization as a framework for reconnecting with each other, ourselves, and land, in a framework of right relations, not exploitation and elimination, speak to each other well. And I think that both speak to the isolation, exploita-

tion, and elimination of trans peoples and communities. I believe really strongly that there can be no liberation or thriving for trans people without also liberation and survival and thriving for all other colonized and oppressed communities. I think that it's true that my liberation is very deeply bound up in the liberation of other people. And I don't see my own or my immediate community's struggle as trans people as separate from any of that.[37]

Hollis refuses the constitution of trans oppression as distinct from—or at least isolable from—the ableist, anthropocentric, capitalist, colonial, and racial projects in which it takes shape. They insist that the policing of gender is never just about gender, but also about a geographically and historically specific power-resistance formation of colonialism. If gender disruption, in whatever forms it comes in, is to flourish, abolition and decolonization must be at the heart of that project. More specifically, Hollis thinks river restoration as intimately connected to trans restoration and they think that connection through working to restore a specific river in concert with a specific trans body. In doing so, Hollis insists on rerooting trans projects in earth justice, body and land together, where the materiality of embankment and embodiment comingle.

Grounded normativity is world work. Queer and trans grounded normativity is reworlding work. And it is work still too rarely recognized as constitutive of trans and gender disruptive liberation. This is not identity politics or intersectional politics, although it is attentive to both identities and intersections. It is, instead, an underflows and undercommons politics—a poetic politics—that stakes futures on the *meaningfully attentive* ways of moving and making, desiring and dreaming, otherwise suffocated by cisheteronormativity and settler colonialism. Trans, in this framework, becomes something sunk, down into the body, down into the land. Trans* becomes trans_. Abolition and decolonization demand the work of undoing and reimagining underground foundations and reconnecting with grounded living. Trans worlding, if it is indeed to contribute to trans liberation, must do the same.

How big is a world? How far and how deep does it stretch? What are the bonds that world it? Much ink has been spilt on the multiplicity of worlds, especially following the work of Argentinian feminist philosopher María Lugones.[38] As important as it is to understand *that* there are different worlds, it is critical to understand that worlds can be *made* different. The shape of worlds—the shape of each world—can and does change. Worlds have not always already existed—nor have they always taken the form they currently have. Alongside thinking the necessary skill of world-traveling (shuttling between worlds), then, one must also think the even more fundamental task of world-building and world-changing—that is, the work of worlding itself. How is it that we world and how is it that we might world? To return to Lugones, this has to be the work of bringing together flesh and blood people. The work of making and sharing languages. The work of building shared, entangled histories and stories. And to turn further back to queer Chicana feminist Gloria Anzaldúa, this also has to be the work of building bridges and blurring the boundaries—for more expansive coalitions, mixed beings, and learning from the land itself.[39]

Trans worlding at the Five Colleges supplements this picture of world-building. As modeled by Smith and Mount Holyoke, world-changing involves building belonging along the lines of shared identity formations or shared histories of discrimination. Expanding real commonalities, then, is one way in which worlds can be transformed. As further demonstrated by #AmherstUprising, world-changing involves tracing tentacles of oppression across the glut of university life, within but especially across different social positions. World-building need not pit one community's needs against another's. Finally, world-changing, following Mason and Hollis, involves digging into the body and the earth in a way that ruptures and reroots its stories; it involves abolition and decolonization, grappling with Indigenous sovereignty as much as the inherent wisdoms of nonhuman life. Such world-building can and should attend to identities and intersections, but also to the mycelial net between and under these things. This is not only to say that trans worlds ought to *trans* coloniality and the Anthropocene. It is also to say that trans worlding should be driven by a sense that there is always something underfoot and underground, something left to be attuned to, a necessary vigilance and humility. We still do not yet know all that trans worlds are made of nor all the ways in which trans worlds might be made.

World is an analytic of trans poetics. It is a frame through which we can access and assess how we are with one another—who the *we* is, and in what ways the *we* and the *how* might change. It is a way of attending and attuning, of pulling something out from a submerged place. It is an angle through the water that illuminates the underflows.

World. Trans worlds and worlding have already come in multiple shapes—some of which we are right to be very proud of and some of which we may not be. Trans worlds, moreover, are not simply inherited and inhabited, but they can be made to shift and slip. In particular, trans worlds can be refashioned so as to challenge troubling formations of trans life and trans studies themselves. Trans worlds can set trans communities tilting. What I have done in this chapter and this book is insist that whatever we think of trans worlds as doing in the university, we must look underneath the policies and protests to get to the everyday ways trans people tell their stories, conduct their struggles, and craft visions of another future. And if we want to build trans worlds differently, from a place of grounded, undergrounded meaning and community, trans poetics is no mere aesthetic ornament; it is an essential element. Trans poetics, for a grounded trans worlding, is the earth and the water, the air and the fire.

coda *Methods, Tangents*

Finding a way out of a project is just as tricky as finding a way to begin. This book was full of false starts and there was a long period during which I felt certain there was no way to craft something cohesive out of the fantastic morass I had accumulated. Over and over again, I redrew its shape, and over and over again it shifted in my hands. I went back to the audio recordings, back to the archival artifacts, back in fact to the land and just stood there and listened. It became clear to me that the story of trans life at the Five Colleges—at least as I could tell it—could not be told chronologically. Nor could it be beholden to passing policy, nor organized simply (e.g., five chapters, five colleges). Just as the Connecticut River twists and turns through the watershed, fed by countless tributaries and siphoned, just as often, by effluent pockets and branching streams, so too this story had to pool and to rush at once, having some direction, certainly, but also being repeatedly waylaid, meaningfully and meanwhile.

A book of poetics needed a poetry to it. This is not simply to say it had to manifest an attention to the work and way of words, although of course it had to do that. But it also had to think and move in ways common to the undercommons. In tracing trans disruptions at the edge of the university, it had itself to disrupt university logics; it had to upset methods that serve the overhead rather than the underfoot. This meant staging competing resonances. Lingering beside tarns of affect and torrents of protest. Staying with the way trans does not settle into plans. It meant refracting trans through crystalline terms—like *scatter*, *glue*, and *risk*—in ways that set it adrift rather than dammed it up. It meant to make sense in out-of-the-way places and by unofficial means, not just in person but on the page and in the prose. And it meant being beleaguered and buoyed by the effort. To come away homed and unhomed in equal measure.

At some point, the book was all but done. And here it is, ready to be set to rest and sent off. What have I learned? How am I different for it? And what will keep buzzing in my ears long after these many marks are set to page and to print? I want to leave readers with what I am left with: questions of method, questions of the paths we take and those we still might.

Throughout this book, I have spoken primarily of trans poetics as a place—a strata or register—where making happens. I have aligned it with edges and cracks, undercommons and underflows, the behind and the beneath. But trans poetics is also a movement, a way of moving in relation to what already moves, but in another direction. It is oriented sideways and at an angle askew from things themselves, and the surfaces and flows that typically distinguish them. Methodologically speaking, then, any analysis that means to enact trans poiesis in its very inquiry (and to track trans poetics in its materiality) has to mimic that movement. It has to assume a *tangential* relation to mainstream inclusive policy work, but also to all kinds of organized knowledge and thought-out projects that have become institutionalized, over the years, because of and on the back of (and as a way of backing out of, because of) poetics.

On Tangents, Then

A whole book could be written about the names under which trans folks organize themselves. In the Five College archive of trans life, there are some unusually resonant ones. GRIN, for example (Gender Identity Resource Network) and T-SWAG (Trans Studies Working Group). Transcending Gender and Gender+ and TransActive. These are names full of attitude and humor, ambition and commitment. But the one I cannot shake (because it keeps shaking me) is "Tangent." At Smith College, in the fall of 2003, the T Committee, a 1998 spinoff of the student LBA, became "Tangent." While the T Committee was primarily a support group for transgender students, offering opportunities for social networking, conference attendance, and educational workshops, Tangent was different.[1] In addition to support work, Tangent was politically active on campus, organized Trans Awareness Week, and advocated with administrators for trans-inclusive health services, bathrooms, a nondiscrimination clause, and such.[2] That is, it intersected with the university itself and, contoured by resistance, drew a line in another direction.

Lucas Cheadle—a Smith neuroscience major, trans man, and citizen of the Chickasaw Nation in Oklahoma—is credited with renaming the group Tangent. In an interview for *The Sophian* in 2004, Cheadle explains the name as follows: "If you have a curve and you have a tangent it follows the slope of the curve. That's the velocity and that's also called the rate of change. So Tangent is representative of a rate of change, and it's also representative of not being silent because you can go off on a tangent about something you believe in."[3] The Latin *tangere*, of course, means "to touch." In mathematics, a tangent is a straight line that touches a curve without crossing it—the way a book might sit on someone's head or a broken fence post might lie across an uneven hill. Insofar as the tangent line is drawn by connecting two infinitesimal points on the curvilinear line, its slope indicates the instantaneous rate of change of the curve. Of course, we typically think of trans as the curvy line that crisscrosses the straight lines of mainstream culture. But Cheadle's proposal is different. Here trans is a line that reveals the change already happening in what, at the micro level of this or that present moment, seems unchanging, but isn't. Trans/tangent names the change already underfoot, already underway. In this context, going off on a tangent means moving in a different direction, but a direction built from a momentary change already at work in things themselves. It is a (mad) transversal movement built from the unapologetically local.

When I think about the methods that have guided me in this book, I think about its tangential vectors of analysis—tangential to the curvilinear lines not only of university knowledges, but also to mainstream trans studies. I am left with, and therefore leave you with, then, two words. Two concepts at the edge of trans, and that set trans on edge. Two invitations that ironically also bring trans home, keeping it closer and more honest than it would be otherwise. They are these: transversality and translocality. In *staying with trans*, I have tried to transverse and transect it. To find in it, rather than outside it, the tensions that strain and stretch it. We need no asterisk when the point itself vanishes. Likewise, in staying with trans *in a place*, I have tried to root it in the rich soils that produce it but also exceed it. To find in the local the mad logics that refuse subsumption and defy transplantation. The hyphen can turn a word in, as much as it can turn a word out. To me, these two terms and two movements summon us to the insides and sideways of trans in place. It is here that I stay as the book takes leave of me.

Transversality

There are innumerable ways to disrupt what becomes solid and solidified, what becomes separable by binaristic logics and made falsely universal. And one of the dangers of that work is to find, slowly forming in one's hands, a weapon of disruption that is itself solidifying, becoming separate, and wielded in isolation from its complicated and complicating contexts. *Trans* is one such weapon in the work of resistance. It is consistently in danger of becoming something divorced from its own disruptive potential. Something purified. As if it were distinguishable from the bodies within which it sits, transected as they are with class, disability, gender, race, and sexuality, to mark only the beginning of enfleshed difference. One way to combat this winnowing of trans, in the service of broader structures of normalization, is to bridge—and branch—outward. Talk about trans+, trans*, trans-. Situate it only always as part of a couplet or conglomerate of sites. This has been the plea of trans studies from its inception. Yet another way, however, is to situate trans in a place and space from which it cannot abscond or be abstracted. To resist normalization through localization. Ultimately, either move injects trans with its own transversality.

The term *transversality* is nothing new to resistance theorizing—or to trans studies for that matter. Developed over a series of decades and in a variety of contexts, transversality today typically refers to the transverse or crosscurrent energies that shape who we are, what we do, and the coalitions we build.[4] More specifically, transversality marks the crossings that shape a marginalized people, fuel their anti-institutional resistance work, and require their allyship with other oppressed peoples. Félix Guattari famously identified transversality as the heart of the antipsychiatry movement in France, which aimed to disorganize psychiatric institutions from the inside out. His comrade Édouard Glissant saw in transversality the relational crosscurrents that define the history and ontology of the Caribbean Sea and Middle Passage. And Lohana Berkins located transversality squarely in travesti/trans life and its capacity to do cross-movement coalition-building in Argentina. In trans studies, transversality has been used to describe the intimacies between transness and blackness, madness, and animality, as well as the trans ecologies of hybridity, borderlands, disciplinary promiscuity, and methodological mischief.[5]

It is, I think, not too much to say that, to date, the sign of transversality par excellence is the asterisk. How can trans studies stay accountable to its tangled histories, build unexpected coalitions, and resist the institutionalization of trans itself? The asterisk insists on drawing trans beyond itself, unsettling it by putting it in relation with the many crosscurrents that transect it—social positions, certainly, but also modalities, geographies and potentialities. Salvation by starfish. The trans* story is, then, never singular, nor isolable. It holds relation at its heart. This sense of transversality is already part of our history, part of our struggle. Think of Stonewall. Or of Leslie Feinberg, who urges that "all those who have the least to lose from changing this ['economic and social system that governs our lives'] get together" to "examine" and "take action."[6] Trans is always more than trans, always *with* more than trans, always working for more than trans. And the paradigmatic way to think this moreness is as a reaching of trans beyond itself.

But what of the turn inward? One of the invitations of Glissant's work in the Carribbean or Guattari's work in psychiatric settings is to think transversality in the context of specific lands and institutions. It is an injunction to place and space. While I find myself starfishing in this book, contextualizing its contents within and stretching beyond broader trans studies literatures, I also do a bunch of barnacling, hewing close to a specific trans community. I do landed thinking, *local theory*. At the Five Colleges, what trans is and means is already under scrutiny and contestation. It is already being pulled apart at its seams. One need not look at trans plus in order to find trans porous, pulverized, parceled. This is not simply—and pedantically—to say that it is impossible to tell the story of trans here without other vectors of identity (e.g., class, disability, gender, race, and sexuality). It is also, and I think more meaningfully, to say that staying with trans in the Five Colleges is enough to get beyond it, between it, behind it, and before it. Staying is disruptive. Staying is upsetting. Staying with and staying in, rather than pulling away or pulling out, gets at the same irremediable instability and self-resistant potentiality at the heart of trans life.

In an age in which trans studies work tries to cross greater and greater distances, and put trans into more adjacent and apposite conversations, with theoretical monographs stringing together largely disconnected artefacts, ... getting local, getting proximal, getting *close* is another way of getting *transed*, trounced by the instability that lies at the heart not just within reach of the (trans) hand. That transing demands a multiplication of logics and loci of concern (a transversality), but it also, perhaps uniquely, harbors an antilogic. A kind of *loco-* that disrupts the *topos*. A *trans*locality.

Translocality

The term "translocality" took social geography by storm in the early twenty-first century.[7] With the steep growth in sociospatial interconnectedness and globalization, producing and produced by increasingly expansive migration flows, exchange circuits, and connective infrastructures (i.e., communication, transportation, and digital mediums), the local seems to have all but vanished. Previously conceptualized as a determinate place, with physical coordinates and palpable borders, the local is now also, and indeed fundamentally, global. Nomadic lifeforms are not external to but germane to even the smallest of worlds. This means that living in place has become just as often and just as much "living in transition."[8] *Translocality* has found a warm welcome in trans studies. In this context, the translocal is always a space of translation, tranimacies, and transnational critiques of nationhood, while trans lives themselves become transregional and transarchipelagic, proliferating trans-mutations, -dislocations, and -disputations. Perhaps unsurprisingly, the term is especially flexed in literatures from and for the Global South.

To be transed from the outside, however, is different from being transed from within. Likewise, to be crosshatched by a sprawling network is different from being a tangled web to begin with. While not incompatible, these different states offer separate resources for thought. The former invites us to think disturbances at the edge, while the latter invites us to think disturbances from the cracks. Both are equally important to the dislocation marked by the term *translocality*. But fewer energies are spent thinking the translocal from the inside out. Imagine a smooth stone teeming with microscopic life that will—slowly but inexorably—disintegrate it over time. Imagine a monad as a deterritorializing surface. What if the local was never as local as people took it to be? This suggests a bivalence to translocality itself. Although typically taken to mean crosslocal, translocal might just as surely mean local-transed or local-crossed. And while there is every reason to resist the tyranny of small-mindedness, there is nothing immediately simple or necessarily unitary about a small world. Air still moves in a bubble—whirling and swirling, churning and chopping, straining against the sides and pulling clean away.

The conceit of trans studies has been that trans is too easily, or too simply territory, and that to save it from itself we must reach outside of it, recontextualizing it within global connections, energy flows, interdependencies, and economies. But there is a way in which this attempt to make trans truer by making it half the hyphen, or one element in the compound, necessarily lends trans more credit than it deserves. It makes trans simpliciter more logical than it actually is. Logic, after all, is a delocalizing affair, tapping into generalizations and universalizations, ways of thinking across difference rather than from difference. Logic quells the loco of the local, so to speak; it is a making sane of what is, in its small world context, always a little off, shaky and a bit askew. Translocality, then, lives not only in the disruption of trans by that which lies beyond it, but in the dysfunction of trans from within. An irrepressibly local madness.

When I think trans in the Connecticut River Valley and at the Five Colleges, there is certainly a way in which those stories are transected by larger worlds, not least Massachusetts politics, US culture, and global gestalts, as well as the quotidian realities of academic production and circulation. People come and go from all over the country and across the world. Millenia-old ideas circulate beside Reddit threads and Tumblr posts. Crosshatch indeed. But this is also a village. As anyone who has really lived here knows, this place is tiny and just plain kookie. And the trans-speciation of gendered bodies at work in these hills hardly begs to differ. The array of gender creativity I have witnessed—whether linguistic, gestural, guttural, textilic, romantic, or otherwise material and enfleshed, brooks no comparison. Making sense here is making nonsense. And that *matters*. When it comes to making one another, attention to *where* we do it, and the peculiarities of place, reveals the real weirdness of trans itself. This, too, is translocality.

If we want to shake a whitening grip of trans on itself, then it helps to train our eyes on the miniscule madnesses—the heterotopias—that shape trans place and space. Such an invitation not only supports the continual work of rupturing trans from its own normalization, but it also does something else. Something beautiful, something unexpected. It takes (trans) people back to place. Place—from which we have been unceremoniously jettisoned, as not belonging and as too different. Place—which we are now too reticent to claim, to love, to honor. Place—where small enclaves of our people are, strung out and sunk in the woodwork. Place—where creatures themselves transgress biological logics every damn day, for us and with us. Here are the exuberant eccentricities from which we come. The unwashed and unsanitized. To sink trans back into place is to put us back into context, to take us home. To think trans and land. Local theory is translocality in action.

In a world in which "people postulate about my existence over cheerios in the morning," as Smith alum Silas puts it, what is it to think trans with *trans-thinking*?[9]

It is, at the very least, to puddle those postulates with the force of real trans poetics—the gritty ways in which we struggle together, tell stories and dream dreams together, and ultimately make one another. You can't catch sight of poetics by staying in the world of postulates, hovering above a bowl of cheerios. You have to get down in a place, down in the divoted dirt, in a sweaty undercommons, or in an actual kitchen. In my case, I had to get on campus, hang out in classrooms and cafes with other trans people, sharing stories around a table, raging together, and imagining other worlds. I had to be part of and adjacent to instances of trans resistant life at the Five Colleges. And I had to do so over time. Part of the trouble with theory is its delocalization, its extraction from community and community building. To catch poetics necessitates showing up where the poetics happens. It requires the local, and from there the relational. Trans studies' always impending turn toward relation, then, can begin here. It need not straightway head toward the canopy. It can start at the roots and then get to the rhizomes.

The attunements I have offered here are transversal, and the analytics translocal. Attunements to the an-archic and to silence, to webs and to hangouts, to the ephemeral and to trash, these cut across traditional ways of telling stories and tracking social movements. They insist on messy intimacies in place of clean distinctions, and on unexpected alliances buried in the brush. They are reasons to link arms across difference, as much as to find difference at the heart. Similarly, analytics such as stash and scatter, thread and glue, fatigue and world expressly enact a refractive method, honoring the multiple, often competing ways in which trans gets constituted and gets constellated in a place. They underscore trans's unsettledness, its constitutive unsteadiness. And they do this by rooting themselves in mad, heterotopic spaces. What does a trans poetics offer, then, through its attunements and analytics, for a trans methodology? It offers notes on the ground—notes from underground—about the crisscross tracks that fabricate who we are and what we do. They trans the trans, and, in doing so, perpetually open a portal.

I also take a transversal and translocal approach to citation politics in the project. In writing this book, I aimed to consult and to write local, story-led theory. I did not aim to write a book that only cites trans theorists, nor did I aim to write a book where all the hottest contemporary trans voices jockey for space. I wanted to write a humble, rhizomatic book that puts the wisdom of Five College trans folks at the forefront of big questions that many people, trans and nontrans, continue to tackle. Through this local work, I am committed to the richness of thinking trans in place.

Poetics puts back in question how we punctuate things like trans life. What would it look like were trans+, trans*, and trans- to become trans_? The underscore—or understrike or underbar—insists on space where space is disallowed. In a system saturated with higher order discourse, where only more words and more links and more things are given value, this insistence on space and place ruptures the rhetoric. Trans_ would insist on a grounding beneath the string of words and prefabricated trans discourse. A grounding in the local, a grounding in the poetic. Such a grounding would give back a sense not of trans as the global, cosmopolitan, urban creature it has become, but of the rural, backwoods, backwater trans it has always been. Trans in the undercommons, trans in the underflows. What might that do to the university? And to the university discourses in which trans circulates? What might that do to trans organizing and trans flourishing? When we think of the intimacies of place, reconnecting to land and landed thinking, to the grounds of our flesh and the flesh of our ground, what else about who we have been, what we do, and who we might become surfaces?

Let's make each other together again, on that edge.

Epilogue

While I was hired at Hampshire on a three-year visiting line in 2015, I was hired away within the first year. Nine months after moving to the most queer and trans affirming place I had ever been, I left. Within a year, I also separated from what was, at that point, my longest-standing, most formative romantic partnership. It was the kind of breakup where you are not sure where all the pieces of you went or if they will ever come back. The decimation was so brutal, there wasn't a core left standing. In a book about how trans people make things and make one another, the nontrans folks who love us—and make us and make things with us (and, because of that, also unmake us)—deserve a moment in the sun. I would not be here, writing this book, without them. But what is patently clear to me, looking back, is that by 2017 when I first organized that fateful trip back to Hampshire to begin interview and archival work, I desperately needed these trans stories. I was starved for belonging in all kinds of ways. I needed them to root me and to help me rebuild some semblance of a life.

My need for connection was acute, but I find the trans need for connection is chronic.

Deep in the archives, I came across a story of the first time trans elders Leslie Feinberg and Ben Power met. It was three years after Ben started the East Coast FTM Group. It was also three years after Leslie had published *Transgender Liberation*, and two years after *Stone Butch Blues*. For the first time, Amherst College's Affirmative Action Office acknowledged transgender issues by sponsoring a lecture by Feinberg. Ben recalls the event like this:

> I met Leslie in 1995. Leslie was speaking at Amherst College prior to publication of *Transgender Warriors* [1996]. She was there to give a lecture about transgender history in this big auditorium of about 800 people and

almost every seat was filled. I came in dressed in a three-piece suit and tie. I was very proud to be dressed like this, going to see Leslie Feinberg for the first time.

The front of the auditorium was very low and Leslie was at the microphone attached to the podium. Since I was late, I was up front trying to find a seat. Leslie stopped her lecture and said to me, "Welcome brother. Don't you look handsome in that suit." The majority of the audience was cisgender, gay, or lesbian. There were maybe a handful of students there that I could identify as trans folk.

So, that was the first word spoken at me from the person and I never forgot that. I took my seat and listened to this lecture about all these figures in trans history. After the lecture, I went up to the podium because people were meeting Leslie, shaking hands and stuff like that. I introduced myself as the curator of the SMA [Sexual Minorities Archives] and Leslie said, "Oh, I know who you are. You belong in my book. I'll be contacting you very soon about it." Leslie told me I belonged in history. I had never been recognized like that before.

This was all pre-internet, so we were corresponding via some emails but mostly letters. After going back and forth about the book, I suggested that Leslie come and do a book signing at the SMA when the book comes out. Leslie and Minnie Bruce came, in 1996 when the SMA was located in Northampton, and did readings. Minnie Bruce read some poetry and Leslie read from *Transgender Warriors*, *Stone Butch Blues*, and *Trans Liberation*. We had a spaghetti dinner—just a real cheap thing to pull off since it was a fundraiser for the SMA. That day, in and out over a six-hour period, I'd estimate we hosted about three hundred people.[1]

Ben was indeed acknowledged, in *Transgender Warriors*, for founding and directing East Coast FTM and the Sexual Minorities Archives, as well as for offering a "heap of help" in the research process.[2] But that is not the point of this story. The point is the poetics. In that auditorium, surrounded by a predominantly "cisgender" and gay audience, Leslie and Ben made one another, at the edge of the university. And that trans making reverberated outward in every direction.

Then: Ben, Leslie, and Minnie Bruce. A three-piece suit, a word of welcome, a spaghetti dinner. A bit of poetry in the archives, around a podium and a table, and then in the streets. A cycle of affirmation and of making home. Together, they—alongside all those they brought together—(re)wrote trans history, locked arms in struggle, and built fierce, collective visions for another world. They were dust particles colliding—sticky, and full of hope.

For the beautifully gender-disruptive people who read these words, I hope this book is like that for you. That you will have been met. That you will have been seen. That you will have been loved.

Not all our stories will be trans stories. *Trans* remains a contested term within and beyond its original Western context. Feinberg offered *Transgender Warriors* as "our-story."[3] But perhaps that book—and certainly this one—are better understood as simply part of our *ourchive*. An ourchive, Mount Holyoke faculty member Ren-yo Hwang writes, is "a self-reflexive, collective-collection of community-led knowledge that remains willfully open, without completion, a process."[4] If *How We Make Each Other* is meant to be anything, I mean it to be a contribution to an archive of gender disruption—an ourchive gender disruptors of all sorts can claim and contest, resonate with, resist, and remake.

As I look up from writing it, then, I look for you.

chronology

This chronology is not meant to be exhaustive or perfectly representative; it is, as our histories are, scattershot in nature. Not all aforementioned people, events, or actions are entered here, nor are all entries developed in the preceding pages. The aim of this record is to provide a contextualizing apparatus for the flows of trans life at the Five Colleges over the last several decades.

1974   The New Alexandria Library for Women is founded in Chicago, Illinois, but quickly renamed New Alexandria Lesbian Library for Women that same year.

1975   Fall: Janice Raymond, author of *The Transsexual Empire* (1979), is appointed visiting assistant professor at the Five Colleges in women's studies and medical ethics. The appointment expired in 1978 when she was hired as the first tenure-track professor in Women Studies by UMass, Amherst, where she is now professor emerita.

1979   Ben Power moves the New Alexandria Lesbian Library to Massachusetts. In 1981, he moves it into his own apartment in Northampton.

1992   Northampton, Massachusetts, is named "Lesbian Ellis Island" on ABC's *20/20*.

                East Coast FTM Group is established by Ben Power in Northampton, Massachusetts.

                The New Alexandria Lesbian Library is renamed the Sexual Minorities Archives by Ben Power.

1995	Ben Power meets Leslie Feinberg for the first time when Feinberg spoke at Amherst College, at the invitation of the Affirmative Action Office. It was a big auditorium, filled with almost eight hundred people.
	Eli Goodwin ('99, he/him) asks for the "T" to be added to the LGBA at Amherst College. The motion was voted on and hit the following year.
	A Mount Holyoke Lesbian and Bisexual Alliance notebook (1995–1997) records plans to make "signs that define heterosexism, homophobia, and transgender." It also lists "Trans Books," including Kate Bornstein's *Gender Outlaw* and Leslie Feinberg's *Stone Butch Blues*, and it records plans to host a "trans-speaker (student) to lead a mtg."
	Enoch Page (UMass, Amherst, anthropology) successfully insists that the Chancellor's Task Force for Gay, Lesbian, and Bisexual Matters include "Transgender" in its title.
1996	Mount Holyoke's Lesbian and Bisexual Alliance flyer welcomes: "Dykes, radicalesbians, riot grrls, lipstick lesbians, raging bisexuals, stone butches, soft butches, femmes, transgenders, queers, in-betweeners, bulldaggers, fruits, drag kings, lesbos, dykes with bikes, lezzies, fans of Hothead, kd lang, Jodie Foster, sappho-followers, closeted and questioning friends."
1997	April 2: Mount Holyoke College's Spectrum student group presents "A Transgender Panel," in Stimson Room, Williston Library. Five trans people speak.
	October: Riki Wilchins, cofounder of Transexual Menace, speaks at Smith College.
1998	*Mount Holyoke News* advertises SYSTA, "a confidential support group for lesbian, bisexual, transgendered, and questioning Women of Color."
	The Transgender Committee forms (as offshoot of LBT Alliance) at Smith College.
	University of Massachusetts's Pride Alliance hosts panel of "out" queer and trans professors, including Enoch Page.

1999	March 26–27: "Transgender Perspectives: Arts, Activism, and Academia," self-described as the first annual Transgender Conference at Smith, occurs. The event includes a showing of *Shinjuku Boys* (1995) and *Stonewall* (1995), a lecture on gender terminology, and a panel on transgender experiences. Of the seven panelists, one was an intersex person.
2000	The Amherst College administration provides space and a part-time paid staff position for an LGBT resource center called the Rainbow Room in the basement of Pratt Dormitory.
	Eli Clare gives his first of many talks in the valley at Food for Thought Books in Amherst, Massachusetts.
	February: Enoch Page (UMass, Amherst) gives a talk at Smith College entitled "Whiteness in Transsexual Activism."
	March: The Transgender Committee at Smith College hosts a second trans conference: "Y2Genders." Kate Bornstein is the keynote speaker.
2001	Transgender Activist Network (TAN) is established by Mitch Boucher, then graduate student in English at UMass, Amherst. The group helps spearhead the Restroom Revolution group (2001–2003), led by AJ Crittendon, then an undergraduate student.
	Spring: T. Aaron Hans first teaches Sociology 397G/397T: Transgender Theory at UMass, Amherst. The course was cofacilitated by trans colleague Alisha Clarke.
	March: A group of students lead a transgender issues workshop at Mount Holyoke College.
	April: Toby Davis ('03) writes and performs *Crossing* at Smith College, a play about a transgender Jesus, to great acclaim. An encore performance is scheduled for UMass, Amherst.
	April: David Valentine gives a talk on "The Transgender Imaginary" at Smith College.
2002	The *Camp Transfeminism* zine is issued at Smith College.
	April: Kate Bornstein gives a talk at Hampshire College on "Entitled America's Least Welcome: Who Are the Outcasts and Why?"

CHRONOLOGY 241

November: The Student Government Association at UMass, Amherst, votes 34–12 to support the creation of "gender-neutral bathrooms."

2003

March: Smith College hires "transgender specialist" Julie Mencher in the counseling center.

March: Toby Davis ('03) writes and directs *The Naked I* play at Smith College.

April: Dean Spade holds the first "Trans 101" workshop in Hampshire College's Women's Center, later renamed the Center for Feminisms (CFF).

April: Dean Spade gives a talk, "Framing a Trans Social Justice Agenda," at UMass, Amherst.

April: Smith students vote to replace she/her pronouns with the gender-neutral term *student* throughout its governing documents. The vote was electronic; 1,115 votes were cast and the initiative passed with a 50-vote margin.

April: Julie Mencher, MSW, leads a "Transgender 101" training at Mount Holyoke College.

October: UMass, Amherst hosts Transcending Boundaries Conference.

November: Smith College student group Tangent (formerly Transgender Committee, or T Committee) hosts Trans Awareness Week.

2004

April: Dean Spade gives talk at Smith College entitled "Economic Justice Issues in Trans Law."

Fall: Milo Primeaux '07 (along with cochair Ryan Berman) establishes the Mount Holyoke Brothers and Others: Association of Transgender Students & Allies student group.

November 1: UMass Pride Alliance, Stonewall Center, and Amherst College Department of English cosponsor a talk by Leslie Feinberg.

November 29–December 3: Mount Holyoke hosts its first Transgender Awareness Week.

2005

TransGeneration, a documentary, is released spotlighting four trans college students, one of whom is Lucas Cheadle, then a student at Smith College.

February: Dean Spade returns to Hampshire College to host second "Trans 101" Workshop in the Queer Community Alliance Center (QCAC).

September: Chase Catalano ('01, '14) offers "Gender Transgression and Transgender Identity" Workshop at UMass, Amherst. He offers it again in October 2006, October 2007, October 2008, and November 2009.

October: *Hedwig and the Angry Inch* film plays at the Academy of Music in Northampton.

2006

S. Bear Bergman ('96 Hampshire alum) publishes *Butch Is a Noun*.

Hampshire College's Transgender Student Alliance (TSA) is established. The group is reconceptualized and renamed Gender Resource Network (GRN) in 2014.

Smith College hosts student Jack Pierson's exhibit, "Pioneering Voices: Trans Experiences in the Valley," for the first time. The project includes interviews and photographs of local trans people.

February: Mount Holyoke hosts the Seven Sisters SGA Conference, during which the issue of transgender students arises.

March: Initial Mount Holyoke Transgender Awareness Committee is convened by Bill Boerner, Residence Life. The group convenes to discuss trans issues on campus and is joined by Chase Catalano (UMass, Amherst). The committee meets regularly through 2009.

March: Smith College screens *Transamerica*.

April: Paisley Currah gives a talk entitled "The Transgender Rights Imaginary" at Amherst College.

May: Mount Holyoke Transgender Committee implements its first event: a panel presentation entitled "Voices Speak: Transgender Students and Alums Share Their Stories."

November 8–17: Transgender Film Festival is hosted by UMass, Amherst.

December: Mount Holyoke hosts "Transgender Studies and Women's Colleges" conference, attended by people from seventeen different institutions.

2007

Mount Holyoke's sexual health education program is renamed to be more trans-inclusive. It was SHE—Sexual Health Educators, but it became In Touch.

April: Smith College hosts Mangos with Chili, a queer and trans of color cabaret group.

2008

February: Kate Bornstein returns to Smith College to speak. Smith's Resource Center for Sexuality and Gender (est. 2006) and the East Coast FTM Group (Ben Power) sponsor the event.

March: *New York Times* publishes "When Girls Will Be Boys," featuring Smith and Mount Holyoke College students.

April: Student Jess Ream ('08) publishes a piece in *Mount Holyoke News* about the necessity of trans inclusion in sports.

October: Smith College hosts alum Toby Davis ('03) and his play *Standards of Care*.

October: Mount Holyoke's Transgender Committee hosts "Trans U: An Introduction to Transgender Issues on Campus," an event offered by Sam Lurie.

November: Around forty people gather in Amherst's Unitarian Universalist meetinghouse for Transgender Day of Remembrance.

2009

Ben Power and others start Noho Trans Pride, which then becomes the New England Trans United (NETU) Pride March and Rally.

Five College Queer Gender and Sexuality Conference is established (and remains active to date).

November 16: Amherst College hosts event "Understanding Trans: Exploring Identities and Creating Supportive Communities," led by Chase Catalano (UMass, Amherst alum); attendees included students from UMass, Amherst and Hampshire.

November 20–22: 6th Transcending Boundaries Conference occurs in Worcester, Massachusetts.

November: Smith student group Tangent is reformulated as Transcending Gender.

December: Students organize a "fireside chat" on trans inclusion at Smith College with then President Carol Christ, Provost Marilyn Schuster, and several deans.

As a matter of policy, UMass, Amherst commits to including gender-inclusive single-stall restrooms in all newly constructed or significantly renovated academic or administrative buildings and residence halls starting January 2010.

2010

Jules Rosskam is hired as visiting assistant professor of film and video production at Hampshire College. At the time, he had produced the widely acclaimed feature film *Transparent* (2005) and feature documentary *Against a Trans Narrative* (2010). In 2012, he shot his third feature film *Thick Relations*. His position expired in 2014.

Jack Pryor is hired as an adjunct at Hampshire College. They are then promoted to half-time visiting assistant professor of Queer Studies and Public Practice (2011–2012). They are involved in establishing the Five College Queer, Trans, and Sexuality Studies Certificate. On April 17, 2012, their contract is not renewed.

Summer: Mateo Medina ('13) creates the "Preferred Gender Pronouns" handout for Hampshire College's orientation.

August: University of Massachusetts, Amherst adds "gender identity and expression" to its nondiscrimination policy.

October: Massachusetts legislators consider a bill called "An Act Relative to Gender-Based Discrimination and Hate Crimes" (HB 1728).

December 1: Paisley Currah gives a talk, "Sex Is as Sex Does," at Amherst College.

2011

The Queer Does Not End Here initiative is established at Hampshire College (and runs through 2013) to demand a permanent

Queer Studies faculty line and to demand that Jack Pryor be considered for the position.

January (circa): Trans Policy Committee (informally known among its members as the "Trans Cabal") is established at Hampshire College and remains active until 2013.

February 16: Eli Clare gives a talk, "Gawking, Gaping, Staring: Living in Marked Bodies," at Mount Holyoke. The talk was reported on in Smith's *Sophian*.

April: Jake Pecht ('12), AKA Gneiss Guy, defends his right to serve as a Gold Key guide for prospective students at Smith College. He simultaneously publishes "'I Am Smith' and I Am Male" in *The Sophian*. Jake is supported by the student group Transcending Gender, led by Robbie Dunning ('11).

October 25: Amherst College hosts Rocco Katastrophe, transgender rapper. The event is co-sponsored by UMass, Amherst's Stonewall Center.

November 17: An incident sets off what would become the #occupybathroom and/or #decolonizebathroom (2011–2013) movement at Hampshire College.

November: More than sixty people gather at Amherst's Unitarian Universalist meetinghouse for Transgender Day of Remembrance.

Massachusetts passes the "Gender Identity Bill" to ensure workplace protection for trans people.

2012

March 3: Amherst College hosts "Five College Transgender Awareness Event" to discuss the Girl Scouts' recent admission of a trans girl and the ensuing controversy. Hampshire's QCAC and UMass, Amherst's Stonewall Center cosponsor.

March 9: The Queer Does Not End Here Hampshire student group submits a letter to the deans regarding "the historical demand for a permanent Queer Studies faculty position."

April 27: Hampshire College president Jonathan Lash is officially inaugurated. During the event, The Queer Does Not End Here conducts a beached whales action, asking "Are we just inconvenient queers?"

July: Amherst College hires Angie Tissi-Galloway (previously health educator at Mount Holyoke) to direct the Queer Resource Center.

October: Ivan Coyote and S. Bear Bergman (Hampshire '96) talk storytelling at Smith College.

November 15: Mara Keisling speaks at UMass, Amherst about the National Center for Transgender Equality and the urgent need for trans advocacy.

2013

February: D'Lo screens *Performing Girl* (2013) at Smith College. The film was directed by Crescent Diamond (Hampshire '99).

February: The Amherst Area Chamber of Commerce sponsors a Brown Bag Lunch on transgender issues in the workplace, led by Genny Beemyn (UMass, Amherst).

February: Mount Holyoke's COGA (Coalition for Gender Awareness) forms. The group organizes a "Trans*Identity Panel at All Women's Colleges," featuring Lynn Pasquerella (MHC President), Genny Beemyn (director, Stonewall Center, UMass, Amherst), Mitch Boucher (UMass, Amherst professor), and students.

March: Stephen Dillon is hired to begin as assistant professor of Queer Studies at Hampshire College in Fall 2013. He leaves Hampshire in 2023.

March 1–2: Five College Queer Gender and Sexuality Conference is held at Hampshire College. Keynote speaker: José Esteban Muñoz.

March: Massachusetts issues guidelines for addressing transphobia in schools and supporting trans students.

March 10: Smith College denies admittance to Calliope Rose Wong, a transgender woman whose FAFSA documents included the sex designation of "M" rather than "F."

March 29: Ben Power releases a video addressing Wong's denial from Smith College.

April: Smith student group Q&A demands Smith admissions policy expressly include trans women.

April 25: Julia Serano, who had offered to come speak, gives talk at Smith College.

Fall: Mount Holyoke College hires Andrea Lawlor (author of *Paul Takes the Form of a Mortal Girl*), who teaches fiction, poetry, queer/trans writing, and fabulist and utopian writing.

Fall: Amherst College hires Sahar Sadjadi, associate professor of Sexuality, Women, and Gender Studies. She studies gender-nonconforming and transgender children.

October: Laverne Cox speaks at UMass, Amherst.

November: Janet Mock speaks at Amherst College. The trans man who reports on the event in *Amherst Student* writes from the closet and uses a pseudonym.

November: COGA introduces preferred names/pronouns to Mount Holyoke Health Services.

2014

January 14: Mount Holyoke hosts "Transgender Student Health Panel" by and for Health Services and Counseling Services staff.

March 7–8: Five College Queer Gender and Sexuality Conference is held at Hampshire College. Keynote speakers: Jiz Lee and Tristan Taormino.

April 24: Smith Q&A organizes Trans Women Belong Here Rally on Smith College campus.

Fall: Sonny Nordmarken (UMass '19, Sociology) offers WGSS 397, "Transgender Politics and Critical Thought," at UMass, Amherst.

September: Mount Holyoke becomes the second all-women's college to accept transgender women applicants, as well as anyone who is not a "cisgender male."

September 26: Smith College's Q&A group hosts a "Transforming Education: Trans Women's Inclusion at Smith" panel, from 4:30–6:30 in the Neilson Library Browsing Room.

October 9: Jennifer Boylan speaks at Mount Holyoke in the wake of its new admissions policy.

October 15: Smith Q&A and Justine Killian (UMass '18) organize another Trans Women Belong Here Rally on Smith's campus.

October 22: Saren Deardorff (Amherst '17), founder of the Trans-Active Five Colleges group, publishes "Being Transgender in the Five Colleges" in *Amherst Student*.

October 30: Mount Holyoke's Dean of College reconvenes new staff/faculty Trans-Identity Committee.

November 18: Hampshire County hosts "Remembering Sylvia Rivera: Transwomen of Color in Context" event.

2015

April: Janet Mock speaks at Smith College.

March 6–7: Five College Queer Gender and Sexuality Conference is held at Hampshire College. Keynote speakers: Lourdes Ashley Hunter and Leah Lakshmi Piepzna-Samarasinha.

May: Smith College announces it will explicitly extend admission to trans women. It will not admit trans men, or genderqueer, or nonbinary students.

Fall: Perry Zurn is hired in School of Critical Social Inquiry at Hampshire College, and as founding faculty of the Ethics and the Common Good Project. He leaves the following year.

Fall: Queer and trans faculty at Hampshire College insist during faculty meetings that faculty also have genders and pronouns, not just students.

October 16: Gender Liberation UMass subscribes to Amherst College's TransActive email listserv, through an email from Nihils Rev to Saren Deardorff.

October 28: UMass, Amherst hosts "Redefining Realness: A Discussion with Janet Mock on Race and Gender." Hampshire's GRN group takes a bus to the event.

November: GLU (Gender Liberation UMass) releases a zine, announcing its formation.

November 12: Amherst Uprising occurs at Amherst College. The statement of demands is signed by the Queer Resource Center and TransActive, among other student groups.

Massachusetts no longer requires surgery for changing sex on birth certificates.

2016

K. J. Rawson launches the Digital Transgender Archive at College of the Holy Cross in Worcester, Massachusetts. The project is supported by an ACL grant (2015–2016).

February 29: Amherst College screens *Tangerine* (2015).

March 4–5: Five College Queer Gender and Sexuality Conference is held at Hampshire College. Keynote speakers: Olympia Perez and Sasha Alexander.

March: Mount Holyoke student government passes a memorandum with proposals to make the college more supportive and inclusive of trans students.

May: *The Amherst Student* publishes a spotlight on Amira Lundy-Harris (they/them), a Black Studies and SWAGS major ('16).

Fall: Amherst College hires Jen Manion (author of *Female Husbands: A Trans History*) as associate professor of history.

Fall: Jeanine Ruhsam is hired to teach trans studies courses in WGSS at UMass, Amherst.

October: Abby Wambach and trans student Emet Marwell ('18) speak about trans-inclusive sport at Mount Holyoke.

October 13: Dean Spade delivers a talk at Amherst College entitled, "Can We Survive Mainstreaming? On the New Visibilities and Invisibilities of Trans Politics."

November: University Health Services at the University of Massachusetts announces it will offer hormone replacement therapy.

November 14–16: Gender Liberation UMass (GLU) stages a "Shit-In."

November 19: First "Trans Futurity Symposium" is held at Hampshire College.

Fall: Ryka Aoki, Talia Bettcher, micha cárdenas, and C. Riley Snorton are the four speakers in UMass, Amherst's Trans* Speaker Series, organized by the university's Women, Gender, and Sexuality Studies department in conjunction with Gender Liberation UMass (GLU), Gender Studies at Mount Holyoke College, and the Five College Women's Studies Research Center.

2017

The Sexual Minorities Archives moves from Northampton to Holyoke, Massachusetts.

February: Mount Holyoke's "MoHo TGNC Facebook Group" forms for trans and gender-nonconforming folks.

March 3–4: Five College Queer Gender and Sexuality Conference is held at Hampshire College. Keynote speaker: T. J. Jourian. Featured speakers: Leah Lakshmi Piepzna-Samarasinha and Morgan M. Page.

April: Laverne Cox speaks at Smith College as the Student Event Committee's (SEC) 2017 Spring Speaker.

April: Sam Davis ('17), senior at Smith College, presents his *In Our Own Words* documentary. As part of the project, Davis also establishes the Trans Archive Oral History Project at Smith College.

April: Gender+ Group hosts "Gender+ Town Hall Meeting" at Mount Holyoke.

May 1: Premiere screening of *Invisible No More: A Queer and Trans History*, documentary directed by Saren Deardorff ('17), at Amherst College.

May: The Sylvia Rivera Community, a queer and trans floor named to honor Latinx trans movement worker and Stonewall veteran Sylvia Rivera, is inaugurated at Amherst College.

Fall: Mount Holyoke College hires Ren-yo Hwang in Gender Studies, Critical Social Thought, and Critical Race and Political Economy.

Fall: Elliot Montague is hired as visiting lecturer in Film and Media Studies at Amherst College.

August: Jxhn Martin (they/them) starts as director of the Queer Resource Center at Amherst College. They remain at Amherst until 2023.

September: Amherst College announces gender-inclusive bathrooms across campus.

October: Amherst College trustee meeting officially adds "gender identity" to its nondiscrimination policy.

October: Cece McDonald speaks at UMass, Amherst following a screening of *Free Cece!*

November: Sahar Sadjadi offers ANTH-353/SWAG-353: Transgender Ethnographies at Amherst College.

November: Amherst College hosts Zachary Drucker, coproducer (with Rhys Ernst, Hampshire '01) of *Transparent*, in an event organized by Jxhn Martin.

Massachusetts passes a law prohibiting discrimination against trans people in public spaces.

2018

Cassils offers an artist lecture at Amherst College.

Jordy Rosenberg (UMass, Amherst, English) publishes *Confessions of the Fox*.

March 2–3: Five College Queer Gender and Sexuality Conference is held at Hampshire College. Featured speakers include Kavindu Ade and Jamila Hammami.

April: Amherst College hosts "Transgender Politics Now" event, including Kai Green, Cecilia Gentili, and Rosza Daniel Lang/Levitsky. Sahar Sadjadi organizes.

April: Mount Holyoke hosts "Surviving and Thriving: An Artistic Celebration for Trans and Nonbinary Students, Staff and Faculty" event featuring Davey Shlasko, Tobias Davis, and Yusef Flores.

April: Cavar ('20) publishes, in *Mount Holyoke News*, "Autistic and Transgender Communities Should Build Solidarity Together."

Summer: Leo Rachman ('20) organizes Mount Holyoke archives exhibit "Trans Lives at Mount Holyoke Today."

Fall: Cameron Awkward-Rich is hired at UMass, Amherst in Women, Gender, Sexuality Studies and offers a course called

"Reading Transgender." His first theory book, *The Terrible We: Thinking with Trans Maladjustment*, appears in 2022.

Fall: Trans Empowerment Series at Amherst College includes non-binary affinity space and a QTPOC dinner with Alok Vaid-Menon.

Fall: Dean Spade and Jen Manion (Amherst College, History) publish public pieces for and against pronoun go-rounds.

September: UMass's Trans Studies Working Group (T-SWAG) by and for grad students hosts its first meeting: Cameron Awkward-Rich offers a job market workshop, "Going on the Market While Trans."

2019

Spring: Jen Manion offers Transgender Histories course at Amherst College.

February: Ace/Aro support group available at Amherst College.

March 1–3: Five College Queer Gender and Sexuality Conference is held at Hampshire College. Keynote speakers: Caleb Luna and Cyree Jarelle Johnson. Featured speakers include Gavin Grimm.

November 16: Second "Trans Futurity" Symposium is held at Hampshire College.

October: UMassAmherst's Stonewall Center Director Genny Beemyn receives first Lou Sullivan Torch Award.

2020

Spring: A new group called "Mx. Holyoke" is established for trans/gender-nonconforming students at Mount Holyoke.

Jen Jack Gieseking (Mount Holyoke '99) publishes *A Queer New York*.

notes

PREFACE

1. At the urging of this moment, I collaboratively reconstructed the story of trans life at American University. See Zurn et al., "The AU Experience: Then and Now."
2. Feinberg, *Stone Butch Blues*.

INTRODUCTION

1. Chess, Kafer, Quizar, and Richardson, "Calling All Restroom Revolutionaries!"
2. Gershenson and Penner, "Introduction," 8; Gershenson, "The Restroom Revolution."
3. Dove, "Mission" email to Restroom Revolution members.
4. For five definitions of failure relevant to activist work, see Zurn, "Work and Failure."
5. See the W. Clyde Fitch (AC 1886) Collection.
6. Lester, "Gay? Straight? Vive la Différence."
7. Cawley, "You Don't Have to Be a Lesbian to Live Here."
8. Cawley, "You Don't Have to Be a Lesbian to Live Here."
9. Power, "Brief Autobiographical Information on Ben Power."
10. Painter, *Sojourner Truth*, 89.
11. For more on the original design and mission of Mount Holyoke College and Smith College, see Horowitz, *Alma Mater*.
12. Patterson, *The Making of a College*.
13. Personal interview with Jorge, October 5, 2017.
14. See UMass alum Siegel, "Transgender Experiences and Transphobia in Higher Education."
15. Awkward-Rich, "I Wish I Knew How It Would Feel to Be Free."
16. See Davis, Trans Archive Oral History Project.
17. Personal interview with Jason, October 4, 2017.
18. I borrow the term *gender disruptors* from Micha Broadnax, Mount Holyoke librarian.
19. Moten, *A Poetics of the Undercommons*, 24.
20. Harney and Moten, *The Undercommons*, 74–75.

21. Harney and Moten, *The Undercommons*, 50; Tsang and Moten, "All Terror, All Beauty," 347.

22. Gossett, Stanley, and Burton, eds., *Trap Door*.

23. Gieseking, *A Queer New York*, 198.

24. Gieseking, *A Queer New York*, 198.

25. Gieseking, *A Queer New York*, xix.

26. Astronomer, "Anniversary in Loneliness."

27. Astronomer, "Anniversary in Loneliness," 8.

28. Horsman, "Astronomer Led Double Life," 1.

29. Tolkien, "Letter to Michael."

1. PROBLEMATIZING TRANS INCLUSION

1. Russell Pollitt, Li, and Grossman, "Chosen Name Use Is Linked to Reduced Depressive Symptoms."

2. Catalano and Shlasko, "Transgender Oppression."

3. Nicolazzo, *Trans* in College*; Pitcher, *Being and Becoming Professionally Other*.

4. Bassichis, Lee, and Spade, "Building an Abolitionist Trans and Queer Movement with Everything We've Got," 30.

5. Medina, "Preferred Gender Pronouns." Another student revised the handout title in 2016 to simply read "Pronouns Handout."

6. Personal interview with Mateo Medina, January 10, 2018.

7. Manion, "The Performance of Transgender Inclusion."

8. Spade, "We Still Need Pronoun Go-Rounds."

9. Rich, "Invisibility in Academe," 218.

10. Manion, *Liberty's Prisoners*; Spade, *Normal Life*.

11. Manion, *Female Husbands*; Spade, *Mutual Aid*.

12. Foucault, "Polemics, Politics, and Problematizations," 118.

13. Foucault, *Fearless Speech*, 74.

14. Foucault, *Fearless Speech*, 74, 171.

15. Foucault, *The Use of Pleasure*, 13.

16. Foucault, "Problematics," 418.

17. Killerman, "Genderbread Person."

18. Ferguson, *The Reorder of Things*.

19. Beemyn, "Serving the Needs of Transgender College Students"; Beemyn, "Making Campuses More Inclusive of Transgender Students"; Beemyn and Rankin, "Transgender Youth and Implications for Higher Education"; Beemyn, "Introduction."

20. Beemyn, Domingue, Pettitt, and Smith, "Suggested Steps to Make Campuses More Trans-Inclusive."

21. Goldberg, Beemyn, and Smith, "What Is Needed, What Is Valued."

22. Personal interview with Crys, July 21, 2020.

23. Nicolazzo, *Trans* in College*, 16.

24. Pitcher, *Being and Becoming Professionally Other*, 191.

25. Personal interview with Crys, July 21, 2020.

2. BECOMING A TRANS PROBLEM

1. Personal interview with Pat, March 16, 2020.
2. Du Bois, *Souls of Black Folk*, 5.
3. Du Bois, *Souls of Black Folk*, 5, 8.
4. Ahmed, *Living a Feminist Life*, 34.
5. Smith, "Mount Holyoke from the Other Side: I."
6. Smith, "Mount Holyoke from the Other Side: I."
7. McCarthy, "Mount Holyoke from the Other Side: III."
8. Ainsworth, "Mount Holyoke from the Other Side: II." As if to underscore this communal character, the issue features a photo of Smith, Ainsworth, and McCarthy sitting together smiling while a large dog nuzzles Smith.
9. Ahmed explicitly roots her thinking of "problem" in Du Bois and Philomena Essed. See Ahmed, *On Being Included*, 152–53; Ahmed, "Black Feminism as Life-Line." Interestingly, in her account of "problems" in *Living a Feminist Life*, where she is committed to citing only women, she uses her own memories of being a problem as her theoretical source.
10. Ahmed, "An Affinity of Hammers."
11. Ahmed, *On Being Included*, 152–53.
12. Ahmed, *Living a Feminist Life*, 37.
13. This chapter was written before Sara Ahmed's *The Feminist Killjoy Handbook* was released, but the latter could certainly guide further analysis.
14. Ahmed, *Willful Subjects*, 2.
15. Ahmed, *Living a Feminist Life*, 172.
16. Ahmed, *Living a Feminist Life*, 74–75; see also 80.
17. Ahmed, *Willful Subjects*, 97, 115.
18. Ahmed, *Willful Subjects*, 137; see also *Living a Feminist Life*, 67, 70, 84.
19. Ahmed, *Living a Feminist Life*, 83; *Willful Subjects*, 144, 150, 164.
20. Ahmed, *Willful Subjects*, 152.
21. Ahmed, *Willful Subjects*, 161, 167.
22. Ahmed, *The Promise of Happiness*, 62.
23. Ahmed, *Living a Feminist Life*, 187–212.
24. See Ahmed, *Living a Feminist Life*, 268.
25. See Ahmed, *The Promise of Happiness*, 70.
26. Ahmed, *Living a Feminist Life*, 261.
27. Ahmed, *Living a Feminist Life*, 255.
28. Ahmed explicitly muses on the willful arm becoming collective in the form of a feminist army. See *Willful Subjects*, 173–204.
29. There is already a certain intimacy between doing and enjoying, often lost in a neoliberal economy. The Latin *fructi* means both to use and to enjoy, while the term *function* stems from the Proto-Indo-European *bhung* meaning "be of use" and its related root *bhrug* meaning "to enjoy."
30. Ahmed, *Queer Phenomenology*.
31. Ahmed, *Living a Feminist Life*, 84, 235.

32. Palmero, "UMass Students Hold 'Sh*t-In'"; Lindahl, "Protestors Demand Gender-Neutral Bathrooms at Mass"; Bowman, "Bathroom Occupation Begins at Whitmore Administration Building"; Foster, "Bathroom Stalls in Whitmore Occupied"; Foster, "Protest for Gender-Neutral Bathrooms Continue for Second Day"; Moye, "UMass Students' Hold 'S**t In.'"

33. Palmero, "UMass Students Hold 'Sh*t-In.'"

34. Moye, "UMass Students' Hold 'S**t In.'"

35. GLU, "What's Up with the Shit-In?" flyer, shared with me by interviewee Justine (personal correspondence, November 22, 2020). The phrase "critical transmisogyny from an intersectional perspective" is an unusual one, utilizing a locution not otherwise used in trans studies or trans activism. I take GLU to mean intersectional transfeminism that focuses critically on deconstructing transmisogyny.

36. Moye, "UMass Students' Hold 'S**t In.'"

37. Bhabha, *The Location of Culture*, 52–56.

38. GLU, "Transgender Health Survey," shared with me by interviewee Justine (personal correspondence, November 22, 2020).

39. GLU, "Letter Draft," shared with me by interviewee Justine (personal correspondence, November 22, 2020).

40. Palmero, "UMass Students Hold 'Sh*t-In.'"

41. Bowman, "Bathroom Occupation Begins at Whitmore Administration Building."

42. GLU, "Monday Marshals," shared with me by interviewee Justine (personal correspondence, November 22, 2020).

43. Moye, "UMass Students' Hold 'S**t In.'"

44. GLU, "GLU 'Shit-In' Sign Up!," shared with me by interviewee Justine (personal correspondence, November 22, 2020).

45. Stryker, Currah, and Moore, "Trans-, Trans, or Transgender," 13.

46. Stryker, Currah, and Moore, "Trans-, Trans, or Transgender," 14.

47. Stryker, Currah, and Moore, "Trans-, Trans, or Transgender," 14.

48. Aizura et al., "Thinking with Trans Now," 131, 134, 135.

49. DiPietro, "Of *Huachafería, Así*, and *M'e Mati*," 70.

50. Bey, *Black Trans Feminism*, 147.

51. Bey, *Black Trans Feminism*, 147.

52. Bey, *Black Trans Feminism*, 147.

53. Bey, *Black Trans Feminism*, 157.

54. Bey, *Black Trans Feminism*, 160.

55. See Malatino, *Side Affects*.

56. Palmero, "UMass Students Hold 'Sh*t-In.'"

57. Bowman, "Bathroom Occupation Begins at Whitmore Administration Building."

58. UMass Fossil Fuel Divestment Campaign, "Divest UMass Stands with Gender Liberation UMass."

59. Lindahl, "Protestors Demand Gender-Neutral Bathrooms at UMass." See UMass Fossil Fuel Divestment Campaign Facebook post (November 14, 2016): "In the meantime, maybe they will feel a little bit as anxious as trans students do just trying to pee."

60. Amanda Jean Fadum Hall was the ally and artist (under the name "Bitty Vicious") who created Gloux. Hall died in May the following spring, as her obituary reports,

"due to complications from an earlier suicide attempt caused by her battle with bipolar disorder." Neither Hall's suicidality nor her bipolar disorder are unique among GLU activists. As such, Gloux appropriately depicts an in-sane, un-stable force at work not only for trans policy, here, but also within an on-the-ground trans poetics. See "Obituary of Amanda Jean Fadum Hall."

61. Palmero, "UMass Students Hold 'Sh*t-In.'"
62. The group here cites a line from Roy, "Confronting Empire."
63. UMass Fossil Fuel Divestment Campaign, "Divest UMass Stands with Gender Liberation UMass."
64. Awkward-Rich, "I Wish I Knew How It Would Feel to Be Free."
65. Harney and Moten, *The Undercommons*, 30.
66. Halberstam, "The Wild Beyond," in Harney and Moten, *The Undercommons*, 3.

3. MOBILIZING TRANS POETICS

Epigraph: Oliver Bendorf, "Split Open Just to Count the Pieces," 417.

1. Aristotle, *Poetics*, 1447a.
2. Aristotle, *Poetics*.
3. Heidegger, *Poetry, Language, Thought*.
4. Bachelard, *The Poetics of Space*.
5. Bachelard, *The Poetics of Space*, xxxv.
6. Anzaldúa, *Borderlands / La Frontera*, 88.
7. Anzaldúa, *Light in the Dark / Los en lo oscuro*, 108.
8. Glissant, *The Poetics of Relation*, 29.
9. Glissant, *The Poetics of Relation*, 1.
10. Glissant, *The Poetics of Relation*, 32.
11. Glissant, *Introduction à une poétique du divers*, 25.
12. Glissant, *Introduction à une poétique du divers*, 43–44.
13. For implications of creolization for politics, see Sealey, *Creolizing the Nation*.
14. Personal interview with Ben, March 21, 2020.
15. See Brown, *Emergent Strategy*.
16. Personal interview with Helder, May 31, 2013.
17. Edwards, "Trans Poetics," 252.
18. Tolbert and Peterson, eds., *Troubling the Line*; Abi-Karam and Gabriel, eds., *We Want It All*.
19. Abi-Karam and Gabriel, *We Want It All*, 3, 4.
20. Tolbert, "Open, and Always, Opening," 9–10.
21. Shipley, "The Transformative and Queer Language of Poetry," 197; Ace, "The Language of the Seeing the Language of the Blind," 436; Tolbert, "The Gifts of the Body Are the Gifts of Imperfection," 465.
22. Bendorf, "Poetics Statement," 422.
23. Peterson, "Being Unreadable and Being Read," 20.
24. Shipley, "The Transformative and Queer Language of Poetry," 198; Edwards, "A Narrative of Resistance," 325; cárdenas, "Statement on Poetics," 396, 398.
25. Day, "Poetics Statement," 387; Bendorf, "Poetics Statement," 422.
26. Myles, "My Boy's Red Hat," 176.

27. Banias, "On Being a Stranger," 64; Luengsuraswat, "Poetics Statement," 86.
28. Bodhran, "Carved Crimson into the Bark of a White Page," 34.
29. Romero, "Poetics Statement," 219; see Bronson, "Poetics Statement," 356.
30. Herman, "Poetics Statement," 42–44; Crandall, "Feeling of My Memory," 169.
31. Herman, "Poetics Statement," 42–44; Selke, "Poetics Statement," 367.
32. Bronson, "Poetics Statement," 356; Hastain, "Poetics Statement," 255.
33. Krawitz, "Poetics Statement," 113.
34. Krawitz, "Poetics Statement," 113.
35. Krawitz, "Poetics Statement," 114; Herman, "Poetics Statement," 43; Hegnauer, "Statement on a Gendered Possibility," 236–37.
36. Oliver Bendorf describes it as a "site of counterintimacies." See Bendorf, "Poetics Statement," 423.
37. D'Lo, "Poetics Statement," 122; see Keer, "Poetics Statement," 227; and Peck, "Real Poetry Transifesto," 408.
38. CAConrad, "Don't Take Any Shit!!," 94.
39. Harris, "Poetics Statement," 159.
40. Personal interview with Ashling, October 4, 2017.
41. Latini, "Gloria Talks Back to Patti Smith."
42. Edidi, *Baltimore*, 21; source of the latter quotation unknown.
43. Theonia, "When You're Trans in the Brooklyn Summertime," 30.
44. Aguhar, "These Are the Axes"; Aguhar, "Litanies to My Heavenly Brown Body."
45. Harney and Moten, *The Undercommons*.
46. Moten, *A Poetics of the Undercommons*, 24.
47. Moten, *A Poetics of the Undercommons*, 34–36.
48. Moten, *A Poetics of the Undercommons*, 30.
49. Harney and Moten, *The Undercommons*, 28, 30, 50, 52, 61, 81, 94, 137–138. Similarly, Halberstam, in his preface to the book, summarizes the peopling of the undercommons as Black, Indigenous, queer, poor, and crazy. See Halberstam, "The Wild Beyond," 6, 11.
50. Harney and Moten, *The Undercommons*, 47, 50.
51. Harney and Moten, *The Undercommons*, 49.
52. Harney and Moten, *The Undercommons*, 50.
53. For more on this relationship, see the work of, for example, Marquis Bey, Che Gossett, Kai Green, Matt Richardson, SA Smythe, and C. Riley Snorton.
54. Tsang and Moten, "All Terror, All Beauty," 347.
55. Tsang and Moten, "All Terror, All Beauty," 52, 105.
56. Halberstam, "The Wild Beyond," 12; Harney and Moten, *The Undercommons*, 81.
57. Harney and Moten, *The Undercommons*, 110.
58. Harney and Moten, *The Undercommons*, 98.
59. Harney and Moten, *The Undercommons*, 98.
60. Harney and Moten, *The Undercommons*, 74–75.
61. Harney and Moten, *The Undercommons*, 82.
62. See Hale in Zurn and Pitts, eds., "Trans Philosophy."
63. See, by way of comparison, Stryker, Currah, and Moore, "Trans-, Trans, or Transgender."

64. Lugones, *Pilgrimages/Peregrinajes*, 214–15.
65. See Davis, "Interview with S"; Personal interview with Emery, March 21, 2020.
66. The name of the group, The Queer Does Not End Here, certainly resonates with José Esteban Muñoz's famous claim, "queerness is not yet here." If queerness is not yet here but constantly deferred, queerness also cannot end here. There will always be a remainder both in the future and in the present.
67. Pryor, *Time Slips*, 139.
68. "The Queer Does Not End Here," Tumblr.
69. *Something Queer Happened Here*.
70. Drowning may occur when the blowhole is obstructed for a lengthy period of time during high tide.
71. See Gibson, "Do You Know Whales."
72. Hampshire Queer Community Alliance Center was formed in 1992, following a takeover of the Cole Science Building by students insisting on "more multi-cultural American education." See Hampshire College, "Dis-Orientation Packet."
73. Zique, "Opening Statement."
74. Personal interview with Spencer, July 24, 2020.
75. Pryor, *Time Slips*, 139.
76. Hollibaugh, *My Dangerous Desires*, 269.

4. ATTUNEMENTS TO TRANS HISTORY

1. Derrida, *Monolingualism of the Other*, 10.
2. Derrida, *Archive Fever*, 10.
3. Derrida, *Archive Fever*, 12.
4. Derrida, *Archive Fever*, 81.
5. Derrida, *Archive Fever*, 90.
6. Derrida, *Archive Fever*, 93, 95.
7. Foucault, *Archeology of Knowledge*, 130.
8. Foucault, *Archeology of Knowledge*, 129.
9. Foucault, *Archeology of Knowledge*, 131.
10. Foucault, "Lives of Infamous Men," 159.
11. Foucault, "Lives of Infamous Men," 158.
12. Cvetkovich, *Archive of Feelings*, 16.
13. Stewart, *Space on the Side of the Road*, 34.
14. Cvetkovich, *Archive of Feelings*, 12 and 17.
15. Cvetkovich, *Archive of Feelings*, 243.
16. Cvetkovich, *Archive of Feelings*, chapters 5, 6.
17. Hartman, "Venus in Two Acts," 2.
18. Hartman, *Scenes of Subjection*; Hartman, *Lose Your Mother*; Hartman, *Wayward Lives*, xiv.
19. Hartman, *Wayward Lives*, xiv; Hartman, *Lose Your Mother*, 11.
20. Hartman, "Venus in Two Acts," 10, 5.
21. Hartman, "Venus in Two Acts," 2–3.
22. Hartman, "Venus in Two Acts," 11.

23. Hartman, "Venus in Two Acts," 12.
24. Hartman, "Venus in Two Acts," 10.
25. Raymond, *The Transsexual Empire*, 104.
26. Card, "Rape as a Weapon of War," 14.
27. Raymond, *Doublethink*, 95; see Raymond, *Transsexual Empire*, xxv.
28. Raymond, *Doublethink*, 95.
29. Raymond, *Passion for Friends*, 8.
30. Raymond, *Passion for Friends*, 25.
31. Raymond, *Passion for Friends*, 19, 27.
32. Personal interview with Micha Broadnax, March 27, 2020.
33. Sandra, "SYSTA," 6.
34. Gerstein, "LBA Celebrates Coming Out."
35. Gamble, "Transgender Panel."
36. Delgado, "SYSTA"; Lim, "SYSTA," 2001.
37. Lim, "SYSTA," 2001; Lim, "SYSTA," 2002.
38. See SYSTA description, *Slip of the Tongue* 2.1 (1999–2000).
39. Johnson, "Reflections on Gay Life at Amherst." See also Johnson's work advocating for the Gay Liberation movement on campus in Johnson and Cleaver, "Gay Lib" and Marks, "Gay Libbers at Amherst."
40. Whittemore, "A Glorious Woman."
41. American Heritage Center, "Technical Writer S. J. Moffat"; American Heritage Center, "Transitioning to Her True Self"; Walsh, "Celebrating LGBTQ Pride."
42. Waggener, "Oral Histories with the S. J. Moffat Family."
43. See, especially, Moffat and Williams, "Book Proposal." Intriguingly, she credits much to her Aunt Mildred (Morton Gilbert), an editor at *Vogue*, for her familiarity with artistic impulse, femme fashion, and queer life.
44. Leeb, "In Memory."
45. It should also be noted that Michelle Allison '64 is a trans graduate of Amherst College, but she transitioned in 2015, at the age of seventy-three. She spoke at Amherst's Reunion in 2019; See Allison, "About Michelle;" Allison, "A View from the Trans* Bridge."
46. Snorton and Haritaworn, "Trans Necropolitics."
47. Deleuze and Guattari, *A Thousand Plateaus*. In *Queer Embodiment*, Malatino argues that state science helps illuminate medical and psychiatric institutions, while nomad or minor science helps elucidate trans modes of embodiment (176). Here I am suggesting there is both a state science and a minor science to trans history and it is the latter I aim to practice.

5. DUST

1. Amato, *Dust*.
2. Guattari and Rolnik, *Molecular Revolution in Brazil*.
3. Marder, *Dust*, xi.
4. Marder, *Dust*, xi.
5. Marder, *Dust*, 24, 21.
6. Marder, *Dust*, 45.

7. Marder, *Dust*, 58.

8. This is perhaps another way to describe the identity processes described by UMass alum Nordmarken, "Coming into Identity."

9. Steedman, *Dust*, 164.

10. Aoki, *Why Dust Shall Never Settle Upon This Soul*, 38.

11. Awkward-Rich, *Sympathetic Little Monster*, 75.

12. "Dust Bunny."

13. Personal interview with Jan, March 9, 2020.

14. *Camp Transfeminism*; GLU, *Gender Liberation UMass*. *Camp Transfeminism* is an oblique reference to Camp Trans, an annual protest, originating in the early 1990s, against trans exclusion from the Michigan Womyn's Festival.

15. *Camp Transfeminism*, 1.

16. *Camp Transfeminism*, 2, 14.

17. *Camp Transfeminism*, 18.

18. Personal interview with Ella, April 29, 2024.

19. Personal interview with Ella, April 29, 2024.

20. Raymond, *The Transsexual Empire*.

21. Minutes of Chancellor's Task Force on G/L/B Matters.

22. Minutes of Chancellor's Task Force for Gay, Lesbian, Bisexual, and Transgender Matters; Memo from David K. Scott to Felice Yeskel. Not incidentally, that same month of May 1995 saw the Stonewall Center come into its name as a way of incorporating trans issues as well. See BG, "Program for LGBT Concerns Changes Name to Stonewall Center."

23. GLBT Task Force Members List, version 1.

24. Fordham, Committee and Member Updates.

25. GLBT Task Force Members List, version 2.

26. Larke, "Queer Profs Speak on Life Experiences."

27. Personal interview with Jadyn, April 3, 2020.

28. Page, "No Black Public Sphere in White Space"; Page, "Academentia," 17. Page's scholarship and teaching on race earned him a critical report; see Wood, "No Escape at U Mass Amherst."

29. Anonymous, "Whiteness in Transsexual Activism," 10; Page and Richardson, "On the Fear of Small Numbers." Page receives a gentle acknowledgment as a "friend of my mind" in Snorton, *Black on Both Sides*, 201.

30. Personal correspondence with Enoch Page, December 15, 2023.

31. Page, Faculty Profile.

32. Personal correspondence with Enoch Page, August 8, 2023.

33. Personal interview with Enoch Page, September 13, 2023.

34. Personal interview with Marta, June 21, 2023.

35. Page, Faculty Profile.

36. Page, *On Being a Witness*.

37. Page, "The Environment"; Page, "Dr. Enoch Page."

38. LGBTQ Religious Archives Network, "The Historical Development of BIPOC Trans-spiritual Leadership."

39. Personal interview with Ben Power, August 8, 2018.

6. STASH

1. "Stash," *Oxford English Dictionary*.
2. A related sense is "to quit," as in the intriguing phrase "stash the glim" which means "put out the light."
3. Clare, *Brilliant Imperfection*, 46.
4. Clare, *Brilliant Imperfection*, 46.
5. Clare, *Brilliant Imperfection*, 114.
6. Raha, "Embodying Autonomous Trans Health Care in Zines," 196n2.
7. Harney and Moten, *The Undercommons*, 26.
8. Harney and Moten, *All Incomplete*, 14, 30–31.
9. Harney and Moten, *All Incomplete*, 167.
10. Davis, "Interview with Davey Shlasko."
11. Simmons, dir., *TransGeneration*.
12. Davis, "Interview with Everett (Izzy) Owen."
13. Davis, dir., *In Our Own Words*.
14. Foucault, *The Order of Things*, xv.
15. Ferguson, *Reorder of Things*, 229.
16. Ferguson, *Reorder of Things*, 230.
17. Ferguson, *Reorder of Things*, 231, 232.
18. "Power & Memory."
19. Personal interview with Lark, October 4–5, 2017.
20. Ferguson, *We Demand*, 91.
21. Rawson, "Accessing Transgender // Desiring Queer(er?) Archival Logics." It should be noted that Rawson developed the Digital Transgender Archive (launched in 2016), in neighboring Worcester and then Boston, which similarly attempts to queer and to trans traditional archival logics in its construction and maintenance. See https://www.digitaltransgenderarchive.net/about/overview.
22. Zinn, "Secrecy, Archives, and the Public Interest," 20.
23. Rosenberg, *Confessions of the Fox*, x.
24. Rosenberg, *Confessions of the Fox*, 122, 124.
25. Rosenberg, *Confessions of the Fox*, 258.
26. Rosenberg, *Confessions of the Fox*, 166.
27. Rosenberg, *Confessions of the Fox*, 315–16.
28. Rawson, "Archival Justice," 184.
29. Rawson, "Archival Justice," 186.
30. Rawson, "Archival Justice," 186.
31. Rawson, "Archival Justice," 186.
32. Rawson, "Archival Justice," 181.
33. Rawson, "Archival Justice," 181.
34. Rawson, "Archival Justice," 184.
35. Rawson, "Archival Justice," 187
36. See Cohen and Duckert, eds., *Veer Ecology*.
37. Barad, *Meeting the Universe Halfway*.
38. Barad, "Transmaterialities," 387.

39. The importance of Yiddish in the Connecticut River Valley ought not go unremarked. The Yiddish Book Center, hosted on Hampshire College's campus, boasts the largest collection of Yiddish texts in the world.

40. Davis, "Interview with Davey Shlasko."

41. Personal interview with Agni, March 25, 2020.

42. Personal interview with Jack, July 7, 2020.

7. SCATTER

1. "Scatter," *Oxford English Dictionary*.
2. Cavar, "Loving Trans into Possible."
3. Derrida, "Différance."
4. Bennington, *Scatter 1*, 2; Bennington, *Scatter 2*, 9.
5. Glissant, *Caribbean Discourse*, 19, 255n1.
6. Glissant, *Poetics of Relation*, 33.
7. By *crip*, I understand a critical positionality and politic that unmasks the ideological co-construction of ability and white cisheteronormativity. See McRuer, *Crip Theory*; and Kim, "Toward a Crip-of-Color Critique."
8. I borrow the term *scatterscram* from Cavar, personal correspondence, May 7, 2023.
9. I offer this trans/crip analytic as supplement to the trans/crip temporalities and microtactics developed by Alexandre Baril and Max Thornton to highlight the shared misfitting of trans and crip life. See Baril, "An Intersectional Analysis of 'Trans-crip't Time'"; and Thornton, "Trans/Criptions."
10. In my retelling, I rely on the student-produced zine covering the incident: *Something Queer Happened Here*, shared with me by interviewee Micah (personal correspondence, October 14, 2018), as well as corroborating accounts offered by multiple interviewees and Pryor's account in *Time Slips*, 168–201.
11. *Something Queer Happened Here*, 3.
12. *Something Queer Happened Here*, 4.
13. *Something Queer Happened Here*, 6.
14. Zurn, "Waste Culture and Isolation"; Zurn, "Bathroom."
15. Manne, *Down Girl*.
16. Cavanaugh, *Queering Bathrooms*.
17. Moore, "Colonial Visions of 'Third World' Toilets," 105–25; Abel, "Bathroom Doors and Drinking Fountains."
18. Lugones, "Heterosexualism and the Colonial/Modern Gender System"; Spillers, "Mama's Baby, Papa's Maybe."
19. Hampshire, "Dis-Orientation Packet."
20. *Something Queer Happened Here*, 21.
21. *Something Queer Happened Here*, 5, 8, 12–13.
22. *Something Queer Happened Here*, 33; Personal interview with Melissa, October 4–5, 2017.
23. Awkward-Rich, *Terrible We*, 55.
24. Awkward-Rich, *Terrible We*, 2; Stryker, "(De)Subjugated Knowledges," 1–2.

25. Awkward-Rich, *Terrible We*, 59.

26. Awkward-Rich, *Terrible We*, 32, 44, 58.

27. Awkward-Rich, *Terrible We*, 93.

28. Awkward-Rich, *Terrible We*, 94, 95, 108.

29. Awkward-Rich, *Terrible We*, 19, 20; McCullers, *Member of the Wedding*, 42.

30. Awkward-Rich, *Terrible We*, 150, 165n16. See also Awkward-Rich's use of the "motley we" in "I Wish I Knew How It Would Feel to Be Free," and "Feeling That Motley We."

31. Harney and Moten, *The Undercommons*, 74.

32. *Something Queer Happened Here*, 21, 20.

33. *Something Queer Happened Here*, 9.

34. *Something Queer Happened Here*, 8, 21, 3, 4.

35. *Something Queer Happened Here*, 2. Two references to *crazy* also occur in Omi Osun/Dr. Joni Jones, "Six Rules for Allies," republished in *Something Queer Happened Here*, 10–12.

36. *Something Queer Happened Here*, 5.

37. *Something Queer Happened Here*, 4.

38. *Something Queer Happened Here*, 32.

39. *Something Queer Happened Here*, 15.

40. As one such exception, consider Davis, "Interview with Miles (Abah) Collins-Sibley."

41. See, by way of comparison, Williams v. Kincaid.

42. Cavar, "Toward transMad Epistemologies;" Burke, "Cis Sense."

43. Cavar, "Keeping It Surreal."

44. Cavar, "In Praise of -Less."

45. T-SWAG (Trans Studies Working Group), 2018–2019.

46. Nordmarken, "Becoming Ever More Monstrous"; Nordmarken, "Queering Gendering."

47. Nordmarken, "Contesting Lyme."

48. Nordmarken, "Contesting Lyme," 437.

49. Cavar, "In-Cite"; see also Nash, "Citational Desires."

50. Zurn, *Curiosity and Power*, x.

8. ATTUNEMENTS TO TRANS RESISTANCE

1. The English word *jam*, in both senses, is apparently of onomatopoetic origin.

2. Hilton, "Mapping the Wander Lines."

3. Other creatures Deligny aligns with the spider include the turtle, the protozoa, the water lizard, and the fossil.

4. Deligny, *The Arachnean*, 54. The term first appears in 1972. See Deligny, *Cartes et Lignes d'Erre*, 6.

5. Deligny, *The Arachnean*, 140; Deligny, *Cartes et Lignes d'Erre*, 12.

6. Deligny, *The Arachnean*, 156.

7. Miguel, "Towards a New Thinking on Humanism."

8. Certeau, *The Practice of Everyday Life*, vol. 1; Certeau, Giard, and Mayol, *The Practice of Everyday Life*, vol. 2.

9. Certeau, *The Practice of Everyday Life*, vol. 1, xix.
10. Certeau, *The Practice of Everyday Life*, vol. 1, 34.
11. Certeau, *The Practice of Everyday Life*, vol. 1, 91–110.
12. Certeau, *The Practice of Everyday Life*, vol. 1, 98.
13. Certeau, *The Practice of Everyday Life*, vol. 1, xii.
14. Certeau, *The Practice of Everyday Life*, vol. 1, 101.
15. Certeau, *The Practice of Everyday Life*, vol. 1, 105.
16. DiPietro, McWeeny, and Roshanravan, eds., *Speaking Face to Face*.
17. Lugones, *Pilgrimages/Peregrinajes*, 211.
18. Lugones, *Pilgrimages/Peregrinajes*, 209.
19. Lugones, *Pilgrimages/Peregrinajes*, 219.
20. Lugones, *Pilgrimages/Peregrinajes*, 224.
21. Lugones, *Pilgrimages/Peregrinajes*, 213, 221.
22. Lugones, *Pilgrimages/Peregrinajes*, 221.
23. Lugones, *Pilgrimages/Peregrinajes*, 215.
24. Tucker, "Catholic School Accepting Change." See also Sister Laura Reicks, "Letter to Parents of Mercy High School"; Morris-Young, "Catholic School Won't Fire Transgender Teacher"; Ford, "Transgender Bodies, Catholic Schools, and a Queer Natural Law Theology of Exploration." Ford points out that Cordileone's appeal to prudential judgment "clarifies nothing," implying that the choice to retain Stein-Bodenheimer is just as legitimate as the choice not to retain him (75).
25. Eliot, "The Love Song of J. Alfred Prufrock."
26. Eliot, "The Love Song of J. Alfred Prufrock," 10–12.
27. Jews in the Woods, "About Jews in the Woods."
28. S., "In the Woods."
29. Bazant, *Timtum*, 1.
30. Kukla, "A Created Being of Its Own."
31. Keefe, "SGA Beat / Students Split on Gender Issues," 2.
32. Porras, "Arguments against Gender Neutral Constitution Shallow and Embarrassing," 10.
33. Robinson, "Transgender Coverage on Fox," 1.
34. Russell, "Groups Take Gender Out of Event Names," 1.
35. Staff Editorial, "Trans Advocates Alienate Students with Vandalism," 8.
36. Staff Editorial, "We Need to Address 'Thought Police' at Smith," 8.
37. Laas, "Senate Votes to Keep Gender Neutral Language in Constitution," 1.
38. Laas, "Senate Votes to Keep Gender Neutral Language in Constitution," 1.
39. Roth, "Dining Changes May Impact Alumnae Gifts," 9.
40. Prosnitz, "Poorly Proposed Dining Hall Changes," 8.
41. "Letters to the Editor," 8.
42. Personal interview with Silas, December 23, 2021.
43. Reimold, "Controversial 'Cashmere and Pearls' Letter."
44. Ford, "Campus Committee Explores New Dining Options," 1.
45. Miller, "Kitchen Work Study Jobs Face Cuts," 3.
46. Hazard, *Underflows*.

9. THREAD

Epigraph 1: Leslie Feinberg, *Trans Liberation*, 101.
Epigraph 2: Rike Frank, *Textiles—Open Letter*, 28–29.
1. See Davis, "Interview with Eddie/Edsuvani Maisonet."
2. Maisonet, "Sounding It Out," 244.
3. Maisonet, "Sounding It Out," 246.
4. Maisonet, "Sounding It Out," 245.
5. On a different register, Maisonet elsewhere speaks of his experience with suicidality and trans lifelines. See Maisonet, "Eddie Maisonet."
6. Maisonet, "Sounding It Out," 245.
7. Maisonet, "Sounding It Out," 245.
8. Personal interview with Joshua, July 10, 2020.
9. See also Smith alum Vaccaro, "Felt Matters" and "Feelings and Fractals."
10. Alvarez, "Finding Sequins in the Rubble."
11. Dormer, *Philosophy of Textile*.
12. Dormer, *Philosophy of Textile*, 4.
13. See Deleuze, *The Fold*.
14. Dormer, *Philosophy of Textile*, 13.
15. Dormer, *Philosophy of Textile*, 47.
16. Dormer, *Philosophy of Textile*, 44.
17. Dormer, *Philosophy of Textile*, 88, 97.
18. Steinbock, *Shimmering Images*.
19. Butler, *Gender Trouble*; Halberstam, *Female Masculinity*.
20. For a study of the challenges of recording some of those histories, see Kumbier, "Archiving Drag King Communities from the Ground Up."
21. Personal interview with Oliver, May 17, 2021.
22. Ferguson, "Clothing Swaps." For the difficult work of thinking neoliberalism's effects on clothing swaps, see Deflorian, "Refigurative Politics."
23. Fenstermacher, "Transgender Awareness Week," 1.
24. "Transgender Awareness Week" flyer.
25. Fenstermacher, "Transgender Awareness Week," 4, citing Milo Primeaux, co-chair of the Trans/Gender and Allies Group.
26. Davis, "Interview with Ryan Rasdall."
27. Personal interview with Blake, February 12, 2021.
28. Personal interview with Blake, February 12, 2021.
29. Spade, *Mutual Aid*.
30. cárdenas, *Poetic Operations*, 144.
31. cárdenas, *Poetic Operations*, 4.
32. cárdenas, *Poetic Operations*, 134.
33. cárdenas, *Poetic Operations*, 158.
34. Stryker, "My Words to Victor Frankenstein," 245.
35. cárdenas, *Poetic Operations*, 134, cp. 131.
36. See also Rachman, "Navigating Personal Masculinities for Trans Men."
37. Rachman, "Desire and Action"; Rachman, "Trans Lives at Mount Holyoke College Today."

38. Personal interview with Leo Rachman, July 16, 2020.

39. Cavar, "The Common Misconception of a 'Sex Binary' Is Damaging"; Cavar, "Autistic and Transgender Communities Should Build Solidarity Together." Rachman and Cavar later joined Kai Chuckas, a Black trans man, and Francesca Eremeeva, a cis woman, as interviewees for Caplan-Bricker, "Who Is a Women's College For?"

40. Booker, "Dysphoria," Artist Statement.

41. Booker, "Dysphoria," Artist Statement.

42. Booker, "Gender Euphoria," Artist Statement.

43. Booker, "Gender Anarchy," Artist Statement.

44. Keats, "Paperback Classics."

45. Keats, "Paperback Classics," 13.

46. Some fields are so flimsy themselves as to be forgiven for their paperbacks. As Keats puts it in a later column, "I have never taken a class in the WAGS department [est. 1987]. And I am sure WAGS is not an easy discipline; the search for even a trace of serious scholarship must be a daunting task indeed." See Keats, "Sex Education," 13.

47. Personal interview with Ean, February 17, 2021.

48. Davis, "Interview with Davey Shlasko."

49. Davis, "Interview with Davey Shlasko."

Epigraph: Rike Frank, *Textiles—Open Letter*, 28–29.

10. GLUE

Epigraph: Virginia Woolf, *A Moment's Liberty*, 184.

1. See Moten, *A Poetics of the Undercommons*, 24.

2. Bergman, "When I Can't Fix It"; Personal interview with Ben, March 21, 2020.

3. "The Story of CIE and Hills House (1960–2018)."

4. Personal interview with Vincente, January 10, 2018.

5. Personal interview with Reese, October 4–5, 2017. Reese further reports that single-stall restrooms were a special target because it was so "funny" they were gendered at all.

6. Personal interview with Fae, February 20, 2018.

7. A Facebook photo announcing this plaque in Franklin Patterson Hall dates August 16, 2012.

8. See, for example, the testimonial of Hampshire student Ide, "No, Seriously, We Need All Gender Bathrooms."

9. With Aster (Erich) Pitcher, personal interview with Cassidy, October 4–5, 2017.

10. Hampshire's student magazine *The Omen* featured "Self-Identified Omen Restroom" on its front cover in Fall 2013.

11. Personal interview with Talia, November 5, 2017.

12. The battle continues. Presently, things have settled into a new normal using signs that read "Bathrooms with Urinals" and "Bathrooms without Urinals." But these, too, are periodically removed or papered over, in protest of their seeming centralization of cisnormative male biology. When Aster (Erich) Pitcher and I first came to Hampshire College in fall 2017 to conduct interviews, for example, the bathroom signs on the main floor of Franklin Patterson Hall were missing.

13. Primeaux, "Trans/Gender and Ally Meeting Minutes."

14. "Transgender Awareness Week" flyer.
15. Karen Jacobus, "Transgender Efforts at MHC," March 23, 2020, private correspondence.
16. Primeaux, "Trans/Gender and Ally Meeting Minutes" (emphasis mine).
17. Fenstermacher, "Transgender Awareness Week," 1.
18. Fenstermacher, "Transgender Awareness Week," 4.
19. Lorde, *The Master's Tools*.
20. *Oxford English Dictionary Online*.
21. Ortega, *In-Between*, 210.
22. *Domus* is the Latin correlate of *oikos* in Greek, from which we get *economics* and *ecology*.
23. Fenstermacher, "Transgender Awareness Week," 1 and 4.
24. GLU, "Gender Liberation UMass."
25. GLU, Million Student March statement (November 2015), private correspondence.
26. GLU, Post from November 5, 2015, Facebook page.
27. GLU, Facebook page.

11. PEBBLE

1. Hayward, "More Lessons from a Starfish"; Hayward, "Spider City Sex."
2. Heidegger, *Fundamental Concepts of Metaphysics*, xii.
3. Derrida, "A Conversation with Jacques Derrida about Heidegger." See also Derrida, *The Beast and the Sovereign II;* and Derrida, *Life Death*.
4. Chen, *Animacies*; Chen, "Tranimacies."
5. For example, Chen would insist we ask how such a schematization informs Heidegger's own anti-Semitism.
6. Clare, *Exile and Pride*, 144–45.
7. Clare, *Brilliant Imperfection*, 49.
8. Clare, *Brilliant Imperfection*, 136.
9. Clare, *Brilliant Imperfection*, 83.
10. Clare, *Exile and Pride*, 152.
11. Clare, *Exile and Pride*, 152.
12. Clare, *Exile and Pride*, 153.
13. Clare, *Exile and Pride*, 145.
14. Clare, *Exile and Pride*, 151.
15. Clare, *Exile and Pride*, 146.
16. Clare, *Exile and Pride*, 155.
17. Clare, *Exile and Pride*, 156.
18. Clare, *Exile and Pride*, 160.
19. Clare, *Brilliant Imperfection*, 169.
20. Personal interview with Hollis, March 20, 2020.
21. Pecht, Just a Gneiss Guy.
22. Pecht, "Of Ultimatums."
23. Pecht, "'I Am Smith' and I Am Male."
24. Pecht, "Of Ultimatums."

25. Pecht, "Of Ultimatums."
26. Pecht, "'I Am Smith' and I Am Male."
27. Pecht, "Eve before Battle."
28. Pecht, "Updates, Requests, and Courses of Action."
29. Facebook, "Support Trans* Students at Smith College!!," April 13 to June 30, 2011.
30. Tallon-Hicks, "54," 31.
31. Tallon-Hicks, "54," 53.
32. Personal interview with Sam, October 4–5, 2017.
33. Anonymous, "Untitled."
34. Anonymous, "Untitled."
35. Jackson, "David and Goliath."
36. Thanks to Andrew Dilts for this reference.
37. I Samuel 17:40 (King James Version).
38. For more on the latter story, see Chapter 3 of this book.
39. Martinez, "45 Minutes with Hexter."
40. Martinez, "45 Minutes with Hexter."
41. SOURCE, "Demands." See also Hampshire's student magazine *The Omen* 30, no. 5.
42. Chen, *Animacies*, 235.
43. Chen, *Animacies*, 235.
44. Derrida, *The Beast and the Sovereign II*, 6.
45. Derrida, *The Beast and the Sovereign II*, 104, 121.

12. ATTUNEMENTS TO TRANS HOPE

1. Mock, *Redefining Realness*.
2. Aoki, *Why the Dust Shall Never Settle Upon This Soul*, 5.
3. Bendorf, *Advantages of Being Evergreen*, 6.
4. Dodge, *My Meteorite*.
5. Lorde, *Burst of Light*, 74.
6. Lorde, *Burst of Light*, 59, 124; Lorde, *Conversations with Audre Lorde*, 38, 72, 176.
7. "Scrutinize," *Oxford English Dictionary Online*.
8. Lorde, *Sister Outsider*, 7–8, 57, 122.
9. Bloch, *Principle of Hope*, 5; see also Bloch, *Spirit of Utopia*.
10. See Bloch, *Principle of Hope*, 115.
11. I borrow the phrase "sideways relationality" from DiPietro, *Sideways Selves*.
12. Bloch, *Principle of Hope*, 214–215.
13. Bloch, *Principle of Hope*, 216.
14. Bloch, *Principle of Hope*, 207.
15. King, *"I Have a Dream."*
16. Muñoz, *Cruising Utopia*, 26.
17. Muñoz, *Cruising Utopia*, 42, see also 65.
18. Muñoz, *Cruising Utopia*, 4, 117.
19. Muñoz, *Cruising Utopia*, 118; Muñoz, "Ephemera as Evidence," 11–12.
20. Muñoz, *Cruising Utopia*, 67, 70, 106, 121, 144.

21. Muñoz, *Cruising Utopia*, 91.
22. Muñoz, *The Sense of Brown*, 2.
23. Muñoz, *Cruising Utopia*, 209.
24. Muñoz, *Cruising Utopia*, 70–71.
25. Muñoz, *Cruising Utopia*, 26.
26. Rosskam, dir., *Dance, Dance Evolution*.
27. Rosskam, dir., *Dance, Dance Evolution*.
28. Rosskam, dir., *Dance, Dance Evolution*.
29. Rosskam, dir., *Dance, Dance Evolution*.
30. Rosskam, dir., *Dance, Dance Evolution*.
31. Personal interview with Anya, June 10, 2021.
32. Personal interview with Jan, March 9, 2020.
33. Personal interview with Phoenix, April 7, 2020.
34. Anonymous, "Trans at MHC."
35. As another example, consider the two locally produced documentaries about queer and trans life at the Five Colleges, both spearheaded by trans folks: Deardorff's *Invisible No More* and Davis's *In Our Own Words*. In Deardorff's documentary, only one interviewee is an out trans woman. In Davis's, while he interviewed a number of trans women, not one would consent to being in the film or in the associated trans oral history archive. Visibility is not liberty.
36. Personal interview with Spencer, July 24, 2020.
37. Personal interview with Helder, May 31, 2023.
38. Personal interview with Reese, October 4–5, 2017.
39. For more on trans men critically engaging their own masculinity, see UMass alum Catalano's work, including "Welcome to Guyland" and "'Trans Enough?'"
40. Personal interview with Silas, December 23, 2021.
41. Personal interview with Langston, February 19, 2021.
42. Personal interview with Finn, April 2, 2020.
43. Davis, "Interview with Davey Shlasko."
44. Davis, "Interview with Cai Sherley."
45. Davis, "Interview with Cai Sherley."
46. Maduro, "An(other) Invitation to Epistemological Humility," 88.
47. Awkward-Rich, *Terrible We*, 26.
48. Tsing, *Mushroom at the End of the World*.

13. FATIGUE

1. Abel, *Sick and Tired*.
2. This expression dates back to the 1700s.
3. Gumbs, *Undrowned*; see also Hersey, *Rest Is Resistance*.
4. "Fatigue," *Oxford English Dictionary Online*.
5. Anderson, *Fracture Mechanics*.
6. "Fatigue," *Online Etymology Dictionary Online*.
7. Personal interview with Jason, October 4, 2017.
8. Davis, "Interview with Cai Sherley."

9. Berlant, *Inconvenience of Other People*, 131.
10. Gustaffson, "Thinking Trans Embodiment," 92.
11. Malatino, *Side Affects*, 15; see also Malatino, *Trans Care*, 19–34.
12. See extended musing on cracks in Zurn and Bassett, *Curious Minds*, 219–31.
13. Ahmed, *Living a Feminist Life*, esp. 210–11.
14. Personal interview with Oliver, May 17, 2021.
15. Hunter, "Every Breath a Black Trans Woman Takes"; see also Stryker, "Breathe."
16. Personal interview with Oliver, May 17, 2021.
17. Personal interview with Oliver, May 17, 2021.
18. Hazard, *Underflows*, 127.
19. Wong's denial came on March 10, 2013. On March 29, Ben Power released a video response entitled "Poem for Calliope."
20. Wong, "Update #3"; Wong, "Good Game."
21. Wong, "Good Game."
22. Wong, *Hyaline Songs*.
23. Wong, *Hyaline Songs*.
24. Wong, "Odyssey." The venue, *Anastomosis*, is the student journal of the Stanford University School of Medicine.
25. Wong, "Odyssey," 21.
26. Wong, "Odyssey," 24.
27. Wong, "Odyssey," 24.
28. Prior to Wong, trans woman author and performance artist Bryn Kelly was also denied admittance to Smith—this time in 2010. She credited the denial to her inconsistent school records (and therefore her readability as trans). Uncannily, Kelly also died by suicide—this time on January 13, 2016. See Kelly, "Transwomen@Smith: Thanks, Again" and Branlandingham, "In Remembrance: Bryn Kelly."
29. Fhlannagáin, "Rest in Peace, Rose Wong."
30. Brush, "She Fought for What Is Right and What Is Fair."
31. Salamon, *Life and Death of Latisha King*, 101.
32. Thank you to Sarah Tyson for this point. See also Stanley's characterization of suicide as "a leap toward death but also away from the death some are already living," in *Atmospheres of Violence*, 97.
33. Piepzna-Samarasinha, *Care Work*, 185–86.
34. Awkward-Rich, *Terrible We*, 144; Malatino, *Side Affects*.
35. Awkward-Rich, *Terrible We*, 147.
36. I understand fatigue to be an analytic that resists the suicidism diagnosed by Baril in *Undoing Suicidism*.
37. Berlant, *Inconvenience of Other People*, 120.

14. RISK

1. Grant, Mottet, and Tanis, "Injustice at Every Turn."
2. Grant, Mottet, and Tanis, "Injustice at Every Turn," 27.
3. Black, "Risk Position."
4. Lawlor, *Position Papers*.

5. Lawlor, "Position Paper #1: Cars," "Position Paper #9: Transitioning," "Position Paper #47: Inherited Wealth," "Position Paper #6: Landfills," and "Position Paper #5: Property," *Position Papers*; Lawlor, "Position Paper #19: Donald Trump" and "Position Paper #20: Positions," *Ploughshares*.

6. Lawlor, "Position Paper #1: Cars," *Position Papers*.
7. Lawlor, "Position Paper #3: Cell Phones," *Position Papers*.
8. Lawlor, "Position Paper #9: Transitioning," *Position Papers*.
9. Dufourmantelle, *In Praise of Risk*, 2.
10. Dufourmantelle, *In Praise of Risk*, 7.
11. Dufourmantelle, *In Praise of Risk*, 103.
12. Dufourmantelle, *In Praise of Risk*, 173, 107.
13. Dufourmantelle and Derrida, *Of Hospitality*, 2.
14. Dufourmantelle, *In Praise of Risk*, 171.
15. Personal interview with Jimena, October 4–5, 2017.
16. Personal interview with Fae, February 20, 2018.
17. Personal interview with Anya, June 10, 2021.
18. Personal interview with Anya, June 10, 2021.
19. See "Scatter," this volume.
20. Personal interview with Talia, November 5, 2017.
21. Personal interview with Talia, November 5, 2017.
22. Newheiser, *Hope in a Secular*, 2.
23. Newheiser, *Hope in a Secular*, 4.
24. Newheiser, *Hope in a Secular*, 154.
25. Newheiser, *Hope in a Secular*, 156.
26. Davis, "Interview with Davey Shlasko."
27. Davis, "Interview with Davey Shlasko."

15. WORLD

Epigraph 1: Helder, Personal interview, May 31, 2023.
Epigraph 2: Samuel Ace, "I Met a Man," *Our Weather Our Sea*, 10.
Epigraph 3: Cameron Awkward-Rich, "Essay on the Theory of Motion," *Sympathetic Little Monster*, 6.
Epigraph 4: Oliver Baez Bendorf, "After a While, We Stop Asking," *Advantages of Being Evergreen*, 7.

1. Stewart, "Afterword," 340.
2. Ahmed, *Queer Phenomenology*, 126.
3. Berlant and Warner, "Sex in Public"; Eng, "The End(s) of Race."
4. Aizura, *Mobile Subjects*, 210.
5. Stanley, *Atmospheres of Violence*, 7, 11.
6. Smith College, "Admissions Policy Announcement."
7. Smith College, "Gender Identity and Expression."
8. Smith Q&A Tumblr, protest photos.
9. Velocci, "'A Very Threatened and Nervous Group of People.'"
10. Smith College, "Gender Identity and Expression."

11. Smith Q&A Facebook, protest photos.
12. Mills College, "Transgender Admissions Policy."
13. Mount Holyoke College, "Inclusive Admission."
14. Mills College, "Report on Inclusion of Transgender and Gender Fluid Students"; see also Stone, "Transitions."
15. Mount Holyoke College, "Transgender Planning Committee."
16. Combahee River Collective, "Combahee River Collective Statement."
17. Lebron, *Making of Black Lives Matter*.
18. Carruthers, *Unapologetic*; Ben-Moshe, Gossett, Mitchell, and Stanley, "Critical Theory, Queer Resistance, and the Ends of Capture"; Ben-Moshe, *Decarcerating Disability*; Ranganathan, "From Urban Resilience to Abolitionist Climate Justice."
19. The effort to remove Amherst's Lord Jeff mascot on grounds of Indigenous justice began at least as early as 1991. See Cooper, "Native Americans Warrant Mutual Respect."
20. Amherst Uprising, "What We Stand For."
21. Editorial Board, "Five Years after Amherst"; De Rosa and Gieger, "Notes from Frost."
22. Amherst College, "Common Language Guide."
23. Amherst Uprising, "What We Stand For."
24. Personal interview with Langston, February 19, 2021.
25. Personal interview with Langston, February 19, 2021.
26. See also Davis, *Abolition Democracy*.
27. Rodríguez, "Statement on Abolition."
28. Nibley, dir., *Two Spirits*.
29. Driskill, *Asegi Stories*; Pyle, "Naming and Claiming"; Pyle, "'Women and 2spirits'"; Simpson, *As We Have Always Done*.
30. Personal interview with Mason, June 23, 2023.
31. Coulthard and Simpson, "Grounded Normativity."
32. Simpson, *As We Have Always Done*, 145.
33. Simpson, *As We Have Always Done*, 151.
34. Simpson, *As We Have Always Done*, 144.
35. Simpson, *As We Have Always Done*, 119.
36. Kimmerer, *Braiding Sweetgrass*, 214.
37. Personal interview with Hollis, March 20, 2020.
38. Lugones, *Pilgrimages / Peregrinajes*.
39. Anzaldúa, *Borderlands / La Frontera*.

CODA

1. Robinson, "Tangent."
2. Tangent homepage.
3. Robinson, "Tangent."
4. Zurn and Martínez, "Genealogies of Transversality."
5. E.g., Snorton, *Black on Both Sides*; Weil, "Psychoanalysis and Trans*versality"; DiPietro, *Sideways Selves*; Stryker, Currah, and Moore, "Trans-, Trans, and Transgender."

6. Feinberg, *Trans Liberation*, 11.
7. Greiner and Sakdapolrak, "Translocality."
8. Weintraub, "At Home in a Liminal World."
9. Personal interview with Silas, December 23, 2021.

EPILOGUE

1. Sexual Minorities Archives, "Interview."
2. Feinberg, *Transgender Warriors*, xvi, 177.
3. Feinberg, *Transgender Warriors*, x.
4. Hwang, "Ourchive."

bibliography

Abel, Elizabeth. "Bathroom Doors and Drinking Fountains: Jim Crow's Racial Symbolic." *Critical Inquiry* 25, no. 3 (2009): 435–81.
Abel, Emily K. *Sick and Tired: An Intimate History of Fatigue*. Chapel Hill: University of North Carolina Press, 2021.
Abi-Karam, Andrea and Kay Gabriel, eds. *We Want It All: An Anthology of Radical Trans Poetics*. Brooklyn, NY: Nightboat Books, 2020.
Ace, Samuel. "The Language of the Seeing, the Language of the Blind." In *Troubling the Line: Trans and Genderqueer Poetry and Poetics*, edited by TC Tolbert and Trace Peterson, 436–38. Callicoon, NY: Nightboat Books, 2013.
Ace, Samuel. *Our Weather Our Sea*. Berkeley, CA: Black Radish Books, 2019.
Aguhar, Mark. "Litanies to My Heavenly Brown Body," *Cultural Disruptions*, March 13, 2012. https://culturaldisruptions.blogspot.com/2012/03/litanies-to-my-heavenly-brown-body.html.
Aguhar, Mark. "These Are the Axes," Tumblr, February 17, 2012. https://markaguhar.tumblr.com/post/17806858973/these-are-the-axes-1-bodies-are-inherently.
Ahmed, Sara. "An Affinity of Hammers." *TSQ: Transgender Studies Quarterly* 3, no. 1–2 (2016): 22–34.
Ahmed, Sara. "Black Feminism as Life-Line." In *Feminist Killjoys* (blog), August 27, 2013. https://feministkilljoys.com/2013/08/27/black-feminism-as-life-line/.
Ahmed, Sara. *The Feminist Killjoy Handbook*. Durham, NC: Duke University Press, 2023.
Ahmed, Sara. *Living a Feminist Life*. Durham, NC: Duke University Press, 2017.
Ahmed, Sara. *On Being Included: Racism and Diversity in Institutional Life*. Durham, NC: Duke University Press, 2012.
Ahmed, Sara. *The Promise of Happiness*. Durham, NC: Duke University Press, 2010.
Ahmed, Sara. *Queer Phenomenology*. Durham, NC: Duke University Press, 2006.
Ahmed, Sara. *Willful Subjects*. Durham, NC: Duke University Press, 2014.
Ainsworth, Sharyn. "Mount Holyoke from the Other Side: II." *Mount Holyoke Alumnae Quarterly* Spring (1969): 3.

Aizura, Aren. *Mobile Subjects: Transnational Imaginaries of Gender Reassignment*. Durham, NC: Duke University Press, 2018.

Aizura, Aren, Marquis Bey, Toby Beauchamp, Treva Ellison, Jules Gill-Peterson, and Eliza Steinbock. "Thinking with Trans Now." *Social Text* 145, 38, no. 4 (2020): 125–47.

Allison, Michelle. "About Michelle." Personal website. N.d. https://www.michelleallisonlmft.com/about-michelle.html.

Allison, Michelle. "A View from the Trans* Bridge." Amherst College Reunion. June 1, 2019. https://www.amherst.edu/alumni/events/reunion/media/2019-reunion/node/744720.

Alvarez, Eddy Francisco. "Finding Sequins in the Rubble: Stitching Together an Archive of Trans Latina Los Angeles." *TSQ: Transgender Studies Quarterly* 3, nos. 3–4 (2016): 618–27.

Amato, Joseph A. *Dust: A History of the Small and the Invisible*. Berkeley: University of California Press, 2000.

American Heritage Center. "Technical Writer S. J. Moffat—Transgender Awareness Week." *Discover History,* November 16, 2015. https://ahcwyo.org/2015/11/16/technical-writer-and-trans-pioneer-s-j-moffat/.

American Heritage Center. "Transitioning to Her True Self: S. J. Moffat's Story." *Discover History,* April 11, 2018. https://ahcwyo.org/2018/04/11/transitioning-to-her-true-self-s-j-moffats-story/.

Amherst College. "Common Language Guide," March 2019. https://www.bostonherald.com/wp-content/uploads/2019/03/Common-Language-Guide_March-2019.pdf.

Amherst Uprising. "What We Stand For." *AC Voice*, November 13, 2015. https://acvoice.wordpress.com/2015/11/13/amherst-uprising-what-we-stand-for/.

Anderson, Ted L. *Fracture Mechanics: Fundamentals and Application*, 4th ed. Boca Raton, FL: CRC Press, 2017.

Anonymous. "Whiteness in Transsexual Activism." *The Sophian* 49, no. 10 (February 3, 2000): 10.

Anonymous. "Untitled." N.d. RB 25 Student Org. Records, Series 13 LGTQA Groups, Box 2, Folder 14 "Trans Experiences at MHC," Archives and Special Collections, Mount Holyoke College, South Hadley, MA.

Anonymous. "Trans at MHC" bingo card. Meme Holyoke, Facebook, April 2, 2020. https://www.facebook.com/groups/236510300107001.

Anzaldúa, Gloria. *Borderlands / La Frontera*. San Francisco: Aunt Lutte Books, 1999.

Anzaldúa, Gloria. *Light in the Dark / Los en lo oscuro*. Durham, NC: Duke University Press, 2015.

Aoki, Ryka. *Why Dust Shall Never Settle Upon This Soul*. Toronto: Biyuti Publishing, 2015.

Aristotle. *Poetics*. Cambridge: Loeb Classical Library, 1995.

Astronomer. "Anniversary in Loneliness." Letter dated September 19, 1975. *Choragos* 9, no. 4 (October 2, 1975): 8.

Awkward-Rich, Cameron. "I Wish I Knew How It Would Feel to Be Free." *Paris Review,* June 11, 2020. https://www.theparisreview.org/blog/2020/06/11/i-wish-i-knew-how-it-would-feel-to-be-free/.

Awkward-Rich, Cameron. *Sympathetic Little Monster*. Toronto: Ricochet, 2016.
Awkward-Rich, Cameron. "Feeling That Motley We." *Audio QT*, January 19, 2021. https://podcasts.la.utexas.edu/audio-qt/podcast/episode-3-feeling-that-motley-we-an-interview-with-cameron-awkward-rich/.
Awkward-Rich, Cameron. *The Terrible We*. Durham, NC: Duke University Press, 2022.
Bachelard, Gaston. *The Poetics of Space*. Boston: Beach Press, 1994.
Banias, Ari. "On Being a Stranger. Instinct, Messiness, Binaries, Failure, Discomfort, and How I Think I Write Poems." In *Troubling the Line: Trans and Genderqueer Poetry and Poetics*, edited by TC Tolbert and Trace Peterson, 63–64. Callicoon, NY: Nightboat Books, 2013.
Barad, Karen. *Meeting the University Halfway: Quantum Physics and the Entanglement of Matter and Meaning*. Durham, NC: Duke University Press, 2007.
Barad, Karen. "Transmaterialities: Trans*/Matter/Realities and Queer Political Imaginings." *GLQ: A Journal of Lesbian and Gay Studies* 21, nos. 2–3 (2015): 387–422.
Baril, Alexandre. "An Intersectional Analysis of 'Trans-crip't Time' in Ableist, Cisnormative, Anglonormative Societies." *Journal of Literary and Cultural Disability Studies* 10, no. 2 (2016): 155–72.
Baril, Alexandre. *Undoing Suicidism: A Trans, Queer, Crip Approach to Rethinking (Assisted) Suicide*. Philadelphia: Temple University Press, 2023.
Bassichis, Morgan, Alexander Lee, and Dean Spade. "Building an Abolitionist Trans and Queer Movement with Everything We've Got." In *Captive Genders: Trans Embodiment and the Prison Industrial Complex*, edited by Eric Stanley and Nat Smith, 15–40. Oakland, CA: AK Press, 2011.
Bazant, Micah. *Timtum: A Trans Jew Zine*, 1999. https://archive.qzap.org/index.php/Detail/Object/Show/object_id/408.
Beemyn, Genny. "Introduction." In *Trans People in Higher Education*, xi–xxxi. New York: SUNY Press, 2019.
Beemyn, Genny. "Making Campuses More Inclusive of Transgender Students." *Journal of Gay and Lesbian Issues in Education* 3, no. 1 (2005): 77–87.
Beemyn, Genny. "Serving the Needs of Transgender College Students." *Journal of Gay and Lesbian Issues in Education* 1, no. 1 (2003): 33–50.
Beemyn, Genny, Andrea Domingue, Jessica Pettitt, and Todd Smith. "Suggested Steps to Make Campuses More Trans-Inclusive." *Journal of Gay and Lesbian Issues in Education* 3, no. 1 (2005): 89–94.
Beemyn, Genny and Susan Rankin. "Transgender Youth and Implications for Higher Education." In *The Lives of Transgender People*, 159–66. New York: Columbia University Press, 2011.
Ben-Moshe, Liat. *Decarcerating Disability: Deinstitutionalization and Prison Abolition*. Minneapolis: University of Minnesota Press, 2020.
Ben-Moshe, Liat, Che Gossett, Nick Mitchell, and Eric A. Stanley. "Critical Theory, Queer Resistance, and the Ends of Capture." In *Death and Other Penalties: Philosophy in a Time of Mass Incarceration*, edited by Geoffrey Adelsberg, Lisa Guenther, and Scott Zeman, 266–95. New York: Fordham University Press, 2015.
Bendorf, Oliver Baez. *Advantages of Being Evergreen*. Cleveland, OH: Cleveland State University Poetry Center, 2019.

Bendorf, Oliver Baez. "Poetics Statement." In *Troubling the Line: Trans and Genderqueer Poetry and Poetics*, edited by TC Tolbert and Trace Peterson, 422–33. Callicoon, NY: Nightboat Books, 2013.

Bendorf, Oliver Baez. "Split Open Just to Count the Pieces." In *Troubling the Line: Trans and Genderqueer Poetry and Poetics*, edited by TC Tolbert and Trace Peterson, 417–18. Callicoon, NY: Nightboat Books, 2013.

Bennington, Geoffrey. *Scatter 1*. New York: Fordham University Press, 2016.

Bennington, Geoffrey. *Scatter 2*. New York: Fordham University Press, 2021.

Bergman, S. Bear. "When I Can't Fix It." In *Butch Is a Noun*, 136–39. San Francisco: Suspect Thoughts Press, 2006.

Berlant, Lauren. *On the Inconvenience of Other People*. Durham, NC: Duke University Press, 2022.

Berlant, Lauren, and Michael Warner. "Sex in Public." *Critical Inquiry* 24, no. 2 (1998): 547–66.

Bey, Marquis. *Black Trans Feminism*. Durham, NC: Duke University Press, 2022.

BG. "Program for LGBT Concerns Changes Name to Stonewall Center." *Campus Chronicle*, September 1, 1995: 8.

Bhabha, Homi. *The Location of Culture*. New York: Continuum, 2012.

Black, Henry Campbell. "Risk Position." *Black's Law Dictionary*, 2nd ed. Minneapolis: West Publishing, 1910. Available online at https://thelawdictionary.org/risk-position/.

Bloch, Ernst. *The Principle of Hope*. 1959. Translated by Neville Plaice, Stephen Plaice, and Paul Knight. Cambridge, MA: MIT Press, 1986.

Bloch, Ernst. *The Spirit of Utopia*. 1918. Translated by Anthony A. Nassar. Stanford, CA: Stanford University Press, 2000.

Bodhran, Ahimsa Timoteo. "Carved Crimson into the Bark of a White Page: A Queer/Trans Womanist Indigenous Colored Poetics." In *Troubling the Line: Trans and Genderqueer Poetry and Poetics*, edited by TC Tolbert and Trace Peterson, 34–35. Callicoon, NY: Nightboat Books, 2013.

Booker, Levi. "Dysphoria," Artist Statement, 2018. Trans Lives at Mount Holyoke College Today, Archives and Special Collections, Mount Holyoke College, South Hadley, MA. https://ascdc.mtholyoke.edu/exhibits/show/student-activism-at-mount-holy/trans-lives-at-mount-holyoke-c/dysphoria.

Booker, Levi. "Gender Anarchy." Artist Statement, 2018. Trans Lives at Mount Holyoke College Today, Archives and Special Collections, Mount Holyoke College, South Hadley, MA. https://ascdc.mtholyoke.edu/exhibits/show/student-activism-at-mount-holy/trans-lives-at-mount-holyoke-c/gender-anarchy.

Booker, Levi. "Gender Euphoria." Artist Statement, 2018. Trans Lives at Mount Holyoke College Today, Archives and Special Collections, Mount Holyoke College, South Hadley, MA.

Bornstein, Kate. *My Gender Workbook*. New York: Routledge, 1997.

Bowman, Bryan. "Bathroom Occupation Begins at Whitmore Administration Building." *Amherst Wire*, November 15, 2016. https://amherstwire.com/17995/campus/bathroom-occupation-begins-at-whitmore-administration-building/.

Branlandingham, Bevin. "In Remembrance: Bryn Kelly." Lambda Literary, January 15, 2016. https://lambdaliterary.org/2016/01/in-remembrance-bryn-kelly/.

Bronson, Lizz. "Poetics Statement." In *Troubling the Line: Trans and Genderqueer Poetry and Poetics*, edited by TC Tolbert and Trace Peterson, 356–57. Callicoon, NY: Nightboat Books, 2013.

Brown, Adrienne Maree. *Emergent Strategy: Shaping Change, Changing Worlds*. Chico, CA: AK Press, 2017.

Brush, Matt G. "She Fought for What Is Right and What Is Fair." *UConn Magazine*, June 22, 2021. https://magazine.uconn.edu/2021/06/22/she-fought-for-what-is-right-and-what-is-fair/.

Burke, Megan. "Cis Sense and the Habit of Gender Assignment." *Journal of Speculative Philosophy* 36, no. 2 (2022): 206–18.

Butler, Judith. *Gender Trouble: Feminism and the Subversion of Identity*. New York: Routledge, 1990.

CAConrad. "Don't Take Any Shit!! A (Soma)tic Poetics Primer." In *Troubling the Line: Trans and Genderqueer Poetry and Poetics*, edited by TC Tolbert and Trace Peterson, 94–95. Callicoon, NY: Nightboat Books, 2013.

Camp Transfeminism zine. 2002. CA-MS-00326, Box 3003.1, Folder 17. Special Collections, Smith College, Northampton, MA.

Caplan-Bricker, Nora. "Who Is a Women's College For?" *Chronicle of Higher Education*, January 20, 2019. https://www.chronicle.com/article/who-is-a-womens-college-for/.

Card, Claudia. "Rape as a Weapon of War." *Hypatia* 11, no. 4 (1996): 5–18.

cárdenas, micha. *Poetic Operations: Trans of Color Art in Digital Media*. Durham, NC: Duke University Press, 2022.

cárdenas, micha. "Statement on Poetics." In *Troubling the Line: Trans and Genderqueer Poetry and Poetics*, edited by TC Tolbert and Trace Peterson, 396–98. Callicoon, NY: Nightboat Books, 2013.

Carruthers, Charlene. *Unapologetic: A Black, Queer, and Feminist Mandate for Radical Movements*. Boston: Beacon Press, 2018.

Catalano, D. Chase. "'Trans Enough?' The Pressures Trans Men Negotiate in Higher Education." *TSQ: Transgender Studies Quarterly* 2, no. 3 (2015): 411–30.

Catalano, D. Chase. "Welcome to Guyland: Experiences of Trans* Men in College." PhD diss., University of Massachusetts, Amherst, August 2014.

Catalano, D. Chase, and Davey Shlasko. "Transgender Oppression." In *Readings for Diversity and Social Justice*, edited by Maurianne Adams, Warren J. Blumenfeld, Carmelita Castaneda, Heather W. Hackman, Madeline L. Peters, and Ximena Zuniga, 423–29. Oxon, UK: Routledge, 2010.

Cavanaugh, Sheila. *Queering Bathrooms: Gender, Sexuality, and the Hygienic Imagination*. Toronto: University of Toronto Press, 2010.

Cavar. "Autistic and Transgender Communities Should Build Solidarity Together." *Mount Holyoke News*, April 20, 2018. https://www.mountholyokenews.com/visibility/2018/4/20/autistic-and-transgender-communities-should-build-solidarity-together.

Cavar. "The Common Misconception of a 'Sex Binary' Is Damaging." *Mount Holyoke News*, November 8, 2018. https://www.mountholyokenews.com/opinion/2018/11/8/the-common-misconception-of-a-sex-binary-is-damaging.

Cavar. "In-Cite: The Mad Possibility of Interethnography." In *Mad Scholars: Reclaiming and Reimagining the Neurodiverse Academy*, edited by Melanie Jones. Syracuse: Syracuse University Press, forthcoming.

Cavar. "In Praise of -Less: [transMad shouts from absent (pl)aces]." *AZE Journal*, August 7, 2022. https://azejournal.com/article/2022/8/4/in-praise-of-less-transmad-shouts-from-absent-places.

Cavar. "Keeping It Surreal: Writing transMad Poetic Realities." Presentation at the Midwest Modern Language Association (MMLA), November 19, 2022. Minneapolis, MN.

Cavar. "Loving Trans into Possible: t4t As Transpollinatory Praxis." *APA Studies in LGBTQ Philosophy* 23, no. 1 (2023): 13–21.

Cavar. "Toward transMad Epistemologies: A Working Text." *Spark: A 4C4 Equality Journal* 4 (2022). https://sparkactivism.com/toward-transmad-epistemologies/.

Cawley, Janet. "You Don't Have to Be a Lesbian to Live Here, But It Doesn't Hurt." *Chicago Tribune*. December 5, 1993, E1.

Certeau, Michel. *The Practice of Everyday Life*, vol. 1. Translated by Steven F. Rendall. Berkeley: University of California Press, 1988.

Certeau, Michel, Luce Giard, Pierre Mayol. *The Practice of Everyday Life*, vol. 2. Translated by Timothy J. Tomasik. Minneapolis: University of Minnesota Press, 1998.

Chen, Mel Y. *Animacies: Biopolitics, Racial Mattering, and Queer Affect*. Durham, NC: Duke University Press, 2012.

Chen, Mel Y. "Tranimacies: An Interview with Mel Y. Chen." *TSQ: Transgender Studies Quarterly* 2, no. 2 (2015): 317–23.

Chess, Simone, Alison Kafer, Jessi Quizar, and Mattie Udora Richardson. "Calling All Restroom Revolutionaries!" In *That's Revolting: Queer Strategies for Resisting Assimilation*, edited by Mattilda Bernstein Sycamore, 216–36. New York: Soft Skull Press, 2004.

Clare, Eli. *Brilliant Imperfection: Grappling with Cure*. Durham, NC: Duke University Press, 2017.

Clare, Eli. *Exile and Pride: Disability, Queerness, and Liberation*. Durham, NC: Duke University Press, 2015.

Cohen, Jeffrey Jerome, and Lowell Duckert, eds. *Veer Ecology: A Companion for Environmental Thinking*. Minneapolis: University of Minnesota Press, 2017.

Combahee River Collective. "The Combahee River Collective Statement." In *Home Girls: A Black Feminist Anthology*, edited by Barbara Smith, 264–74. New Brunswick, NJ: Rutgers University Press, 2000.

Cooper, Ben. "Native Americans Warrant Mutual Respect: Dump Jeff." *Amherst Student* 121, no. 7 (October 23, 1991): 23.

Coulthard, Glen, and Leanne Betasamosake Simpson. "Grounded Normativity / Place-Based Solidarity." *American Quarterly* 68, no. 2 (2016): 249–55.

Crandall, EC. "Feeling of My Memory." In *Troubling the Line: Trans and Genderqueer Poetry and Poetics*, edited by TC Tolbert and Trace Peterson, 168–69. Callicoon, NY: Nightboat Books, 2013.

Cvetkovich, Ann. *An Archive of Feelings: Trauma, Sexuality, and Lesbian Public Cultures*. Durham, NC: Duke University Press, 2003.

D'Lo. "Poetics Statement." In *Troubling the Line: Trans and Genderqueer Poetry and Poetics*, edited by TC Tolbert and Trace Peterson, 122–24. Callicoon, NY: Nightboat Books, 2013.

Davis, Angela. *Abolition Democracy: Beyond Empire, Prisons, Torture, Empire*. New York: Seven Stories Press, 2005.

Davis, Sam, dir. *In Our Own Words: On Being Trans at Smith*. 2017.

Davis, Sam. Trans Archive Oral History Project, 2017. CA-MS-01201, Archives and Special Collections, Smith College, Northampton, MA.

Davis, Sam. "Interview with Miles (Abah) Collins-Sibley." Trans Archive Oral History Project, 2017. CA-MS-01201. Archives and Special Collections, Smith College, Northampton, MA.

Davis, Sam. "Interview with Cai Sherley." Trans Archive Oral History Project, 2017. CA-MS-01201. Archives and Special Collections, Smith College, Northampton, MA.

Davis, Sam. "Interview with Davey Shlasko." Trans Archive Oral History Project, 2017. CA-MS-01201. Archives and Special Collections, Smith College, Northampton, MA.

Davis, Sam. "Interview with Eddie/Edsuvani Maisonet." Trans Archive Oral History Project, 2017. CA-MS-01201. Archives and Special Collections, Smith College, Northampton, MA.

Davis, Sam. "Interview with Everett (Izzy) Owen." Trans Archive Oral History Project, 2017. CA-MS-01201. Archives and Special Collections, Smith College, Northampton, MA.

Davis, Sam. "Interview with Ryan Rasdall." Trans Archive Oral History Project, 2017. CA-MS-01201. Archives and Special Collections, Smith College, Northampton, MA.

Davis, Sam. "Interview with S." Trans Archive Oral History Project, 2017. CA-MS-01201. Archives and Special Collections, Smith College, Northampton, MA.

Day, Meg. "Poetics Statement." In *Troubling the Line: Trans and Genderqueer Poetry and Poetics*, edited by TC Tolbert and Trace Peterson, 387. Callicoon, NY: Nightboat Books, 2013.

De Rosa, Natalie, and Livia Gieger. "Notes from Frost: Amherst Uprising, Five Years On." *The Amherst Student,* February 15, 2021. https://amherststudent.com/article/notes-from-frost-amherst-uprising-five-years-on/.

Deardorff, Saren, dir. *Invisible No More: Queer and Trans History,* 2017. Amherst College. https://www.amherst.edu/campuslife/our-community/queer-resource-center/queer-history-at-amherst.

Deflorian, Michael. "Refigurative Politics: Understanding the Volatile Participation of Critical Creatives in Community Gardens, Repair Cafes, and Clothing Swaps." *Social Movement Studies* 20, no. 3 (2021): 346–63.

Deleuze, Gilles. *The Fold: Leibniz and the Baroque*. Translated by Tom Conley. Minneapolis: University of Minnesota Press, 1992.

Deleuze, Gilles, and Félix Guattari. *A Thousand Plateaus: Capitalism and Schizophrenia*. 1980. Translated by Brian Massumi. Minneapolis: University of Minnesota Press, 1987.

Delgado, Karla. "SYSTA." *Mount Holyoke News* 81, no. 3 (September 24, 1998): 9.

Deligny, Fernand. *The Arachnean and Other Texts*. Translated by Drew S. Burk and Catherine Porter. Minneapolis: University of Minnesota Press, 2015.

Deligny, Fernand. *Cartes et Lignes d'Erre / Maps and Wander Lines: Traces du Réseau de Fernand Deligny 1969–1979 et Journal de Janmari*. Paris: Éditions L'Arachnéen, 2013.

Derrida, Jacques. *Archive Fever: A Freudian Impression*. 1995. Translated by Eric Prenowitz. Chicago: University of Chicago, 1996.

Derrida, Jacques. *The Beast and the Sovereign II*. Translated by Geoffrey Bennington. Chicago: University of Chicago Press, 2011.

Derrida, Jacques. "A Conversation with Jacques Derrida about Heidegger." Edited and translated by Katie Chenoweth and Rodrigo Therezo. *Oxford Literary Review* 43, no. 1 (2021): 1–61.

Derrida, Jacques. "Différance." In *Margins of Philosophy*. Translated by Alan Bass, 3–27. Chicago: University of Chicago Press, 1982.

Derrida, Jacques. *Life Death*. Translated by Pascale-Anne Brault and Michael Naas. Chicago: University of Chicago Press, 2020.

Derrida, Jacques. *Monolingualism of the Other—Or the Prosthesis of Origin*. 1996. Translated by Patrick Mensah. Stanford, CA: Stanford University Press, 1998.

DiPietro, PJ. "Of *Huachafería, Así*, and *M'e Mati*: Decolonizing Transing Methodologies." *TSQ: Transgender Studies Quarterly* 2, no. 4 (2016): 67–76.

DiPietro, PJ. *Sideways Selves: The Decolonial Politics of Transing Matter across the Américas*. Austin: University of Texas Press, forthcoming.

DiPietro, PJ, Jennifer McWeeny, and Shireen Roshanravan, eds. *Speaking Face to Face: The Visionary Philosophy of María Lugones*. New York: SUNY Press, 2019.

Dodge, Harry. *My Meteorite*. New York: Penguin Random House, 2020.

Dormer, Catherine. *A Philosophy of Textile*. London: Bloomsbury, 2020.

Dove, Amanda M. "Mission" email to Restroom Revolution members, November 14, 2001. Restroom Revolution Folder, Stonewall Center Archives, University of Massachusetts, Amherst, Amherst, MA.

Driskill, Qwo-Li. *Asegi Stories: Cherokee Queer and Two-Spirit Memory*. Tucson: University of Arizona Press, 2016.

Du Bois, W. E. B. *Souls of Black Folk*. Radford, VA: Wilder Publications, 2008.

Dufourmantelle, Anne. *In Praise of Risk*. Translated by Steven Miller. New York: Fordham University Press, 2019.

Dufourmantelle, Anne, and Jacques Derrida. *Of Hospitality*. Translated by Rachel Bowlby. Stanford, CA: Stanford University Press, 2000.

"Dust Bunny." *Wikipedia*. https://en.wikipedia.org/wiki/Dust_bunny. Accessed April 29, 2024.

Edidi, Lady Dane Figueroa. *Baltimore—A Love Letter*. Self-published, 2015.

Editorial Board. "Five Years after Amherst Uprising, What Should Campus Activism Look Like?" *Amherst Student*, November 11, 2020. https://amherststudent.com/article/five-years-after-amherst-uprising-what-should-campus-activism-look-like/.

Edwards, Kari. "A Narrative of Resistance." In *Troubling the Line: Trans and Genderqueer Poetry and Poetics*, edited by TC Tolbert and Trace Peterson, 323–25. Callicoon, NY: Nightboat Books, 2013.

Edwards, Rebekah. "Trans Poetics." *TSQ: Transgender Studies Quarterly* 1, no. 1–2 (2014): 252–53.

Eliot, T. S. *Prufrock and Other Observations*. London: The Egoist LTD, 1917.

Eng, David L. "The End(s) of Race." *PMLA* 123, no. 5 (2008): 1429–93.

Feinberg, Leslie. *Stone Butch Blues*. Ithaca, NY: Firebrand Books, 1993.
Feinberg, Leslie. *Transgender Warriors: Making History from Joan of Arc to Marsha P. Johnson and Beyond*. Boston: Beacon Press, 1996.
Feinberg, Leslie. *Trans Liberation: Beyond Pink and Blue*. Boston: Beacon Press, 1998.
Fenstermacher, Erica. "Transgender Awareness Week Is a Huge Success." *Mount Holyoke News* 87, no. 12 (December 9, 2004): 1, 4.
Ferguson, Roderick. *The Reorder of Things: The University and Its Pedagogies of Minority Difference*. Minneapolis: University of Minnesota Press, 2012.
Ferguson, Roderick. *We Demand: The University and Student Protests*. Oakland: University of California Press, 2017.
Ferguson, Sian. "Clothing Swaps Can Be a Lifeline for Queer and Trans People." *Racked*, October 17, 2017. https://www.racked.com/2017/10/17/16466176/clothing-swaps-lgbtqa.
Fhlannagáin, Eilís Ní. "Rest in Peace, Rose Wong." Medium.com, February 10, 2021. https://medium.com/@dirtycitybird/rest-in-peace-rose-wong-6acffa42c44d.
Fitch, W. Clyde (AC 1886) Collection, MA.00116. Archives and Special Collections, Amherst College, Amherst, MA.
Ford, Craig A. "Transgender Bodies, Catholic Schools, and a Queer Natural Law Theology of Exploration." *Journal of Moral Theology* 7, no. 1 (2018): 70–98.
Ford, Heather. "Campus Committee Explores New Dining Options." *The Sophian* 53, no. 4 (October 2, 2003): 1, 3.
Fordham, Diana. Committee and Member Updates, October 19, 1998, RG 30.2.6, unprocessed box. Special Collections and University Archives, University of Massachusetts, Amherst, Amherst, MA.
Foster, Stuart. "Bathroom Stalls in Whitmore Occupied During First Day of Gender Liberation Union Actions." *Daily Collegian*, November 15, 2016. https://dailycollegian.com/2016/11/bathroom-stalls-in-whitmore-occupied-during-first-day-of-gender-liberation-union-actions/.
Foster, Stuart. "Protest for Gender-Neutral Bathrooms Continue for Second Day in Whitmore." *Daily Collegian*, November 16, 2016. https://dailycollegian.com/2016/11/protests-for-gender-neutral-bathrooms-continue-for-second-day-in-whitmore/.
Foucault, Michel. *The Archeology of Knowledge*. 1969. New York: Pantheon Books, 1972.
Foucault, Michel. *Fearless Speech*, edited by Joseph Pearson. Los Angeles: Semiotext(e), 2001.
Foucault, Michel. "Lives of Infamous Men" (1977). In *Power*, edited by James Faubion, 157–75. New York: New Press, 2003.
Foucault, Michel. *The Order of Things: An Archeology of the Human Sciences*. 1966. New York: Vintage Books, 1994.
Foucault, Michel. "Polemics, Politics, and Problematizations: An Interview with Michel Foucault." In *Ethics, Subjectivity, and Truth*, edited by James Faubion, 111–19. New York: New Press, 1997.
Foucault, Michel. "Problematics." In *Foucault Live: Collected Interviews, 1961–1984*, edited by Sylvere Lotringer, 416–22. New York: Semiotext(e), 1989.
Foucault, Michel. *The Use of Pleasure*. 1984. New York: Vintage, 1985.

Frank, Rike. *Textiles—Open Letter*. London: Sternberg Press, 2015.
Gamble, Sarah. "Transgender Panel." *Mount Holyoke News* 79, no. 21 (April 10, 1997): 1.
Gershenson, Olga. "The Restroom Revolution: Unisex Toilets and Campus Politics." In *Toilet: Public Restrooms and the Politics of Sharing*, edited by Harvey Molotch and Laura Noren, 191–207. New York: New York University Press, 2010.
Gershenson, Olga, and Barbara Penner. "Introduction: The Private Life of Public Conveniences." In *Ladies and Gents: Public Toilets and Gender*, edited by Olga Gershenson and Barbara Penner, 1–32. Philadelphia: Temple University Press, 2009.
Gerstein, Julie. "LBA Celebrates Coming Out." *Mount Holyoke News* 79, no. 5 (October 10, 1996): 1.
Gibson, Andrea. "Do You Know Whales Will Follow Their Injured Friends to Shore, Often Taking Their Own Lives So to Not Let Their Loved Ones Be Alone When They Die?" *Homesick: A Plea for Our Planet*, October 20, 2020. https://andreagibsonpoetry.bandcamp.com/.
Gieseking, Jen Jack. *A Queer New York*. New York: New York University Press, 2020.
GLBT Task Force Members List, version 1, n.d., RG 30.2.6, unprocessed box. Special Collections and University Archives, University of Massachusetts, Amherst, Amherst, MA.
GLBT Task Force Members List, version 2, n.d., RG 30.2.6, unprocessed box. Special Collections and University Archives, University of Massachusetts, Amherst, Amherst, MA.
Glissant, Édouard. *Caribbean Discourse: Selected Essays*. 1981. Translated by J. Michael Dash. Charlottesville: University Press of Virginia, 1989.
Glissant, Édouard. *The Poetics of Relation*. Ann Arbor: University of Michigan Press, 1990.
Glissant, Édouard. *Introduction à une poétique du divers*. Paris: Gallimard, 1996.
GLU. Facebook. 2015–2018. https://www.facebook.com/groups/312327738955427.
GLU. *Gender Liberation UMass* zine 2015. University of Massachusetts, Amherst.
GLU. "Transgender Health Survey," October 7, 2015.
GLU. Letter Draft, June 3, 2016.
GLU. "GLU 'Shit-In' Sign Up!," Google Form Survey, 2016.
GLU. "What's Up with the Shit-In?" flyer, November 14, 2016.
GLU. "Monday Marshals," November 15, 2016.
Goldberg, Abbie, Genny Beemyn, and JuliAnna Z. Smith. "What Is Needed, What Is Valued: Trans Students' Perspectives on Trans-Inclusive Policies and Practices in Higher Education." *Journal of Educational and Psychological Consultation* 29, no. 1 (2019): 27–67.
Gossett, Reina, Eric A. Stanley, and Johanna Burton, eds. *Trap Door: Trans Cultural Production and the Politics of Visibility*. Cambridge, MA: MIT Press, 2017.
Grant, Jaime M., Lisa A. Mottet, and Justin Tanis. "Injustice at Every Turn: A Report of the National Transgender Discrimination Survey." National Center for Transgender Equality, 2011. https://transequality.org/sites/default/files/docs/resources/NTDS_Report.pdf.
Greiner, Clemens, and Patrick Sakdapolrak. "Translocality: Concepts, Applications, and Emerging Research Perspectives." *Geography Compass* 7, no. 5 (2013): 373–84.

Guattari, Félix, and Suely Rolnik. *Molecular Revolution in Brazil*. Los Angeles: Semiotext(e), 2008.

Gumbs, Alexis Pauline. *Undrowned: Black Feminist Lessons from Marine Mammals*. Chico, CA: AK Press, 2020.

Gustafsson, Ryan. "Thinking Trans Embodiment: On Contingent 'Home' and Trans Fatigue." In *Trans Philosophy*, edited by Perry Zurn, Andrea Pitts, Talia Bettcher, and PJ DiPietro, 81–98. Minneapolis: University of Minnesota Press, 2024.

Halberstam, Jack. *Female Masculinity*. Durham, NC: Duke University Press, 1998.

Halberstam, Jack. "The Wild Beyond: With and for the Undercommons." In Stefano Harney and Fred Moten, *The Undercommons*, 2–13. Brooklyn, NY: Automedia, 2013.

Hampshire College. *Dis-Orientation Packet*, 2017–2018. https://www.hampshire.edu/disorientation-packet.

Harney, Stefano, and Fred Moten. *All Incomplete*. London: Minor Compositions, 2021.

Harney, Stefano, and Fred Moten. *The Undercommons*. Brooklyn, NY: Automedia, 2013.

Harris, Duriel. "Poetics Statement." In *Troubling the Line: Trans and Genderqueer Poetry and Poetics*, edited by TC Tolbert and Trace Peterson, 158–59. Callicoon, NY: Nightboat Books, 2013.

Hartman, Saidiya. *Lose Your Mother: A Journey Along the Atlantic Slave Route*. New York: Farrar, Straus and Giroux, 2006.

Hartman, Saidiya. *Scenes of Subjection: Terror, Slavery, and Self-Making in Nineteenth-Century America*. Oxford: Oxford University Press, 1997.

Hartman, Saidiya. "Venus in Two Acts." *Small Axe* 26 (2008): 1–14.

Hartman, Saidiya. *Wayward Lives, Beautiful Experiments: Intimate Histories of Riotous Black Girls, Troublesome Women, and Queer Radicals*. New York: W. W. Norton, 2019.

Hastain, J/J. "Poetics Statement." In *Troubling the Line: Trans and Genderqueer Poetry and Poetics*, edited by TC Tolbert and Trace Peterson, 253–55. Callicoon, NY: Nightboat Books, 2013.

Hayward, Eva. "More Lessons from a Starfish: Prefixial Flesh and Transspeciated Selves." *Women's Studies Quarterly* 36, no. 3/4 (2008): 64–85.

Hayward, Eva. "Spider City Sex." *Women and Performance: A Journal of Feminist Theory* 20, no. 3 (2010): 225–51.

Hazard, Cleo Wölfle. *Underflows: Queer Trans Ecologies and River Justice*. Seattle: University of Washington Press, 2022.

Hegnauer, HR. "Statement on a Gendered Possibility." In *Troubling the Line: Trans and Genderqueer Poetry and Poetics*, edited by TC Tolbert and Trace Peterson, 236–37. Callicoon, NY: Nightboat Books, 2013.

Heidegger, Martin. *Fundamental Concepts of Metaphysics: World, Finitude, Solitude*. Bloomington: Indiana University Press, 1995.

Heidegger, Martin. *Poetry, Language, Thought*. New York: Perennial, 1971.

Herman, Aimee. "Poetics Statement." In *Troubling the Line: Trans and Genderqueer Poetry and Poetics*, edited by TC Tolbert and Trace Peterson, 42–44. Callicoon, NY: Nightboat Books, 2013.

Hersey, Tricia. *Rest Is Resistance*. Boston: Little, Brown Spark, 2022.

Hilton, Leon. "Mapping the Wander Lines: The Quiet Revelations of Fernand Deligny." *Los Angeles Review of Books,* July 2, 2015. https://lareviewofbooks.org/article/mapping-the-wander-lines-the-quiet-revelations-of-fernand-deligny/.

Hollibaugh, Amber. *My Dangerous Desires: A Queer Girl Dreaming Her Way Home.* Durham, NC: Duke University Press, 2000.

Horsman, Susan. "Astronomer Led Double Life." *Choragos* 9, no. 5 (October 9, 1975): 1, 3.

Hunter, Lourdes Ashley. "Every Breath a Black Trans Woman Takes Is an Act of Revolution." *HuffPost,* February 6, 2015. https://www.huffpost.com/entry/every-breath-a-black-tran_b_6631124.

Hwang, Ren-yo. "Ourchive." Ren-yo Hwang (website). http://www.renyohwang.com/ourchive. Accessed April 29, 2024.

Jackson, Jesse. "David and Goliath." Political Rally at Tendley Baptist Church, January 16, 1984. https://www.youtube.com/watch?v=6H6vazOz018.

Jews in the Woods. "About Jews in the Woods," 2011. https://web.archive.org/web/20110726203438/http://jewsinthewoods.org/aleph/.

Johnson, Raphaela. "Reflections on Gay Life at Amherst." *Amherst Student* 102, no. 33 (March 5, 1973): 2.

Johnson, Raphaela, and Richard Cleaver. "Gay Lib: 'Cause Which Is Common to Us All." *Amherst Student* 102, no. 7 (October 2, 1972): 2, 5.

Keats, Jonathan. "Paperback Classics Reflect Downfall of Societal Values." *Amherst Student* 120, no. 14 (February 6, 1991): 13.

Keats, Jonathan. "Sex Education." *Amherst Student* 123, no. 6 (October 20, 1993): 13.

Keefe, Sarah. "SGA Beat / Students Split on Gender Issues." *The Sophian* 52, no. 15 (March 6, 2003): 2.

Keer, Gr. "Poetics Statement." In *Troubling the Line: Trans and Genderqueer Poetry and Poetics,* edited by TC Tolbert and Trace Peterson, 227–28. Callicoon, NY: Nightboat Books, 2013.

Kelly, Bryn. "Transwomen@Smith: Thanks, Again." Bryn Kelly (blog), March 13, 2013. https://brynkelly-blog.tumblr.com/post/45282140322/transwomen-smith-thanks-again.

Killerman, Sam. "Genderbread Person." Sam Killerman (website). November 2011. https://www.samkillermann.com/work/genderbread-person/.

Kim, Jina B. "Toward a Crip-of-Color Critique: Thinking with Minich's 'Enabling Whom?'" *Lateral* 6, no. 1 (2017). https://csalateral.org/issue/6-1/forum-alt-humanities-critical-disability-studies-crip-of-color-critique-kim/.

Kimble, Paige. *Tangent: Challenge the Paradigm.* 2003. https://web.archive.org/web/20080630073357/http:/sophia.smith.edu/tangent/.

Kimmerer, Robin Wall. *Braiding Sweetgrass: Indigenous Wisdom, Scientific Knowledge, and the Teachings of Plants.* Minneapolis, MN: Milkweed Editions, 2013.

King, Martin Luther. "I Have a Dream." In *A Testament of Hope,* edited by James Melvin Washington, 217–20. San Francisco: HarperCollins, 1991.

Krawitz, Cole. "Poetics Statement." In *Troubling the Line: Trans and Genderqueer Poetry and Poetics,* edited by TC Tolbert and Trace Peterson, 113–14. Callicoon, NY: Nightboat Books, 2013.

Kukla, Rabbi Elliot. "A Created Being of Its Own: Toward a Jewish Liberation Theology for Men, Women, and Everyone Else." *TransTorah*, 2006. http://www.transtorah.org/PDFs/How_I_Met_the_Tumtum.pdf.

Kumbier, Alana. "Archiving Drag King Communities from the Ground Up." In *Ephemeral Material: Queering the Archive*, 121–54. Sacramento, CA: Litwin Books, 2014.

La Fountain-Stokes, Lawrence. *Translocas: The Politics of Puerto Rican Drag and Trans Performance*. Ann Arbor: University of Michigan Press, 2021.

Laas, Molly. "Senate Votes to Keep Gender Neutral Language in Constitution." *The Sophian* 53, no. 18 (April 8, 2004): 1, 11.

Larke, Dylan. "Queer Profs Speak on Life Experiences." *Daily Collegian* (April 9, 1998): 1, 3.

Latini, Lilith. "Gloria Talks Back to Patti Smith." *Feminist Wire*, October 3, 2013. https://thefeministwire.com/2013/10/3-poems-by-lilith-latini/.

Lawlor, Andrea. "Position Paper #19: Donald Trump." *Ploughshares* 43, no. 1 (2017): 115. https://www.pshares.org/issues/spring-2017.

Lawlor, Andrea. "Position Paper #20: Positions." *Ploughshares* 43, no. 1 (2017): 114. https://www.pshares.org/issues/spring-2017.

Lawlor, Andrea. *Position Papers*. Amherst, MA: Factory Hollow Press, 2016.

Lebron, Christopher. *The Making of Black Lives Matter: A Brief History of an Idea*. Oxford: Oxford University Press, 2017.

Leeb, Stu. "In Memory: Shannon Moffat '50." *Amherst Magazine*, 2009. https://www.amherst.edu/news/magazine/in_memory/1950/shannonmoffat.

Lefkowitz Horowitz, Helen. *Alma Mater: Design and Experience in the Women's Colleges from Their Nineteenth-Century Beginnings to the 1930's*. New York: Knopf, 1984.

Lester, Joan. "Gay? Straight? Vive la Différence." *Chicago Tribune* (May 14, 1993): D21.

"Letters to the Editor." *The Sophian* 53, no. 5 (October 9, 2003): 8.

LGBTQ Religious Archives Network. "The Historical Development of BIPOC Trans-spiritual Leadership" (December 2023). https://exhibits.lgbtran.org/exhibits/show/bipoc-trans-spiritual.

Lim, Un Jung. "SYSTA." *Mount Holyoke News* 84, no. 8 (November 1, 2001): 7.

Lim, Un Jung. "SYSTA." *Mount Holyoke News* 84, no. 22 (April 18, 2002): 11.

Lindahl, Chris. "Protestors Demand Gender-Neutral Bathrooms at Mass by Occupying Stalls at Administrative Building." *Daily Hampshire Gazette*, November 14, 2016. https://www.gazettenet.com/UMass-students-occupy-Whitmore-administration-building-to-demand-gender-neutral-bathrooms-6132456.

Lorde, Audre. *A Burst of Light: and Other Essays*. Ithaca, NY: Firebrand Books, 1988.

Lorde, Audre. *Conversations with Audre Lorde*. Edited by Joan Wylie Hall. Jackson: University Press of Mississippi, 2004.

Lorde, Audre. *The Master's Tools Will Never Dismantle the Master's House*. New York: Penguin, 2018.

Lorde, Audre. *Sister Outsider: Essays and Speeches by Audre Lorde*. 1984. Berkeley, CA: Crossing Press, 2007.

Luengsuraswat, Bo. "Poetics Statement." In *Troubling the Line: Trans and Genderqueer Poetry and Poetics*, edited by TC Tolbert and Trace Peterson, 86. Callicoon, NY: Nightboat Books, 2013.

Lugones, María. "Heterosexualism and the Colonial/Modern Gender System." *Hypatia* 22, no. 1 (2007): 186–209.

Lugones, María. *Pilgrimages/Peregrinajes: Theorizing Coalition against Multiple Oppressions.* Lanham, MD: Rowman and Littlefield, 2003.

Maduro, Otto. "An(other) Invitation to Epistemological Humility: Notes Toward a Self-Critical Approach to Counter Knowledges." In *Decolonizing Epistemologies: Latino/a Theology and Philosophy*, edited by Ada Mara Isasi-Daz and Eduardo Mendieta, 87–104. New York: Fordham University Press, 2011.

Maisonet, Eddie. "Sounding It Out." In *Outside the XY: Queer, Black and Brown Masculinity*, edited by Morgan Mann Willis, 241–46. Riverdale, NY: Riverdale Avenue Books, 2016.

Maisonet, Eddie. "Eddie Maisonet." TMI Project: Black Trans Stories Matter, October 4, 2022. https://www.youtube.com/watch?v=vdpbE5mbJpI.

Malatino, Hil. *Queer Embodiment: Monstrosity, Medical Violence, and Intersex Experience.* Lincoln: University of Nebraska Press, 2019.

Malatino, Hil. *Side Affects: On Being Trans and Feeling Bad.* Minneapolis: University of Minnesota Press, 2022.

Malatino, Hil. *Trans Care.* Minneapolis: University of Minnesota Press, 2020.

Manion, Jen. *Female Husbands: A Trans History.* Cambridge: Cambridge University Press, 2020.

Manion, Jen. *Liberty's Prisoners: Carceral Culture in Early America.* Philadelphia: University of Pennsylvania Press, 2015.

Manion, Jen. "The Performance of Transgender Inclusion." *Public Seminar,* November 27, 2018. https://publicseminar.org/essays/the-performance-of-transgender-inclusion/.

Manne, Kate. *Down Girl: The Logic of Misogyny.* Oxford: Oxford University Press, 2017.

Marder, Michael. *Dust.* London: Bloomsbury, 2016.

Marks, Andy. "Gay Libbers at Amherst: Playing It by Ear." *Amherst Student* 102, no. 8 (October 5, 1972): 1 and 4.

Martinez, Steven Emmanuel. "45 Minutes with Hexter." *Inside* 1, no. 1 (2008F): 12.

McCarthy, Sheryl. "Mount Holyoke from the Other Side: III." *Mount Holyoke Alumnae Quarterly* Spring (1969): 5.

McCullers, Carson. *The Member of the Wedding.* 1946. New York: Mariner Books, 2004.

McRuer, Robert. *Crip Theory: Cultural Signs of Queerness and Disability.* New York: NYU Press, 2006.

Medina, Mateo. "Preferred Gender Pronouns," Hampshire College (website), August, 2011. https://www.hampshire.edu/sites/default/files/shared_files/Preferred_Gender_Pronouns_for_Faculty.pdf.

Memo from David K. Scott to Felice Yeskel regarding Name Change of Task Force, May 1, 1995. RG 30.2.6, unprocessed box. Special Collections and University Archives, University of Massachusetts, Amherst, MA.

Miguel, Marlon. "Towards a New Thinking on Humanism in Fernand Deligny's Network." In *Structures of Feeling: Affectivity and the Study of Culture*, edited by Devika Sharma and Frederik Tygstrup, 187–98. Munich: De Gruyter, 2015.

Miller, Ruth. "Kitchen Work Study Jobs Face Cuts." *The Sophian* 53, no. 15 (February 19, 2004): 3, 11.

Mills College. "Report on Inclusion of Transgender and Gender Fluid Students: Best Practices, Assessment, and Recommendations." Gender Identity and Expression Subcommittee of the Diversity and Social Justice Committee, Mills College. April 2013. https://www.smith.edu/admission/studygroup/docs/Mills-College-Report-on-Inclusion-of-Transgender-and-Gender-Fluid-Students-Best-Practices-Assessment-and-Recommendations.pdf.

Mills College. "Transgender Admissions Policy." Mills College (website). March 17, 2021. https://web.archive.org/web/20210317150526/https://www.mills.edu/admission-aid/undergraduate-admissions/how-to-apply/transgender-admission-policy.php.

Minutes of Chancellor's Task Force on G/L/B Matters, January 30, 1995. RG 30.2.6, unprocessed box. Special Collections and University Archives, University of Massachusetts, Amherst, MA.

Minutes of Chancellor's Task Force for Gay, Lesbian, Bisexual, and Transgender Matters, March 29, 1995. RG 30.2.6, Box 3, Folder 33. Special Collections and University Archives, University of Massachusetts, Amherst, MA.

Mock, Janet. *Redefining Realness: My Path to Womanhood, Identity, Love and So Much More*. New York: Atria, 2014.

Moffat, Shannon, and Betsy Friar Williams. "Book Proposal," for *The Father Who Became a Woman*, n.d. S. J. Moffat Collection, Accession #11046-02-11-11, Box 25, "Book Proposal" Folder. American Heritage Center, University of Wyoming, Laramie, WY.

Moore, Alison. "Colonial Visions of 'Third World' Toilets: A Nineteenth-Century Discourse That Haunts Contemporary Tourism." In *Ladies and Gents: Public Toilets and Gender*, edited by Olga Gershenson and Barbara Penne, 105–25. Philadelphia: Temple University Press, 2009.

Morris-Young, Dan. "Catholic School Won't Fire Transgender Teacher." *National Catholic Reporter*, May 12, 2016. https://www.ncronline.org/blogs/ncr-today/catholic-school-wont-fire-transgender-teacher.

Morton, Timothy. *The Poetics of Spice*. Cambridge: Cambridge University Press, 2000.

Moten, Fred. *A Poetics of the Undercommons*. Brooklyn, NY: Sputnik and Fizzle, 2016.

Mount Holyoke College. "Transgender Planning Committee." 2019-2020-035, Health Education Records, Box 4. Archives and Special Collections, Mount Holyoke College, South Hadley, MA.

Mount Holyoke College. "Inclusive Admission." Mount Holyoke College (website). https://www.mtholyoke.edu/admission/inclusion. Accessed November 15, 2022.

Moye, David. "UMass Students' Hold 'S**t In' Demanding Gender Neutral Bathrooms." *Huffington Post*, November 17, 2016. https://www.huffpost.com/entry/umass-shit-in-gender-neutral_n_582df2cae4b099512f816aef.

Muñoz, José Esteban. *Cruising Utopia: The Then and There of Queer Futurity*. New York: New York University Press, 2009.

Muñoz, José Esteban. "Ephemera as Evidence: Introductory Notes to Queer Acts." *Women and Performance: A Journal of Feminist Theory* 8, no. 2 (1996): 5–16.

Muñoz, José Esteban. *The Sense of Brown*. Durham, NC: Duke University Press, 2020.

Myles, Eileen. "My Boy's Red Hat." In *Troubling the Line: Trans and Genderqueer Poetry and Poetics*, edited by TC Tolbert and Trace Peterson, 176–77. Callicoon, NY: Nightboat Books, 2013.

Nash, Jennifer. "Citational Desires: On Black Feminism's Institutional Longings." *Diacritics* 48, no. 3 (2020): 76–91.

Newheiser, David. *Hope in a Secular Age: Deconstruction, Negative Theology, and the Future of Faith*. Cambridge: Cambridge University Press, 2020.

Nibley, Lydia, dir. *Two Spirits*. Riding the Tiger Productions, 2009.

Nicolazzo, Z. *Trans* in College: Transgender Students' Strategies for Navigating Campus Life and the Institutional Politics of Inclusion*. Sterling, VA: Stylus, 2017.

Nordmarken, Sonny. "Becoming Ever More Monstrous: Feeling Transgender In-Betweenness." *Qualitative Inquiry* 20, no. 1 (2014): 37–50.

Nordmarken, Sonny. "Coming into Identity: How Gender Minorities Experience Identity Formation." *Gender and Society* 37, no. 4 (2023): 1–30.

Nordmarken, Sonny. "Contesting Lyme." In *The Oxford Handbook of the Sociology of the Body and Embodiment*, edited by Natalie Boero and Katherine Mason, 431–46. Oxford: Oxford University Press, 2020.

Nordmarken, Sonny. "Queering Gendering: Trans Epistemologies and the Disruption and Production of Gender Accomplishment Practices." *Feminist Studies* 45, no. 1 (2019): 36–66.

"Obituary of Amanda Jean Fadum Hall." Murphy and Associates Funeral Directors, 2017. https://www.murphyfuneraldirectors.com/obituaries/amanda-fadum-hall. Accessed November 12, 2023.

The Omen 41, no. 5 (Fall 2013), front cover. https://archive.org/details/hampshireomen/Volume%2041/Omen.41.5/mode/2up.

The Omen 30, no. 5 (April 11, 2008). https://archive.org/details/hampshireomen/Volume%2030/Omen.30.5/mode/2up.

Online Etymology Dictionary, 2001–2023. https://www.etymonline.com/.

Ortega, Mariana. *In-Between: Latina Feminist Phenomenology, Multiplicity, and the Self*. Albany: SUNY Press, 2016.

Oxford English Dictionary Online. Oxford: Oxford University Press, 2023.

Page, Enoch. "Academentia: Physiological Stress, Toxic Work Sites and the Neutralization of Blackness by the Whiteness Standards of Professionalization." Presentation at the *Sixth Annual National Conference, People of Color in Predominantly White Institutions (POCPWI)*, October 31–November 1, 2001. Lincoln, NE. https://digitalcommons.unl.edu/pocpwi6/.

Page, Enoch. "Dr. Enoch Page." Interview by Carol Marie Webster, April 18, 2021. https://vimeo.com/538383532.

Page, Enoch. "The Environment." Interview by Carol Marie Webster, August 5, 2021. https://vimeo.com/583557750.

Page, Enoch. Faculty Profile. University of Massachusetts, Amherst. Last updated March 2003. https://people.umass.edu/hepage/.

Page, Enoch. "No Black Public Sphere in White Space." *Transforming Anthropology* 8, nos. 1–2 (1999): 111–28.

Page, Enoch. *On Being a Witness* (blog). Last updated May 2012. https://onbeingawitness.wordpress.com/.

Page, Enoch, and Matt Richardson. "On the Fear of Small Numbers: A Twenty-First-Century Prolegomenon of the U.S. Black Transgender Experience." In *Black Sexualities: Probing Powers, Passions, Practices, and Policies*, edited by Juan Battle and Sandra L. Barnes, 60–71. New Brunswick, NJ: Rutgers University Press, 2009.

Painter, Nell Irvin. *Sojourner Truth: A Life, a Symbol*. New York: W. W. Norton, 1996.

Palmero, Tyler. "UMass Students Hold 'Sh*t-In' for Gender-Neutral Bathrooms." *Campus Reform*, November 16, 2016. https://www.campusreform.org/?ID=8409.

Patterson, Franklin. *The Making of a College: Plans for a New Departure in Higher Education*. Cambridge, MA: MIT Press, 1966.

Pecht, Jake. "Eve before Battle." *Just a Gneiss Guy* (blog), April 11, 2011. https://gneissguy-blog.tumblr.com/post/4539855184/eve-before-battle.

Pecht, Jake. "'I Am Smith' and I Am Male." *The Sophian* 60, no. 20 (April 14, 2011): 10.

Pecht, Jake. *Just a Gneiss Guy* (blog), 2011–2013, https://gneissguy-blog.tumblr.com/.

Pecht, Jake. "Of Ultimatums at Smith College and Decisions to Be Made." *Just a Gneiss Guy* (blog), April 12, 2011. https://gneissguy-blog.tumblr.com/post/4555557924/of-ultimatums-at-smith-college-and-decisions-to-be.

Pecht, Jake. "Updates, Requests, and Courses of Action." *Just a Gneiss Guy* (blog), April 13, 2011. https://gneissguy-blog.tumblr.com/post/4594316846/updates-requests-and-course-of-action.

Peck, Monica/Nico. "Real Poetry Transifesto." In *Troubling the Line: Trans and Genderqueer Poetry and Poetics*, edited by TC Tolbert and Trace Peterson, 408–10. Callicoon, NY: Nightboat Books, 2013.

Peterson, Trace. "Being Unreadable and Being Read." In *Troubling the Line: Trans and Genderqueer Poetry and Poetics*, edited by TC Tolbert and Trace Peterson, 15–22. Callicoon, NY: Nightboat Books, 2013.

Piepzna-Samarasinha, Leah Lakshmi. *Care Work: Dreaming Disability Justice*. Vancouver: Arsenal Pulp Press, 2018.

Pitcher, Aster (Erich) N. *Being and Becoming Professionally Other: Identities, Voices, and Experiences of US Trans* Academics*. New York: Peter Lang, 2018.

Porras, Isabel. "Arguments against Gender Neutral Constitution Shallow and Embarrassing." *The Sophian* 52, no. 15 (March 6, 2003): 10.

Power, Ben. "Brief Autobiographical Information on Ben Power." 1992. *Digital Transgender Archive*. https://www.digitaltransgenderarchive.net/downloads/fn106z07m.

Power, Ben. "Poem for Calliope," Nycii Vanderhoff (channel). March 29, 2013. https://www.youtube.com/watch?v=cQvwQ9XulEs.

"Power and Memory: 50 Years of Struggle, Shared Legacies of Resistance." Exhibit, Harold F. Johnson Library, Hampshire College, Amherst, MA. March 20–April 10, 2017.

Primeaux, Milo. "Trans/Gender and Ally Meeting Minutes," November 8, 2004. Health Education Records, Box 4, Transgender Issues: MHC Approach/Policies Folder. Archives and Special Collections, Mount Holyoke College, South Hadley, MA.

Prosnitz, Beth. "Poorly Proposed Dining Hall Changes." *The Sophian* 53, no. 13 (February 5, 2004): 8.

Pryor, Jack. *Time Slips: Queer Temporalities, Contemporary Performance, and the Hole of History*. Evanston, IL: Northwestern University Press, 2017.

Pyle, Kai. "Naming and Claiming: Recovering Ojibwe and Plains Cree Two-Spirit Language." *TSQ: Transgender Studies Quarterly* 5, no. 4 (2018): 574–88.

Pyle, Kai. "'Women and 2spirits': On the Marginalization of Transgender Indigenous People in Activist Rhetoric." *American Indian Culture and Research Journal* 43, no. 3 (2019): 85–94.

"The Queer Does Not End Here." Tumblr, April 14, 2013. https://web.archive.org/web/20130414164806/http://thequeerdoesnotendhere.tumblr.com/.

Rachman, Leo. "Desire and Action: The Development of Black Studies at MHC," 2018. Digital Exhibits of the Archives and Special Collections, Mount Holyoke College, South Hadley, MA. https://ascdc.mtholyoke.edu/exhibits/show/student-activism-at-mount-holy/desire-and-action---the-develo.

Rachman, Leo. "Navigating Personal Masculinities for Trans Men." *Mount Holyoke News*, April 15, 2018. https://www.mountholyokenews.com/visibility/2018/4/15/navigating-personal-masculinities-for-trans-men.

Rachman, Leo. "Trans Lives at Mount Holyoke College Today," 2018. Digital Exhibits of the Archives and Special Collections, Mount Holyoke College, South Hadley, MA. https://ascdc.mtholyoke.edu/exhibits/show/student-activism-at-mount-holy/trans-lives-at-mount-holyoke-c#.

Raha, Nat. "Embodying Autonomous Trans Health Care in Zines." *TSQ: Transgender Studies Quarterly* 8, no. 2 (2021): 188–98.

Ranganathan, Malini. "From Urban Resilience to Abolitionist Climate Justice." *Antipode* 53, no. 1 (2019): 115–37.

Rawson, K. J. "Accessing Transgender // Desiring Queer(er?) Archival Logics." *Archivaria* 68 (2009): 123–40.

Rawson, K. J. "Archival Justice: An Interview with Ben Power Alwin." *Radical History Review* 122 (2015): 177–87.

Raymond, Janice. *Doublethink: A Feminist Challenge to Transgenderism*. North Geelong, Australia: Spinifex, 2021.

Raymond, Janice. *A Passion for Friends: Toward a Philosophy of Female Affection*. Boston: Beacon Press, 1986.

Raymond, Janice. *The Transsexual Empire: The Making of the She-Male*. Boston: Beacon Press, 1979.

Reicks, Sister Laura, President of the West Midwest Community of Sisters of Mercy. "Letter to Parents of Mercy High School," May 11, 2016. https://www.scribd.com/doc/312408489/Letter-to-parents-of-San-Francisco-s-Mercy-High-School-students-released-May-11#download.

Reimold, Dan. "Controversial 'Cashmere and Pearls' Letter in Smith College Newspaper Spurs Campus, Media Frenzy." *College Media Matters*, March 1, 2012. https://collegemedia.wordpress.com/2012/03/01/controversial-cashmere-and-pearls-letter-in-smith-college-newspaper-spurs-campus-media-frenzy-acpsea/.

Rich, Adrienne. "Invisibility in Academe." In *The Broadview Anthology of Expository Prose*, edited by Don LePan, Julia Gaunce, Laura Buzzard, Mical Moser, and Tammy Roberts, 217–21. New York: Broadview Press, 2011.

Robinson, Kate. "Transgender Coverage on Fox." *The Sophian* 52, no. 21 (May 15, 2003): 1.

Robinson, Kate. "Tangent: No, It Didn't Come Out of Nowhere." *The Sophian* 53, no. 18 (April 16, 2004): 5.

Rodríguez, Dylan. "Statement on Abolition." *Abolition Journal,* July 17, 2015. https://abolitionjournal.org/dylan-rodriguez-abolition-statement/.

Romero, Fabian. "Poetics Statement." In *Troubling the Line: Trans and Genderqueer Poetry and Poetics*, edited by TC Tolbert and Trace Peterson, 219–20. Callicoon, NY: Nightboat Books, 2013.

Rosen, Shelley. "No, Seriously, We Need All Gender Bathrooms." *The Omen* 40, no. 5 (Spring 2013): 6–7. https://archive.org/details/hampshireomen/Volume%2040/Omen.40.5/page/6/mode/2up.

Rosenberg, Jordy. *Confessions of the Fox.* New York: One World, 2018.

Rosskam, Jules, dir. *Dance, Dance Evolution.* MamSir Productions, 2019.

Roth, Julie Casper. "Dining Changes May Impact Alumnae Gifts." *The Sophian* 53, no. 14 (February 12, 2004): 9.

Roy, Arundhati. "Confronting Empire." *The Nation,* February 20, 2003. https://www.thenation.com/article/archive/confronting-empire/.

Russell, Gina. "Groups Take Gender Out of Event Names." *The Sophian* 53, no. 4 (October 2, 2003): 1.

Russell, Stephen T., Amanda M. Pollitt, Gu Li, and Arnold H. Grossman. "Chosen Name Use Is Linked to Reduced Depressive Symptoms, Suicidal Ideation, and Suicidal Behavior among Transgender Youth." *Journal of Adolescent Health* 63, no. 4 (2018): 379–80.

S., Ilana. "In the Woods." *Jews in the Woods*, 2011. https://web.archive.org/web/20110726203234/http://jewsinthewoods.org/aleph/into-the-woods/.

Salamon, Gayle. *The Life and Death of Latisha King: A Critical Phenomenology of Transphobia.* New York: NYU Press, 2018.

Sandra. "SYSTA." *Mount Holyoke News* 81, no. 1 (September 10, 1998): 6.

Sealey, Kris. *Creolizing the Nation.* Evanston, IL: Northwestern University Press, 2020.

Selke, Lori. "Poetics Statement." In *Troubling the Line: Trans and Genderqueer Poetry and Poetics*, edited by TC Tolbert and Trace Peterson, 366–67. Callicoon, NY: Nightboat Books, 2013.

Sexual Minorities Archives. "Interview: How Leslie Feinberg's Personal Research Library came to the SMA." Sexual Minorities Archives (blog), February 26, 2018. https://sexualminoritiesarchives.org/interview-how-leslie-feinbergs-personal-research-library-came-to-the-sma/.

Shipley, Eli. "The Transformative and Queer Language of Poetry." In *Troubling the Line: Trans and Genderqueer Poetry and Poetics*, edited by TC Tolbert and Trace Peterson, 197–98. Callicoon, NY: Nightboat Books, 2013.

Siegel, Derek P. "Transgender Experiences and Transphobia in Higher Education." *Sociology Compass* (2019): e12734.

Simmons, Jeremy, dir. *TransGeneration.* World of Wonder, 2005.

Simpson, Leanne Betasamosake. *As We Have Always Done: Indigenous Freedom Through Radical Resistance.* Minneapolis: University of Minnesota Press, 2021.

Slip of the Tongue 2.1 (1999–2000). RG 25, Series 13, Box 2, *Slip of the Tongue* folder. Archives and Special Collections, Mount Holyoke College, South Hadley, MA.

Smith College. "Admissions Policy Announcement: FAQ." Smith College. https://www.smith.edu/studygroup/faq.php. Accessed November 6, 2022.

Smith College. "Gender Identity and Expression." Smith College. https://www.smith.edu/about-smith/equity-inclusion/gender-identity-expression. Accessed November 14, 2022.

Smith Q&A Facebook. Protest Photos, October 25, 2014. https://www.facebook.com/profile.php?id=100072345275695.

Smith Q&A Tumblr. Protest Photos, April 24, 2014. https://web.archive.org/web/20140610223743/http://smith-q-and-a.tumblr.com/.

Smith, Barbara. "Mount Holyoke from the Other Side: I." *Mount Holyoke Alumnae Quarterly* Spring (1969): 2.

Spillers, Hortense J. "Mama's Baby, Papa's Maybe: An American Grammar Book." *Diacritics* 17, no. 2 (1987): 64–81.

Snorton, C. Riley. *Black on Both Sides: A Racial History of Trans Identity*. Minneapolis: University of Minnesota Press, 2017.

Snorton, C. Riley, and Jin Haritaworn. "Trans Necropolitics: A Transnational Reflection on Violence, Death, and the Trans of Color Afterlife." In *The Transgender Studies Reader 2*, edited by Susan Stryker and Aren Aizura, 65–76. New York: Routledge, 2013.

Something Queer Happened Here zine, 2011. Hampshire College.

SOURCE. "The Demands as Presented by Members of SOURCE." *Action Awareness* (blog), April 2, 2008. https://actionawareness.wordpress.com/.

Spade, Dean. *Mutual Aid: Building Solidarity during This Crisis (and The Next)*. New York: Verso, 2020.

Spade, Dean. *Normal Life: Administrative Violence, Critical Trans Politics, and the Limits of the Law*. 2011. Durham, NC: Duke University Press, 2015.

Spade, Dean. "We Still Need Pronoun Go-Rounds: A Response to Jen Manion." *Public Seminar*, December 3, 2018. https://publicseminar.org/essays/we-still-need-pronoun-go-rounds/.

Staff Editorial. "Trans Advocates Alienate Students with Vandalism." *The Sophian* 53, no. 9 (November 13, 2003): 8.

Staff Editorial. "We Need to Address 'Thought Police' at Smith." *The Sophian* 53, no. 18 (March 11, 2004): 8.

Stanley, Eric. *Atmospheres of Violence: Structuring Antagonisms and the Trans/Queer Ungovernable*. Durham, NC: Duke University Press, 2021.

Steedman, Carolyn. *Dust*. Manchester, UK: Manchester University Press, 2001.

Steinbock, Eliza. *Shimmering Images: Trans Cinema, Embodiment, and the Aesthetics of Change*. Durham, NC: Duke University Press, 2019.

Stewart, Kathleen. "Afterword: Worlding Refrains." In *The Affect Theory Reader*, edited by Melissa Gregg and Gregory J. Seigworth, 339–54. Durham, NC: Duke University Press, 2010.

Stewart, Kathleen. *A Space on the Side of the Road*. Princeton, NJ: Princeton University Press, 1996.

Stone, Moya. "Transitions: The Transgender Policy." *Mills Quarterly*, Summer (June 22, 2022). https://quarterly.mills.edu/transitions-the-transgender-policy/.

Stone, Sandy. "The 'Empire' Strikes Back: A Posttransexual Manifesto." *Camera Obscura* 29 (1992): 151–76.

Stryker, Susan. "Breathe: Histories and Futures of Trans* Life Now." Lecture at Central European University, February 2016. https://www.youtube.com/watch?v=JLRgJsK4yEc.

Stryker, Susan. "(De)Subjugated Knowledges: An Introduction to Transgender Studies." In *The Transgender Studies Reader* 1, edited by Susan Stryker and Stephen Whittle, 1–17. New York: Routledge, 2006.

Stryker, Susan. "My Words to Victor Frankenstein above the Village of Chamounix." *GLQ: A Journal of Gay and Lesbian Studies* 1, no. 3 (1994): 237–54.

Stryker, Susan, Paisley Currah, and Lisa Jean Moore. "Trans-, Trans, or Transgender." *Women's Studies Quarterly* 36, nos. 3 and 4 (2008): 11–22.

Tallon-Hicks, Yana. "54: An Archive of the Queer Mod." Division III Thesis, Hampshire College (2006).

"The Story of CIE and Hills House (1960–2018)." College of Education, University of Massachusetts, Amherst. https://www.umass.edu/cie/news/story-cie-and-hills-house-1960–2018. Accessed July 23, 2021.

Theonia, Charles. "When You're Trans in the Brooklyn Summertime." In *Which One Is the Bridge*, 30–31. New York: Topside Press, 2015.

Thornton, Max. "Trans/Criptions: Gender, Disability, and Liturgical Experience." *TSQ: Transgender Studies Quarterly* 6, no. 3 (2019): 358–67.

Tolbert, TC. "The Gifts of the Body Are the Gifts of Imperfection." In *Troubling the Line: Trans and Genderqueer Poetry and Poetics*, edited by TC Tolbert and Trace Peterson, 465–66. Callicoon, NY: Nightboat Books, 2013.

Tolbert, TC. "Open, and Always, Opening." In *Troubling the Line: Trans and Genderqueer Poetry and Poetics*, edited by TC Tolbert and Trace Peterson, 7–14. Callicoon, NY: Nightboat Books, 2013.

Tolbert, TC, and Trace Peterson, eds. *Troubling the Line: Trans and Genderqueer Poetry and Poetics*. Callicoon, NY: Nightboat Books, 2013.

Tolkien, J. R. R. "Letter to Michael" (March 6–8, 1941). In *The Letters of J. R. R. Tolkien*, edited by Humphrey Carpenter, 48–49. Boston: Houghton Mifflin, 1981.

"Transgender Awareness Week" flyer (2004). 2019–2020–035, Health Education Records, Box 4, "Transgender Issues: MHC Approach/Policies" Folder. Archives and Special Collections, Mount Holyoke College, South Hadley, MA.

Tsang, Wu, and Fred Moten. "All Terror, All Beauty: Wu Tsang and Fred Moten in Conversation." In *Trap Door: Trans Cultural Production and the Politics of Visibility*, edited by Reina Gossett, Eric A. Stanley, and Johanna Burton, 339–48. Cambridge, MA: MIT Press, 2017.

Tsing, Anna. *The Mushroom at the End of the World: On the Possibility of Life in Capitalist Ruins*. Princeton, NJ: Princeton University Press, 2015.

Tucker, Jill. "Catholic School Accepting Change." *San Francisco Chronicle* (May 13, 2016): D1.

UMass Fossil Fuel Divestment Campaign. "Divest UMass Stands with Gender Liberation UMass." Facebook, November 14, 2016. https://www.facebook.com/divestumass.

Vaccaro, Jeanne. "Feelings and Fractals: Wooly Ecologies of Transgender Matter." *GLQ: A Journal of Lesbian and Gay Studies* 21, nos. 2 and 3 (2015): 273–93.

Vaccaro, Jeanne. "Felt Matters." *Women and Performance: A Journal of Feminist Theory* 20, no. 3 (2010): 253–66.

Velocci, Beans. "'A Very Threatened and Nervous Group of People': Public Scrutiny of Sexuality at Smith College in Two Historical Moments." Senior Honors Project, Smith College, 2011.

Waggener, Leslie. "Oral Histories with the S. J. Moffat Family" (2019). Collection #12749, American Heritage Center, University of Wyoming, Laramie, WY. https://archiveswest.orbiscascade.org/ark:/80444/xv176874.

Walsh, Morgan. "Celebrating LGBTQ Pride: The S. J. Moffat Collection." *Discover History*, June 29, 2020. https://ahcwyo.org/2020/06/29/celebrating-lgbtq-pride-the-s-j-moffat-collection/.

Weil, Abraham B. "Psychoanalysis and Trans*versality." *TSQ: Transgender Studies Quarterly* 4, no. 3–4 (2017): 639–46.

Weintraub, Pamela. "At Home in a Liminal World." *Nautilus*, December 12, 2013. https://nautil.us/at-home-in-the-liminal-world-234691/.

Whittemore, Katharine. "A Glorious Woman." *Amherst Magazine*, April 22, 2022. https://www.amherst.edu/amherst-story/magazine/issues/2022-spring/a-glorious-woman.

Williams v. Kincaid, 45. F.4th 759, 763 (4th Cir. 2022). https://www.glad.org/cases/williams-v-kincaid/.

Wood, Tom. "No Escape at U Mass Amherst." National Association of Scholars, January 22, 2008. https://www.nas.org/blogs/article/no_escape_at_u_mass_amherst.

Woolf, Virginia. *A Moment's Liberty: The Shorter Diary*. New York: Harcourt, 1990.

Wong, Calliope. "Good Game." *Trans Women @ Smith*, May 3, 2015. https://calliowong.tumblr.com/post/118031024736/good-game.

Wong, Calliope. *Hyaline Songs*, 2015. https://calliopewong.bandcamp.com/album/hyaline-songs.

Wong, Calliope. "Odyssey." *Anastomosis* 2, no. 1 (Spring 2019): 21–26.

Wong, Calliope. "Update #3—In the Same Night/Morning." *Trans Women @ Smith*, August 16, 2012. https://calliowong.tumblr.com/post/29541869651/update-3-in-the-same-nightmorning.

Zinn, Howard. "Secrecy, Archives, and the Public Interest." *Midwestern Archivist* 2, no. 2 (1977): 14–26.

Zique. "Opening Statement." Queer Studies Memorial, Hampshire College, Amherst, MA. April 21, 2012. https://www.youtube.com/watch?v=Q5RYhTZYZm8.

Zurn, Perry. "Bathroom." In *Keywords in Gender and Sexuality Studies*, edited by Aren Aizura, Aimee Bahng, Amber Jamilla Musser, Karma Chavez, Mishuana Goeman, and Kyla Wazana Tompkins, 21–22. New York: New York University Press, 2021.

Zurn, Perry. *Curiosity and Power: The Politics of Inquiry*. Minneapolis: University of Minnesota Press, 2021.

Zurn, Perry. "Waste Culture and Isolation: Prisons, Toilets, and Gender Segregation." *Hypatia: A Journal of Feminist Philosophy* 34, no. 4 (2019): 668–89.

Zurn, Perry. "Work and Failure: Assessing the Prisons Information Group." In *Active Intolerance: Michel Foucault, the Prisons Information Group, and the Future of Abolition*, edited by Perry Zurn and Andrew Dilts, 75–91. New York: Palgrave, 2016.

Zurn, Perry, and Dani S. Bassett. *Curious Minds: The Power of Connection*. Cambridge, MA: MIT Press, 2022.

Zurn, Perry, Matt Ferguson, Stephen Masson, Hana Henzen, Scout Pruski, Leslie Nellis, and Erica Bethel. "The AU Experience: Then and Now," Spring 2019. https://storymaps.arcgis.com/stories/012f7283c8204e3aae21721d32d47f80.

Zurn, Perry, and Juliana Martínez. "Genealogies of Transversality: A Critical Trans Studies Framework," unpublished manuscript.

Zurn, Perry, and Andrea Pitts, eds. "Trans Philosophy: The Early Years." *APA Newsletter on LGBT Issues in Philosophy* 20, no. 1 (2020): 1–11.

Index

Bold page numbers refer to figures

ableism, 4, 16, 38, 114, 117, 133, 199, 215, 219, 223
abolitionism, 6, 24, 53–54, 58, 71, 105, 205, 214, 218–24
Ace, Samuel, 215
An Act Relative to Gender-Based Discrimination and Hate Crimes (HB 1728, Massachusetts), 245
Ade, Kavindu, 252
affinity housing, 29, 167
Agni, 105
Aguhar, Mark, 56
Aguirre, Sandra, 75–76
Ahmed, Sara, 36–40, 43–44, 195–96, 214, 257n9, 257n13, 257n28
Ainsworth, Sharyn, 37, 257n8
Aizura, Aren, 44, 214
Alexander, Sasha, 250
Allison, Michelle, 262n45
Alvarez, Eddy Francisco, 137
American Heritage Center, 79
Americans with Disabilities Act (ADA), 41, 112, 115
American University, ix, 28, 255n1
Amherst Area Chamber of Commerce, 247
Amherst College, 3, 16, 76–77, 218, 220, 224, 243–46, 248, 250, 253; Affirmative Action Office, 235, 240; alums, 4, 79–80, 240, 262n45; class at, 146–47; Common Language Guide, 219; Department of English, 242; endowment of, 8; Frost Library, 219; and Hampshire College founding, 8; history of, 7; Lord Jeff (mascot), 219, 275n19; Office of Diversity and Inclusion, 219; Queer Resource Center (QRC), 11, 34, 59, 139, 219, 247, 249, 251; Rainbow Room, 241; Sylvia Rivera Community, 251; trans inclusion at, 24–25, 30, 252
Amherst College Police Department, 219
Amherst Magazine, 77, 79
Amherst Student, 146, 248–49
Amherst Uprising, 218–20, 249
#AmherstUprising, 224
an-archive, 67–69, 71–72, 76, 80, 95–99, 102, 234
animacy, 46, 162, 170; tranimacy, 84, 232
Anthropocene, 221, 224
anti-blackness, 191, 218–19
anticolonialism, 52, 222
Anya, 183, 209–10
Anzaldúa, Gloria, 51, 199, 224
Aoki, Ryka, 86, 157, 250
archival praxis, 84, 87, 105
archive fever, 68
archive theory, 67
Arendt, Hannah, 57
Aristotle, 51, 146
asterisks, 62, 71, 102, 115–16, 229–30
Awkward-Rich, Cameron, 9, 48, 86, 112–13, 115, 187, 218, 252–53
AZT, viii

Bachelard, Gaston, 51
Baldwin, James, 142
ball culture, 137–40, 167
Barad, Karen, 103
Baril, Alexandre, 265n9, 273n36
Bassichis, Morgan, 22
bathrooms/restrooms, ix, 14, 29, 49, 109, 112, 114, 116, 122, 151–52, 153, 188, 228; and ADA compliance, 41; Bathroom Domination Project, 153–56; #DecolonizeBathroom, 111, 246; gendered, 3, 45, 111, 131, 153–54, 209, 269n5; gender-neutral, 3–5, 23, 28, 30–32, 36, 41, 46, 87, 110–11, 150, 157, 195, 211, 219, 242, 245, 252; #OccupyBathroom, 110, 246; People in Search of Safe and Accessible Restrooms (PISSAR), 1; Restroom Revolution, ix, 1–2, 241; Shit-In, 40–**47**, 157, 250, 258n35
Bazant, Micah: *Timtum,* 129–30
Beauchamp, Toby, 44
becoming a problem, 26–27, 33, 36–44, 48
becoming a question, 44
becoming a question mark, 44
Beemyn, Genny, 29–30, 34, 247, 253
Ben, 52–53, 150–51
bending, 16, 139, 161, 179, 182, 194, 196–200
Bendorf, Oliver Baez, 49, 220, 260n36
Bergman, S. Bear, 243, 247
Berkins, Lohana, 230
Berkshire Mountains, 6
Betasamosake Simpson, Leanne, 222
Bettcher, Talia, 157, 250
Bey, Marquis, 44
Bhabha, Homi, 41
Black Femme Lives Matter, 100–101
Black fugitive study, 12
Black Lives Matter, 48, 77, 100–101, 218
blackness, 44, 53, 57–58, 90, 185, 218, 230
Black Panther Party, 10
Black studies, 76, 142, 250
Black Teacher Archives Project, 75
Black Trans Lives Matter, 48, 100–101
Blake, 115, 140
Bloch, Ernst, 177, 179–81, 183
blue star tattoo, 16
Bodhran, Ahimsa Timoteo, 55
Boerner, Bill, 243

Booker, Levi: "Dysphoria," 142–**43**; "Gender Anarchy," 145; "Gender Euphoria," 142, **144–45**
Borges, Jorge Luis, 100
Bornstein, Kate, 14, 66, 241, 244; *Gender Outlaw,* 240; *My Gender Workbook,* 88
Boucher, Mitch, ix, 2, 241, 247
Boylan, Jennifer, 248
Broadnax, Micha, 74–77, 255n18
Brown, Michael, 218
brown commons, 180, 182
butches, 10, 74, 104–5, 150–51, 155, 161, 164, 240

cache, 95, 97, 104, 105
Cahun, Claude, 129
Cai, 193–94
California: San Francisco, viii, 128
Cameron, Loren, 14, 66
Camp Trans, 263n14
Camp Transfeminism, 87–88, 241, 263n14
capitalism, 16, 50, 102, 125, 189, 191, 220, 222–23
Card, Claudia, 73
cárdenas, micha, 140–41, 157, 250
Cassidy, 153
Cassils, 252
Catalano, Chase, 243–44
Cavar, 116–17, 142, 252, 269n39
Cawley, Janet, 4
Cedar Falls, 162
Certeau, Michel de, 123, 125–27
Cheadle, Lucas, 98, 228–29, 243
Chen, Mel, 162, 170, 270n5
chevêtres, 124
Chickasaw Nation, 228
Christ, Carol, 245
Christianity, 162, 175
Chuckas, Kai, 269n39
Cichy, Bruce, 132
cisheteronormativity, 4, 12, 21, 38, 43–46, 55, 59–60, 81, 91, 116, 133, 150, 155–56, 159, 165, 195, 220, 223, 265n7; foundation of universities, 21, 32
cissexism, 114, 136, 194, 217
Clare, Eli, 95–96, 113, 163–65, 167, 170, 241, 246
Clarke, Alisha: Transgender Theory (course), 241

Clarke School for the Deaf, 6
classism, 4, 16, 215, 218–19
clothing swaps, 139–40
College of the Holy Cross, 250
colonialism, 51–52, 111, 114, 117, 129, 221, 224; neo-, 219; settler colonialism, 4, 6, 16, 133, 163, 165, 208, 222–23. *See also* decolonization
Combahee River Collective, 218
concreteness, 15, 25, 101, 130, 177, 179–83, 188–89, 208
Connecticut College: LGBT Resource Center, 25
Connecticut River Valley, viii, 6, 13, 163, 232, 265n39
constellations, 16–17, 31, 87
constitutive intimacy, 116
Cordileone, Salvatore J., 128, 267n24
Coulthard, Glen, 222
COVID-19 pandemic, 2, 10, 115, 208, 210
Cox, Laverne, 14, 66, 248, 251
Coyote, Ivan, 247
creative commons, 50
creolization, 52, 108
critical fabulation, 71
Crittendon, AJ, 241
cruel optimism, 176
Currah, Paisley, 44, 159, 243, 245
the cut, 138, 140–42, 150
Cvetkovich, Ann, 67, 70–71

Daily Collegian, 90
Daly, Molly, 95–96
Danny, 167
Davis, Sam, 10, 186; *In Our Own Words*, 87, 98–99, 251, 272n35
Davis, Tobias, 252; *Crossing*, 241; *The Naked I*, 242; *Standards of Care*, 244
Deardorff, Saren, 249; *Invisible No More*, 251, 272n35
DeClue, Jennifer: Documenting Queer Lives (course), 98–99
decolonization, 51, 111, 114, 141, 207, 220–24
#DecolonizeBathroom, 111, 246
DEI (diversity, equity, and inclusion) work, 27, 30, 77, 221
DeLarverie, Stormé, 75
Deleuze, Gilles, 81, 188

Deligny, Fernand, 123–27, 266n3
DeLine, Elliott, 113
Demosthenes, 211
Dene people, 222
Derrida, Jacques, 67–68, 108, 162, 171, 207
desire lines, 39, 201
Diamond, Crescent: *Performing Girl*, 247
différance, 108
Digital Transgender Archive, 250, 264n21
Dillon, Stephen, 247
DiPietro, PJ, 44
dirt-divoting, 183
disability, 10, 29, 56, 60, 88, 95–96, 111, 124, 156, 163, 181, 193, 209, 219, 230–31; and becoming a problem, 35, 38; disability solidarity, 41; and transness, 81, 109, 112–18. *See also* Americans with Disabilities Act (ADA)
disability justice, 218
disability studies, 95, 112, 199
D'Lo, 55, 247
dodd, jayy, 44
Dormor, Catherine, 137–38
drag, 138–40, 154, 240
Drucker, Zachary, 252
Du Bois, W. E. B., 36–37, 44
Dufourmantelle, Anne, 206–7
Dunning, Robbie, 246
dust, 2, 14, 61, 66–69, 81, 83–94, 151, 237

Ean, 146
East Coast Female-to-Male (FTM) Group, viii, 5, 235–36, 239, 244
edge of the university, definition, 12
Edidi, Lady Dane Figueroa, 56
Edwards, Rebekah, 54
Elah Valley, 169
el cenote, 51
Eliot, T. S., 128
Ella, 88
Ellison, Treva, 44
entanglement, 75, 103, 109, 112–13, 224
ephemerality/ephemera, 9, 55, 108, 122, 132, 137, 153, 177, 180–81, 188–89, 208, 234; and archives, 67, 70–71, 76, 81, 97–98, 100; and hope, 14, 180–83
Eremeeva, Francesca, 269n39
Ernst, Rhys, 252

Ethel, 52–53
Eurocentrism, 52
exhaustion, 191–96, 199–201. *See also* fatigue

Facebook, 47, 157–58, 166, 185, 251, 258n59
Fae, 3, 5, 56, 152, 208
fatigue, 15, 115, 189, 191–202, 234. *See also* exhaustion
Feinberg, Leslie, viii–ix, 44, 75, 135, 230, 242; *Stone Butch Blues,* vii, 235–36, 240; *Transgender Warriors,* 235–37
feminism, vii, 57, 60, 141, 195, 214, 223, 242; Black, 37, 191; Chicana, 51, 199, 224; eco-, 205; feminist killjoy, 38–40, 43, 257n13; feminist philosophers, 73; feminist theorists, 36–37; second-wave, 88; trans exclusionary radical feminism (TERF), 42, 56, 72–74, 88, 169, 184–85; transfeminism, 42, 87–88, 241, 258n35
femmes, 3, 42, 87, 153, 161, 183, 240, 262n43; Black, 100–101; hard, 219; trans, 10–11, 87–89, 146, 156, 184, 186–87, 208
Ferguson, Roderick, 100–101
Finn, 185
Fitch, Clyde, 4
Five College Queer, Trans, and Sexuality Studies Certificate, 245
Five College Queer Gender and Sexuality Conference, 139, 157, 180, 244, 247–53
Five Colleges, 59, 73, 80, 90, 114, 123, 134, 139, 146, 165, 181, 188–89, 192, 221, 224, 227, 231, 233–34, 239, 272n35; archives of, 14–15, 66–68, 84, 87, 89, 91, 102, 128, 130, 150, 176–77, 195, 214, 228; bathroom activism at, 40; cross-campus organizations, 157; history of, 6–7; and methodology of book, 8–11; trans faculty at, 209; trans inclusion at, 3–5, 23, 30, 183–85. *See also* Amherst College; Hampshire College; Mount Holyoke College; Smith College; University of Massachusetts, Amherst
Five College Transgender Awareness Event, 246
Five College Women's Studies Research Center, 251
Flores, Yusef, 252
Ford, Craig A., 267n24
Foucault, Michel, 26–28, 30, 67, 69, 73–74, 99

Frank, Rike, 147
Free Cece!, 252
FTM International, viii
fugitivity, 12, 48, 57–60, 71, 107, 113, 129

Garner, Eric, 218
Gender+, 228, 251
gender-affirming healthcare, 14, 36, 66, 195, 211; hormone therapy, 31, 41–42, 53, 73, 96, 250; improvements in, 4, 28–30; policies for, 2, 28–32, 49, 219; as transgender justice, 24
Genderbread person, 29
gender dysphoria, 42, 115
Gender Identity Bill (H3810, Massachusetts, 2011), 246
Gender Identity Resource Network (GRIN), 228
Gender Liberation UMass (GLU), 156, 251; Shit-In, 40–**47,** 157, 250, 258n35; zine, 88–89, 157–**59,** 249
gender studies, 76, 248, 251
Gentili, Cecelia, 252
Gershenson, Olga, 1
Gieseking, Jack, 16–17, 142, 253
Gilbert, Morton (Aunt Mildred), 262n43
Gill-Peterson, Jules, 44
Girl Scouts, 246
Glissant, Édouard, 52, 108, 230–31
Global South, 232
Gloux, 46, 258n60
glue, 15, 134, 146, 149–60, 227, 234
Goodwin, Eli, 240
Gore, Al, 60
Green, Kai, 252
Grimm, Gavin, 253
Grisé, Sibelle, 45–46
grounded normativity, 222–23
Guattari, Félix, 81, 188, 230–31
Gumbs, Alexis Pauline, 191

Halberstam, Jack, 66, 260n49
Hall, Amanda Jean Fadum, 258n60
Hamer, Fannie Lou, 191
Hammami, Jamila, 252
Hampshire College, 3, 5, 11, 59, 72, 87, 100, 110–11, 118, 151, 153, 156, 167, 181, 184, 208, 235, 241, 244, 248, 250–51; alums, 185,

193, 247, 252; Center for Feminisms, 60, 242; Cultural Center, 170; drag ball, 139; Ethics and the Common Good Project, 249; Harold F. Johnson Library, 56, 60; history of, 8; Mod 54, 167; Music and Dance Building, 114; Queer Community Alliance Center (QCAC), 56, 139, 170, 243, 246, 261n72; Queer Does Not End Here, 60, 245–46, 261; SAGA, 56, 169; Students of Under-Represented Cultures and Ethnicities (SOURCE), 169–70; Transgender Policy Committee, 23; Transgender Student Alliance (TSA)/Gender Resource Network (GRN), 243, 249; trans inclusion at, 23–24, 30; Trans Policy Committee, 152, 211, 246; Women's Center, 170, 242; Yiddish Book Center, 265n39
hangouts, 15, 52, 59, 123, 126–34, 233–34
Hans, T. Aaron: Transgender Theory (course), 241
Haritaworn, Jin, 80
Harney, Stefano, 12–13, 48, 57–59, 97, 113
Hartford-Springfield Knowledge Corridor, 7
Hartman, Saidiya, 67, 71
Harvard University, 75, 146
Hazard, Cleo Wölfle, 134, 188
healthcare. *See* gender-affirming healthcare
Hedwig and the Angry Inch, 243
Heidegger, Martin, 51, 161
Helder, 53–54, 184, 213
Hemphill, Essex, 90
Hersey, Tricia, 191
Hexter, Ralph J., 167, 169
HIV/AIDS, viii, 61, 67, 203
Hollibaugh, Amber, 61
Hollis, 165, 222–24
Holyoke Range, 6
homophobia, 4, 77, 111, 218, 240
hope, ix–x, 33, 47–48, 59, 123, 129, 213, 215, 237; and advocacy, 168; and archives, 65, 72; attunement to, 175–89; and becoming a problem, 40, 43; and bending, 197; and fatigue, 192–93, 199–202; feminist, 195; for more words, 105; and multiplicity, 116; passive, 37; and risk, 204–12; and trans poetics, 14–15, 61; and the undercommons, 97
hospitality, 207
Hubbard, Gardiner Greene, 6

Hunter, Lourdes Ashley, 249
Hwang, Ren-yo, 237, 251

identity politics, 218, 223
index cards, 97, 99, 101, 105
institutionalization, 24–25, 34, 42, 102, 228, 230
intersex people, 25, 88, 241
Ireland, 128
Ivy League, 146

Jack, 105
Jackson, Jesse, 169
Jan, 87
Jason, 11, 193–94
Jews in the Wood, 129
Jimena, 208
Johnson, Cyree Jarelle, 253
Johnson, Tamara, 77–80
Jordan, June, 90
Joshua, 115, 136
Jourian, T. J., 251

Katastrophe, Rocco, 246
Keats, Jonathan, 146, 269n46
Keisling, Mara, 247
Kelly, Bryn, 273n28
Killian, Justine, 46, 249, 258n35, 258nn38–39, 258n42, 258n44
Kimmerer, Robin Wall, 222
King, Martin Luther, Jr., 180
knowledge production, 13, 50, 58, 99, 101, 221
Kwatami Territory, 163

Lang/Levitsky, Rosza Daniel, 252
Langston, 220
Lark, 100
Lash, Jonathan, 59, 246
Latini, Lilith, 56
Lawlor, Andrea, 248; "Position Papers," 205; "Transitioning," 206
Lee, Alexander, 22
Lee, Jiz, 248
lesbians, 10, 17, 37, 67, 73–74, 104, 123, 128, 239; at Amherst College, 236; and blue star tattoo, 16; at the Five Colleges, 4–6, 70, 87; lesbian history, 70, 184; at Mount Holyoke College, 75, 240; at Smith College, 97–98, 131

LGB March on Washington, 4
librarians, viii, 100, 255n18
libraries, vii–viii, ix, 26, 135, 184, 218–20; disruption of, 97, 99; student critiques of, 100–102; trans collections in, 31–32. *See also individual libraries*
local theory, 9, 231, 233
locker rooms, ix, 29, 31
Lorde, Audre, 177–78, 181, 183
Lugones, María, 123, 126–27, 223–24
Luna, Caleb, 253
Lundy-Harris, Amira, 250
Lurie, Sam, 244
lying crossways, 200–201
Lyon, Mary, 7

madness, 26, 46, 54, 57–58, 93, 108–9, 112, 113, 126, 181, 199, 202, 229, 230, 232–33; trans-, 116–17
Magic Files, 98–99
Maisonet, Eddie/Edsuvani, 136
maladjustment, 110, 112–14, 197, 200, 253
Malatino, Hil, 262n47
Mangos with Chili, 244
Manion, Jen, 24–26, 32, 250, 253
March, Vanessa, 154
Marder, Michael, 85
Martin, Jxhn, 251–52
Maryland: Montgomery County, 23
masculinity, 46, 104, 110, 193, 212; toxic, 185–86; trans, 10–11, 87, 112–13, 118, 147, 184–87
Mason, 221, 224
Massachusetts cities: Amherst, 6, 9, 241; Boston, 264; Cambridge, 179; Holyoke, viii, 7, 93, 102, 251; Northampton, 4–7, 9, 48, 102, 199, 209, 236, 239, 243, 251; South Hadley, 6–7, 9; Springfield, 7; Sunderland, 6; Worcester, 245, 264
McCarthy, Sheryl, 37, 257n8
McCullers, Carson, 113
McDade, Tony, 48
McDonald, Cece, 252
Medina, Mateo, 24–26, 32; Preferred Gender Pronouns handout, 23, 34, 245, 256n5
Mencher, Julie, 242
Mercy High, 128
methodology of book, 8–11

Middle Passage, 71, 230
Mills College, 197; Gender Identity and Expression Subcommittee, 216
Miss New England Trans Pageants, 5
Mock, Janet, 14, 66, 248–49
Moffat, Shannon, 79–80
MoHo TGNC, 251
Montague, Elliot, 251
Moore, Lisa Jean, 44, 159
moreness, 9, 23, 33, 50, 182, 231
Morris, Jan, 79
Moten, Fred, 12–13, 48, 57–59, 97, 113
Mount Holyoke Alumnae Quarterly, 37
Mount Holyoke College, 3–4, 145, 168–69, 222, 224; African American Society, 37; alums, 16, 53, 105, 115–16, 140, 165, 218; Bathroom Domination Project, 153–56; Coalition for Gender Awareness, 247; and Hampshire College founding, 8; history of, 7; Initial Mount Holyoke Transgender Awareness Committee, 243; Lesbian and Bisexual Alliance (LBA), 75–76, 228, 240; Mount Holyoke Brothers and Others, 242; Mx. Holyoke, 253; Pat the Mannequin, 139–40; professors at, 103, 205, 237; race at, 37, 142; Spectrum, 75–76, 240; SYSTA, 74–76, 80, 240; trans activism at, 139–40, 153–56, 241–53; Trans/Gender and Allies Group, 153; Transgender Awareness Week, 242; Transgender Committee, 216, 243–44; Trans-Identity Committee, 249; trans inclusion at, 30, 197, 216; trans life at, 75–76; trans women at, 184; True Colors, 153
Mount Holyoke Health Services, 248
Mount Holyoke News, 75, 142, 154, 240, 244, 252; *Voices,* 75–76
Moye, David, 43
Muñoz, José Esteban, 177, 180–81, 183, 199, 247, 261n66
Murray, Pauli, 90
Myles, Eileen, 55

National Center for Transgender Equality, 247
National Coming Out Day, 75
Nazis, 179
neoliberalism, 176, 187, 220, 257n29

nepantla, 51, 199
New Alexandria Lesbian Library for Women, 5, 239
Newheiser, David, 211
New York City, 16, 79
New York State: Buffalo, 16
Nicolazzo, Z, 30
Nishnaabeg people, 222
Noho Trans Pride/New England Trans United (NETU) Pride Mark and Rally, 244
nonbinary people, 10–11, 28–29, 44, 186; at Amherst College, 146; at Hampshire College, 153, 208; at Mount Holyoke College, 105, 142; at Smith College, 61, 136, 193–94, 215–16, 249; at UMass Amherst, 35, 40, 88
nondiscrimination policies, ix, 28–32, 49, 219, 228, 245, 252
Nordmarken, Sonny, 117, 248
Northampton Trans Pride, 5
Not-Yet-Conscious, 179

obstructing feeling/function, 40, 43
#OccupyBathroom, 110, 246
Occupy Hampshire, 111
Occupy Wall Street, 111
Ohio State University, 162; GLBT Student Services, 29
Oliver, 139, 195–96
Oregon, 163
Oregon Fairview Home, 95
Owen, Everett, 98

Packer, Tobias, 131
Page, Enoch, 89–92, 240–41, 263n29; *On Being a Witness*, 93
Page, Morgan M., 251
Pasquerella, Lynn, 247
Pat, 35–37, 40
patriarchy, 71, 73, 110–11, 114, 117, 185–86, 218; cishetero-, 16
Patterson, Franklin, 8, 35
pebble, 2, 15, 56, 134, 161–71, 176, 180, 209, 211–12
Pecht, Jake "Gneiss Guy," 165–67, 170, 246
People in Search of Safe and Accessible Restrooms (PISSAR), 1
Perez, Olympia, 250
Peterson, Trace, 55

PFLAG, 157
phenomenology, 33, 113, 214
Phoenix, 184
Piepzna-Samarasinha, Leah Lakshmi, 199–200, 249, 251
Pierson, Jack, 243
Pioneer Valley, 6. *See also* Connecticut River Valley
Pitcher, Aster (Erich), 33, 269n12
planning, 58–59, 126
poem-bodies, 11–12, 55, 66
poem-lives, 68, 70
poetics. *See* trans poetics
poetics of relation, 52
poetics of resistance, 121–34, 160
poetry, 2–3, 16, 44, 75, 96, 97, 117, 149, 188, 196, 227, 236, 248; and fatigue, 200, 202; and hope, 181; and risk, 210; as tool of scrutiny, 178; and trans poetics, 12–13, 50–51, 54–57, 207, 227
poiesis, 12, 50–51, 57, 125–26, 207
Point Foundation, 198
Polk, Khary, 76
Power, Ben, viii–ix, 5, 11, 102–3, 235, 239–40, 244, 247
Pratt, Minnie Bruce, 236
praxis, 15, 84, 87, 105, 116–17, 123, 150, 181
Primeaux, Milo, 154, 242
problematization, 41, 48, 151; of trans inclusion, 21–34
pronouns, 4, 14, 34, 147, 168–69, 194, 249, 253; policies for, 22–28, 30–32, 42, 49, 66, 130–31, 211, 219, 242, 248
Pryor, Jack, 60–61, 245–46; Performing Identities (course), 110

QPOC, 157
Quabbin Reservoir, 6
Queer Creek, 163
queer feeling, 70
queer liberation, 24
queer studies, 11, 60–61, 110, 245–47
queer theory, 76, 100

Rachman, Leo, 145, 252, 269n39; "Desire and Action" exhibit, 142; "Trans Lives at Mount Holyoke College Today" exhibit, 142, 252

racial justice, 24, 47, 207, 218
racism, 4, 16, 37–38, 40, 92–93, 111, 136, 169, 178, 191, 195, 215, 218–19. *See also* anti-blackness; white supremacy
#RadicalCompassion, 219
Rainbow Elders, 157
Rawson, K. J., 250, 264n21
Raymond, Janice, 80, 185; *Doublethink,* 73; *A Passion for Friends,* 74; *The Transsexual Empire,* 42, 72–74, 88, 239
Ream, Jess, 244
Red Barn, 139
Reddit, 105, 232
Reese, 152, 184, 269n5
Restroom Revolution, ix, 1–2, 241
restrooms. *See* bathrooms/restrooms
Rev, Nihils, 249
reworlding, 220, 223
Rice, Tamir, 218
Rich, Adrienne, 24
risk, 2, 15, 61, 189, 192, 197, 203–12, 227
river restoration, 165, 220–23
Rodríguez, Dylan, 220
Roman Catholic Archdiocese of San Francisco, 128
Rosenberg, Jordy, 102, 252
Rosskam, Jules: *Dance, Dance Evolution,* 181–83, 188; *Thick Relations,* 245; *Against a Trans Narrative,* 245; *Transparent,* 245, 252
Roy, Arundhati, 47
Ruhsam, Jeanine, 250
Ryan, 140

Sadjadi, Sahar, 248, 252
scatter, 14, 17, 40, 55, 68, 74, 81, 83–87, 97, 102, 107–18, 145, 192, 199, 227, 234
Schuster, Marilyn, 245
Scott, David K., 90
seam, 43, 133, 137–38, 141–42, 145, 149–50, 159, 231
Serano, Julia, 184, 248
settler colonialism, 4, 6, 16, 133, 163, 165, 208, 222–23
Seven Sisters, 7–8, 184, 197
Seven Sisters SGA Conference, 243
sexism, 4, 38, 40, 191, 218; cis-, 114, 136, 194, 217. *See also* transmisogyny

Sexual Minorities Archives (SMA), viii, 1, 5, 93, 94, 102, 103, 209, 236, 239, 251
Shay's Rebellion, 6
Shepard, Jack, 102
Shepard, Matthew, 79
Sherley, Cai, 186, 194
the shift, 140–41
Shinjuku Boys, 241
Shlasko, Davey, 24, 97–98, 104, 146–47, 212, 252
sideways relationality, 179, 271n11
Silas, 131–33, 233
silence, 65–72, 75–76, 80, 87, 103, 105, 117, 156, 164, 178, 234
Sisters of Mercy, 128
Situationists, 125
Smith, Barbara, 37, 142, 218, 257n8
Smith, Sophia, 7
Smith College, 3–5, 10, 185–86, 224, 243, 251; Admissions Policy Study Group, 216; alums, 24, 61, 87, 88, 128, 136, 140, 147, 166, 184, 193, 212, 233; Boys Night Out, 59; class at, 132, 146–47, 166; and Hampshire College founding, 8; Hillel, 136; history of, 7; Queers and Allies (Q&A), 197, 216, 247–49; Resource Center for Sexuality and Gender, 244; Save Our Smith (SOS), 131–32; Student Government Association (SGA), 130–32; Tangent/T Committee/Transcending Gender, 130, 166, 228, 240–42, 245–46; trans inclusion at, 30, 97–99, 130–32, 197–99, 215–18; Trans Women Belong at Smith, 157, 248; Trans Women Belong Rally, 249; Women for the World campaign, 215
snapping, 39, 46, 195–96, 201
Snorton, C. Riley, 80, 157, 263n29
Something Queer Happened Here, 87, 265n10
The Sophian, 98, 131–32, 228, 246
Spade, Dean, 22, 24–26, 32, 242–43, 250, 253
Spencer, 61, 184
Stanley, Eric, 214, 273n32
stash, 14, 56, 81, 85, 95–105, 108, 116, 234
Steedman, Carolyn, 86
Steinbock, Eliza, 44
Stein-Bodenheimer, Gabriel, 128–30, 267n24
Stewart, Kathleen, 70, 214
the stitch, 55, 136, 138, 140–42, 145, 149

Stone, Sandy, 72
Stonewall (film), 241
Stonewall Rebellion, 161, 230, 251
streetwalkers (callejeras), 126–27, 137
Stryker, Susan, 44, 112, 141, 159
study, 58–60
suicide, 21, 77, 87, 112, 115, 122, 133, 192–93, 198–200, 203, 258n60, 268n5, 273n28, 273n32, 273n36
Sullivan, Lou, viii
Sunshine Club, 5
Sylvia Rivera Law Project, 25

tactics *vs.* strategies, 125–26
Talia, 153, 211
Tallon-Hicks, Yana, 167
Tangerine, 250
Taormino, Tristan, 248
theft, 96–99, 105
Theonia, Charles, 56
things-being-done, 61
things-in-the-doing, 61
things-that-are, 61
third space, 41–42, 192, 196, 201
Thornton, Max, 265n9
thread, 15, 58, 61, 89, 96, 123–24, 134–47, 185, 220, 234
Tissi-Galloway, Angie, 247
Title IX, 42
Tolbert, TC, 55
tranimacies, 84, 232
Trans 101, 28, 30–32, 66, 129, 150, 196, 219, 242–43
TransActive, 157, 219, 228, 249
Transamerica, 243
Trans Archive Oral History Project, 251
trans belonging, 43, 46, 59–60, 141–42
Transcending Boundaries Conference, 242, 245
trans/crip analytic, 265n9
trans exclusionary radical feminism (TERF), 42, 56, 72–74, 88, 169, 184–85
Transexual Menace, 240
trans feeling, 47, 70, 76, 96
transfemininity, 10, 89, 183, 185, 187
transfeminism, 42, 87–88, 241, 258n35
Trans Futurity Symposium, 250, 253
Transgender Activist Network (TAN), 5, 241

transgender awareness weeks, 154, 228, 242
Transgender Day of Remembrance, 244, 246
Transgender Network (TNET), 5
Transgender Perspectives: Arts, Activism, and Academia conference, 241
Transgender Special Outreach Network (TSON), 5
Transgender Studies and Women's Colleges conference, 244
TransGeneration, 97–98, 243
trans hope. *See* hope
transhumanism, 83–84, 159, 165, 210
transing, 25, 43–46, 59, 85, 124, 159, 177, 186, 200, 214, 220, 231
trans liberation, 24, 109, 184–85, 218, 220, 223
translocality, 15, 229, 231–34
transMadness, 116–17
transmasculinity, 10–11, 61, 76, 87, 98, 112–13, 118, 139, 147, 183–87, 212
transmaterialities, 103
transmisogyny, 41, 88, 168, 183–84, 199, 258n35. *See also* cissexism; sexism
transphobia, ix, 4, 11, 88, 111, 133, 167–68, 186, 193, 195, 199, 247. *See also* trans exclusionary radical feminism (TERF)
trans poetics, 3, 5, 80, 96, 139, 141, 151, 165, 224–25, 228, 233–34, 236; and archives, 66–76, 84, 89, 93, 105; definition, 11–13; and disability, 112–14, 117; and fatigue, 193, 201–2; of history, 105; of hope, 14–15, 61, 179, 181, 183, 187–89, 202, 204; and methodology of book, 9; mobilizing, 49–62; and poetry, 12–13, 50–51, 54–57, 207, 227; and policy, 22, 33, 43; of resistance, 121–34, 160; and risk, 210, 212; and scatter, 109, 116; and the undercommons, 48
trans pollination, 108
trans studies, 2, 42, 60, 74, 100, 112, 140, 150, 162, 224, 229–33, 250, 258n35; and disability, 112–13, 116–17; foundational texts in, 72; inclusion in, 13; and library collections, 31; and maladjustment, 112–13; and scatter, 109, 113; transing in, 43–44; trans poetics in, 57. *See also* Transgender Studies and Women's Colleges conference
trans-thinking, 233
transversality, 47–48, 55, 68, 84, 94, 123, 130, 132, 164, 177, 216, 219, 229–31, 234

INDEX 309

trans world-building, 3, 152, 156, 162–63, 170, 214, 224
trans worlding, 134, 189, 213–16, 221, 223–25
trash, 15, 88–89, 177–83, 187–88, 234
Troubling the Line, 54
Trump, Donald, 10, 208
Truth, Sojourner, 6
Tsing, Anna, 189
TSQ, 54
Tumblr, 60, 105, 197, 232
Two Spirits (film), 221
Tyson, Sarah, 273n32

undercommons, 13, 33, 48, 57–58, 81, 97, 99, 113, 177, 187, 210, 223, 228, 233–34, 260n49
underconcepts, 58
underflows, 134, 177, 188, 201, 210, 223–24, 228, 234
Underground Railroad, 6
Unitarian Universalist Church, 157, 244, 246
University of California, Santa Barbara, 1
University of Connecticut (UConn), 198
University of Massachusetts, Amherst, ix, 3, 7, 52, 86, 102, 112, 135, 189, 245; Access and Affordability, 157; alums, 35, 117, 150, 240–41, 243–44, 248–49; Black Student Union, 157; Chancellor's Task Force for Gay, Lesbian, and Bisexual Matters, 89–90, 240; Coalition to End Rape Culture, 157; Department of Anthropology, 92; Department of English, 241–42; Department of Sociology, 117, 241; Department of Women, Gender, Sexuality Studies (WGSS), 41–42, 48, 72, 89, 239, 250–51; Gender Liberation UMass (GLU), 40–47, 87–89, 156–**59**, 249–51, 258n35; and Hampshire College founding, 8; history of, 7; Janice Raymond at, 72–74; Multicultural Organizing Bureau, 157; Queer People of Color Group, 42; race at, 9, 90–93; RA Union, 157; School of Education, 150; Stonewall Center, 1, 29, 139, 157, 242, 246–47, 253, 263n22; Student Government Association, 242; Student Labor Action Project, 157; Students for Justice in Palestine, 157; Transgender Film Festival, 244; trans inclusion at, 30; Trans Studies Working Group (T-SWAG), 228, 253; UMass Fossil Fuels Divestment Campaign, 47; UMass Pride Alliance, 157, 240, 242; University Health Services, 42, 250
University of Missouri, 218
University of Wyoming, 79

Vaid-Menon, Alok, 253
Valentine, David, 241
van Fritsch, Karl, 124
Vermont, 163
Vervoodt, Axel, 138
Vincente, 152

Walter, 162–63
Wambach, Abby, 250
wander lines, 123–25, 127
Watson, Lindsay, 130
weaving, 5, 15, 51, 55, 71, 84, 124–25, 129, 136–38, 141, 145, 222
webs, 17, 83, 123–25, 127–28, 130–34, 155–56, 162, 214, 232, 234
welcome mats, 22, 25–26, 33
We Want It All, 54
whales, 60–61, 246
white supremacy, 36, 71, 219
Whittemore, Katharine, 77
Wilchins, Riki, 240
Wilde, Oscar, 4
willful subject, 37–39, 43
Wilson, Tonya, 132
Wolfe, Tim, 218
Women's College Coalition, 197
Wong, Calliope Rose, 197–99, 215, 247, 273n19
Woolf, Virginia, 149
world, 213–25

Y2Genders conference, 241
Yale University, 146, 218
Young Lords, 100

Zique, 60–61
Zurn, Perry, 249

www.ingramcontent.com/pod-product-compliance
Lightning Source LLC
LaVergne TN
LVHW091226090925
820435LV00034B/126